LINCOLN

AND THE

WAR GOVERNORS

LINCOLN

AND THE

WAR GOVERNORS

William B. Hesseltine

1955

NEW YORK :: ALFRED A KNOPF

THIS IS A BORZOI BOOK,
PUBLISHED BY ALFRED A. KNOPF, INC.

PUBLISHED MAY 24, 1948
SECOND PRINTING, AUGUST 1955

Preface

IT WAS Alexander H. Stephens, sometime irreconcilable
Vice President of the Southern Confederacy, who first gave
convincing argument that the American Civil War should
be called a "War between the States." His was, he said, a
"constitutional view," and he repeated, in a lawyer's heavy
tome, all the arguments that the years had made to prove
that the American states were "sovereign," that they had retained their sovereignty when they formed the Constitution,
that the federal government was only an agency of the sovereign states, and that secession was a legal exercise of the
rights of the states. The argument was not new, but the ex-
Confederate gave currency to the term he used to describe
the conflict. Since Stephens's day, defenders of the "Lost
Cause" have insisted on naming the American conflict the
"War between the States."

In actual fact, the caption favored by the South is inadequate to describe even the constitutional aspects of the war.
Rather than a war among the American states, the conflict
of 1861–5 was a war between the states on the one hand and
the growing power of the national government on the other.
In popular speech, the Southern Confederacy symbolized
the particularist principles of states' rights, and the United
States embodied the national creed. But, as in most wars,
neither side had a clear monopoly of either contending
dogma. Within the confines of the Confederacy, ardent
Southern nationalists battled unceasingly with the adherents
of state sovereignty, while in the North the struggle between
nation and state went on steadily.

This latter struggle is the theme of this book. When the
smoke of the Civil War had lifted from the battlefields, it

was seen that a new nation had been erected on the ruins of
the old federal union. But though the fact of national sovereignty was distinct, the process by which Abraham Lincoln,
architect of the nation, had used the exigencies of war and
politics to build a new structure was not so readily evident.
Only by tracing the relations between the federal government and the states during the war years can the foundation
of the new nation be made clear.

In personal and political terms the struggle between
states' rights and nationalism in the North involved a conflict between Abraham Lincoln, President of the United
States, and the ill-assorted governors of twenty-five Northern
and border states. In the beginning the governors possessed
power as commanders-in-chief of the states' military force,
and had prestige by virtue of their leadership of the domi-
nant political party in their respective states. In the early
part of the war they used both power and prestige to force
Lincoln's hand and to drive the President to accept their
policies. But the shrewd prairie lawyer was more than a
match for the governors. Slowly, with many a skillful maneuver and many a clash of personalities, the President proved
that he alone could direct the war and that only he could
win elections. In the end Abraham Lincoln had control of
the Republican Party — the political instrument in nation-
alization — and of the military force that made the nation.

When the war between the states and the nation ended,
the bodies of those who had died that "this nation, under
God, shall not perish from the earth" rested in neat rows in
national cemeteries.

The opening of the Robert Todd Lincoln Collection of his
father's papers has brought to light the last major body of
source material relating to Abraham Lincoln. These papers
enable the historian to check the accuracy of previously
printed letters, and they throw a revealing light on which of
all the problems that came before him in these years Abraham
Lincoln deemed important. The hundreds of letters from the

governors in this collection attest again the important place that the state executives held in Lincoln's thinking.

I am under deep obligations to many persons and institutions who have aided in my work: to the officials of the Illinois State Historical Society, the Wisconsin State Historical Society, the Michigan Historical Collections, the Detroit Public Library, the Henry E. Huntington Library, the Ohio State Archeological and Historical Society, the Maryland Historical Society, and the Library of Congress, who made available their manuscript and printed materials; to Miss Hazel Wolf of Peoria, Illinois, and Professor Bessie L. Pierce of the University of Chicago, who furnished advice and notes from their own files; to Professor and Mrs. Horace S. Merrill of the University of Maryland, who labored with me and for me in the Robert Todd Lincoln Collection; to Miss Livia Appel of the University of Wisconsin, who made penetrating criticisms and performed major operations on the literary form; to Professor T. Harry Williams of Louisiana State University and to Professor Richard N. Current of Mills College, who read and criticized the manuscript; to the students in my seminars who studied many of these problems with me; and to the research committee of the University of Wisconsin's graduate school for a semester's leave of absence.

W. B. H.

Contents

LINCOLN

AND THE

WAR GOVERNORS

Chapter 1

The Birth of Republicanism

Viewed in the long perspective of history, the American
Civil War appears to have been, as it has been aptly called, a
second American Revolution. It was a revolution in more
ways than one, for it embraced several different, though related conflicts. There was a clash between economic systems
—a new, expanding industrialism and an old, established
agrarianism; the factory and the plantation and farm. There
was a clash between opposing constitutional views: the doctrine of national supremacy and the dogma of states' rights.
There was a clash between incompatible ideas of the proper
relations of man to man: an idea of slavery and an idea of
freedom. In the war, industrialism and national supremacy
and freedom won out. The result was a revolutionary transformation, from top to bottom, of American society.

But history's long perspective, giving a broad view of the
effect of the war upon society, neglects the impact of the war
upon men as individuals. Such vague and colorless terms as
industrialism and agrarianism hide the activities of countless
workers who listened to the clatter of machines or watched a
glistening plowshare fold spring's moist earth into serried
pleats. Slogans like "Union" or "States' Rights" conceal the
private ends of personal security, preferment, or profit for
which men struggled. The concepts of slavery or freedom
cover the separate aspirations of millions who in one fashion
or another were seeking a more congenial way of life.

To call a war a revolution, then, is but to summarize a complex and contradictory host of human aims and acts. The men on the victorious side of the Civil War who made policies or administered affairs were as often bewildered and irrational as they were clear-sighted and judicious. Bickering among themselves, they frequently lost sight of the evils they sought to destroy and the positive goals they sought to attain. Many of them stood ready to sacrifice basic principles for immediate benefits. Eventually, as in most other revolutions, a leader appeared who grappled with conflicting forces and contending men, mastered them, and gave meaning and direction to events.

The man whom the Civil War revealed was Abraham Lincoln. As the war gathered momentum, this inexperienced prairie politician whom accident had elevated to the Presidency grew in mental stature, in moral fiber, and in political skill. Though he had little formal education, he possessed the keenest insight into other men's minds and hearts and an unusual capacity to learn from experience. One by one he mastered his problems and put down rival leaders until finally he assumed direction of the struggle. In the end he came to personify the revolution. The history of the Civil War merges into the biography of the man in the White House.

In 1861, however, Abraham Lincoln was only nominally the head of the nation and of the Republican Party, which had so recently come into power. In truth, he was only one of many "chief executives" in the country. For in 1861 there existed no truly national Republican organization to recognize either Lincoln's right or his capacity to lead. The party that won the election of 1860 was then but a conglomerate of many local groups bound together by a common enmity rather than a common loyalty. In the later evolution of the party there were some strange paradoxes. It was a paradox that a party resting upon state organizations and gaining control by pooling state grievances was to sacrifice states' rights in return for national power. It was paradox, too, that the party that would destroy slavery was also to destroy so many of the ancient rights of free men. Only in the growing character of Abraham Lincoln do these paradoxes become resolved. It was Lincoln who gave the Republican Party a national task and used the party, amid the exigencies of war, to transform a federal union into a new nation.

In the course of that transformation the ancient doctrine of states' rights was seriously impaired. In 1861 the seceding states repeated the trite formulas of Jefferson and Calhoun. The seceders were actuated by economic motive, it is true: they were erecting an agrarian defense against a rising industrialism. Yet in both their arguments and their actions they followed the compact theory of the state. This doctrine proved to be an unstable foundation for the Southern Confederacy: it was to hasten the collapse of the government of Jefferson Davis.

However, the states' rights theory was not confined to the South. Throughout the North there were Jeffersonians and disciples of Calhoun who believed in a strict construction of the Constitution. Many of them, confronting local problems and moral issues, left the decaying, Southern-controlled Democratic Party and looked for place and profit in the new Republican organizations. But they carried their constitutional doctrines along and were reluctant to give them up. Against these notions of states' rights Lincoln battled constantly until he succeeded in scotching them and establishing in their place a firm belief in national supremacy.

In the North the governors were the jealous guardians of the rights of the states. The federal union devised by the founding fathers had left enormous power, both political and military, in the governors' hands. They were the commanders-in-chief of the state militias, the agents through whom the nation's commander-in-chief must work. They were the political heads of their states and controlled the organizations that sent delegates to national conventions. Thus they were important personages who must be cajoled, conciliated, and controlled. The curtailment of their power and prestige was one aspect of the revolution. As the exigenices of war permitted a concentration of authority in the national government, Abraham Lincoln with his superior political ability was able eventually to dominate his rival executives. It was no easy task, however. The struggle was long, sometimes confused, often awkward. But in the end Lincoln ruled, and never did the governors recover the prestige they had enjoyed for three quarters of a century.

Before he could dominate the governors Lincoln had to gain control of his party. In 1860 the Republicans, lacking an accepted leader and a coherent program, forming a conglomerate of local groups, and possessing no experience in handling National affairs, could give no warrant that they were equipped to deal with a national crisis.

The Republican Party had been born of the political opposition and moral indignation kindled by the Kansas-Nebraska Act. No sooner had Stephen A. Douglas, in January 1854, introduced his bill to open these territories to settlers who should themselves decide whether or not to admit slavery than a storm suddenly broke about his head. Northern congressmen, mindful of the antislavery sentiments of their constituents, denounced the bill and assailed the Pierce administration. The "Little Giant," they charged, was bidding for support for the Presidency. Whatever Douglas's dream may have been — and he was at least as much interested in launching a Pacific railroad scheme as in promoting his own candidacy — the bill did provide others with a political cause. To Senator William H. Seward, of New York, already the acknowledged leader of the antislavery "Conscience" Whigs, it opened an avenue by which to advance his own presidential aspirations. His eyes flashing fire, the sharp-featured Senator became Vengeance incarnate as he rose to challenge the specious arguments of the bill's proponents. Step by step he reviewed the history of slavery and the compromises it had occasioned. Like some dark master of magic, he summoned the shade of Henry Clay to testify that the Compromise of 1850 had not been intended to repeal the Missouri Compromise. Seward was no orator and his dramatic powers were slight, but the learning and the zeal he invested in his speech temporarily clothed him with glamour and made him a likely candidate for any opposition party. Years later Gideon Welles, who hated him, was to charge that Seward had deliberately inspired the repeal of the Missouri Compromise in order to create the Republican Party.

The politically sensitive congressmen who cheered Seward had not misjudged their constituents. The telegraphic spark that spelled out the news of Douglas's proposal unleashed a tempest of popular fury. Antislavery enthusiasts were wroth that the Missouri Compromise, accepted for a generation as a solemn dedication of the territories to freedom, should be so cavalierly ignored. Home-seekers avid for fertile farms in the Missouri Valley were beside themselves with frustration. Local politicians fanned the widespread resentment into a flaming crusade. Throughout the North, while Congress debated the Kansas-Nebraska bill, people met in schools and churches and, without regard for political ties, banded into new organizations to damn the measure and oppose its passage.

Whig politicians privately confessed to one another that their party was doomed, that its ancient principles had lost their magic appeal. The protection of industry, the national bank, internal improvements — in fact, the whole set of glittering promises that Henry Clay had incorporated in his American system — no longer gathered Northern voters.

In any event the basic economic program of the Whigs had been submerged in the growing conservatism of the party. As a national organization the Whigs, like the Democracy, had fallen into the paralyzing grip of Southern slave-owners. Few of the "Cotton Whigs" had any use for the economics of the American system; they were Whigs because the party was conservative, and their influence helped to keep it so. After the fiasco of 1852, when the unknown Franklin Pierce had defeated the war hero Winfield Scott, Northern Whigs had looked about for a new issue. They recognized that their economic program of tariffs, internal improvements, and a national bank, lacking in imaginative appeal as it was, might best be advanced under cover of a moral crusade. So for a time, and in scattered places, they had experimented with temperance, and sundry St. Georges had assailed the demon rum. Others had discovered Mormonism with its shocking tenet of polygamy. Now at last, in the Nebraska bill, they had a real issue, whose potency had already been demonstrated. As repercussions came in from the states, politicians in Congress saw the wisdom of riding the crest of the ground swell. The day after the Nebraska bill passed, some thirty representatives, mostly Northern Whigs, met in answer to the call of Israel Washburn of Maine and solemnly agreed that the moment had come to launch a new party.

The Republican Party was born, however, in the states of the West. On Washington's Birthday 1854, the "Free Democracy" of Michigan met at Jackson and nominated a state ticket on a platform denouncing slavery and the Nebraska bill. A few days later Wisconsin dissentients assembled at Ripon to resolve that if the bill passed they would abandon the old parties and form a new one opposed to the extension of slavery. At another Wisconsin meeting, in March, it was suggested that the new party be called "Republican." This name was promptly adopted by local mass meetings in Illinois and presently by organizations in other states.

Soon there was clamor for state-wide organizations. The Illinois mass meetings began it, and other states followed. In May the "Free Democrats" of Michigan called for a mass convention "springing from thousands, irrespective of political organization." On July 13, the anniversary of the Northwest Ordinance, opponents of the Nebraska iniquity assembled in Madison, Indianapolis, Columbus, and even Montpelier, Vermont, and a few weeks later in Illinois, New York, and Iowa. Resolutions were adopted and candidates named for local offices. All pledged themselves to return the nation to "free principles" by restoring Kansas and Nebraska to the status of free territories, repealing the Fugitive Slave Law and preventing the admission of new slave states to the Union. In other states the Whig organizations hastened to place themselves in the vanguard of the popular surge. Even as they did so they deserted the Southern branch of the party and made easy the transition to the Republican fold.

In the elections that fall the unknown candidates carried the day, and before the year was out the Republican organizations had taken firm root in many of the states. The Whig Party had received its deathblow, and everywhere politicians looked for opportunities to preen themselves in the new party. The next year the Republicans improved their position in the Western states and got a firmer foothold in the East. In New York Senator Seward, who the year before had preferred to retain the Whig organization, now came out for the Republicans: "Ye men of Erie, the Republican party is sounding throughout all our border a deep-toned alarum for the safety of the Constitution, of Union and of Liberty!" In September, when the Whig and Republican state conventions both met in Syracuse, Seward was asked by a friend which he ought to attend. The reply was that it would make no difference, for if they went in by two doors, they would come out by one. Seward was right. Against the protests of some of the "Silver Grays" or "Cotton Whigs," the Whigs walked in a body to the Republican meeting.

In 1856 the Republican organizations were strong enough to launch a national party. In January the chairmen of eight state committees — those of Maine, Vermont, Massachusetts, Pennsylvania, Ohio, Michigan, Indiana, and Wisconsin — united in a call for a national mass convention to be held in Pittsburgh on Washington's Birthday. There the party was organized and arrangements made for a nominating convention at Philadelphia. A few weeks later Seward, through his debate with Douglas over Kansas, made himself the logical candidate for the nomination. But his political partner, Thurlow Weed, after surveying the prospects, concluded that the Republicans could not carry Pennsylvania against the Democratic nominee, James Buchanan; and without the Keystone State they could not hope to win the election. Regretfully

Seward acquiesced in Weed's judgment and in the nomination of John C. Frémont, "Pathfinder of the West," by the Philadelphia convention. The fall election confirmed Weed's shrewdness. The Republicans, having failed to carry Pennsylvania and Indiana, whose votes would have elected Frémont, were decisively defeated in the national poll.

Yet within the states the campaign had accomplished much. It had overthrown the old parties in the East and had snatched from the Democracy several more of the Western states. The new party carried all of New England and New York, Ohio, Michigan, Wisconsin, and Iowa. In five other states — New Jersey, Pennsylvania, Indiana, Illinois, and California — its organizations had been so strengthened as to offer a real challenge to Democratic supremacy.

In these early days of the party a number of men emerged from relative obscurity to assume leadership in the states. They were mostly young men still untried in any political arena: idealistic youths eager to give themselves to a cause, political aspirants with an eye to the main chance, able tyros itching to have a try at personal leadership. Comparatively young, albeit not unknown men had led the national meetings at Pittsburgh and Philadelphia. Presiding at Pittsburgh was Francis P. Blair, Jr., of Maryland, scion of an influential Democratic family who was destined to a stormy career in Maryland and Missouri, in the army, and in both the Republican and the Democratic Party. The committee on permanent organization included George W. Julian, old-line abolitionist from Indiana, and Edwin D. Morgan, prominent merchant, banker, and broker of New York City, who had sponsored the creation of Central Park and was soon to become Governor of his state. Serving on the committee on resolutions were Ebenezer R. Hoar, of Boston's Back Bay aristocracy, and William Dennison and Oliver P. Morton, who were to become the war Governors of Ohio and Indiana.

At the Philadelphia meeting were Louis P. Harvey, who was to be Governor of Wisconsin in 1862; Gideon Welles, the Connecticut editor later to be "Father Neptune" in Lincoln's cabinet; David Wilmot of Proviso fame; Joshua R. Giddings, who was seeing a lifetime of antislavery agitation bear fruit; Alexander Ramsey, representing the new party in the newly created territory of Minnesota on the distant frontier; and Salmon P. Chase, "attorney general for run-away niggers," an ambitious Ohio abolitionist with eyes already trained on the White House. All these men to whom the national organization was entrusted were important figures in their states, though only a handful had yet tested their strength in the national arena. Comparatively young men as most of them were, they brought youth's vigor to a movement that was both a political campaign and a moral crusade.

During the four years of the Buchanan administration the Republican Party and its unfledged generals matured. Drawing strength from Democratic weakness, the party perfected its organizations in the several states. Seizing every opportunity offered by national developments, it formulated its program, always with an eye to winning over new groups of proselytes. Taking full advantage of Democratic dissensions in Congress, it built up a record to be used in the campaign of 1860. As an opposition party without responsibility for the actual conduct of government, it was in a position to capitalize upon every significant event.

In succession the Republican leaders seized upon the Dred Scott decision and Buchanan's veto of a homestead bill to proclaim themselves the friends of freedom and of free land for small farmers in the territories. They pounced upon Hilton R. Helper's dull statistical volume, *The Impending Crisis of the South,* and commended its labored denunciation of Southern "lords of the lash" to the voters of 1858.

Similarly the Republicans made political capital of the panic of 1857. Despite the fact that neither the government's fiscal nor its administrative policies could have been responsible for the collapse of banks, railroads, insurance companies, and factories, they charged the entire calamity to Democratic incompetence and misfeasance. Of special importance for their strategy was the impact of the panic on the iron industry of Pennsylvania. There the ironmongers, ascribing their plight to the new Democratic tariff, revived the agitation for protection, and succeeded in projecting the issue into other sections. In Massachusetts both the *Boston Journal* and Samuel Bowles's *Springfield Republican* condemned the existing tariff, and in New York Horace Greeley resumed his ancient protectionism. Thus supported, the Pennsylvanians redoubled their efforts; the *Philadelphia North American* ran a series of articles by the arch-protectionist Henry Carey and employed a lecturer to instruct the city's mechanics on the rewards of a high tariff. When Republicans of the state nominated David Wilmot for governor, a candidate whose position on slavery extension was sound, but who had once been a free-trade Democrat, the protectionist elements determined to smoke him out. They finally extracted from him a statement that he was primarily interested in maintaining "the dignity and rights of free labor against the degrading competition of the labor of the slave," but was "equally in favor of protecting our American labor against a ruinous competition with the cheap labor of the old world." This consignment of the tariff issue to second place did not help his cause. The Democrats won an easy victory.

The lesson of the campaign was not lost, either inside or outside of Pennsylvania: the slavery issue alone might not be enough to carry the Keystone State. The situation was made for the protectionists, for without Pennsylvania the Republicans could not hope to win the election of 1860. In line with the program of the *North American*, which had voiced its dream of a national "People's Party" built on protection, they established such an organization. When it carried the city elections in the spring of 1858 and a few months later elected eighteen of the state's twenty-five congressmen, it gave the Republicans notice that they might be blackmailed in 1860.

Still, most Republican leaders continued to doubt the wisdom of making protectionism an election issue. Greeley, while he asserted that workingmen favored the tariff, questioned whether the party could endorse protection. Seward too was cautious, and New England was only lukewarm. Western Republicans were for the most part actively opposed. True, the *Chicago Tribune* came out gingerly for protection, and some of the old Whig elements of Ohio welcomed the movement, but the majority of Westerners saw no advantage in tariff agitation. Meantime, in 1859, the "People's Party" again swept Pennsylvania, dispelling the last doubt that the protectionists would hold the balance of power in 1860. As one of them wrote Justin Morrill, "We carried Pennsylvania . . . and can do so next year for any reasonable candidate who is right on the tariff, by 25,000 majority."

Taking heed, Republicans began to build up a tariff record in Congress. Justin Morrill of Vermont presented to the House a bill acceptable to Pennsylvania. Henry Carey arrived in Washington to lobby, and satellite New Jersey lent support. Western Republicans gave lip-service in the debate, voted for the measure with tongue in cheek, and secretly prayed for its defeat in the Democratic Senate. Their prayer was granted, and tariff protection entered the presidential campaign with Pennsylvania cracking a whip over the party.

While Pennsylvania was thus making its contribution to the growing body of Republican doctrine, Illinois was reaffirming the party's original program. In 1858 Stephen A. Douglas, repudiating an administration bill to admit Kansas under a proslavery constitution, quarreled with Buchanan and the Southerners. Republicans in Congress, gleeful over the prospect of a Democratic split that might in the end spell victory for their own party, sat in cheerful silence as Douglas and the Southerners exchanged excoriations over the Lecompton Constitution. They received a rude jolt, however, when Eastern politicos, more concerned with other issues than slavery, began to propose that Douglas be admitted to the party. Thoroughly alarmed, the Republicans of Illinois rejected the cautious and time-serving advice of the Easterners and found a champion to battle the "Little Giant."

The man of their choice was the Springfield lawyer Abraham Lincoln. When Douglas, still in Washington, heard of it, he admitted that he would have his hands full. "He is the strong man of his party — full of wit, facts, dates — and the best stump speaker, with his droll ways and dry jokes, in the West." The tall, ungainly Lincoln, long a practitioner in local politics, was already well known in Illinois. Early in the state's history he had distinguished himself in a legislative fight over the location of the capital. Once he had served, without distinction, as a Whig congressman. For years he had followed the life of a lawyer on the judicial circuits. Among fellow lawyers and among politicians and citizens who had had business before the courts he was known and well liked. As a storyteller he was celebrated among his colleagues of the bar, some of whom realized that his endless store of yarns was the key to a mind that thought in parables. Untutored and unschooled, he was nevertheless the master of an elevated literary style. Neither the high pitch of his voice, nor the typical twang of the Sucker State, nor his habit of pronouncing "such" as "sich," estranged his Illinois audiences. At the beginning of the Republican movement he had joined in the denunciation of Douglas and the Kansas-Nebraska bill, but when Illinois abolitionists had begun to organize for the campaign of 1854 he had pointedly avoided their meetings. When a state convention assembled in Springfield, Lincoln left town; and when it placed him on the permanent committee, he repudiated the action. Not until the death of the Whig Party was assured did Lincoln identify himself with its successor. By that time the Republican Party had been partly purged of the taint of abolitionism.

From the beginning of his campaign against Douglas, Lincoln concentrated upon the territorial issue. Slavery, he insisted, was already a decaying institution when the Constitution was written; its expansion into the territories would give it new life. Unless that was prevented, it would go on until it became "lawful alike in all the States, old as well as new, North as well as South." This, the basic doctrine of the "House Divided" speech, became his central theme. About it he wove the charge that Douglas, Taney, Pierce, and Buchanan — "Stephen, Roger, Franklin, and James" — had conspired to extend slavery into the territories. Douglas indignantly denied the accusation and counterattacked with the charge that the "Black Republicans" favored Negro equality. Painstakingly Lincoln laid out the proof that Republicans were not abolitionists; skillfully he demolished the Senator's prophecy that a Republican victory would produce a war upon Southern institutions. Again and again, throughout the state, the "Living Dog" pinned the label of proslavery upon the "Dead Lion" as he elaborated his own thesis that slavery must not enter the territories. When the two candidates met in the famous series of seven joint debates, the whole country watched expectantly. Douglas, whose entire future was at stake, was bent on committing his party to a program that would empower the people of the territories to decide the question of slavery for themselves. Lincoln too was defining the policies of his party. By the time the debates were ended, the Springfield lawyer had become the spokesman of Republicans throughout the entire Middle West.

Only one of the surcharged events of this four-year period gave the Republicans pause. John Brown's futile raid at Harpers Ferry shocked moderate Northerners quite as much as it frightened Southerners. Democrats of both North and South promptly circulated the charge that John Brown was the embodiment of Black Republicanism. Radical abolitionists, drawing upon long experience in exploiting martyrs, embarrassed the Republicans still more by claiming Brown. In 1856 they had complained that the party's platform — consisting of the single plank "to keep slavery out of Kansas provided the actual settlers there did not want it in" — was a "very small platform for a great party to stand upon." In gratitude for "very moderate mercies," they had given support, but without enthusiasm. Now they endorsed both Brown and the Republicans, while moderates, daring neither to condemn nor to endorse, teetered dangerously. It was unfortunate that the episode should have introduced an inharmonious element just at the moment Lincoln's speeches and the Helper affair were producing agreement on the basic territorial question, but in the end it did not seriously harm the Republicans. At his trial the great bearded martyr conducted himself with impressive dignity while the hysterical Virginians bungled both his prosecution and his execution. The immoderate assaults that Southerners had directed against Brown and the entire North served only to discredit the Democrats still further.

Thus in these formative years the Republicans strove valiantly to broaden their party base. Eagerly snatching straws from the wind of circumstance, they made use of every issue to confound their opponents. Immune from responsibility, Republican congressmen invited into the party all the disaffected elements of the North, however inharmonious: farmers, ironmongers, merchants, and manufacturers; radicals, conservatives, and moderates; Know-Nothings, Free Soilers, anti-Lecompton Democrats, and old-line Whigs. Young men among them had visions of a new, free nation; old men, hardened in the ways of politics, dreamed of new power. Perhaps none of them fully understood that they were forging a tool that was to convert the nation's economic life from agriculture to industry, and transform the federal union into a new nation. In solving some human problems they were to create a host of new ones. Perhaps they were indeed a "blundering generation."

Chapter 2

John Andrew and His
Conservative Neighbors

FOR the first six years bitter opposition to the South-ridden Democracy was the governing attitude of Republican leaders. Ringing all the changes upon it, they damned the Dred Scott decision, flayed the Democrats for the panic of 1857, denounced the extension of slavery, and hurled Helper's damning statistics at the "lords of the lash." But all this was negative, and a political party built on negation could not long endure. Such a campaign of invective might attract those who were already through with the Democrats. It could not hold them unless they were carefully organized under a positive program.

And that was no simple task. The coteries that made up the infant party were much too diverse to be rallied by a single battle cry. In the national forum Republican congressmen and spokesmen, journalists and publicists and pundits, however they might anathematize the common enemy, were powerless to weld together the multifarious interests of their allies. That was work which had to be done in the states. There the issues were simpler, the conflicting elements easier to handle, and the rewards for politicians more certain and more immediate. For six years, therefore, from 1854 to 1860, the Republican parties took form in the states. From rock-bound Maine to sunny California — the phrase was already trite in the fifties — nonconformists of many varieties banded

[17]

together in "Republican" organizations, invented suitable formulas, and settled upon state leaders. Yet even as they did so, they looked forward to the national convention and the presidential campaign of 1860.

In the east, from the slopes of the Alleghenies to the sea and from Mason and Dixon's line to the forests of Maine, abolitionism contended with the old Whig principles of the American system for the control of the new party. Within these states, where industry and commerce were supreme and where the financial centers of the land were located, conservatism — with one exception — won the victory. Here politicians learned the art of translating conservative economic objectives into humanitarian terms until the new Republican Party became little more than an enlarged Whig Party disguised in a new vocabulary.

The exception to the rule of Eastern conservatism was the Old Bay State of Massachusetts — the most influential of the far Eastern group of commonwealths. Within her boundaries lay the nucleus of much that was New England's distinctive contribution to American society: Boston, and the commerce that poured through her harbor, and Harvard College, which dominated the intellectual life of the region. From Massachusetts' leaders the other states were accustomed to take their cues.

For years the Whigs, representing the "men of quality," had eclipsed every other political element in the state. The Democratic Party, composed largely of humble Irish immigrants, had existed chiefly for federal patronage and had subsisted upon it. Early in the fifties, however, the emergence of the Free-Soil Party had disrupted political alignments in the Old Bay State. The Free-Soilers had combined with Democrats to elect a Governor and to send Charles Sumner to the United States Senate. Hardly had the state returned to sane Whig ways after this shock when Know-Nothingism racked it again. By 1855 the Whig Party was done for, and its members were hopefully surveying the new Republican movement. Within a couple of years an unstable combination of old Whigs, some Know-Nothings, and the erstwhile Free-Soilers were united under the Republican label, with Nathaniel P. Banks, a former Democrat, as their candidate for governor. In 1857 they elected Banks and killed off both the Know-Nothing and the Democratic opposition. Promptly, however, a fight began between the moderates and the radicals in the Banks party.

From 1858 until the election of 1860 the two factions dueled for supremacy. The suave and persuasive Banks, a veteran in politics, was a compromiser both by nature and by conviction. As Governor he tried to conciliate all elements in his party — old Whigs and former Free-Soilers, anti-Nebraska Democrats, and Know-Nothings. With an even hand he dealt out the executive patronage between the politically dead Know-Nothings and the vigorously alive radicals. On issues of policy and administration he yielded now to this group, now to that. But his compromise tactics served only to give the ever vigilant radicals the opportunity time and again to consolidate their own position. In the end they wrested control from him and the moderates.

The leader of the coterie of stand-pat radicals in the Banks party was John Albion Andrew, a native of Windham, Maine. Andrew was forty years old when Banks became Governor and had already displayed the uncompromising nature of the zealot. As a boy of fifteen he had read the first issue of Garrison's *Liberator* and from that day had been an ardent abolitionist. Like the true reformer of his generation, he had soon added temperance to his repertoire of crusades. Indeed, the young orator was equally ready to declaim poetry, expound the evils of intemperance, debate theology with the Baptists, or recite the rhetorical periods of the abolitionist journals. At Bowdoin College he sat at the feet of Longfellow, but apparently imbibed little interest in literature. His talents were manifestly vocal, and he soon distinguished himself as a member of the least important of the student literary societies. He served also in the honorary capacity of class poet, organized a peace society, and contributed generously to the verbal orgies of the college antislavery society. Sententiously the graduating adolescent wrote in a friend's album: "Stand fast, hold on, fear not; a few bullet holes through the bodies of reformers, though they destroy mortal life, are only so many sky lights for the truth to shine through and so much sooner will its light illumine the nations."

Such a character was predestined for the legal profession. In 1840, having read law in a Salem office, he was admitted to the Massachusetts bar and began to practice in Boston. But his progress was slow. Endowed though he was with an excellent speaking voice, which he put to service at every opportunity, he attracted few clients. To begin with, he was a far from prepossessing figure, conforming in no way to the popular stereotype of the statesman established by "Godlike Daniel Webster." From a feeble infant he had grown into an untidy, pudgy adult, large in frame, considerably overweight. Curly blond hair, hanging in ringlets about his forehead, framed an oily countenance from which peered a pair of bright blue eyes.

Had this want of physical grace been redeemed by exemplary professional conduct, he might have fared better. But Andrew was never a scholar; instead of applying himself to the study of law he dissipated his energies in all manner of unconventional philanthropies and moral causes. He visited the prisons and freely gave legal counsel to the inmates. He affiliated with the Church of the Disciples and became its Sunday-school superintendent. He was active in the Boston Port Society, organized to give religious instruction to sailors. With it all, he was in constant touch with the most fervent of the Boston abolitionists, preparing antislavery propaganda for the church papers. In politics, which offered a natural outlet for his talents, he was a staunch Free-Soiler. His closest political friend was Charles Sumner.

With his marriage, in 1848, Andrew found it expedient to withdraw for a time from many of his humanitarian enterprises and devote himself more seriously to his profession.

But he continued his relations with the Free-Soilers, and when the Kansas-Nebraska bill came up, he returned to active work in the party. In 1854 he was chairman of the state committee of extremists that nominated Henry Wilson for governor. After Wilson's defeat and subsequent defection to the Know-Nothings, Andrew retired from public view for the moment, but emerged again in 1856 as an unsuccessful candidate for attorney general on the "Honest Man's" ticket.

The next year, 1857, Andrew stood for the lower house of the General Court on the Banks ticket and was elected. Thereupon he promptly assumed the leadership of the clique opposed to Banks's policy of conciliation. During the first weeks of his term he debated the issues of the Dred Scott decision with Democrat Caleb Cushing. He was in no way Cushing's equal, either as a lawyer or as an orator, yet he managed to use the occasion to draw the radicals to him. His political dexterity and his friendship with Sumner, who was leading the antislavery fight in Congress, combined to make Andrew, next to Sumner himself and Henry Wilson, the most influential man in Massachusetts. Early in 1858 he again commended himself to the radicals by a direct assault on Banks. The Governor had denied the Massachusetts Anti-Slavery Society the customary privilege of meeting in the chamber of the House of Representatives, and Andrew elected to make an issue of the incident. A vote was taken in the House, the result of which stood 85 for Andrew and 81 for Banks. It was plain that the Governor's hold on his party was becoming precarious.

The rift was deepened by a more significant issue, involving a court reorganization. Under Andrew's leadership the radicals forced through a resolution demanding that Banks rescind the commission of a county probate judge who had surrendered a fugitive slave to its owner. Characteristically Banks embraced both horns of his dilemma by removing the judge and at the same time recommending repeal of the state's personal-liberty law. Once more, by compromising with the radicals instead of risking a fight, he strengthened this element in his party.

By 1859 Boston's rumor-mongers knew that all was not well at the statehouse. Every noon the public servants gathered at the Parker House, but in two separate dining-rooms: in one the Banks Club, moderates all, and in the other the Bird Club of legislators and leading lights of Boston abolitionism. The radicals, yielding to political considerations, avoided an actual break with the Banks party, but they overlooked no opportunity to bore from within. Whereas Banks had been re-nominated and re-elected without opposition in 1858, he thereafter steadily lost control to the radicals. In 1859 his party, at the same time that it renominated him, adopted resolutions drafted by Andrew that damned him with faint praise.

Presently the radicals, now in real control of the party, faced a new test of strength. When news came of John Brown's raid, the Banks men unhesitatingly condemned the deed of the fanatic. But not so John A. Andrew. He openly endorsed Brown, proclaimed him a martyr, and took up a collection for his defense. Privately he advised three Bostonians who had supplied Brown with arms and money to flee the state lest Banks honor a Virginia demand for their extradition. And when his zeal brought him a summons to appear before a congressional investigating committee, he took a bold stand before Democrats and Southerners, reiterated that Brown had been right, and returned home in high feather.

He now threw himself into the fight over delegates to the Republican nominating convention. Banks had momentary hope of getting the delegation, but since he did not come out openly as a candidate, Massachusetts radicals were able to undermine him. They were determined to send an anti-slavery delegation to Chicago and to press for the nomination of an avowed antislavery man. At the state convention, which was controlled by Andrew and his fellow radicals, a preponderantly radical delegation was chosen and instructed for William H. Seward. But the New Yorker had turned moderate, and Andrew, as he entrained for Chicago, was privately resolved to defeat his nomination.[1]

Neighboring states looked on as Massachusetts politicians jousted, but none of them repeated the performance. New Hampshire, Maine, and Connecticut passed from the old Whig ranks into the Republican camp with scarcely a skirmish. In New Hampshire Edward E. Rollins and William E. Chandler took the anti-Democratic forces in hand and welded them into an effective political unit. They succeeded in electing the radical William Huile Governor in 1857 and in keeping him in office for a second term. With Huile's administration, however, the high point in the state's radicalism had been reached. In 1859 the political bosses, seeing the expedience of greater moderation, gave the nomination to Ichabod Goodwin, a solid New England conservative of sixty-five.

Goodwin was a well-to-do merchant of Portsmouth. He had been a prosperous shipowner, had dabbled in local manufacturing enterprises, and was now president of two railroads. His lifelong quest for riches had not, however, occupied him to the exclusion of equally worthy services to society. Throughout the years he had been a faithful Whig, a delegate to national party conventions, and six times a member of the state legislature. Several times he had run unsuccessfully for Congress and once, in 1856, for governor. As the eminently conservative candidate of the well-organized Republicans, he won handily in 1859 and was renominated without opposition in 1860.

New Hampshire's campaign in the early months of 1860, as the first state campaign in a presidential year, attracted wide attention. At the Republican convention in January, party managers had shrewdly decided to postpone the selection of delegates to Chicago until after the election. Their coy delay brought its reward. Weed and Seward sent speakers, Banks

[1] Fred H. Harrington: "Nathaniel P. Banks," unpublished doctoral dissertation, New York University, 1935; H. G. Pearson: *Life of John A. Andrew*, I, 3.

lent aid, and Abraham Lincoln came on to make four speeches for Goodwin. Campaign managers supplemented the borrowed oratory with copies of the Helper compend and appealed to the Irish vote with the cardinal Republican precept of "Land for the Landless and Homes for the Homeless without money and without price." The result of it all was a gratifying 4,500 majority for Goodwin. The election over, the party convention selected Rollins, Huile, and eight others — all "judicious and reliable" men — to go to Chicago without instruction. Abraham Lincoln was to profit by the sagacity of New Hampshire's political managers. On the first ballot at Chicago seven of the state's ten votes went to the man from Illinois.[2]

In Connecticut the Republican Party, though it was born of the slavery issue, inherited both the economic program and the basic conservatism of the Whigs. Until 1857 its margin of supremacy over the Democrats was narrow, but with the panic of that year it was able to capitalize on the prevailing economic disorder. In 1858 it nominated for the governorship a rubber-goods manufacturer, William A. Buckingham, for whom a state convention of businessmen and bankers had expressed its esteem. In the face of this support from solid business interests, the recent panic, and the candidate's unassailable reputation, victory was a foregone conclusion.

The new Governor was an old Whig completely untouched by Know-Nothingism. Endowed with the major New England virtues, he already had behind him, at fifty-four, a career of financial prosperity and quiet respectability. After leaving the academy at Colchester he had mounted the ladder of success step by step; he was successively teacher in a district school, farm worker on his father's acres, dry-goods clerk, storekeeper at twenty-two, carpet manufacturer at twenty-six, and in 1848, ten years before he became Governor, organizer of a rubber company. Only thrift, industry, and rectitude could produce such a rise in Connecticut, and so his fellow

2 Hobart Pillsbury: *New Hampshire: A History,* Vol. III.

citizens recognized when they made him treasurer, then
mayor, of Norwich. His election to the governorship in 1858
was followed by seven successive re-elections, though often
by narrow margins. Thus his eight years in the gubernatorial
office carried him through the war. He was to be one of the
most dependable and most efficient of Lincoln's war governors.

Buckingham's political strength lay in his talent for keeping
before his constituents the close connection between moral
and economic issues. In his first inaugural, which was largely
given over to the need for rigid economy and banking reform, he deplored the federal government's extension of "the
system of human bondage" as a contradiction of "principles
involving our business and our civil liberty." And again in
1859: "The citizens of Connecticut regard slavery as a system that paralyses industry, dries up the sources of prosperity,
obstructs education, civilization, and Christianity." An energetic Congregationalist, the Governor was well equipped to
expound the interrelations between morals and economics.
The *Springfield Republican* rejoiced, after his election in
1859, that the Connecticut party now had "greater moral and
intellectual strength," "new and abler representative men,
and broader and more popular principles."

Buckingham's formula was attractive, but it did not ensure
a landslide. State politics were still close enough to sustain
the hope of the Democrats. The spring elections of 1860, like
those of other New England states, were being closely followed throughout the nation, and observers were therefore
more than casually interested when Connecticut Democrats
nominated the most popular man of their party — Thomas
H. Seymour, who had been Pierce's Minister to Russia. The
campaign attracted outside money, brought in visiting speakers, and inspired the formation of marching clubs of "Wide-
Awakes" and "Chapultapers," who made more noise than
staid old Connecticut had heard since Jackson's day. Speech-
makers harangued their audiences on the fallacies of Republican doctrine, warning manufacturers that disunion and ruin

would follow in the wake of a Republican victory. The result of the fanfare and campaign oratory was to swell the Democratic vote from 8,000 in 1859 to 9,000 in 1860 and to reduce Buckingham's majority to 541. But the Republican victory was nevertheless significant. It infused new hope in the delegates who were to assemble in Chicago six weeks later.[3]

The neighboring state of Vermont had long outshone even Massachusetts and Connecticut in the fervency of her abolitionism. For years she had proudly boasted of having abolished slavery in her first constitution, leading attacks upon the Southern system, and of her personal-liberty laws. No sooner had the Senate passed the Kansas-Nebraska bill than Vermonters appealed to all enemies of iniquity to join in protest. In co-operation with the Westerners they launched a Republican Party, into which Free-Soilers and Whigs slid without undue difficulty.

But Vermont Republicans had more than one string to their bow. They too had long been aware of the close connection between antislavery and industrial progress. At their convention of 1854 they advocated "a tariff for revenue with proper discrimination in favor of American industry." This endorsement of protection — the first in the history of the Republican Party — was supplemented by a long list of other planks: homesteads, internal improvements, cheaper postal rates, and prohibition. With this well-rounded program, so prophetic of the future, the party carried the election and sent a Republican delegation to Congress.

Most conspicuous of the Vermonters in Congress was Justin Morrill, long a student of tariff problems. Morrill sponsored two measures that were ultimately to become cardinal tenets of the Republican creed. One was a protective tariff, which delighted Pennsylvania's avid ironmongers; the other a bill to promote agricultural education in the states by federal loans. When Buchanan vetoed the second of these meas-

[3] Samuel G. Buckingham: *The Life of William A. Buckingham*, pp. 31–53; *New York Times*, March 22, 23, 26, 1860.

ures, the Republican Party promptly became the farmer's friend and added education to its ever lengthening agenda.

Vermont's contributions to the party's ideology gave the state an intellectual prestige quite unwarranted either by the size of her electoral vote or by the personal influence of her leaders. As the election of 1860 approached, the chief aspirants for the Republican nomination angled for her support. From Massachusetts came Banks's men to spend long evenings with Vermont politicians, and from New York Seward's supporters, bearing promises of money from Thurlow Weed. But the canny Green Mountain Boys foresaw that an uninstructed delegation would have power in Chicago. Although the ten delegates were evenly divided between Banks and Seward, they agreed to cast their first vote for a favorite son, Jacob Collamer, and after that to fish in the stream of events.[4]

Powerful as abolitionism was in New England politics, the experience of the minuscule but turbulent state of Rhode Island proved that alone it was not enough to turn the scale. There the more vociferous of the Free-Soilers appropriated the rising Republican movement, recklessly snubbing the conservative Whigs and the Know-Nothings. Early in 1860 a Republican state convention elected as its chairman an uncompromising Garrisonian and nominated a state ticket of "straight-out" abolitionists. Over the protests of the "ex-Whigs" they tendered the nomination for governor to one Seth Padelford, a wealthy grocer who had shown commendable zeal but was altogether wanting in political experience. The *Providence Journal* withheld its endorsement of the candidate, and cautious Republicans outside the state groaned despairingly. It took no seer to predict where such crusading blindness would lead.

The Democrats knew their cue. At once they assembled and assigned their leading role to William Sprague, a veritable

[4] G. G. Benedict: *Vermont in the Civil War*, Vol. I, *passim;* W. H. Crockett: *Vermont: the Green Mountain State*, III, 419 *et passim.*

glamour boy of politics. Just past his twenty-ninth birthday, Sprague was admittedly the handsomest man in all the length and breadth of Rhode Island. He was also the richest. From his father he had inherited cotton mills that had survived without a tremor the crashes of 1857 and that were to multiply his wealth many times over with the coming of war contracts. His father had been murdered — possibly, it was said, because he had refused to permit the Providence council to issue a liquor license. This tragedy and the removal of paternal authority did not strengthen young William's shallow character, but merely gave it free rein. For a time the boy attended academies, but the world of learning held no attraction for him. More to his taste was the tinseled glint of bayonets on the parade ground of the Providence Marine Artillery Company. When this martial-sounding unit elected him its colonel, he reciprocated by outfitting the entire company with Zouave uniforms, which he selected personally in France. These purchases he was bringing home, late in January 1860, when he learned of his nomination for governor. The Democrats had set the stage for a rousing campaign; a salute from hundreds of guns welcomed the traveler home from abroad; the marine artillerists, in gaudy array, marched down the streets of Providence rending the air with their cheers; and the city's elder citizens gave munificent banquets in his honor.

The conservative Republicans — ex-Whigs and Americans — withdrew their support from the abolitionist grocer and transferred it to Sprague. By so doing they ensured his election. The lesson was taken deeply to heart by all the men who were speculating about Chicago. Unless that meeting brought forth a conservative, Republicans generally would play into the hands of the Democrats. To Abraham Lincoln, watching from Springfield, the close vote in Connecticut and the "quasi defeat" in Rhode Island made Seward's chances in New England seem very dubious. Yet Sam Bowles, editor of the *Springfield Republican,* continued to assure Weed that all the New

England delegates save a few from Connecticut would go to Seward. Apparently the real issue in New England was whether Seward could satisfy both the radical abolitionist and the conservative, antislavery businessman.[5]

In the middle Atlantic states politicians no longer blinked the necessity for conservatism. True, Andrew's star was rising in Massachusetts, but the conservative Banks was still Governor, and in the rest of New England conservative businessmen of the Whig tradition were leading the Republican Party. Even less sympathetic with antislavery excesses were the businessmen of New York, New Jersey, and Pennsylvania; in these states the party must rest on a solid economic foundation. To Senator Seward, coveting the party's nomination, New England's spring elections came as both opportunity and challenge, and he rose in the Senate to speak. What he said on the issues was unimportant; what he said about himself was significant. His moderate and conciliatory words and his soft speech and gracious manner were meant to assure the men of the North that he was a conservative to whom the government could be safely entrusted.

Deft though he was, Seward could not at one stroke wipe out a lifetime of antislavery agitation. His failure to denounce slavery cost him the confidence of the radicals, and his new-found conservatism did not ring true among conservatives. The Know-Nothings, a real force in Republican ranks, could not forget old scores; no political nativist could escape certain misgivings about a man who had repeatedly assured foreigners and Catholics of his friendship. Contributing further to the general skepticism was the notorious corruption of the New York legislature, a byword throughout the land, which reflected no credit on bosses Weed and Seward. And finally, unknown to Weed and minimized by the Senator, there was

[5] H. W. Shoemaker: *The Last of the War Governors*, pp. 3–14; *New York Times*, January 9, 13, 30, April 6, 1860; G. A. Tracy (ed.): *Uncollected Letters of Abraham Lincoln*, pp. 141–2; E. D. Fite: *The Presidential Campaign of 1860*, p. 120; Thurlow Weed: *Memoir*, II, 260–1.

Horace Greeley's secret enmity. In 1854 the eccentric editor of the *New York Tribune* had gagged at the necessity of supporting his journalistic rival Henry J. Raymond of the *Times* for the lieutenant-governorship. At the close of the campaign he had written Seward a petulant letter informing him of the "dissolution of the political firm of Seward, Weed, and Greeley, by the withdrawal of the junior partner." Thereafter he had nursed his grievances in silence, storing up venom against the day of vengeance.

Thus Seward was handicapped. Yet he could not be ignored by the ambitious Republicans. For he and his alter ego, Thurlow Weed, controlled the state of New York and its large electoral vote. In 1858, at the party's convention in Syracuse, Weed had worsted his opponents and thereafter wielded control over the Republicans as he once had over the Whigs. Token of his pre-eminence was the party's acceptance of his choice for governor, Edwin D. Morgan.

Governor Morgan, forty-eight, able, dignified, and physically attractive, was a man to arouse confidence. His tall, well-built figure was surmounted by a magnificent head, and his handsome countenance was illumined by expressive, lustrous eyes. The inner man behind this personable exterior was also well endowed; a good mind and practical ability were combined with a moral character that had kept unblemished both his private and his public life. His long and respectable business career had begun in his native state of Connecticut, where as a young man he had been a successful grocer and a member of the Hartford city council. At the age of twenty-five he had removed to New York, where he had established a wholesale grocery. To this he had added in time a banking and brokerage business, which during his first term as Governor sold thirty million dollars' worth of bonds for the state of Missouri and the city of St. Louis. His political career, too, had been without reverses. He had served as a member and as president of New York's board of aldermen; he had been a senator at Albany; and he had been commissioner of immigration. In 1856 he was made chairman of the Republican

National Committee, and this onerous post he retained until 1862.

Morgan's first administration was marked by both honesty and conservatism. He vetoed bills for granting franchises to corrupt railway companies in New York City, and he set an example of calm business judgment in the midst of sectional controversy. In January 1860 he delivered to the legislature a message that reflected the growing conservatism of Seward and Weed. Following a few short paragraphs on federal-state relations, it presented a complete balance sheet of the affairs of the commonwealth. Morgan professed his attachment to the "strongest Republican creed." In actual fact he embodied the most conservative interests of the party over whose councils he presided.[6]

It was in Pennsylvania, however, that conservative forces bore down the hardest and radicalism was most effectively silenced. So repugnant to most Pennsylvanians was the antislavery agitation of Republicans elsewhere that even the party name was rejected in favor of another, the "People's Party." The only issue that had vote-catching appeal was the tariff.

The unanimity on protection did not, however, heal the breach that divided the ranks of Pennsylvania politicians. In 1854 the Know-Nothings had elected a Whig Governor and a Democratic canal commissioner and had control of a majority in the legislature. After the election Simon Cameron, railroad lawyer and aspiring politician, had deserted the Democracy and had announced simultaneously his affiliation with the Know-Nothings and his candidacy for the United States Senate. His opponent was Andrew Gregg Curtin, secretary of the commonwealth and promoter of a rival railroad. Cameron's defeat of Curtin was only the immediate result of the senatorial contest. The enmity it engendered between the two men was to divide Pennsylvania politics for a generation.

[6] D. S. Alexander: *A Political History of the State of New York*, II, 248 ff.; Weed: *Memoir*, II, 277; Fite: *Election of 1860*, pp. 120–1; *New York Times*, January 4, 1860.

Curtin consoled himself for the loss of the senatorship by devoting himself to the duties of his office. As ex-officio superintendent of schools, he sponsored larger appropriations for education and established a number of normal schools. These and other services to his community won him many friends, as did his personal qualifications. His fine six-foot, broadshouldered, symmetrical figure was a splendid vehicle for his powerful oratory, which made up in rhetoric and wit what it lacked in grammar and literary finish. In his profession of the law he had never been a scholar, but the charm of his personality, the dignity of his bearing, and the roaring torrent of his words had made their impression on juries and played their part in his political career. He was right on most of the things that counted. He gave generously to churches. He talked convincingly about education. And he was sound on the tariff.

In 1860 it was evident that Curtin could carry the state. But to Simon Cameron he was still an enemy. When the People's Party met in convention at Harrisburg on Washington's Birthday, the Senator marshaled his forces in support of Congressman John Covode, who had made a name for himself investigating Democratic corruption in Washington. Covode had a personal following, and Cameron had influence with the anti-Nebraska and Know-Nothing elements. Throughout a long, wearisome night the opposing forces battled, only to arrive at compromise in the morning. Curtin was nominated for governor and selected to head the People's Party delegation to the Republican convention in Chicago. But the delegates were pledged to support Cameron for the Presidency. They understood that Cameron personally supported Seward, and that they were expected to vote once for their favorite son and then throw their support to the New Yorker. But some of them were Curtin men, sharing their leader's deep hatred for the unscrupulous Senator.[7]

[7] A. K. McClure: *Abraham Lincoln and Men of War Time*, pp. 41, 248 f.; W. H. Egle: *Andrew Gregg Curtin*, pp. 103 f., 444 ff.; S. L. Davis: *Pennsylvania Politics, 1860–1863*, pp. 53–65; *Philadelphia Pennsylvanian*, February 22, 1860.

Neighboring New Jersey, possessing only four electoral votes, could expect no stellar role in the unfolding political drama. Its Republican Party was merely a satellite revolving in the orbit of the more powerful organizations in New York and Pennsylvania. But though it shone only in reflected light and generated no heat of its own, the reflection was nevertheless a faithful one. As in Pennsylvania, the party eschewed the Republican cognomen and adopted another, the "Opposition Party." Preponderantly old Whig and Know-Nothing in composition, it too was more interested in the tariff than in the abolition crusade.

New Jersey's Governor was Charles Smith Olden, a Quaker in whose modest, retiring person all the conservatism of the "old opposition" found harbor. From his Quaker ancestors he had inherited a talent for business, which he had used to amass a fortune. After a long career as merchant and trader in Princeton, Philadelphia, and New Orleans he had returned to Princeton, built himself a mansion, and settled down to the tranquil, leisurely life of a gentleman farmer. For a time his seclusion was interrupted only by his duties as director of a Trenton bank. In 1845, however, the Whigs, recognizing that his eminent respectability was political capital, persuaded him to run for the state senate, where he served his county until 1851. In 1859 Olden seemed the most available gubernatorial candidate for the new-forming quasi-Republicans. They nominated him, and his popularity in the rural districts bore him to victory. His inaugural address, sane, moderate, and devoid of pyrotechnics, promised reform in the treatment of prisoners and the insane and the enforcement of the Fugitive Slave Act. Despite his Quaker faith, he worked also for improvement in the state's militia system.

New Jersey's conservatism, albeit a reflection of local conflicts elsewhere, aroused hope in the breast of a favorite son, William L. Dayton. What was needed, as local observers saw it, was a candidate who was an avowed Republican, who had demonstrated his "backbone," and who was right on the tariff. They realized that Seward, who had Cameron's support in

Pennsylvania but not Curtin's, could not carry the state. Judge Dayton, on the other hand, a "Republican conservative," sound on both slavery and the tariff, might carry both Pennsylvania and New Jersey. And so they permitted themselves to hope that the fires of controversy in adjoining states would leave the party no choice but their own candidate.[8]

Thus was the East committed to moderation, to conservatism in economics, and to expediency in politics. Except for John Andrew's strident tones, the voice of the East was the voice of the old Whig Party. John Andrew's neighboring governors were solid substantial men, more devoted to the rights of property than to agitation about the rights of man. To states' rights, too, each in his own way was devoted.

[8] *Dictionary of American Biography;* J. T. Sherman to Tweedy, March 2, 1860, Tweedy MSS.; *New York Times,* January 19, 1860.

Chapter 3

A Gallery of Western Governors

s Eastern Republicans came out with mild and conciliatory programs and safe and sane tickets, Republicans of the Middle West retreated from their early extremism. Had they been in an intransigent mood, Westerners might have claimed a lien on the party they had ushered in and have refused to cooperate with the moderate men of the old American-system Whiggery, which the boiling political pot was bringing to the surface. But few of the men of the West were obstinate. After the experience of 1856 it was clear that ultimate victory depended on their readiness to yield ground.

Principles, the men of the West realized, must be redefined in a way to broaden the party base. As the Eastern lessons became clear, political leaders sought for a formula that would incorporate the non-extension of slavery, but would remove from the party the taint of abolitionism. Forewarned, the Republicans of the West, and especially of Ohio, Indiana, and Illinois, got to work. These three states were the political and economic center of the Middle West. Upon their achievements hung the party's fate in the nation.

Ohio was not yet competing with Virginia for the title of "Mother of Presidents," but even in 1860 she was fostering a number of presidential candidates. Oldest of the Middle Western states, she was the most developed industrially and commercially, and thus saw more clearly the emerging conflict between agriculture and industry and voiced it more explicitly. Railroads, canals, and the Ohio River traffic entered con-

stantly into the calculations of Ohio's men. The internal
conflict was intensified also by the operation of certain ances-
tral influences. The Western Reserve migrants from New
England had in their makeup a strain of crusading zeal that
went far to explain not only their adoption of abolitionism,
but the vigor they infused into it — a vigor it never had
in Garrison's Massachusetts — and the eventual fruition of
the movement as a political force. In the southern counties the
descendants of Virginia's colonial soldiers held title to the
military bounty lands, practiced agriculture, and thought
Southern thoughts. Commercial Cincinnati, whose golden
life-blood flowed from her Southern trade, turned her back on
the state to watch Kentucky and guard her Southern markets.
Thus divided internally, Ohio could not present a united
front to the nation, but the very intensity of her intra-state
conflicts seemed to breed a swarm of presidential aspirants.

The Western Reserve presented to the nation its Senator, a
rough-hewn man whose crudity of manner and bluntness of
speech had earned him the title of "Bluff" Ben Wade. Senator
Wade had learned the lessons of antislavery from the crusading Joshua R. Giddings and had whetted his political sense on
the rough rocks of Ohio politics. In Congress, where he functioned as a Whig, he had endeared himself to abolitionists by
calling the bluff of the haughty Southerners. These were the
turbulent days of the 1850's, when Southerners were wont to
challenge their antislavery opponents to meetings on the field
of honor. Northerners were unaccustomed to such personal
combats; indeed, most Northern states had long since out-
lawed dueling and had denied office to anyone who gave or accepted a challenge. Thus the sensitive Southern honor was
quite safe until Bluff Ben Wade arrived on the senatorial
scene.

At the first opportunity the new Ohio Senator accepted a
challenge and named squirrel rifles at thirty paces as his weapons. There the matter ended, however. It was obvious to the
Southerner that a man who could suggest such ignoble weap-

ons for an affair of honor was a quite unworthy opponent for
one of gentle breeding. On another occasion Wade listened
attentively while a proslavery orator, with tears in his eyes,
whimpered that the Republican territorial policy would prevent his taking the family's old Negro mammy into Kansas.
"We have not the slightest objection," interjected Wade. "We
only insist that he shall not be empowered to sell her after
taking her there." Such brutal jabbing of the Southern balloon infuriated the Southerners and endeared Wade to the
radical antislavery forces. But he was too coarse-grained a person to be seriously considered as a presidential candidate.
Nevertheless he was quite willing to serve and stood on the
crags vainly hoping the lightning would strike him.

A more finished gentleman but one no less radical in his
antislavery principles was pompous Salmon Portland Chase.
With his tall, heavy-set frame, his stately bearing, his firm
mouth and well-shaped head, the Ohio Senator's physical as-
sets would have betokened only supreme moral strength and
probity had it not been for his somewhat shifty eyes and
slightly drooping eyelids. These revealed the politician beneath the shell of the statesman. Ignorant of human nature,
deficient in his judgment of men, he pinned his hope of political preferment on his rigid adherence to abolitionist principles. More convinced of his own worth than any of his fellows,
he was for two decades a perennial presidential aspirant. He
could never understand why, with his tireless energy, massive
eloquence, and shrewd intellect, successive parties should all
pass him by for lesser men.

He had begun as a Democrat. Later he joined the Free-
Soilers, and in 1849 a coalition of Democrats and Free-Soilers
sent him to the Senate. There he opposed the Nebraska bill
and fought against Douglas and Buchanan. At the end of his
term a Democratic legislature replaced him with George
Pugh.[1] But Chase was not through. He ran for governor, was
elected in the face of his abolitionism, and devoted his admin-

[1] Whitelaw Reid: *Ohio in the Civil War*, I, 17–19.

istration to reforming the state militia. Meantime he sought
to square himself with the rising tide of Republican conservatism. He discovered, when the tariff men began their campaign, that he had always favored protection. Surely, he declared, there could be no difference among Republicans on
this issue. "I am a practical man," he added hopefully. "No
man deserves the name of an American Statesman who would
not so shape American legislation and administration as to
protect American industry." [2]

Chase's efforts to ingratiate himself with conservatives were
largely gratuitous, for in 1859 it was the abolitionists who
were in control of Ohio's Republican convention. So insist-
ently did the antislavery sentiment cry for expression there
that the meeting demanded a repeal of the Fugitive Slave Act.
To Abraham Lincoln, watching every move from Springfield,
this seemed a mistake, for it played into the hands of those
who charged Republicans with opposition to the Consitution.
"And it is the very thing," he said, "that will greatly endanger
our cause, if it is not kept out of our national Convention." [3]
As for Chase personally, Lincoln supposed him to be "right-
minded," but still not the right man for the Presidency. To
Chase himself Lincoln declared that the introduction of such
a plank would "explode the national convention." [4]

During the campaign that fall, Lincoln came into Ohio to
define the narrow line between the non-extension of slavery
and its abolition. "The Republican party," he told a Columbus audience, "believes that there is great danger of the institution of slavery being spread out and extended until it is
ultimately made alike lawful in all the States of the Union."
To forestall this was "the original and chief purpose" of the
party. Of course, once in power, it would have to attend to
"all the other matters of national housekeeping," but the
"chief and real purpose of the Republican party is eminently

[2] *New York Times,* October 25, 1859.

[3] Lincoln to Sam Galloway, July 28, 1859 in *Writings of Abraham
Lincoln,* V, 30–1.

[4] Paul M. Angle: *New Letters and Papers of Lincoln,* pp. 206–7.

conservative." [5] Again at Cincinnati he promised that Republicans would not interfere with slavery where it already existed, and would not withhold an efficient fugitive slave law. But they would forestall the extension of slavery, the revival of the African slave trade, and the enactment of a territorial slave code.[6]

However radical the course of Ohio's Republicans in denouncing the Fugitive Slave Act, they were guided by conservative counsel in their choice of a gubernatorial candidate. William Dennison was sufficiently conservative, respectable, and wealthy to have met the needs of any one of the New England states. Scion of a family prominent in the Miami Valley, he had married the daughter of a wealthy stagecoach magnate. As lawyer, banker, and railroad man he had reached a position of eminence, which he graced with impeccable social connections, elegant manners, and ultra-fashionable attire. He had a reputation for financial ability and for large-scale administration. His political experience was meager, but it included one term in the state senate, where he had led a successful movement to repeal Ohio's "Black Laws." He had joined the Republicans at the beginning, had attended the Pittsburgh convention, and had served as chairman of the state's delegation at Philadelphia.

As nominee for governor Dennison surprised even his supporters by his ability on the stump. Matched against the popular Judge Rufus P. Ranney, he proved himself the judge's intellectual superior. Yet though the majority of Ohioans voted for him in October, they were never quite sure but that he was a man "wholly frittered away in polish." For unfortunately Dennison lacked the common touch. He could compliment the people's intellects, but he could not reach their hearts. His inaugural address, prolix and stilted, missed entirely the emotional basis of the Republican crusade. If the South seceded, he declared, a standing army "would be the Succedaneum for the security conferred by a common government."

[5] *Writings of Lincoln,* V, 38–9.
[6] Ibid., p. 109.

Such aristocratic pig-Latin disgusted the radicals of the Western Reserve. Thenceforth Dennison was the "succeedaneum Governor," never quite trusted even by his followers.[7]

A few days after his inauguration Dennison proclaimed his conservatism by playing host to the legislatures and governors of Kentucky and Tennessee. Heralded as a great Union-saving movement, the joint meeting of the three legislatures was actually no more nor less than a junket inspired and sponsored by the Louisville & Nashville Railroad. Himself a railroad man — president of the Columbus & Xenia Railroad — Dennison appreciated the necessity of saving the Union for the railroads. On other grounds Governor Magoffin of Kentucky, too, repudiated any desire to dissolve the Union. "Sirs," said he to Dennison's banquet guests, "we have no hearts nor arms for fraternal strife, but, sirs, we have millions of brave hearts and powerful arms ready to preserve this whole Union." All this hobnobbing with Southerners did Dennison no good with the radicals of his own party.[8]

Hopelessly divided though it was, the Ohio contingent to Chicago gave early promise of being important in the councils of the party.[9] The delegation went half pledged to support John McLean, Supreme Court justice. An old Jacksonian, McLean had watched the shifting sands of politics from the bench and awaited an opportunity to commend himself to some new party. With an eye on the coming campaign he had written a dissenting opinion on Dred Scott. But it was now too late. McLean was too old to be seriously considered, although Lincoln did seem to concede the possibility of his nomination. Believing him to be stronger than Seward in Illinois, Lincoln speculated whether, if McLean should be nominated and elected, the Republicans could prevent the Democrats from appointing his successor on the bench. Perhaps Lincoln was merely telling off the objections to any candidacy but his

[7] Reid: *Ohio in the War,* I, 26–7, 1017–19.

[8] E. O. Randall and D. J. Ryan: *History of Ohio,* IV, 152–3.

[9] Murat Halstead: *The Caucuses of 1860: A History of the National Political Conventions,* p. 122.

own. "The taste is in my mouth a little," he confessed, "and this, no doubt, disqualifies me to some extent, to form correct opinions." Yet not even the anxious Lincoln took McLean — or any other Ohio candidate — very seriously.[10]

In Indiana the Republican situation was somewhat less confused. Hoosiers along the Ohio River were of Southern descent and of Democratic, proslavery sentiments. Those north of the Old National Road had come from New England and the middle Atlantic states. So evenly divided was the population in ancestry and interests that Indiana had long been — and would long continue to be — a doubtful state. This very uncertainty gave the state an undue influence. Because in most elections the touch of a feather would turn the scale either way, all parties used gold-tipped feathers to push it the right way. There was probably no conspiracy between opposing politicians to keep the Hoosier State doubtful, but they certainly profited from the situation.

At the beginning of the Republican movement Indiana's Free-Soilers and Whigs united in a People's Party, which after the fiasco of 1856 offered the Know-Nothings also a political haven. From the first, Indiana Republicans showed more interest in winning elections than in the party's principles. Activated as they were by a practical realism, their course was seldom complicated by deep convictions or crusading idealism.

In 1856 they nominated for governor the handsome, intellectually gifted, and magnetic Oliver Perry Morton. Morton had lived his whole thirty-three years in the state, having been brought up on its frontier. He brought to politics a mind hardened but not refined by the Scotch Presbyterianism of his ancestors. After studying at Miami University, where he had distinguished himself as a debater, he had read law and been admitted to the bar. For eight months, as a Democrat, he had served as a county judge. In 1854, sensing a political opportunity rather than a moral obligation, he deserted the Democracy and threw in his lot with the Republicans. He had been

[10] Tracy: *Uncollected Letters of Lincoln,* pp. 142–4.

an avowed free-trader, and he did not abandon the popular
issue with his defection to the Republicans. He had been a
hard-money Democrat; he became a hard-money Republican.
Not until long after the Civil War, when Indiana became in-
flationist, did he advocate paper money. Thus Morton was an
opportunist who adapted his principles to the demands of
politics.

Irresistible as Morton's qualifications may have seemed —
personal attractiveness combined with popular ideas — they
did not save him from defeat. Moreover, he had seriously impaired his political future by an overzealous exegesis of his
new-found antislavery principles. Four years later the Hoosier
Republicans were determined to carry their state at all costs,
for Indiana's electoral vote was necessary to a national victory.
If they played their cards right — that is, if they were sanely
conservative — they stood a good chance of defeating the
state's Democracy, sadly divided over the burgeoning conflict
between Stephen A. Douglas and President Buchanan. They
settled on Henry S. Lane, old-time Whig, for governor. Morton they nominated for lieutenant governor to pacify antislavery men who were finding it hard to stomach this sudden
moderation of the party. Even so, it was generally understood
that if the Republicans carried the legislature, Lane would
go to the Senate and Morton would become governor.

Since Lane was really running for the Senate, the national
aspects of the campaign devolved upon him, and Morton
undertook to convert the wavering Hoosiers to Republicanism. On March 18 Morton opened his campaign at Terre
Haute with an exhaustive disquisition on Republican principles. Popular sovereignty, he told his audience, was wrong
in principle and destructive in operation. The correct constitutional view was that the territories were dependent on
the national will. The Republican Party, advocating no mere
sectional dogmas, would preserve the territories for freedom
and the benefit of the whole nation. The Republican Party
was conservative, whereas the Democrats were flirting with
radical constitutional ideas. As for John Brown, his acts were

deplorable, the skillful orator admitted, but the blame rested squarely upon the South for inciting disorders in Kansas. The Democrats were bent on extending slavery into the territories, and their agent in the foul plot was the Supreme Court. "That body," charged Morton, was "an irresponsible tribunal, the members of which hold their offices for life, and who are not elected by nor responsible to the people: a tribunal which, for many years, has been used as a place of retirancy for broken, spavined, and asthmatic politicians." Under the Democrats the Court had been "converted into an engine for the subversion of free institutions and the propagation of human slavery." The Republican Party would see that it was reformed. The party recognized the right of the South to a fugitive slave law. It was not an abolitionist party. It was in favor of protection to industry, but opposed to monopoly. It was in favor of a homestead law.[11]

Meanwhile Lane was working industriously on the problem of the coming Chicago convention. When Weed approached him, promising to spend enough money to carry Indiana for both Lane and Seward, the Hoosier candidate was tempted but did not fall. Weed's reputation was unsavory, and Seward's radicalism and anti-Know-Nothingism were serious if not insuperable obstacles in Indiana.[12] Frankly looking for a candidate, Lane listened to the supporters of Edward Bates, McLean, Chase, and Banks, but made no promises. The situation was made for Abraham Lincoln. Already able to count on a few friends in the Indiana delegation, he induced Jesse Dubois and David Davis to "confer" with the delegates, who arrived in Chicago a week early. Before the convention met they had thrown in their lot with Lincoln.[13]

Meantime, in Illinois, Lincoln was carefully nurturing his budding prospects. After his Douglas debates he let no one

[11] W. M. French: *Life . . . of Oliver P. Morton*, pp. 21 ff.; W. D. Foulke: *Life of Oliver P. Morton*, I, 72.

[12] William E. Baringer: *Lincoln's Rise to Power*, p. 273.

[13] Tracy: *Uncollected Letters of Lincoln*, p. 146.

forget what his part had been in the party's development. In 1857 and 1858 he had been alarmed by the proposal of Greeley and other Easterners that Illinois Republicans let Douglas win re-election and thus defeat Buchanan's schemes in Kansas.[14] In accepting the senatorial nomination of the Republican ticket, Lincoln let it be known that he espoused the hopeless cause in order to save the party in Illinois. After his defeat he continued to work for the same end. When Douglas went south to repair the damage his Freeport Doctrine had wrought, Lincoln predicted that the majority of the Democratic politicians "mean to kill him." But he doubted that they would select the best means. If they put him to no new test and defeated him in convention, the Little Giant could not desert the ticket. But if they pushed a slave code on him, he would bolt and appeal to all Northern men to make common cause against the slave power. Then "the struggle in the North will be, as it was in Illinois . . . whether the Republican party can maintain its identity, or be broken up to form the tail of Douglas's new kite." [15] To Salmon P. Chase he insisted that he had saved the party. "Had we thrown ourselves into the arms of Douglas as re-electing him by our votes would have done, the Republicans' cause would have been annihilated in Illinois and, as I think, demoralized and prostrated everywhere for years, if not forever." [16]

Having established his lien on the Republican Party and his right to interpret its doctrines, the Springfield politician carefully guarded his position. When one old friend proposed a unification of all opposing forces under the slogan "Opposition to the opening of the Slave Trade; and eternal hostility to the rotten democracy," Lincoln retorted that such weasel words would "probably carry Maryland," but no other state. The Republican Party had been founded on opposition to the extension of slavery; it could not abandon that ground.[17] And when John J. Crittenden, Clay's successor in the Senate, sought to don the great compromiser's mantle by proposing

---

[14] Tracy: *Uncollected Letters of Lincoln*, pp. 82–4.
[15] Ibid., pp. 96–8.　　[16] Ibid., p. 109.　　[17] Ibid., pp. 111–13.

unity on a platform of "the Constitution, the Union, and the enforcement of the laws," Lincoln sagely reminded him that the Constitution had been "the shibboleth of every party of malcontents" from the Hartford Convention to John C. Calhoun. The platform would be meaningless. In any case, he added sententiously, "compromises of principles break of their own weight." [18]

This rigid adherence to correct dogmas and devotion to party interests brought its rewards. Illinois observers had begun to notice that old-line Whigs were none too happy over the prospects of Seward's nomination. Egypt, watching the divisions in the Democracy, was beginning to waver, but it would never go for the New Yorker. Businessmen suspected him, despite his recent avowals of conservatism, and looked favorably upon Edward Bates of Missouri. But Bates could no more carry the Germans than Seward the Know-Nothings. Lincoln's moderation, on the other hand, appealed to all factions, and in the winter and spring of 1860 one newspaper after another placed his name at its masthead. County conventions endorsed him, and editors and politicians of neighboring states, skeptical of Eastern influences and of Seward's chances, sent up trial balloons to test his strength.[19]

But as all this made the taste stronger in Lincoln's mouth, he began to realize that he must have the undivided support of his own state. "I am not in a position where it would hurt much for me not to be nominated on the national ticket," he explained to Norman Judd, "but I am where it would hurt some for me not to get the Illinois delegates." [20] And getting the Illinois delegates depended upon harmony in the state convention at Decatur. To realistic politicians of Illinois, Lincoln's chances for the Chicago nomination seemed remote: their primary concern was to carry the state.

Rivals for the gubernatorial nomination were Norman B. Judd, ex-Democrat, and Leonard Swett, old-line Whig. Judd

[18] Ibid., pp. 120–1.
[19] A. C. Cole: *The Era of the Civil War*, p. 189.
[20] *Writings of Lincoln*, V, 120.

was the abler of the two, but he had many enemies, notably "Long John" Wentworth of the *Chicago Democrat;* moreover, his opponents charged him with having betrayed Lincoln in 1856 and abused his confidence in 1858. Judd's friends besought Lincoln to deny these accusations, and Lincoln did so, taking pains to add that he wanted no part in the developing controversy.[21] Stymied, the slander-mongers now turned on Lincoln, who appealed to Judd to save him in the state convention. The situation was made for a dark horse with a flair for compromise, and it was not long before one appeared on the horizon.

Richard Yates was a veteran politician of Illinois. Ever since his emigration from Kentucky thirty years before, he had participated in the Whig politics of the state. He had served one term in Congress, where he had voted with his Whig colleagues against the repeal of the Missouri Compromise. When he stood for re-election his opponents had fastened the charge of Know-Nothingism on him, and not even Lincoln's help availed to save him from defeat. After that he had practiced law, interested himself in railroads, and nursed his hope for political rewards.[22]

Fortunately situated as he was in the geographical center of the state, Yates believed that he had a better chance of carrying his old congressional district than either Judd or Swett. He approached both Judd's friends and his enemies, extracting from each vague promises of second-choice support. To the general surprise, the desire for harmony was strong enough to give Yates the nomination. Lincoln was content. He had not favored Yates, but the choice of the dark-horse candidate buried the internal dissensions, and the Illinois delegation was pledged to support its favorite son at Chicago.[23]

[21] *Writings of Lincoln,* V, 114–16.

[22] Angle: *New Letters of Lincoln,* pp. 131–2; Tracy: *Uncollected Letters of Lincoln,* pp. 51–2; J. G. Nicolay and J. Hay: *Complete Works of Abraham Lincoln,* VI, 37.

[23] Yates to Thomas A. Marshall, January 18, and to Wentworth, March 10, 1860; letters of J. C. Howell, January 23, L. P. Norton, Febru-

To the north and west of Illinois, Indiana, and Ohio, and forming a crescent around them, lay another group of states with a different pattern of politics. Michigan, Wisconsin, Minnesota, and Iowa were still only sparsely settled, and still close to the frontier stage of development. Being younger, they were more dependent upon the national government, though no less attached to doctrines of states' rights. Having recently been territories themselves, they were actively interested in popular sovereignty and opposed to the extension of slavery. Embracing large groups of Germans, Scandinavians, and New Englanders, they were predisposed to a New England brand of abolitionism. Being undeveloped, but possessing great natural resources, they might welcome an alliance with Eastern finance.

Even Michigan, oldest of these states, was still an immature frontier community, as was evidenced by its wooden capitol with churchlike steeple peering over the treetops of forested Lansing. The state had been the first to marshal Northwesterners against the Kansas-Nebraska Act and was thus a contender for the title of birthplace of the Republican Party. As elsewhere, a host of dissentients united on no issue save opposition to the extension of slavery flocked to the standard of the new party. In 1856 Republicans got control of the state, only to run afoul of so many misfortunes as to make their victory a dubious one. The panic of 1857, rising taxes, and crop failures inevitably produced ill feeling and carping criticism of the handling of affairs in the statehouse. Nor did the Republican politicians improve. They won the state elections of 1858, but the succeeding administration of Moses Wisner only increased their troubles. Their only hope was found in the divisions among the Democrats. Local Democratic quarrels reflected the differences between Democratic leaders in Washington, and made the Republicans, to Michigan voters, appear the lesser of two evils.

Strangely enough, as the campaign of 1860 drew near,

ary 13, A. Tomlin, February 21, and A. W. March, April 5, 1860, to Yates; Yates MSS. Cole: *Era of the Civil War*, p. 190.

Michigan Republicans paid little attention to the sporadic booms for Midwestern candidates. Ignoring Chase, McLean, Bates, and Lincoln, Michigan gave adherence to Seward. Perhaps the Republicans of Michigan were more radical than their neighbors. In 1857 they had sent Zachariah Chandler to the United States Senate, and Free-Soil elements had maintained a tight hold on the Michigan party. In 1860 Austin Blair, rising Republican radical and old abolitionist, was second only to Chandler in the party's councils.

Austin Blair had descended from abolitionist forebears. Both his parents had been active abolitionists in Caroline, New York. After attending Hamilton and Union colleges, Blair was admitted to the bar and moved to Jackson, Michigan, where he immediately entered politics as an antislavery Whig. Slightly built, intense and nervous in manner, Blair gave the appearance of a devout crusader. In the state legislature of 1848–9 he advocated giving the ballot to Negroes. In 1848 he joined the Free-Soilers, and as a Free-Soiler he took a leading part in the Jackson mass meeting that launched the Republican Party. In 1859 he was the extremist candidate for the Senate against the slightly more moderate Chandler. After he was defeated, his supporters recompensed him in 1860 with the gubernatorial nomination and the chairmanship of the state's delegation to Chicago. Michigan delegates were pledged for Seward, and Blair had taken the lead in organizing the New Yorker's forces in the Northwest.

Even more inclined toward abolitionism were the Republicans of Wisconsin. There the party had been born and christened, and there it had pledged itself to prevent the extension of slavery. Representative of the state's radicalism was its Governor, Alexander William Randall. Other states had felt it necessary to select moderate and conservative men, but not the Badger Republicans.

Randall had lived in Wisconsin since 1840, when he had emigrated to the territory from his native state of New York. Originally a Whig, he had soon shown Democratic leanings, and Polk had appointed him postmaster of Waukesha. In 1846, as a delegate to a first, abortive constitutional convention, he had favored Negro suffrage. This allied him with the "Barnburner" group of Democrats, and soon led him into the Free-Soil Party and thence into the Republican fold. In 1857, at the age of thirty-eight, he was elected Governor, although Carl Schurz, running with him for lieutenant governor, was defeated. In 1859 he was re-elected.

With impressive manner and a dignity of bearing that delighted the Madison ladies in the gallery, Randall delivered his second inaugural. In a clear firm voice he made a report on state affairs that was eminently pleasing to his Republican constituents. Ignoring, or perhaps not comprehending, the precarious condition of the state's banking system — to which the outbreak of the Civil War brought collapse — the Governor reported the lightest tax burden in years, a surplus in the treasury, and a state free from debt. Continuing in the same practical business tone, he passed on to a lengthy exposition of slavery and the Republican Party. The party, he declared, deplored John Brown's raid, but it still believed that slavery must be eradicated. To Wisconsin Republicans his words and manner seemed conservative enough, but they were a far cry from those of leading politicians in the older states.

When it came time to instruct the state's delegation to Chicago, Abraham Lincoln was ignored, though the previous year Wisconsin politicians had been impressed with the moderation of an address he had delivered to a state-fair crowd in Milwaukee. Carl Schurz, leading German of the state and captain of the movement to support Seward, had done his work well. Although Randall, persuaded of the wisdom of conservatism, favored Lincoln, the delegation was pledged to support the New York Senator.[24]

Still closer to the frontier was the new state of Minnesota, with a population of some 170,000, clustered about the Mis-

[24] *Wisconsin State Journal*, January 3, 12, 1860; *New York Times*, January 20, April 17, 1860.

sissippi and St. Croix rivers. Large areas were still unsettled
and virtually unexplored, the habitation of a few thousand
Chippewa and Sioux Indians not yet reconciled to the inex-
orable advance of the white man's frontier. Upon its admission
to the Union under Democratic auspices in 1858, the new
state had immediately been converted into a political battleground. In 1859 the Republicans nominated Alexander Ramsey for governor and called upon party leaders throughout the
nation to come and help them overthrow the Democratic
reign. Carl Schurz, hero of the Germans, lent his talents, as
did the gracious Schuyler Colfax of Indiana, Galusha Grow,
representing Ohio's brand of abolitionism, and young Francis
Blair of Missouri, scion of an ancient Democratic family. Nor
was local inspiration lacking; Ignatius Donnelly, master of a
potent and iridescent prose, and perhaps the most brilliant
orator Minnesota was ever to have, conducted a masterful
campaign for lieutenant governor. All this eloquence undoubtedly contributed a good deal to the final outcome. In
any event, Ramsey, who two years before, amid circumstances
redolent of corruption, had been counted out by the narrow-
est of margins, was now safely elected by a majority of nearly
four thousand over his friend and political rival, Henry Has-
tings Sibley.

Alexander Ramsey, when he came to Minnesota in 1849 to
serve as territorial governor, had already had a successful political career in his native Pennsylvania. Orphaned at ten, he
had taught himself to read, had learned the carpenter's trade,
had taught school, studied briefly at Lafayette College, and
read law. After his admission to the bar he became active as a
Whig politician. In 1840, as he was entering his twenty-fifth
year, he had been a Clay elector. The next year he was chief
clerk of the Pennsylvania House of Representatives. In 1843
he began the first of two terms in Congress; he was one of the
small group who encouraged David Wilmot to offer his famous Proviso and remained a consistent supporter of the antislavery measure. In 1848 he was again a Whig elector, and

President Taylor appointed him Governor of Minnesota Territory. When removed from office by Pierce, he stayed on in Minnesota to engage in what became a remunerative real-estate enterprise.

At the time of his election in 1859 Ramsey was still a vigorous young man under forty-five, broad-shouldered and deep-chested. His massive head, his large muscular frame, and his open countenance bespoke many homely virtues. He was no intellectual, but he had strength of character and much personal dignity. With his firmness and decision of manner was combined an unfailing good humor that undoubtedly contributed much to his wide popularity. One of his friends felt that for this virtue he could thank the fact that he had the "best stomach in America," a good stomach being the "foundation of a strong man." Ramsey was no orator, but his obvious sincerity, freedom from all eccentricities, and practical ability earned for him a well-deserved reputation for clear-headedness and common sense. His personal integrity was unassailable. When, some years before, he had been charged with corruption by disgruntled traders dissatisfied with his honest administration of Indian affairs, not even a Democratic investigative body could find anything to fasten on him.[25]

Lying closest to the two territories whose future was at stake in 1860 was the state of Iowa. Though longer in the Union than Minnesota and Wisconsin, it too was only partially developed. The Kansas-Nebraska agitation had struck close to Iowans, for the state's future was bound up with the territorial question. Across her borders had passed most of the New Englanders who had established homes in Kansas, and within her own confines dwelt a sizable New England element. By 1856, two years after the party's establishment, Republicans had gained the ascendancy. But despite their pronounced anti-

[25] W. W. Folwell: *A History of Minnesota*, II, 61 f.; J. H. Baker: *Lives of the Governors of Minnesota*, pp. 1 ff.; *Wisconsin State Journal*, January 10, 1860.

slavery views, they nominated a moderate for governor in 1859.

Samuel Jordan Kirkwood, a native of Maryland, had moved to Iowa after a varied career in Ohio as teacher, drug clerk, surveyor, farmer, and lawyer. Once he had served as a prosecuting attorney, and in 1850 he had been a member of the state's constitutional convention. Five years later he had followed his wife's people to Iowa and had settled down to manage a brother-in-law's farm and flour mill near Iowa City. His successive ventures had given him maturity and common sense, virtues that his new neighbors were quick to discover and to reward. Within a year he had become a Republican candidate for the state senate from a strongly Democratic district. His victory commended him to the party, and in 1859 he was nominated to run for governor against the popular Augustus Cæsar Dodge.

The tall, broad-shouldered Samuel Kirkwood looked every inch an honest man of the people. His austere, sharply chiseled countenance, with high cheekbones like an Indian's, bespoke only simple integrity and unwavering rectitude. His deep-set eyes were steady in their gaze, his brow high and furrowed as became a thinker. Adding to the general impression of dignity and rugged strength, a shock of slightly graying hair fell about his large ears, which were flanked by a pair of snow-white sideburns. Nevertheless, he was careless, even uncleanly, in his dress, but that did not count against him on the rough frontier. The voters decided he was their man and elected him in the face of Dodge's great personal popularity.

Governor Kirkwood did nothing to disabuse the voters of their confidence in him. In his inaugural he condemned John Brown's acts, but had only praise for the "unflinching courage and calm cheerfulness" with which he had suffered. Without drama or flourish he assumed the administration of the state's business and his party's politics. As a conservative, he favored the choice of a conservative presidential candidate. He dissuaded the state convention from instructing its delegates for Seward, and Iowa went to Chicago with its eight votes distributed two each for Lincoln and Seward, and one apiece for Cameron, Bates, Chase, and McLean.[26]

Thus by the middle of May 1860 were the states aligned. Where abolitionism was strong, the Republican politicians were radicals who favored Seward, or even Chase, as the party's nominee. But the radicals were in a minority. Conservative businessmen and the shrewder politicians saw that Republicans must espouse a broad program and nominate a moderate. If they acted wisely, victory was within their grasp, for the Democratic convention at Charleston had split between the Southerners and Stephen A. Douglas, and the breach seemed irreparable. But to make a wise choice they must subordinate emotion to intelligence and wisdom.

[26] C. Cole: *Iowa through the Years*, pp. 260–72; S. M. H. Byers: *Iowa in War Times*, pp. 29–30.

Chapter 4

Lincoln the Nominee

WHEN the Republicans assembled in Chicago, most of the emotion was on the side of Seward. While the hopeful New Yorker remained in ostentatious seclusion in Albany awaiting his transfiguration, his cohorts descended on the Windy City. Confident of success, they began to celebrate their victory even before they arrived. On the incoming train they were hilarious, "singing songs not found in hymn books" and imbibing plentiful quantities of whisky to show that the Republicans were absorbing "the spirit as well as the substance of the old Democratic Party." Upon their arrival they paraded to party headquarters serenaded by their own band and flanked by rollicking "Irrepressibles" under the leadership of Tom Hyer, noted pugilist. Throughout the convention they drank, swore, sang, ridiculed those who were "too d—d virtuous," and conducted themselves in a manner "that would do honor to Old Kaintuck on a bust." The New York politicians, decided one observer, "are a peculiar people."

But other New Yorkers were there to work and serve. Thurlow Weed, heading the delegation, had no time for premature celebration. He met the incoming trains, visited doubtful delegations in their hotel rooms, counseled with kindred souls from other states. He knew, if his hell-raising entourage did not, that Seward's nomination depended on the support of Indiana, Pennsylvania, and Illinois. He could count on Cameron, but unfortunately at least half of Pennsylvania's delegation belonged to the Curtin faction. In Indiana and Illinois he had a handful of supporters, but most of the delegates were looking for a man to beat Seward. The New Englanders were safer, but even they were not fully persuaded that Seward's conservation was more than a politician's mask. Weed had his hands full, but he had the support of Edwin D. Morgan, chairman of the national committee; of Carl Schurz, who thought he could control the German votes; and of Austin Blair, who might work upon the Midwesterners.

The first cloud to cast a shadow on Weed's fair hopes was the arrival of Horace Greeley upon the scene. Having been defeated for a delegate's place, Greeley appeared with a proxy from far-off Oregon. For a long time now the indomitable editor of the *Tribune* had nursed in silence his grievances against Weed and Seward. Six years before, he had privately revealed his enmity to Seward; now he publicly announced his opposition to Seward's nomination. Upon his otherwise cherubic face, fringed with a graying beard, he wore a look of grim determination. His long linen duster streaming behind him — some wag pinned a Seward ribbon on it — he strode from one delegation to another denouncing the New York Senator, sowing dissension among the loyal and doubts among the wavering. He was a "d—d old ass," said the Irrepressibles. He was a tower of strength, thought Seward's opponents. He was a thorn in the flesh of Thurlow Weed.

Unassessed as an injury to Seward's cause was the damage done by Seward's alcoholic rooters. Puritans from New England and sons of Puritans from the Western Reserve were horrified. Most of the old abolitionists were temperance men, and they brought temperance with them into the Republican Party. Staid conservatives, too, were deeply shocked.

Chicago was bedecked for the convention as for a county fair. Across the streets hung welcoming banners; from homes and shops and public buildings floated hundreds of yards of patriotic bunting; and all through the night the parading Wide-Awakes, clad in their oilcloth capes and bearing aloft their flaming torches, surged through the city's thoroughfares. The transparencies of the night and the banners of the day bore pictures of Lincoln, "Honest Abe," the "Rail-Splitter." The excitement and effervescent enthusiasm of the crowds that churned about the Wigwam and piled over one another in its galleries all seemed very spontaneous and artless by contrast with the alcoholic maundering of the New Yorkers. Present were the leading Republicans of Illinois, Judge David Davis, candidate Richard Yates, editor Wentworth, Gustav Koerner, and ex-candidates Norman Judd and Leonard Swett, all united in pushing Illinois' favorite son for a place on the national ticket, all prepared to capitalize upon the emotional content of the moment.

The first business of the convention after its organization was the adoption of the party's platform. This was a hodge-podge of all the opposition's ideas since 1854. It denounced slavery as an evil and opposed its extension into the territories. This was basic doctrine, to which was appended a long list of irrelevant vote-catching items. The party stood for free lands in the West, for a Pacific railroad, for agricultural education, for the rights of labor, for the tariff, which was Pennsylvania's price. Every minute segment of discontent got a vague mention or an ambiguous allusion that on the stump could be stretched into a generous promise. The convention endorsed the Constitution and even, after some discussion, the Declaration of Independence. No longer did the Republicans rest their case upon a single issue; the party stood for anything that would attract votes. In the phrase of the day, its platform was like a pair of suspenders, large enough for any man, small enough for any boy.

The platform having been adopted, the convention turned to the more important task of choosing a candidate. Seward was nominated and endlessly seconded while the Irrepressibles burst into deafening cheers. Behind him were the solid delegations of New York, Michigan, Wisconsin, Minnesota, Massachusetts, California, and Kansas. In the New England states he was only nominally the second choice, and scattered delegates from Pennsylvania, Ohio, and even Illinois preferred him. Bates of Missouri, who believed that he could unite the conservatives of the country, had Missouri, Delaware, and Oregon. Cameron, who supported Seward, was nominated — and cheered by a part of Pennsylvania's delegation. New Jersey offered William M. Dayton, hoping that conservatives would perceive his eminent availability. But when Lincoln was nominated, the Chicago crowd in the galleries sent their whoops echoing among the rafters. That was local pride, which could be discounted and then ignored.

What the convention could not ignore was the deep undercurrent of opposition to Seward. Primarily it was opposition from the states, and sprang from the belief that the New Yorker's nomination would endanger the party in the critical states of New Jersey, Pennsylvania, Illinois, and Indiana. Curtin and his mentor and henchman Alexander K. McClure spread the word throughout the convention that Seward could not carry Pennsylvania. However sound he might be on the tariff, his opposition to the Know-Nothings would cost him many votes. Not even Curtin's self-admitted popularity could carry Seward through the elections. Curtin was concerned with his own chances; and partly because he feared Seward and partly because he hated Cameron, he sought for another presidential candidate. New Jersey politicians, echoing Curtin, gave warning that Seward would also have difficulty in New Jersey; and Henry S. Lane took up the refrain and protested that his own defeat would follow Seward's nomination.

The situation was made for the men of Illinois. Yates, too, declared that he would be defeated if Seward were the candidate, and David Davis began to work on the discontented and the wavering. Greeley preferred Bates, but soon discovered that the Missourian had no support. Lane preferred McLean, but Ohio's divided delegation could not unite upon anyone, making McLean's chances hopeless. Davis quickly enrolled both Missouri and Ohio under the Lincoln banner. There was dissent from the Massachusetts delegation, which was pledged to Seward. But John A. Andrew, who headed that delegation, had from the start intended to thwart Seward's nomination if it could be managed. Gathering a handful of like-minded Bay Staters he began to call on other doubtful New England delegations. Only Vermont wavered, but finally decided to join its neighbors and cast its vote for Lincoln.

All through the sweltering night David Davis dragged his great hulk from one delegation to another. Lincoln wired his agents that he would be bound by no promises, but Davis ignored the warning. To Indiana he promised a cabinet office and clinched the delegation's support. In Pennsylvania he had Curtin's support, but not Cameron's. Finally he promised Cameron the secretaryship of the treasury, and the delegation agreed to cast its first vote for Cameron, its second for Mc-Lean, and its third for Lincoln. Virginia's Republicans, strong in convention however impotent at the polls, agreed to abandon Seward for Lincoln after a ballot. Hour after hour, from dusk until sunrise, Henry Lane, pale and haggard, his usually jaunty cane tucked under his arm, labored first with his own and then with other groups, cajoling, arguing, bargaining. A morning rumor had it that Curtin, Lane, and Yates, candidates for governor in their respective states, would withdraw if Seward was nominated.

The first ballot on Thursday morning was a test of strength. Seward led with 173½, but Lincoln came second with 102. Cameron had 50½, Bates 48, Chase 49, Dayton 14, McLean 12, Collamer 10, Wade 3, Sumner and Frémont one each. Weed was crestfallen. He, too, had worked through the night, promising unlimited money to carry the states. He had hoped for success on the first ballot. The Illinois men sat breathless, hoping that the promises of the night would bear up in the light of day. Seward needed only 60 votes for a majority. If Cameron's 50 and New Jersey's 14 . . .?

With the second ballot the hopes of the men of Illinois soared. Seward picked up eleven votes to show 184½, but Pennsylvania, not waiting for the third ballot, gave her vote to Lincoln, who picked up enough more to show 181. All the others had declined, Chase to 42½, Bates to 35, Dayton to 10, McLean to 8, and Cameron to 2. The contest was clearly between Lincoln and Seward.

The third ballot was mercifully brief. While the delegates and galleries sat so still that the scratching pencils of the tally clerks could be heard, the votes came in. Even before the official announcement was made, the delegates knew that the vote stood 180 for Seward, 231½ for Lincoln. Chase still held 24½, Bates had 22, McLean 5, and only 2 were scattered. Before the chairman could announce the vote an Ohio delegate was on his feet to announce the transfer of four votes from Chase to Lincoln. "I had imagined Ohio would be slippery enough for the crisis," commented the *Cincinnati Commercial's* Murat Halstead.

Not emotion born of the place and the moment but shrewd political calculation had brought about the choice of Abraham Lincoln, sage and seer of the Western Republicans. As sage he had drawn more clearly than anyone else the narrow line that separated Republicans from Democrats; he had defined the party's opposition to the extension of slavery and had shown where it differed from popular sovereignty; he had carefully distinguished between antislavery and abolitionism. As seer he had foreseen Seward's disadvantages, decided that the New Yorker stood no chance in the West, and trimmed his own sails accordingly. He was no abolitionist, no radical. He was a conservative, mild in manner, sound on the tariff, in favor of homesteads for farmers, a railroad to the Pacific, and support for industry. Had the party been concerned only with finding a statesman to enunciate its principles and embody its ideals, the nomination would still have been unassailable. Yet it was upon quite other grounds that it actually rested. The exigencies of politics demanded a candidate who could carry Indiana and Pennsylvania. Without these key states the party's hopes were doomed. Thus in the last analysis state politics and the state governors dictated the outcome. They forced the convention to pass over Seward and name "Honest Abe" as its candidate.

From the cannon that had been wheeled to the door of the Wigwam the news was boomed to the waiting mob outside. Inside the building, gallery and floor burst into pandemonium. Someone brought out a huge crayon portrait of the Rail-Splitter. Illinois, Indiana, and Ohio delegates screamed like wild men. Henry Lane leaped upon a table, swinging hat and cane, grinning but uttering no distinguishable sound. A beneficent smile wreathed the cherubic face of Horace Greeley. Heaving a sigh of relief, David Davis mopped anxiety's perspiration from his brow. New York, Michigan, and Wisconsin sat stupefied. The Irrepressibles had been repressed.

Later that afternoon the convention nominated Hannibal Hamlin of Maine for the vice-presidency — a sop to Seward and the abolitionists. Then it adjourned to mingle with Chicago's ebullient crowds. The telegraph carried the news to a sad man in Albany and to a man in Springfield who, strangely enough, was even sadder.

The convention had chosen wisely, though wisdom had not guided the choice. Fundamentally, the choice had sprung from the political situation in the individual states. Despite the "national" framework of its platform, the Republican party was not yet a national organization. It was, in fact, a conglomeration of state parties united by expediency and not by principle. As they entered the campaign, Lincoln was nowhere recognized as a national leader.[1]

As the delegates in the Chicago Wigwam grew more and more hoarse with cheering and shouting, they gradually recovered some semblance of sobriety. The country had expected them to nominate Seward. Would the people share the convention's enthusiasm for the Western commoner, or would they reject him? Already the editor of the Democratic *Herald* of New York was composing an editorial branding

[1] Halstead: *Caucuses of 1860*, pp. 127 ff.; D. S. Alexander: *Political History of New York*, II, 281 f.; Baringer: *Lincoln's Rise to Power*, pp. 232–73; Pearson: *Andrew*, I, 112 ff.; Davis: *Pennsylvania Politics*, pp. 103–5; Fite: *Election of 1860*, pp. 122–6; *New York Times*, May 16–21, 1860.

the nomination as "a remarkable indication of small intellect growing smaller." The delegates had passed over Seward, Chase, and Banks — "statesmen and able men" — to "take up a fourth-rate lecturer, who cannot speak good grammar, and who, to raise the wind, delivers his hackneyed, illiterate compositions at $200 apiece." In Troy the *Whig* editorialist was preparing to shed crocodile tears for Seward, victim of the "Molochs of Availability and Expediency." [2]

Crocodile tears were no monopoly of the critics. In the convention itself many were none too comfortable as they thought of the people back home. John A. Andrew suddenly recalled that Massachusetts Republicans had instructed their delegation for Seward. Rising to second a motion to make Lincoln's nomination unanimous, his cherubic face the picture of innocence, Andrew told the delegates that "it had not been for old Massachusetts to strike down William Henry Seward." So saying, the orator launched into a panegyric on the glories of the Old Bay State. It was Andrew's first trip west of the Hudson, and it had probably come as a shock to him to discover that Massachusetts did not loom quite so large in the nation as in New England. In token of his state's importance he promised Lincoln a majority of a hundred thousand. [3]

The speech of the hour came from Michigan's Austin Blair. With some evidence of real sincerity he told his hearers that Michigan had "nothing to take back. She has not sent me forward to worship the rising sun, but . . . to say that, at your behests here today, she lays down her first, best loved candidate, to take up yours, with some bleeding of the heart, with some quivering in the veins; but she does not feel that the fame of Seward will suffer, for she knows that his fame . . . will be written, and read, and be loved long after the temporary excitement of this day has passed away." Michigan would follow Seward "in the grand column which shall go out to battle for Abraham Lincoln of Illinois." [4]

[2] Quoted in the *New York Tribune*, May 21, 1861.
[3] Halstead: *Caucuses of 1860*, pp. 150–1.
[4] Frederick W. Seward: *Seward at Washington*, p. 452.

Having tendered their apologies to the man whose dearest hope they had shattered, the heads of the state delegations entrained for Springfield to give Lincoln formal notice of his nomination. Privately many of them hoped that the sight of the candidate would remove their numbing doubts. All Springfield was gathered at the depot to welcome them. Cheers went up from the crowd, and three brass bands poured confidence into the twilight air. In a body the party proceeded to Lincoln's home, where the candidate was awaiting them. His simplicity drove the last vestige of doubt from their hearts. More at ease than his guests, Lincoln shook hands with each of them in turn, holding up the line only twice. Once was when the Kentucky delegate, Blakie, came along and prodded Lincoln into reminiscences of his own Kentucky boyhood. The other was when tall Judge Kelley approached.

"What's your height?" demanded Lincoln, straightening up.

"Six feet three. What is yours?" asked the Pennsylvanian.

"Six feet four," answered the nominee.

"Then Pennsylvania bows to Illinois," exclaimed Judge Kelley. "My dear man, for years my heart has been aching for a President that I could *look up to,* and I've found him at last in the land where we thought there were none but *little* giants."

Not all the delegates were so orotund, but all of them were delighted. One New Englander, who had feared he would meet a "gigantic rail splitter with the manners of a flatboatman," was overjoyed to find the nominee "a complete gentleman." John Andrew was moved to characteristic comment. "We claim you, Mr. Lincoln," he beamed, "as coming from Massachusetts, because all the old Lincoln name are from Plymouth Colony." But Lincoln was not overwhelmed by the honor. "We'll consider it so this evening," he said briefly.[5]

More satisfied with their choice than they had dared hope, the committeemen hurried home to face "ratification" meetings of local Republicans. It was a load off their minds to

[5] *New York Tribune,* May 25, 1860.

find that in general their parties were ready to accept the explanation that it had not been practical to nominate Seward. In Maine one observer expressed his fear that the party was paralyzed, but even he took courage from the Democrats' lack of vitality.[6] Rhode Island Republicans, having recovered from their surprise, were soon assuring one another that Lincoln's conservatism would give them the support of Sprague's followers. In New York City Horace Greeley entered an elaborate — and mostly incoherent — explanation of his conduct at Chicago, claiming that he had always preferred Bates to any other candidate. But upstate Republicans were ready to accept the assurance that "Lincoln will get all the votes that Seward would, and a great many beside." [7] Wisconsin politicians privately admitted that they had had their misgiving about Seward all along,[8] though publicly they repeated that he had been, in Governor Randall's words, their "star and guide." Randall looked so serious, standing with hands folded, quoting Scripture, that Democrats thought he might "commence lining for the meeting." [9]

In Pennsylvania, amid many assurances that Seward could not possibly have carried the state, there was great rejoicing over the tariff. Simon Cameron told an audience at Harrisburg that Lincoln's record on protection was "clear, emphatic, and beyond suspicion." In Philadelphia the People's Party talked of the Republican nominee as a friend of the poor, a lover of liberty, and a "conspicuous advocate" of protection, river and harbor improvements, a Pacific railroad, and free homesteads.[10] Senator Trumbull came from

[6] Hunt: *Washburn*, pp. 72–3.

[7] *New York Times*, May 25, 1860; *New York Tribune*, May 22, 26, 1860.

[8] C. C. Sholes (Kenosha) to Doolittle, May 21, 1860, in the James Doolittle MSS. in the State Historical Society of Wisconsin.

[9] *Wisconsin Patriot*, May 26, 1860; *Wisconsin State Journal*, May 21, 1860.

[10] *New York Tribune*, May 21, 28; *Philadelphia Inquirer*, May 28, 1860.

Illinois to bolster these assurances. But still the People's
Party moved cautiously. Though they endorsed Lincoln and
the Chicago platform, they did not abandon their separate
party organization, nor did they wax demonstrative over Lincoln. Few, in fact, could go along with John Andrew in his
sirupy ecstasy. Andrew thought Lincoln's countenance proclaimed "the benignity and beauty of a noble soul." "I would
trust my case with the honesty and with the intellect, with
the heart and with the brain of Abraham Lincoln as a lawyer," he told a Springfield, Massachusetts, audience. "I would
trust my country's cause in his care . . . while the wind
blows and the water runs." [11]

The defeated candidates received the news of Lincoln's
nomination with various emotions. Edward Bates, pasting a
clipping in his diary, penned a note prophesying that the
Republican Party would pass into a decline and eventually
fall to pieces. He had pictured himself as the savior of the
party, the only man who could unite old Whigs, disorganized Know-Nothings, and new Republicans into a winning
team. But since Lincoln's views were right, Bates would support him.[12] Salmon Chase swore his continued adherence to
Republican principles, which were dearer to him than mere
personal considerations. "I rejoice," he told a slightly incredulous audience in Columbus, "that, although I was not
nominated, my principles were." [13]

Most disgruntled was the candidate whose hopes had been
highest. Seward blamed Greeley for the outcome and predicted that the editor's egotism and ambition would wreck
the party. When that happened, he hoped that his friend
Weed would step in to save the cause.[14] At the moment,
however, Weed was more interested in getting a little rest
than in looking to a future role as political savior. So he put

11 *New York Tribune*, May 28, 1860.
12 *Diary of Edward Bates*, edited by Howard Beale, p. 128.
13 *Wisconsin State Journal*, May 26, 1860; *New York Tribune*, May
26, 1860.
14 Barnes: *Memoir of Thurlow Weed*, p. 270.

off Lincoln's Chicago managers when they made overtures to him, and he went over into Iowa to recoup his energies. He was soon sufficiently restored to map out a course of action. Greeley had plotted against Seward, but for this neither Lincoln nor his working friends were responsible. So, en route home from his brief vacation, Weed stopped off in Springfield. There he found in Lincoln a kindred spirit — a politician "sagacious and practical." For five hours they talked together. Weed became more and more impressed with Lincoln's good sense, his "intuitive knowledge of human nature," and his "familiarity with the virtues and infirmities of politicians." He returned to Albany to wait with Seward until the time came to save the party.[15]

Within ten days after the Chicago convention the state Republican leaders had agreed that Lincoln was agreeable, capable, respectable, conservative, and acceptable. He was a rail-splitter with drawing-room manners, a man of the people whom the conservatives could trust, a politician of insight, acumen, and integrity. But not one expected that he would bring these virtues to bear on the ensuing campaign. However shrewd as a politician, Lincoln was not to participate in his party's councils. He was a figure apart. He was "Honest Old Abe," the subject, not the author, of oratory.

The role that Republican strategists assigned him accorded with the American tradition. Eight years before, Winfield Scott had broken with tradition to make campaign speeches in his own behalf and had met the well-deserved fate of the nonconformist. Warned by Scott's experience, Lincoln remained modestly in Springfield, an interested spectator without voice or vote in the campaign. Occasionally a delegation waited on him and listened to innocuous words. Now and then someone reported his observations on the political weather. But Abraham Lincoln was not yet the leader of the Republican Party.

Lincoln's personal friends in Illinois constituted a flying

[15] Barnes: *Memoir*, p. 272; Weed: *Autobiography*, pp. 602–3.

squadron to keep in touch with the campaign managers in the other states. Sometimes they were trouble-shooters, harmonizing discordant elements with promises of patronage; sometimes they concocted formulas to synthesize divergent dogmas. David Davis, judicious but jovial, Leonard Swett, shrewd in analysis, and Norman Judd, experienced and energetic, kept the candidate informed of the progress of the campaign. Lincoln read letters, studied newspapers, chatted with politicians who dropped past Springfield. He worried over Pennsylvania and inquired about Cameron's opinion, became alarmed over rumors of trouble in Maine, and on several occasions reassured his personal friends in Indiana. When the opposition accused him of having been a Know-Nothing, he privately denied it but refused to make a public statement. When asked about his attitude on fugitive slaves, he referred the catechist to his printed speeches.[16]

With Lincoln silent, the national committee should have shouldered the campaign. But the national organization was hardly more active than the candidate. Governor Edwin D. Morgan, who headed the committee, gathered funds in the East to spend in the West, but he never guided the party's work. He was Governor of New York, busily seeking re-election, and subservient to Thurlow Weed. It was the Albany editor himself who took control and gave the national campaign all the direction it had. As Seward had predicted, Greeley was worthless in the canvass.

Somehow, between them, Weed and the Lincoln men got things moving. Lincoln's friends approached Bates and asked him to take the stump in Illinois. This invitation Bates declined, but he did publish a letter, which was so well received that he was prompted to write several more and soon

16 A. K. McClure: *Abraham Lincoln and Men of War Times*, p. 37; Nicolay and Hay: *Abraham Lincoln*, II, 286–7; Nicolay and Hay: *Complete Works*, I, 646–7; V, 141; VI, 42, 47–8; A. B. Lapsley, ed.: *Writings of Abraham Lincoln*, V, 183, 190; Tracy: *Uncollected Letters of Abraham Lincoln*, pp. 153–4; Judd to Trumbull, June 24, 1860, in the Trumbull MSS.; *New York Herald*, October 20, 1860.

was preening himself on the power of his quill.[17] Carl
Schurz, immigrant on the make, took charge of the "foreign
part" of the campaign, promising to do the work of a hundred men. He boasted that his efforts were "almost super-
human," but distinctly worth while. He said the Germans
were coming over to the Republicans by the thousands; "the
Old Pennsylvania Dutch follow me like little children." [18]
No doubt he honestly believed that the Germans would vote
for Lincoln. Actually he did little to remove the stigma of
Know-Nothingism from the party. A local candidate who
accurately represented Wisconsin sentiment insisted: "We
don't want to borrow any Dutch votes, nor trade them any
white votes. If they don't want to vote our ticket, let them
go to Hell." [19] And in Wisconsin, Schurz's home state, the
Germans voted solidly for the Democrats.[20]

More fruitful than the work of Bates and Schurz was that
of Seward. The Senator awaited the propitious moment,
then announced that he would tour the Northwest. In Madison, Wisconsin, he was introduced by Governor Randall
with new avowals of affection. Lincoln was "our Moses," but
Seward was "our great High Priest." [21] Aaron-like, Seward
erected a golden calf in the wilderness, promising prosperity
to all who would support the Chicago platform. The Northwest, intoned Seward, was the future seat of power; its duty
was to call the federal government back to its original principles. In Michigan and Minnesota he blessed his loyal supporters, then passed on to St. Louis. Here he told his audience that if Missouri had been a free state it would now
have a population of four million. He noted, with a glance
at the German vote, that the state was fortunately in a fair
way to being "Germanized" into a liberal attitude. "It was

[17] *Diary of Bates*, pp. 132, 137, 145.

[18] Carl Schurz: *Works*, II, 116–21, 158.

[19] *Madison Patriot*, October 6, 1860.

[20] Joseph Schafer: "Who Elected Lincoln?" *American Historical Review*, XLVII, 51–63 (October 1941).

[21] *Wisconsin State Journal*, September 12, 1860.

through the Germans Germanizing Great Britain," he said, "that Magna Charta was obtained." [22]

The touring high priest's remarks were a token of the lack of very specific issues in the Republican campaign. The *New York Times* vaguely remarked that Lincoln's weakness in safe New England was an argument for him in doubtful Western areas.[23] The rival *Herald* warned the conservative East against Seward's supposedly dangerous ideas: Republican success would place abolitionists in federal judgeships and fanatics in other offices of the national government. Negro insurrections would multiply, and fugitives would flood the North.[24] Instead of replying, Republicans merely sang:

> Come all you landless freemen
> That want good land to till,
> Elect old honest Abraham
> And get the Homestead Bill.
> Oh will you, won't you, don't you
> Want to come and vote with me?

Thus rosy prophecies and gilded promises were the substitutes for tangible issues in the campaign oratory. Indeed, no other course was feasible. The conglomerate structure of the Republican Party made it impossible either to discuss vital issues or to wage the campaign with a consistent national program. Years later Charles Francis Adams, Jr., was to shudder as he looked back on the summer of 1860. He remembered the Wide-Awakes with their nocturnal parades, their smoking flares, and their deafening fireworks. But he also remembered how little anyone had understood the profound significance of the coming election. When young Adams and his father accompanied Seward on his Northwestern tour, none of the party had any idea of the bitterness of Southern

[22] Barnes: *Memoir of Weed*, II, 297; *New York Times*, September 19, October 6; *New York Herald*, October 1, 2, 1860.

[23] *New York Times*, September 19, 1860.

[24] *New York Herald*, October 1, 1860.

feeling. "We all dwelt in a fool's Paradise," he confessed. "We fully believed it would all end in gasconade!" [25]

Yet the Republicans won. They won without an integrated program, without an organized national campaign, and without any realization of the terrible train of events they had set in motion. They won with a candidate whose availability had been stressed and whose ability had been ignored. Their victory was due partly to their well-organized campaign in the separate states, partly to their opponents' paralysis. The campaign was not a battle: it was a series of skirmishes against a demoralized foe.

The division among the Democrats had deep roots. It was perhaps the inevitable consequence of their long tenure of office. In the sixty years since Jefferson's election in 1800 his party had relinquished its hold on the federal government only three times, and then only briefly when John Quincy Adams, William Henry Harrison, and Zachary Taylor had been President. Moreover, even when a Whig sat in the executive mansion, the Democrats usually had control of Congress.

Their long supremacy had profound effects on the party. Inevitably it made for conservatism. Thomas Jefferson's liberal philosophy, even mysticism, and the Jackson Democrats' politically inspired concern for the masses gradually gave way to a spirit of reaction. As the crusading zeal declined, the party stood more and more solidly against reform. Meantime the party passed into the hands of the Southerners, who used its doctrine of states' rights to extend and preserve the South's "peculiar institution" of slavery. Finally the party had developed a bureaucratic clique of officeholders maintained by patronage, who were able to whip recalcitrants into line with Southern or conservative wishes.

It was primarily against this élite that Douglas rebelled when he challenged Buchanan on the Lecompton Constitution. In the popular mind the Little Giant represented

25 Charles Francis Adams, Jr.: *Autobiography*, p. 69.

"Young America," and Buchanan the "Old Fogyism" of the Democracy. As the conflict developed, the President threw the full weight of federal patronage against the Illinois Senator. But Douglas won his fight for re-election in 1858, used his own dwindling patronage to secure followers in the Northern states, and sent his cohorts into the party's convention at Charleston to force his own nomination or break up the party.

The Southerners accepted the challenge. In February, Jefferson Davis of Mississippi rose in the Senate to tell Douglas that the South would demand that Congress protect slavery in the territories. Democratic conventions in the South instructed their delegates to withdraw from the Charleston meeting if Southern interests were sacrificed to expediency. Southerners were quite as determined as the Douglasites to rule or ruin.[26]

For ten days the two factions wrangled, first over the organization of the convention, then over the platform. When the Douglas men ultimately gained control and forced through a platform endorsing popular sovereignty and the Freeport Doctrine, delegates from several Southern states withdrew. Unable to nominate a candidate, the convention adjourned on May 3, to meet again in Baltimore.

Before the Democrats reassembled, two other conventions had placed candidates in the field. The Republicans had nominated Lincoln. Another new group, containing remnants of the old Whigs, former Know-Nothings, and a scattered assortment of conservatives called itself the Constitutional Union Party and nominated John Bell of Tennessee and Edward Everett of Massachusetts for president and vice president. Now the seceders from the Charleston convention, conferring in Richmond, agreed to launch a fourth party and candidate if the Baltimore convention did not repent of the Charleston program.

But repentance was far from the thoughts of the Douglas

[26] R. H. Luthin, *The First Lincoln Campaign*, pp. 120–135; Avery Craven, *The Coming of the Civil War*, pp. 394–416.

men as they rode roughshod over their Southern opponents
and Buchanan's henchmen. At Baltimore they excluded the
delegates who had walked out at Charleston, readopted the
platform which had split that meeting, and nominated Douglas. A few Southern delegations that had hoped to effect a
compromise by staying in the convention now withdrew,
and so did many administration men from Northern states.
Reconvening, they proclaimed themselves the true Democracy and nominated John C. Breckinridge for president.

The Douglas men from the Northwest were bitter. In Baltimore's barrooms they roundly cursed the Southerners. An
Indianian insulted them with the taunt that the valley of
the Wabash was "worth more than all the country between
the Potomac and the Rio Grande, niggers included." An
Ohio delegate chipped in with the gibe that Cincinnati was
worth more "than the whole damned State of Alabama."
Another proclaimed that he thought more of Black Republicans than of Southerners, and if there was to be a fight, he
was for his own side of the Ohio. On the train across the
mountains one disappointed Douglasite shouted that he
hoped the South would be "made to sweat under an Abolition President." The fugitive slaves could go to Canada or
to the devil for all he cared — and their masters with them.[27]

In slightly better humor one rhymester ruefully regarded
the wreckage:

> "Abe and his rails." O worse than idle tale —
> We Democrats can lay you on the shelf.
> Boast of a man who's only split a rail?
> Our good old party's gone and split itself.

Though the irate Douglas men threw the blame on the
Southerners, the split in the party was not simply horizontal.
Northern Democrats were not unanimous for Douglas, nor
Southern men for Breckinridge. Douglas' running mate was
Hershel B. Johnson of Georgia, and the vice-presidential
candidate of the seceding Democrats was Joseph Lane of

[27] Halstead: *Caucuses of 1860*, p. 230.

Oregon. In every Northern state there was a strong Breckinridge following, composed in part of states' rights conservatives who shared the South's constitutional views, in part of businessmen whose trade bound them to the South, and in part of politicians whose offices were the reward for long support of the administration. In the states these administration Democrats nominated candidates for Congress and for state offices.

Taking stock after the nominations, observers came to the easy conclusion that Lincoln would be the next president. Although Douglas had supporters in the lower South, the contest there was between Breckinridge and Bell. In the upper South, where mild men continued to hope for compromise between the extremes, the Democratic division made Bell a likely winner. In the North neither Bell nor Breckinridge stood a chance, but their candidacies would prevent Douglas from carrying the states. Observers noted, too, that the Democratic campaign lacked spirit; neither faction expected victory, and yet both seemed to draw an "amazing amount of consolation" from the prospect. The *New York Times* was happy to observe that its opponents were "all steadily settling down to the satisfactory conclusion that worse things might happen than the election of Lincoln." [28]

The Republicans' only fear was that their opponents would put up coalition electoral tickets. It was the obvious thing to do, and Democratic leaders began at once to sound out the possibilities. The *Philadelphia Press* and the *New York Tribune* both reminded Democrats that the Baltimore convention had selected Douglas, and they quoted with malicious delight the statements of Douglas leaders who rejected tenders of fusion.[29] In the South the worried *Richmond Enquirer* proposed that Breckinridge tickets give way in the North and Douglas tickets in the South, and thus, by beating Lincoln in the sections, throw the election into the

[28] *New York Times,* May 21, July 4, 9, 1860.
[29] *New York Tribune,* July 7; Philadelphia Press, July 11, 1860.

House of Representatives.[30] In Pennsylvania the two factions
agreed upon a joint electoral ticket whose members were to
cast the state's electoral vote for any Democrat who could
be elected.[31] In New York the Bell and Douglas men made a
similar arrangement, which the Breckinridge forces refused
to join.[32] But only in Rhode Island and New Jersey was fusion successful. In New Jersey a coalition gave Douglas three
of the state's seven electoral votes. Throughout the rest of
the Northern states Breckinridge, Douglas, and Bell men
campaigned against each other in the full knowledge that
they were delivering the victory to the Republicans.

Yet the bitter feud between the Democratic factions,
though it prevented both wings of the party from waging an
effective campaign, would not in itself have ensured Lincoln's election in November. The Republicans were also
hampered in organizing a national campaign; their funds
were low, and authority was divided between the Morgan-
Weed-Seward national committee and Lincoln's flying squadron from Illinois. Had the election depended either upon
the efforts of the divided Democrats or upon the Republican
national organization, the outcome might have been doubtful. In the final analysis the Republican victory belonged to
the Republican organizations in the separate states. The election of 1860 represented the sum total of a series of separate
state contests.

[30] Quoted in the *New York Tribune,* July 13, 1860.
[31] *Philadelphia Press,* July 16, 18, August 10, 11, 1860.
[32] *New York Tribune,* July 12, 20, 23, August 9, 10, 15, 17, 1860.

Chapter 5

The Governors Elect Lincoln

ERHAPS no national election in American history hinged so largely on state campaigns as did the election of 1860. But no political party had ever before been so largely a coalition of state parties. The Republican victory in November could not be attributed to the national committee: it was weak, impoverished, and ineffective. Nor could it be credited to Abraham Lincoln: he was acceptable, but inarticulate — bound by tradition to hide his political skill and bide his days in almost monastic seclusion. Not even Democratic division could have given the election to the Republicans had they not had tested state organizations, eager and ready to conduct the canvass. In the end the governors won their state campaigns, and their combined successes put Abraham Lincoln in the White House.

By 1860 twenty-two of the thirty-three states had an organized Republican Party. In ten of the twenty-two there were no significant state contests in the campaign. Three of these ten — Kentucky, Maryland, and Delaware — were slaveholding and traditionally Democratic. Oregon and California also had Democratic governors, but the Democrats there, as in the East, were divided, while the Republicans, coming fresh from the campaigns of 1859, were vigorous, well-organized, and aggressive. The remaining five states — New Jersey, Ohio, Wisconsin, Minnesota, and Iowa — were safely Republican. They had Republican governors and recently successful Republican organizations full of zest for the campaign.[1]

[1] *New York Times,* July 26, 1860; Nicolay and Hay: *Lincoln,* II, 292.

In these five states the campaign of 1860 was almost a routine affair. The governors and state officials took charge, put the party workers back into harness, and ran the canvass with efficiency and dispatch. Iowa's Kirkwood was so sure of himself and his organization that he declined a Democratic challenge to joint debate, although only the year before he had himself been the challenger and had welcomed the opportunity to share the Democrats' audiences.[2] Minnesota's campaign was quiet: Ramsey was popular, and the Republicans had shown a commendable interest in economy. The state's Republicans extended a warm welcome to Seward, whose visit was the high point of the campaign.[3] In Wisconsin, Governor Randall and Secretary of State Louis Harvey gave the Republicans skillful leadership, though Democrats, sneering at Randall as a combination of moron and hypocrite, delighted to point out that the Governor always made the same speech. "Argument," they explained, "is not the Governor's *forte*. He can tell a story well, and is capital at an anecdote, especially when it is positively smutty and has an oblique moral tendency." They sneered too when the Governor, addressing a Sunday-school convention, dwelt on the "importance of virtue" and the "beneficent influence of Christianity." Yet not all of Randall's energies were consumed in oratory. By appointing one Democrat to a judgeship and by a judicious distribution of the state printing, he made a working agreement with the Breckinridge Democrats that kept the opposition divided.[4] Ohio had a surplus of Republican talent, ranging from prolix Governor Dennison to pompous Salmon Chase and pugnacious Ben Wade. The party organization, divided though it had been at Chicago, had come through the conflicts intact and was now able to marshal all its forces against the Democracy. East of the

---

[2] Lathrop: *Kirkwood*, pp. 101–3.

[3] Folwell: *Minnesota*, II, 61 ff.

[4] *Madison Patriot*, June 9, July 11, September 6, 13, October 11, 12, 17, 26, 1860; *Wisconsin State Journal*, June 13, August 24, October 22, 1860; James Doolittle MSS., May 29, 1860, and *passim*.

Alleghenies, New Jersey was the only Republican state in which there was no gubernatorial contest in 1860. There the well-disciplined party workers assembled and assumed their campaign duties in encouraging contrast to the "Bell-Everett-Breckinridge-fusion-Douglas-Democratic confusion meetings." [5]

In each of these states the Republicans went through the traditional motions of the politician's guild: they beat their breasts in agony over the nation's peril and herded the voters to the polling booths. Each state had its Wide-Awakes, garbed in oilcloth capes, who paraded in the weird glare of their burning torches and made the nights hideous with their raucous shouting and singing. But in these Republican strongholds the state organizations had little fear of the outcome.

In the five Democratic states that held no gubernatorial elections in 1860, the local Republicans used the campaign to strengthen their position and toughen their organization. On the far-off Pacific coast both California and Oregon were Democratic, but there, as elsewhere, Democrats were divided on local issues and on national problems. In Oregon a Douglas faction challenged Joseph Lane's power and patronage and gave Republicans their opportunity. The Republican Party had organized in April 1859, had run a candidate for Congress in the elections of that year, and in the spring of 1860 had secured a balance of power in the state legislature. This they used to effect a working agreement with the Douglas Democrats, in accordance with which the legislature chose two non-secessionist senators to go to Washington. In the Presidential campaign the growing Republican organization reached its peak; it succeeded in giving Oregon's three electoral votes to Lincoln by a plurality of 270.[6]

California's political circus had featured a major fight be-

[5] *New York Tribune,* July 18, August 9, 1860.

[6] *New York Times,* June 15, 1860; C. H. Carey: *History of Oregon,* pp. 631–45.

tween William M. Gwin, heading the "Chivalry" wing of the Democracy, and David Broderick, an immigrant from Tammany Hall who had organized the Irish of San Francisco. Both were senators, but Gwin had absolute control of the federal patronage in the state. In the gubernatorial campaign of 1859 each faction had run a candidate, and so completely had they engrossed the public interest that Republican Leland Stanford, polling only ten thousand votes, had concluded that he was a mere political curiosity. In an aftermath of the election Senator Broderick was killed in a duel with a judge of the state Supreme Court. The episode left one Democratic faction leaderless and the other in ill-repute. The Republicans promptly grasped this obvious opportunity, began to build their organization, and went into the campaign of 1860 with arguments for homesteads and a Pacific railroad. While the Democratic factions slung mud at each other, the Republicans furnished entertainment. "Genuine" Lincoln-split rails arrived from Illinois, the Wide-Awakes formed an "Uncle Abe's Choir," which specialized in mauling wedges in a log as an accompaniment to the anvil chorus, humorous speakers entertained the crowds, and barbecues fed the hungry. In the end the Douglas candidates captured both houses of the state legislature, but the Lincoln electors carried the state by a plurality of 750, and the Republicans had at their command an organization that was to make Stanford Governor the next year.[7]

In Delaware, Kentucky, Maryland, and Missouri — the only slave states with Republican parties — the campaign permitted Republicans to strengthen their organization, but offered no hope of immediate victory. The task of Repub-

[7] R. G. Cleland: *A History of California*, pp. 345–55; H. H. Bancroft: *History of California*, pp. 726–30; G. T. Clark: *Leland Stanford*, pp. 87–90; *San Francisco Bulletin*, January 22, September 7, October 2, 10, 30, November 6, 8, 9, 1860; *Sacramento Union*, January 19, March 1, June 21, July 30, 31, August 1, 3, 4, 16, 18, 21, 31, 1860; *New York Times*, October 24, 1860.

lican leaders was to persuade the electorate that the party
was conservative and devoted to the Union. In Delaware the
indignation over the alleged corruption of the Buchanan administration was so intense that even some slaveholders were
driven to support the Republican ticket. In November the
Lincoln electors polled 3,815 votes of a total of 16,041, and
Republicans were satisfied.[8]

Missouri and Maryland were held by the Blair family. In
Maryland, Henry Winter Davis challenged Montgomery
Blair's leadership, but a threat to disrupt the organization
was averted.[9] Missouri presented a unique set of problems.
The rivalries that appeared in 1860 were deep-rooted, running back to the days when Thomas Hart Benton had ruled
Missouri as a satrapy, during the "reign" of Andrew Jackson. Later, when Benton had split with President Polk and
the Southerners, administration followers had disrupted the
Democratic Party. By 1860 the Bentonites were led by Frank
Blair, son of Jackson's fiery editor, Francis Preston Blair. To
the Bentonian faction Blair added Germans from St. Louis
to form a Republican Party avowedly abolitionist and radical. With the Benton element out of the party, the Democrats were able to heal the Douglas-Breckinridge breach at
least long enough to unite in nominating Claiborne Fox
Jackson for the governorship. But when Jackson, personally
known as a Breckinridge man, announced his preference for
Douglas, the Breckinridge forces again pulled up stakes and
entered a weak candidate against him. In August, Jackson
won. After the election he switched his allegiance to Breckinridge in a futile effort to save the state from the Constitutional Union Party in the presidential campaign. The most
significant result of the election, however, was the triumph
of Frank Blair's radical Republicans in St. Louis. They carried the city, sent Blair to Congress, and remained to harass

[8] *New York Tribune,* May 2, 1860; Conrad: *History of Delaware,* I,
194–5.

[9] *New York Tribune,* May 11, July 4, 1860; William E. Smith: *The
Blair Family in Politics,* I, 487.

both Claiborne Jackson and Abraham Lincoln in the years ahead.[10]

In each of these eleven states the Republican Party strengthened itself by electioneering exercises, but in none of them was the situation ever desperate. The presidential election of 1860 was decided in eleven other states, stretching from Maine to Illinois, where contests for the governorship determined the outcome. This group possessed the largest bloc of electoral votes, the greatest concentration of wealth, and a majority of the population. Without Republican victory in these state contests Lincoln would not have been President.

Three of the New England states had already elected governors in the spring. Rhode Island had chosen the erratic Democrat Sprague, partly because the Republicans had been divided into moderate and radical wings. This experience had taught its lesson: as the followers of Breckinridge and Douglas divided the Democracy, the Republicans stilled their own quarrels to present a united front and march to victory. In Connecticut, under the leadership of the recently elected Buckingham, they regarded the national election as a continuation of the state campaign. Their organization was good, the Wide-Awakes went into hilarious encampment at Hartford, and the party workers performed their allotted tasks without worry. The voters, too, were calm, apparently content with having spoken their minds in the spring. Had the Democrats been united, they might have challenged the Republican control. As it was, twelve thousand Democratic voters stayed away from the polls in November, and Douglas and Breckinridge evenly divided the remainder. Lincoln, although he carried the state by ten thousand, polled fewer votes than the Democrats had mustered in the spring cam-

[10] B. Leopard and F. Shoemaker: *Messages and Proclamations of the Governors of Missouri*, III, 318–20; *New York Times*, April 26, June 12, July 26, September 4, 1860; Smith: *Blair Family*, I, 462; *New York Tribune*, August 13, 17, 20, 1860; Laughlin: *Missouri Politics during the Civil War*, pp. 13–27.

paign.[11] The New Hampshire machine, under Rollins and Chandler, worked with equal effectiveness. In June, Governor Goodwin discussed the national situation with calm assurance. "Threats of disunion," he told the state legislature, ". . . are not unusual upon the recurrence of each presidential canvass." Those who stirred up sectional animosity, he felt sure, would be rebuked by "true patriots and right men." "As good citizens it becomes us not to despair and as wise men not to be frightened by mere bluster and despair." [12] In November, New Hampshire's patriots took his advice and rebuked the Democrats.

The first Northern elections after the Chicago convention were held in Vermont and Maine. In neither state did Republicans have cause for alarm. Maine's politics had long been known as among the most extreme in the nation. There the temperance forces had imposed the first prohibition law and there abolitionism had had some of its strongest — and strangest — adherents. The Republican Party had controlled the state since 1857. It was compounded of a number of factions, all extremist, which frequently stymied one another and then united on moderate candidates: abolitionists, Conscience Whigs, Free-Soil Democrats, and "Ramrod" temperance men. Hannibal Hamlin, candidate for vice president, had been a Free-Soil Democrat; Neal Dow, the "Father of Prohibition," kept the party austerely "dry."

Comparatively moderate — for Maine Republicanism — was gubernatorial candidate Israel Washburn, eldest of six famous brothers. Washburn had been in Congress for ten years. In 1854 he had called upon the congressional opponents of the Kansas-Nebraska bill to launch a new party, and he shared the honor of having given the Republican organization its name. Though short in stature, serious, almost

[11] *New York Times,* July 28, 1862; Crofutt and Morris: *Connecticut during the War,* p. 29: J. R. Lane: *Political History of Connecticut during the Civil War,* pp. 122–40.

[12] *Boston Post,* September 5, 1860.

scholarly, in demeanor, nearsighted, and high-voiced, Israel Washburn impressed people as a solid, hard-working man of erudition and integrity. His appearance and reputation were valuable to the party, for the Democrats, weary of assailing Republican eccentricities, had begun to charge the party with extravagance and corruption.[13]

The prosiness of the Republican campaign and the Democratic charges alarmed Hannibal Hamlin, who predicted that the Democrats would carry two congressional districts and reduce Washburn's majority to less than six thousand. This in turn frightened Lincoln, who told his running mate that such an outcome would "put us on the downhill track, lose us the state elections in Pennsylvania and Indiana, and probably ruin us on the main turn in November." [14]

Vermont's campaign stirred up even less excitement. In June the Republicans nominated for governor the elderly Erastus Fairbanks, manufacturer and vendor of the numerous items, from cast-iron plows to platform scales, that his brother Thaddeus invented. The Fairbanks company had doubled in value every three years from 1842 to 1857, but Erastus had never neglected his public responsibilities while building the family fortune. He had represented St. Johnsbury in the legislature, had been a Whig presidential elector in 1844 and 1848, and Governor in 1852. He had been devoted to education, to the Congregational Church, and to prohibition. The nomination of such a man in Vermont was equivalent to election. In September the voters ratified the party's choice.[15]

If moderation and caution determined the candidates in most of New England, other forces operated in Massachusetts. At the last moment the moderate Nathaniel P. Banks,

[13] Hunt: *Washburn*, pp. 69 ff.

[14] *New York Tribune*, May 24, July 13, 1860; *Writings of Lincoln*, V, 191; *New York Times*, September 12, October 23, 1860.

[15] *New York Times*, June 27, October 18, 1860; L. E. Chittenden: *Recollections of President Lincoln*, p. 8.

who had been Governor for three years and who was entitled by long custom to one more nomination, withdrew from the race. Having failed to win higher political honors at Chicago, he accepted the presidency of the Illinois Central Railroad and prepared to abandon the governorship of Massachusetts.

Banks knew that John Andrew, his hated rival, could — and probably would — seize the Republican nomination. Consulting his advisers, the Governor determined to keep his decision a secret until the eve of the Republican state convention. The meeting was scheduled for Wednesday, August 29. Banks planned to withhold his announcement until the Friday before — too late for the weekly rural papers to carry the news. Meantime his moderate friends would marshal the conservatives of western Massachusetts for Henry L. Dawes. But Banks made one misstep. On the morning of the 24th he showed his announcement to a friend of Senator Charles Sumner.

"Give me my boots," exclaimed the radical Senator as he heard the news. "John A. Andrew must be the next governor of Massachusetts."

Hastily Sumner, Andrew, and the radicals went to work. They promoted two other conservatives to split Dawes's support, and they browbeat delegates into supporting Andrew. By the time the Worcester convention met, Andrew had control and was nominated on the first ballot.

Conservatives were aghast. Sam Bowles of the *Springfield Republican* assured his readers that Andrew had "a warm heart but a cool head" and that the responsibilities of office would make him wise and politic. But even Bowles could not hide his fear that Andrew's extremism, his Garrisonian affiliations, and his John Brown speeches and sympathies would be "trumpeted far and wide" to injure Lincoln.

No one expected the Democrats to carry the state, for as elsewhere they were hopelessly divided. The Douglas faction nominated Erasmus Beach, who had a reputation as a "liberal"; the Breckinridge wing entered Benjamin F. Butler, who had charm in the eyes of the foreign elements. The Constitutional Unionists, forsaking consistency in the very home of their vice-presidential candidate, offered Amos Lawrence, "the man who furnished John Brown's rifles," to the voters. The three groups tried, and failed, to get together. They had only one thing in common — a consuming hatred of John Andrew and an abhorrence of his radicalism. The burden of their speeches was translated by street urchins into a ditty:

> Tell John Andrew
> Tell John Andrew
> Tell John Andrew
> John Brown's dead.

But only the body of John Brown lay a-moldering in the grave; his soul went marching on with John Albion Andrew. Throwing himself heart and soul into the campaign, he moved the radicals to ecstasy and the moderates to despair. He could lose ten thousand votes and still carry the state, admitted Sam Bowles and Butler and Lawrence and Beach. But he lost no ten thousand votes. In November the radical Andrew fell only a thousand behind the moderate Lincoln, and the Republican majority was forty thousand. The thousand votes, said the poet Whittier, was the price of Andrew's John Brownism.[16]

Massachusetts' campaign with a radical candidate was paralleled in one other state. In Michigan, too, the Republicans were radical and considered abolitionism to be the central issue. When scandal touched the administration of Moses Wisner, they were able to divert public scrutiny by pointing to the infamies of slavery. For instance when asked by a heckler to explain the loss of fifty thousand dollars in canal

[16] *Boston Transcript,* September 12, 13; *New York Herald,* October 2; *New York Times,* August 27, November 2, 1860; *Boston Post,* August 29 *et passim;* Pearson: *John A. Andrews,* I, 117 ff.; Merriam: *Life of Bowles,* I, 206–7; Schuyler: *Massachusetts in the War,* pp. 2–3.

frauds, a state official demanded: "How dare any Democrat to raise his voice and ask such a question when there are four million human beings in bondage?" And the audience shouted approval.[17]

Political expediency combined with radicalism to make Austin Blair the Republican nominee for governor. Though Blair had shown himself a willing party worker and an able stump speaker, he had failed thus far to receive from his party the recognition he so ardently desired. He had long been ambitious for a seat in Congress, but his home in Jackson was in the same congressional district as Detroit, and both in 1856 and in 1858 the machinations of Detroit politicians had forestalled his nomination. Each time the party managers had promised to support him at the next election. But when the time came in 1860, they made "certain cozy little arrangements" in the district which required that Blair be put off again. Accordingly in the state convention the Detroiters wangled a unanimous gubernatorial nomination for Blair and persuaded him to accept it by solemnly promising that he could be United States senator in 1862.[18]

The Democrats characterized "Our Blair" — so called to distinguish him from "Old Man Blair" and his two "cubs" — as a bitter politician and a chronic office-seeker who had been "holding out his hand crying 'give, give'" until finally he had been nominated for a place for which he had neither inclination nor ability. The Democrats, united on the governorship though divided on the Presidency, nominated John S. Barry, promised economy and honesty, and imported Douglas to enlighten the electorate. But the Republicans countered with Seward and Chase, drummed up support of Blair and Lincoln with the Wide-Awakes, and watched with satisfaction the ebbing of the Douglas wave. November's count put Blair ahead of Lincoln, and both twenty thousand votes ahead of the Democrats.[19]

[17] *Detroit Free Press,* June 5, 1860.
[18] Ibid., May 10, June 5, 8, 23, 1860.
[19] Ibid., May 16, June 20, 21, July 4, 1860, June 1, 1861; *New York*

Michigan's neighbors, Indiana and Illinois, were less surely Republican. Illinois, with two presidential candidates, became a caldron of activity. In Dick Yates the Republicans had a gubernatorial candidate who made up in mediocrity what he lacked in moderation. Democrats assailed his radicalism, but found little in his personality to capitalize upon. Even the Republicans themselves paid little attention to him; they were much more interested, locally, in electing a legislature that would return Trumbull to the United States Senate. In the end, after a campaign that was a nightmare of Wide-Awake parades, *Chicago Tribune* editorials, reckless expenditures, oratorical harangues, and shrewd plots of one sort and another, they succeeded in electing Lincoln and in gaining control of the legislature by a single seat, which they got with a bare majority of seven at the polls. Thus Trumbull's return to Washington was assured. Yates's election as Governor was incidental to the general success of the party.[20]

In Indiana, on the other hand, it was the gubernational contest that determined the outcome in November. Indiana was an "October state," — that is, it held its state and congressional elections in October — and the politicians of all parties found it profitable to keep it in the doubtful column. At every election both parties sent out piteous pleas for aid from Eastern party angels. In return they usually produced a play that thrilled the spectators.

For the leading role in Indiana's 1860 drama, the Republicans cast Harry Lane, billed as "the Zouave of popular orators," an actor with a keen sense of the distinction between comedy and buffoonery. After introducing himself to his delighted audiences with "Ladies and gentlemen, the

Times, August 29, September 7, October 12, 1860; F. B. Streeter: *Political Parties in Michigan, 1837–1860,* pp. 270 ff., 288 ff.

[20] White: *Trumbull,* p. 109; *Chicago Tribune,* July 12 *et passim;* Barnes: *Weed,* II, 301; notes on Allen's speech at Jacksonville, Yates MSS., July 7, 1860; James Doolittle to his wife, October 26, 1860, Doolittle MSS.

next governor of Indiana," he would instantly transform himself into a powerful crusader against the evils of the day. Abandoning his initial humor for biting sarcasm, he would launch into an exposé of Democratic corruption and ineptitude. Playing opposite him was the Democrats' Thomas A. Hendricks, only slightly inferior in histrionic talents. A political acrobat, Hendricks had just deserted the Buchanan administration to declare himself a Douglasite. The two candidates, engaging in joint debate, hurled invective at each other while the audience stamped and cheered. Before the play was over, others strode across the political stage: Jesse Bright, Schuyler Colfax, George W. Julian, Carl Schurz, George E. Pugh, and Clement L. Vallandigham. Behind the scenes, part understudy and part prompter, waited Oliver P. Morton, the man who was actually to become Governor. Both audience and players knew that Lane's candidacy was only make-believe: if he was elected he would go to the Senate, and Morton, who was too radical for the spotlight now, would then preside at the statehouse.

The campaign's opening gave a portent of the Indiana Democracy's fate. The Douglas Democrats, with much ballyhoo, announced a Great Ratification Meeting for the 18th of July. Handbills promising lively entertainment appeared on fence posts and the walls of grogshops. Bandsmen polished up their trumpets. No preparation was neglected except to consult the almanac. When the day came, the sun went into eclipse. The crowd stayed home, and the imported exhorters wasted their words on the darkened air.

Republicans, too, were in an agony of fear during the long, oppressive summer. In August it looked as though the Bell men might organize. If they did, it might go hard with Lincoln. Really alarmed, the Republicans hastily called in David Davis and feverishly begged him to extract ten thousand dollars from Thurlow Weed and Chairman Morgan. Uncertain whether the danger was real or merely a part of the plot, the Easterners sent the money. Nor did they know in October, when Lane carried the state by nearly ten thousand, thus making sure that there would be no hitch in the last act in November.[21]

But it was in the East that the financial problems of the election of 1860 were most serious. Neither New York nor Pennsylvania could be carried without money, and in both states campaign solicitors met with many rebuffs. In New York even Thurlow Weed, a past master at extracting contributions from potential beneficiaries of the Republican program, became discouraged in the face of the Southern threats of secession, which would jeopardize Northern business.

Conservative businessmen of New York were in a quandary, for if Lincoln won and the South seceded, the established Southern trade would be destroyed. At the same time, less well-established and more speculative financial interests had been angered by Morgan's vetoes of railroad bills in the previous session of the legislature. Neither group of businessmen would contribute heavily to either the national or the state war chests. Lacking adequate resources, Weed early abandoned hope of carrying New York City and concentrated his efforts in the upstate area. By so doing he hoped to gain enough to compensate for an expected twenty-five-thousand Democratic majority in the metropolis.

Governor Morgan not only had alienated the railroad speculators but had also incurred Seward's displeasure by failing to support him more effectively at Chicago. This might have turned Weed against the Governor had Weed not been too much a realist in politics to suppose that Morgan could be repudiated. When the Republicans assembled in state convention at Syracuse, it was obvious that they must bury their internal dissensions. Already the Douglas and Bell forces were uniting in the state, and there was an imminent possibility that the Breckinridge men would join

[21] Woodburn: *"Party Politics in Indiana,"* 227 f.; French: *Morton,* pp. 18 f.; *New York Tribune,* July 18; *New York Times,* July 24, August 8, 22, September 19, October 12, 1860; Barnes: *Weed,* II, 299–300; K. M. Stampp: Indiana Politics during the Civil War.

them. In an "industrious convention" that ran "as if it had been wound up," Morgan was renominated "if not by acclamation, at least by acquiescence." [22] So convincing was the pretense of perfect concord that cynics began to suspect that Morgan's vetoes had been an "honesty dodge." They pointed to the apparent harmony between Senator, editor, and Governor. The combination was not especially conducive to raising money, but it carried the state for Morgan and Lincoln, even though New York City gave a thirty-thousand majority to the fusion candidates.[23]

Despite New York's size and its abundance of political talent, however, Pennsylvania was the pivot in the election of 1860.[24] Results in this "October state" had so regularly presaged national elections that politicians had become superstitious about its role. Without Pennsylvania's twenty-seven electoral votes — that is, without Andrew Curtin's victory in October — Lincoln could not be elected in November.[25] At best the Republicans, disunited by the long-standing feud between their two leaders, would have had no field day. But to make matters more difficult, Pennsylvania's Democrats were united behind Henry D. Foster, an able politician of quasi-Breckinridge sympathies. Despite the national situation, the Democrats in Pennsylvania were less divided than their opponents.

Throughout the campaign the bitter fires of the Cameron-

[22] *New York Times,* August 21, 24, 1860.

[23] Ibid., July 12 *et passim;* cf. especially editorials of August 17, 21, 22, 23, 24, September 6, November 7; *New York Tribune,* July to November, and editorials of July 11, August 15, 16, 20, 1860; Barnes: *Weed,* II, 273–4, 297 f., 300; Pearson: *Wadsworth,* p. 49; Tracy: *Uncollected Letters of Lincoln,* p. 160; S. D. Brummer: *Political History of New York during the Civil War,* pp. 34–5; Fite: *Election of 1860,* p. 233.

[24] This belief, generally held by politicians, was based on the logical assumption that New Jersey's vote would swing in Pennsylvania's orbit. See J. G. Blaine: *Twenty Years of Congress,* I, 206–7.

[25] McClure: *Abraham Lincoln and Men of Wartime,* pp. 41–4, and *Old Time Notes,* pp. 409, 419; Davis: *Pennsylvania Politics,* pp. 114–18; Nicolay and Hay: *Lincoln,* VI, 54.

Curtin feud smoldered, threatening momentarily to break into consuming flame. Early in the campaign Curtin prevented Cameron from securing control of the People's Party machinery. The state central committee, evenly divided between Curtin and Cameron men, had scheduled a meeting at Cresson. The night before was spent in revelry, but Curtin's cohorts remained sober while they plied their rivals with wine. Promptly at ten the next morning, the hour set, Chairman A. K. McClure called the meeting to order. Present were the sleepy but sober Curtin men, absent the majority of Cameron's cohorts. With feverish dispatch Curtin presented his plan for the campaign, McClure stifled discussion and put it to a vote, and the chairman appointed committees and adjourned the session. All was over before Cameron's drowsy fighters staggered in to discover that they had been outwitted. Hotly they demanded another meeting, but McClure never found it convenient to call the committee together again. Instead he did all the work himself, organizing subcommittees of Curtin's followers in each election district and coercing party workers to labor without pay. Disgusted and disgruntled, Cameron's friends appealed to Lincoln. Davis and Sweet came in to make an inspection, but reported only that McClure had built up an efficient, well-knit organization. From Springfield, Lincoln replied that he never interfered in quarrels between friends! [26]

Cameron was not the only one who was disgruntled. The political firm of Weed, Seward, and Morgan also refused to do business with the Curtin faction. Seward had not forgiven Curtin for his part at Chicago, and the national headquarters withheld both moral and financial support from the Pennsylvanians. With a united party McClure could certainly have raised money in so rich a state to send elsewhere.

[26] McClure: *Old Time Notes*, pp. 417–33. *Philadelphia Press*, April to October, *passim;* see especially July 16, August 27, 28, 1860. *New York Tribune*, August 10, 1860; *New York Herald,* October 2, 8, 9, 10, 1860; *New York Times*, October 5, 8, 10, 1860; *Harrisburg Patriot*, August 3, 27, 30, September 6, 13, 20, 27, 1860.

As it was, the wealthy men of Philadelphia closed their purses to him, and he raised only twelve thousand dollars for the campaign. Late in the summer, with Weed's consent, he obtained forty-three hundred dollars in New York to save two Pennsylvania congressmen who were in danger, but he got no help for the state campaign. Only organization and hard work saved the day. Curtin spoke at least twice in each county of the state, quashing Know-Nothing rumors that he was a Catholic, reiterating his devotion to the common man and the laborer, and rising to eagle flights of oratory — without benefit of grammar — as he extolled the virtues of a high tariff.

The tariff was the sole issue in Pennsylvania, and both parties were for it. They vied with each other only in protesting their devotion to a protectionist philosophy. Candidate Foster and the Democrats proclaimed that they alone were the true tariff men, and professed to believe that the "People's Party" of Curtin and McClure was only the Republican Party in disguise. The Republicans, they said, were abolitionists, who would embroil the country in a war to keep slavery out of the territories and would vote for free homesteads in the West. They were really free-traders, and Hannibal Hamlin was an old free-trade Free-Soiler. Pennsylvanians, they insisted, were interested in none of these things: they only wanted a tariff, and only the Democrats could give it to them. To such assertions Curtin made evasive reply. The People's Party, he professed, was not interested in slavery, in the territories, or in homesteads. It was concerned only with protection — and Lincoln was a high-tariff Whig!

The campaign orators made more noise than sense. But the people of Pennsylvania remembered that in the last Congress Republicans had sponsored a tariff bill. The babel of party names neither confused nor dispersed them; in fact, they understood only too well that the retention of the "People's Party" enabled them to hold a whip over the Republicans. In October they gave a thirty-thousand majority to Curtin, making Lincoln's election, a month later, a certainty. People's Party nominees also won eighteen of the state's twenty-five congressional seats.[27]

"Pennsylvania has spoken. She is lost," bemoaned the Democratic *New York Herald*[28] as it recorded the October vote. At the same time Indiana and Ohio went Republican, and the *Herald* concluded that New York was the last forlorn hope of the Democrats. Try as they might, the Democrats could not make themselves believe that Pennsylvania's People's Party was anything but the Republican Party, or that Bell would make inroads on its vote in November.[29] The *Harrisburg Patriot* was honest: "We say frankly that the election of Andrew G. Curtin makes the defeat of Abraham Lincoln hopeless. It is useless to attempt to keep up appearances by affecting a hope that we do not feel."[29] Yet the editors of the *Patriot* and the *Herald* were right when they observed that the results in Pennsylvania were no endorsement of radicalism on the slavery and territorial questions.[30]

After the October elections interest flagged. In several states, notably Pennsylvania and New York, the Democrats made frantic efforts to get together with one another and with the Bell men, but it was then too late. Had they succeeded, the results might have been different, but the rifts between them were too wide to be bridged even in an emergency. While they continued to oppose each other the Republican state organizations kept up their work. In November, Andrew, Morgan, Yates, and Blair carried their states, and Lincoln with them. The Republican Party in the states had elected a President for the nation. But there was still no national Republican Party.

[27] *New York Herald,* October 10, 1860.
[28] Ibid., October 11, 1860.
[29] *Harrisburg Patriot,* October 11, 1860.
[30] Ibid., October 18, 25; *Herald,* October 16, 1860.

Chapter 6

Moderate Counsel and a Radical Answer

T HE FIRST result of Republican success in the election
of 1860 was confusion. The governors and the state organizations had won the election, but there was no agreement
among them on the meaning of their victory. Neither Eastern conservatives, giving lip-service to homesteads and humanitarianism, nor Western radicals with their tongue-in-cheek
endorsements of a protective tariff dominated the party. It
was a situation in which each faction could claim a share of
the victor's spoils and each could assume a mandate for its
principles. Few of those who planned to claim the victory
considered that Abraham Lincoln might have a mind of his
own.

"God has laid the great responsibility upon us," wrote the
poet Whittier to Salmon P. Chase in a letter liberally sprin-
kled with the "thee's" and "thou's" of his melodious and
courtly Quaker speech.

Whether they conceded divine intervention or not, the
old abolitionists were agreed that the responsibility was indeed great, calling for careful planning and vigorous action.
For two months they plotted, maneuvered, and outlined
their strategy. The aging abolitionist editor Joshua Leavitt
was sure that the "permanance of our power" depended on
the resurgence of the "Old Benton Democracy." And he
found the prospects heartening. "Thank God! Lincoln is

chosen! It is a joy to have lived to this day," he had exulted in a congratulatory note to Chase. "Let the future take care of its own exigencies," he had added as he set himself to outlining recommendations for the new cabinet. A few weeks later, toward the close of November, some fifty old Barnburners gathered in New York and appointed a committee to promote abolitionists for Lincoln's cabinet — Chase, David Dudley Field, James Wadsworth. Until the turn of the year no misgiving clouded their vision of a Republican administration dominated by Free-Soil, Barnburning, Old Bentonian abolitionists.[1]

In the far South, at the opposite pole of politics, the fire-eating Breckinridge Democrats likewise saw Lincoln's election as the triumph of abolitionism. They too prepared for action. In South Carolina, where devotion to democracy had never induced politicians to trust the people's judgment in a presidential election, the legislature had been convened to appoint the state's electors. The moment the telegraph gave them the disheartening news of Lincoln's victory, the legislators called a state convention. In other states the governors hastily called their legislatures into special session, and in frantic messages urged instant secession. Within a few weeks conventions had been called; and before the end of January, Florida, Georgia, Alabama, Mississippi, Louisiana, and Texas — the whole cotton kingdom along the Gulf coast — had followed South Carolina into secession.

One after another the seceders issued labored rationalizations of their actions. Once again South Carolina elaborated the well-worn argument that the Constitution was a contract between sovereign states, which the North had violated. "Those states have assumed the right of deciding upon the propriety of our domestic institutions. They have denounced as sinful the institution of slavery. . . . They have encour-

---

[1] Letters to Salmon P. Chase from Joshua Leavitt, November 7, J. G. Whittier, November 9, and H. B. Stanton, November 30, December 7, 1860, in "Diary and Correspondence of Salmon P. Chase," in American Historical Association: *Annual Report, 1902,* II, 283–9.

aged . . . thousands of our slaves to leave their homes."
Worse still, they had "united in the election of a man to the
high office of President of the United States whose opinions
and purposes are hostile to slavery." Henceforth the South
would be excluded from the territories, the Supreme Court
would be the organ of sectional interests, and war would be
waged against slavery to its extinction. "The guarantees of
the Constitution will then no longer exist: the equal rights
of the states will be lost." [2] Other states, possessed of similar
fears, repeated these arguments.

Thus Southern apprehensions concurred with abolitionist
hopes and purposes. But abolitionists had no clear field in
the North. No two of the state organizations that had secured Lincoln's election agreed on any concrete and positive
body of principles. Indeed, there was no unanimity within
any of them. Each faction was free to place its own interpre-
tation upon the election returns and to press for the adoption of its own particular program by the party. No individual, no group, had the authority or the prestige or the power
to formulate a national policy.

The Republican Party, thought Edward Bates, was merely
the old Whig Party under a new name. Its dominance would
be assured if only it would be "moderately wise," distributing its patronage liberally, "prudently" protecting industry, "moderately but persistently" promoting commerce and
internal improvements, "preserving peace, and giving careful consideration" to all the problems before it. [3]

In Pennsylvania both parties conceded that the tariff issue
had carried the state—thanks to Republican double-dealing,
the Democrats insisted. By a conspiracy of silence, they
charged, Republicans had concealed their real purposes and
had deluded voters into believing that "by supporting Curtin they were not identifying themselves with abolitionism."
Curtin himself had ignored the slavery issue throughout the
state campaign, and on the very eve of the November elec-

---

[2] *The Rebellion Record,* edited by Frank Moore, I, 3–5.

[3] Bates: *Diary,* pp. 152–3.

tions he had traveled to Boston to assure a Faneuil Hall audience that the entire campaign had turned upon protection for iron and coal. With never a mention of slavery, he had urged Massachusetts voters to elect men of good Whig antecedents.[4]

Yet on the morning after the election the *Boston Transcript* was not persuaded that the people had followed Curtin's advice. The editor admitted that the President-elect was an old Henry Clay Whig, holding all Clay's views on the tariff and internal improvements, but he noted that Lincoln had nevertheless received support from free-traders and Democrats. What the vote really represented, thought the staid *Transcript,* was the "average opinion" of a majority of the people on slavery extension. The *New York Times,* heady with victory, foresaw a "marked and most important change" in the government. The election had checked slavery's political power and its territorial extension; and guaranteed that the Constitution would cease to be a "mere instrument for fortifying and increasing" that institution. Above all, the *Times* rejoiced that a "rule of honesty and patriotism" would replace the "corruption, imbecility, and intrigue" of the Democratic regime.[5]

But all this was simply unbridled intoxication with success. The mere fact of victory had resolved no differences, pacified no enemies. And so Editor Henry Raymond, as he learned of South Carolina's belligerency, dedicated his editorial and news columns to the dual task of conciliating the South and reassuring the North. While his rival of the *Tribune,* Horace Greeley, advised Northerners to let the "erring sisters depart in peace," Raymond sought to prove by extensive quotations from Lincoln's debates with Douglas that the President-elect was an "eminently just, upright and conservative statesman, pledged by his opinions, his declarations, and his life against any invasion of Southern rights." True, he

[4] *New York Herald,* October 16, 1860; *Harrisburg Patriot,* October 18, 25, November 1, 8, 22, 1860.
[5] *Boston Transcript* and *New York Times,* November 7, 1860.

regarded slavery as an evil and would oppose its extension and the reopening of the African trade. But farther he would not go. He would be "tolerant and considerate" of the South, would recognize the sovereignty of the states, would oppose Negro suffrage, and would discountenance social equality.

Day after day the *Times* repeated that Lincoln was a moderate man. Daily, too, it presented evidence that Union sentiment remained strong in the South. Communications from Southern correspondents filled its columns, telling hopefully that there were moderates in Virginia, who had no fear of the state's secession, that Georgia's Governor did not approve of a Southern convention, that Unionists were organizing in Virginia, Texas, and Maryland. Some symptoms of resentment were to be expected, thought the moderate editor. "We are not surprised — nor in the least alarmed. . . . We have never supposed the South would sit down quietly and submit at once to Republican ascendancy. . . . They are compelled to go ahead, if only to prove they weren't hypocrites. . . . We look, therefore, for a great deal of violent talk." But the South would soon learn, he prophesied, that it had nothing to fear from Lincoln and the Republicans.

At the same time Editor Raymond warned the Southerners they must not mistake the government's determination to preserve the Union. South Carolina might with impunity withdraw her congressmen, refuse to accept United States mail, and refrain from using the federal courts, but if she should commit any positive, aggressive act of war — if a vessel in Charleston's port should refuse to pay customs duties, or if Carolina troops should seize Fort Moultrie — the government would not hesitate to use force.

Half hidden behind Raymond's mingled warnings and reassurances was an admonition for Lincoln. The editor intended his long quotations from the debates both to reassure the people, North and South, and to impress upon Lincoln himself what was expected of him. The election, Raymond pointed out, had given Lincoln no mandate on any score. It had confirmed the power of Congress to exclude slavery from the territories, "but practically, there is no necessity for exercising the power at the present time." The party's program should be one of masterly inactivity, keeping public opinion "right" and waiting in patience for the territories to grow up in freedom. If Lincoln and his cohorts would merely be moderate, conservative, and inactive, Southerners would realize that they had nothing to fear and would not be precipitated into irretrievable ruin by a "few disappointed demagogues." [6]

Indeed, their fears could be stilled at once, Raymond suggested, if Lincoln would nationalize his administration by including in his cabinet such Southerners as John Bell, John Minor Botts, Emerson Etheridge, or Henry Winter Davis. This would prove that the new administration contemplated no encroachment on Southern rights.

In urging such a course upon the party and its nominal leader, the *Times* voiced the sentiments of conservatives in general. In the Middle West, they hoped, Indiana's Governor-elect, Henry S. Lane — sagacious, prudent, economical, well informed, steady, and courageous — would be their spokesman.[7] Lane did not disappoint them. At a victory jubilee in Indianapolis the incoming Governor pleaded eloquently for a conciliatory attitude toward the misguided Southerners.[8] In Philadelphia, where a public dinner for state chairman McClure capped the victory celebration, one committee after another of businessmen waited upon McClure and Curtin and implored them to say nothing that could possibly offend the South. So the two leaders, weighing their words, urged justice for all sections, pledged the most sacred regard for the South's constitutional rights, and pleaded for the preservation of the Union.[9] In Boston the

[6] *New York Times,* November 1860; see especially the editorials of November 9, 12, 23.

[7] Ibid., November 15, 1860.

[8] C. M. Walker: *Oliver P. Morton,* p. 43.

[9] S. L. Davis: *Pennsylvania Politics, 1860–1863,* pp. 143–4; *Pennsyl-*

conservatives, with the aid of police, disbanded a meeting
called by the radicals to commemorate John Brown's death,
and passed resolutions that "no virtuous and law abiding
citizens of this commonwealth ought to countenance, sympa-
thize with, or hold communion with any man who believes
that John Brown and his aides and abetters . . . were
right." [10]

While the conservatives strove to commit Lincoln and the
Republicans to a moderate course, the radicals, too, were
busy. [11] The ex-Barnburners of New York agreed that Salmon P. Chase should go into the cabinet, and they combed
their ranks for other prospects. [12] Detroit's Senator Zach
Chandler, believing that Trumbull had influence with Lincoln, wrote the Illinois Senator that he favored a "regular
General Jackson administration" and no compromise, despite the "howl" he knew would go up from the mercantile
centers, which would always rather buy immunity than
fight. [13]

At the same Indianapolis meeting at which Lane spoke
soft words of conciliation, Oliver Perry Morton breathed
fire. He insisted that the government could not permit South
Carolina to withdraw, and that it had no choice but to force
the state's submission. For if the South should leave the
Union, the Pacific coast would follow, and in the end the in-
land states would be cut off from the seaboard and suffer
political, social, and commercial death. If it had been worth
a bloody struggle to create the nation, Morton concluded
fiercely, surely it was worth another to preserve it. Better a
seven years' war than a purchased peace! [14]

---

vania Gazette, December 5, 1860; A. K. McClure: *Old Time Notes,* I,
467–75.

[10] Pearson: *Andrew,* I, 131.

[11] S. H. M. Byers: *Iowa,* pp. 32–3.

[12] *Chase Diary and Correspondence,* pp. 483, 291, 292; S. D. Brummer: *Political History of New York . . . during the Civil War,* p. 129.

[13] W. C. Harris, *Chandler,* pp. 51–2.

[14] W. M. French: *Life, Speeches . . . of Governor Oliver P. Morton,*
pp. 112 f.

Both radicals and conservatives were looking to Lincoln. But the President-elect was not yet head of his party, not yet in a position to speak with authority. His voice would only have added noise to the general clamor. Just before the November election, when the October results had made his victory almost certain, he had told George Prentice, editor of the *Louisville Journal,* that "bad men" of the South would pounce upon any new statement he made and label it an evidence of timidity. Even after the election, as business slumped in the face of the future's uncertainties, Lincoln still refused to speak. "Nothing is to be gained by fawning around the 'respectable scoundrels' " who had "got up" the panic, he said. "Let them go to work and repair the mischief of their own making." And again, when Henry J. Raymond, voicing the moderate hopes of New York's business interests, pressed him for a statement, Lincoln replied that "these political fiends are not half sick enough yet. . . . 'They seek a sign, and no sign shall be given them.' " [15]

But if Lincoln failed to reassure the conservatives, neither did he commit himself to the radicals. Wendell Phillips thought he was hardly an antislavery man, and certainly no abolitionist — merely a pawn in the political chess game.[16] The Barnburners of New York, having made little progress, waylaid Trumbull on his way to Congress to seek his aid in gaining Lincoln's ear. But Trumbull could only tell them that he had no influence.[17] Rumor had it that Lincoln was satisfied that Morton's incendiary speech "covers the whole ground, and declares the necessary policy of the government"; [18] but the abolitionists found no confirmation in words or acts from Springfield. One of them, Congressman Owen Lovejoy, commenting on Joshua R. Giddings's aspira-

[15] Nicolay and Hay: *Complete Works of Lincoln,* VI, 66–7; V, 654; Nicolay and Hay: *Abraham Lincoln, A History,* III, 282.

[16] Cf. A. C. Cole: "Was Lincoln's Education a Threat to the South?" *American Historical Review,* XXXVI, 755.

[17] White: *Trumbull,* p. 139.

[18] W. D. Foulke: *Oliver P. Morton,* I, 96.

tion for a cabinet post, concluded that there was probably "nothing so good in store for us." Lincoln, he complained, "has not as yet called on me for advice." [19]

In the face of Lincoln's failure to translate the election results into concrete terms, both radicals and conservatives turned anxiously to Congress. But the Thirty-seventh Congress, full of lame ducks who had just been repudiated by the people, was in no position to offer leadership. On the eve of the session that was to open on December 1 Thurlow Weed published the first of a series of editorials in his *Albany Journal* urging moderation and compromise, and Henry Raymond's *New York Times* and Sam Bowles's *Springfield Republican* echoed this advice. The conciliatory Seward arrived early in Washington to try to influence his colleagues, but he found the Republican Party "as uncompromising as the Secessionists of South Carolina." He could only hope that a month's consideration would show them the wisdom of moderation. [20]

To the lame-duck Congress the lame-duck President sent an able message. With elaborate but sound argument Buchanan confronted the lawmakers with a constitutional paradox: a state had no right to secede, and the federal government had no power to prevent secession. It was a dilemma that could be resolved only by compromise — which, after all, was the very essence of the American system. Ever since the day the founding fathers had constructed the Constitution by mutual tolerance and concession, the Union had been held together by a series of compromises. The President's recommendation was based upon the clear recognition that in politics toleration and compromise were the American way.

Perhaps it was inevitable, in view of Buchanan's unpopularity, that his appeal should have been ignored. He had been identified with the Breckinridge Democrats so long that whatever recommendation he might have made would

[19] Lovejoy to Giddings, November 23, 1860. Joshua R. Giddings MSS.
[20] Weed: *Memoir*, II, 308–9; *New York Times*, December 4, 6, 1860.

almost certainly have been suspect. Moreover, it was obvious to Republicans that if they accepted compromise of any kind, they would be admitting that they had contemplated the injustices that Democrats and Southerners feared. The political climate was not favorable for growing hybrid compromises.

Each branch of Congress, however, referred Buchanan's message to a special committee. The House Committee of Thirty-three, being overwhelmingly Republican, was from the first a graveyard for all compromise proposals. The Senate Committee of Thirteen, representing all factions and sections, was better balanced, but it, too, was doomed to failure. Its members from the far South took the intransigent position that they would accept no compromise that did not have the full approval of the Republican members. Thus they signified their intention of throwing the entire onus of failure upon their political opponents.

On the floors of both houses serious debate gave way to recrimination. Southerners and Democrats pounced upon the personal-liberty laws of a dozen Northern states and demanded their immediate repeal. Since these laws were the only tangible evidence they could muster to support their prophecies of impending doom, they wrung the last drop of oratory from them. Moderate Republicans, conceding the unconstitutionality of such legislation, endorsed proposals to abolish it, but argued that the "harsh and unjust" Fugitive Slave Act of 1850 should also be modified.[21]

The radicals met every move toward conciliation and compromise with vociferous scorn. "It cannot be done," Preston King had told Thurlow Weed when the editor first advocated moderation. "You and Seward should be among the foremost to brandish the lance and shout for war." Charles Sumner hastened to New York to denounce Weed and his plans for conciliation.[22] Radicals were sure that Lincoln, the

[21] *Congressional Globe,* 36th Congress, 2nd session, part I, pp. 6 ff.; *New York Times,* December 7, *et seq.,* 1860.

[22] *Memoir of Thurlow Weed,* II, 308–9.

moment he was inaugurated, would adopt an "affirmative" policy. Joshua Giddings, for one, returned from a trip to Springfield confident that Lincoln would "stand firmly by our doctrines." [23] From Washington, Lyman Trumbull advised Lincoln to act "with calm dignity in such a way as if possible we may ride out the storm." As he saw it, "inactivity and a kind spirit" were the only course until the 4th of March.[24]

As Lincoln remained silent and it became manifest that Congress was hopelessly paralyzed, Weed and the other moderates bethought themselves of the governors as a last hope. In the South the chief executives of the states had taken the reins; they had led the movement for secession, summoning legislatures into special session, inditing venomous secession messages, and sending to one another personal representatives who co-ordinated their actions. To Thurlow Weed it looked very much as if they were knitting a united South, against which a divided North might find itself impotent. Taking a lesson from the Southern procedure, Weed urged that Republican governors join forces and collectively bring their influence to bear on both Congress and the President-elect. "With wisdom and justice," Weed told Lincoln as he apprised him of a forthcoming conference of governors, "we can unite the North in upholding the supremacy of the Constitution and laws, and thus united, your administration will have its foundation upon a rock." [25]

This was the first move that threatened seriously to tip Lincoln's hand. Hitherto he had remained unperturbed by the conflict between the radical and conservative forces in his party, but now he moved quickly to prevent the situation from getting beyond control. First he offered Seward the State Department in the coming administration, adding cautiously that the job did not include control of the federal patronage in New York. Then, through Judge Davis and

---

[23] Giddings to son, December 10, 1860. Giddings MSS.
[24] Nicolay and Hay: *Lincoln,* III, 254, 255.
[25] Ibid., 252–3.

Leonard Swett, his liaison men of the election campaign, he invited Weed to visit Springfield, ostensibly to give advice on the cabinet. And, finally, he authorized Weed to speak for him at the convention of governors Weed had mentioned. "Tell them," he said, "you judge from my speeches that I will be inflexible on the territorial question: that I probably think either the Missouri line extended, or Douglas's and Eli Thayer's popular sovereignty would lose us everything we gained by the election." As for secession, the President-elect added, no state could lawfully get out of the Union, and it would be "the duty of the President and other government functionaries to run the machine as it is." [26]

Seward, too, wanted Weed to go to Springfield. Republicans in Congress could not commit themselves to any compromise unless they could bank on the support of the new administration. So Weed went to Illinois. He canvassed the situation with the President-elect, urged him to select two Southerners for his cabinet, and registered a protest against old Frank Blair's "cub," Montgomery, becoming postmaster general. Lincoln expressed doubt whether any Southerners could be induced to remain loyal and dismissed Weed's objections to Blair with a humorous story. [27]

Lincoln did, however, transmit a message to the Republican congressmen. The day Weed had arrived in Springfield, Senator J. J. Crittenden, occupying Henry Clay's seat and hoping to wear the Great Compromiser's toga, had introduced resolutions to write the Missouri Compromise, the Fugitive Slave Act, and a guarantee of slavery into the Constitution. [28] Weed entrained for Washington carrying to Trumbull, Hannibal Hamlin, and Seward a memorandum and an oral message from the titular head of the party. The memorandum suggested that Seward introduce three resolutions, declaring that the Fugitive Slave Act should be enforced, that the personal liberty laws conflicting with it

[26] Lapsley (ed.), *Writings of Lincoln*, V, 197.
[27] *Memoir of Weed*, I, 301; II, 605–10.
[28] *Congressional Globe*, 36th Congress, 2nd session, pp. 112, 114.

should be repealed, and that "the Federal Union must be preserved." [29] Orally Weed was to warn the Republicans that Lincoln would repudiate any compromise that, even nominally, permitted slavery in the territories. This message the President-elect reinforced with letters to congressmen warning them not to "demoralize" the cause by entertaining any compromise on the extension of slavery. "There is no compromise upon it," he said, "but which puts us under again, and leaves all our work to do over again." Obviously Lincoln did not agree with Weed that the territorial issue was mere verbiage without practical reality. "On that point hold firm," he said, "as with a chain of steel." [30]

A few days after sending Weed to Washington, Lincoln heard that Buchanan was about to consent to the surrender of the federal forts in Charleston harbor. The *New York Times* had also heard the rumor and was demanding that the President be impeached for treason.[31] Thus assured of even conservative support, Lincoln sought Trumbull's advice. "I will, — if our friends in Washington concur — announce publicly at once that they are to be retaken after the inauguration. This will give the Union men a rallying cry and preparation will proceed somewhat on their side, as well as on the other." [32]

Lincoln's refusal to entertain a compromise and his willingness to furnish a rallying cry, privately expressed though they were, indicated his growing strength. Less than six weeks after election day he had begun to take a grip upon the party. In a sense his strength was only relative: he was less muddled than the Republican congressmen. In part, his growing power resulted from his skillful handling of the patronage. After listening carefully to the hordes of visitors

[29] *Writings of Lincoln,* V, 199; Lincoln to Trumbull, December 21, 1860, Tracy: *Uncollected Letters,* p. 172; H. White: *Trumbull,* p. 112.

[30] Lincoln to E. B. Washburne, December 13, 1860, *Writings of Lincoln,* V, 196.

[31] *New York Times,* December 20, 21, 1860.

[32] December 24, 1860, Tracy: *Uncollected Letters,* p. 173.

who streamed into Springfield, he had begun wisely to select his cabinet from the sundry elements of his chaotic party. Already he had determined to give Seward the secretaryship of state, feeling "under moral, or at least party duress," to do so. In a courteous gesture he allowed the Vice-President-elect to name a New Englander, and Hamlin selected for the navy post Gideon Welles of Connecticut, a former Democrat. To Edward Bates, staid representative of the old-line Whigs, Lincoln offered the post of attorney general; and to balance Bates and strengthen the administration in the border states, he decided on Montgomery Blair. He recognized the claims of the Free-Soil element by promising Salmon P. Chase a place. These made a far from harmonious group of men, but, for the moment at least, all of them were bound to Springfield's master politician, and he could now speak, if need be, for his party.[33]

But one problem remained even after the leading elements in the party had thus been brought into temporary harmony. Pennsylvania had not yet been fixed in the Republican ranks, nor were her rival leaders content. At the Chicago convention Judge Davis had promised the Treasury Department to Cameron, who now expected Lincoln to fulfill the bargain. When a whole month passed without a confirming gesture, Cameron first sent his friends and then went himself to Springfield. After a long conference Lincoln agreed that Cameron should have a place in the cabinet, though he did not specify what place. Jubilant over his victory, Cameron hurried home to rally his forces and to consider ways to force Lincoln to give him the Treasury. Before long the news was out, and McClure sped to Springfield to lodge a vigorous protest.

In the meantime Curtin — with an eye on Cameron — had asked Lincoln what attitude he should take in his com-

[33] C. McCartney: *Lincoln and His Cabinet*, p. 104; White: *Trumbull*, p. 141; *Memoir of Weed*, I, 602–14; Bates: *Diary*, pp. 152, 164; Nicolay and Hay: *Works of Lincoln*, I, 657; W. A. Buckingham to Lincoln, December 28, 1860, R. T. Lincoln MSS.

ing inaugural address. Thus pressed, Lincoln yielded a little. He advised Curtin to "express without passion, threat, or appearance of boasting, but nevertheless with firmness, the purpose of yourself, and your State to maintain the Union at all hazards." Also, if he could, he should get the legislature to pass strong Union resolutions. Now McClure went to Springfield to explain that Curtin's support had its price. Late at night, after a long session with McClure, Lincoln sat down and wrote to Cameron: "You will relieve me from great embarrassment by allowing me to recall the offer." This request did not, he explained, spring solely from McClure's protest, but "from an unexpected complication." In any event, Lincoln promised, he would make no appointment from Pennsylvania until he came to Washington.[34]

In truth, as Lincoln realized, no single Pennsylvanian held the key to the state. Personal rivalries, mutual suspicions, and ever deepening jealousies nourished a factionalism that no nice balance of patronage could dissolve. On only one issue, protection, were the state politicians united, and upon the enactment of a tariff measure Pennsylvania's position still depended. Fully aware that his state held the whip hand, Cameron moved in the Senate to consider the Morrill bill for re-establishing protective duties. Although recalcitrance delayed action, the Senate finally referred the measure to a special committee, and early in February it came up for debate. By that time many of the Southern senators had gone home. Those who still remained denounced the bill as the fruit of a corrupt bargain between Pennsylvania and the Republicans — "the monstrous offspring of a

[34] Davis: *Pennsylvania Politics*, pp. 142, 155–6; McClure: *Old Time Notes*, I, 445; Angle: *New Letters of Lincoln*, p. 260; E. Hertz: *Abraham Lincoln*, II, 795–6; Bates: *Diary*, pp. 170–2, 389–90; *Memoir of Weed*, I, 607–10; McCartney: *Lincoln and His Cabinet*, pp. 30–3; White: *Trumbull*, p. 144; Goings: *Wilmot*, p. 549; *New York Times*, December 31, 1860, January 1, 1861; Lincoln to Cameron, January 3, 1861, Cameron MSS.; J. A. Andrew to Dr. C. N. Ray, January 8, Andrew to Lincoln, January 20, Curtin to Lincoln, January 14, 1861, R. T. Lincoln MSS.

conjunction betwixt greed of gain and political ambition," said Roger Pryor of Virginia. "The importunate protectionists of Pennsylvania," he charged, "more clamorous and insatiable than the daughter of the horseleech, after higgling with every party for a stipend from the treasury, at last caught the Republicans in a moment of exigent need, and from their lust for place extorted the promise of a bounty to iron." The Pennsylvanians themselves recognized the truth of the charge, and they minced no words. While the bill was before Congress, one of them told John Sherman that "the loose aggregation in our State known as the People's Party can be knit together and crystallized into a genuine Republican party — by the passage of the Morrill Bill. . . . Save the Bill and you make a party in Pennsylvania!" With the Southerners gone, the Pennsylvanians put through their bill, and two days before his term expired, the Pennsylvanian in the White House signed it.[35]

To Thurlow Weed and other conservatives Lincoln's growing strength, his flat refusal to accept a compromise, and the number of radicals he had already chosen for his cabinet were most disquieting. Upon returning to Albany the editor renewed his determination to marshal neighboring governors against the swelling radical tide. Governor Morgan supported him and urged Israel Washburn, en route to Maine, to stop in New York for a conference of governors.[36] August Belmont, wealthy banker, solemnly impressed upon Rhode Island's Governor Sprague, wealthy manufacturer, "that all the leaders of the Republican party in our State and city, with a few exceptions of the ultra radicals, are in favor of concessions, and that the popular mind of the North is ripe for them." [37]

Within the sphere of Weed's influence, three governors

[35] T. Pitkin: "Pennsylvania and the Tariff" (Ph.D. MSS. dissertation, Western Reserve University), Ch. vii; Lincoln to Trumbull, January 7, 1861, Tracy: *Uncollected Letters*, pp. 173–4.

[36] Hunt: *Washburns*, p. 83.

[37] Alexander: *History of New York*, I, 337–8.

came out openly for a policy of compromise. Early in January Governor Morgan told the New York legislature that
while he regarded secession as treason and recognized that
the Constitution and the laws should be obeyed and the administration supported, he believed the South had good reason to be alarmed. The North could quell that alarm. Let
New York "set an example," he pleaded, by repealing her
personal-liberty law; "let her oppose no barrier, but let her
representatives in Congress give ready support to any just
and honorable sentiment." [38]

From New Jersey and Pennsylvania came answering
echoes. Governor Olden, too, hoped a compromise could be
achieved, and denounced the agitators who were trying to
prevent it. Jerseymen, he promised, would "make all reasonable and proper concessions" to save the Union.[39] Pennsylvania's retiring Governor Packer, a Buchanan Democrat,
proposed not only the repeal of the state's personal-liberty
law but also legislation to give Southern masters temporary
permits to retain their slaves in Pennsylvania. In addition,
he pressed for an amendment extending the 36°30′ line to
the Pacific.[40]

Even more responsive to these suggestions for preserving
the Union were the governors of the border slave states.
Early in December Virginia's Governor, John Letcher, and
Kentucky's Beriah Magoffin had proposed to send peace
commissioners to South Carolina.[41] Maryland's Governor,
Thomas Hicks, had from the first advised the South to be
deliberate and calm, and to reflect carefully before it took
irrevocable action. When commissioners from the seceding
states called upon him, he refused to receive them, and he

[38] Lincoln (ed.) : *Messages of the Governors of New York*, pp. 249–
305; *New York Tribune*, January 3, 1861; *New York Times*, January 1,
3, 1861.

[39] *Appleton's Annual Cyclopedia, 1861*, I, 514–15; J. Y. Foster: *New
Jersey and the Rebellion*, p. 23.

[40] *Harrisburg Patriot*, January 3, 1861; *New York Times*, January 3,
1861.

[41] *New York Times*, December 6, 1860.

persistently turned a deaf ear to all who demanded a special
session of the legislature. He suggested to the governors of
Virginia, Tennessee, Kentucky, and Missouri that they consult together. To Delaware's Governor Burton he broached
the possibility of a "middle confederacy" to harmonize the
differences between North and South. Burton, whose legislature listened attentively to his despairing message and
passed resolutions endorsing the Crittenden Compromise,
replied that Delaware was bound to the North by economics
and geography, and he did not, therefore, believe that her
people would consider such a confederacy. In the end the
border states agreed to co-operate in a peace conference
called by Virginia.[42]

As neighboring conservatives were thus fostering conciliation, and the border-state governors were expressing their
willingness to co-operate, Governor Nathaniel P. Banks, in
the very heart of New England radicalism, struck his parting
blow for the Union. Obtaining permission from the Massachusetts legislature for an unprecedented act, he sent the
legislators a valedictory message. The South, he declared,
could not secede, but Massachusetts should remove the first
cause for secession by repealing at once the state's personal-
liberty law. If the cause were removed, there would be no
secession, and no civil war.[43]

Weed and his fellow conservatives, who had inspired the
governors, applauded their conciliatory utterances. But their
work was largely wasted. Except for Morgan and Olden, the
conservative governors were leaving office, and radicals were
replacing them. As Democrats or onetime Whigs, the retiring governors, like their colleagues of the border states, pre-

[42] H. E. Buchholz: *Governors of Maryland,* p. 174; G. L. P. Radcliffe: *Governor Thomas H. Hicks of Maryland and the Civil War,*
pp. 36–7, 43; H. C. Conrad: *History of Delaware,* I, 196–7; Powell: *History of Delaware,* pp. 251–7; *New York Times,* December 29, 1860; *New
York Tribune,* January 3, 11, 1861.

[43] *Appleton's Annual Cyclopedia, 1861,* I, 451; William Schouler:
Massachusetts in the Civil War, pp. 5 ff.; *New York Tribune,* January 4,
1861.

ferred the old Union based upon the American way of compromise. Not so the new governors.

Even as the conservatives were exploring the possibilities of conciliation and seeking means of influencing Lincoln, Massachusetts' newly elected Governor, John Andrew, was kindling the fires of radicalism. Southern society, he declared, must be entirely reorganized, and the federal government ought to be driven to aid in the work. There must be no "weak-kneed" measures. "I am for unflinching firmness in adhering to . . . all our principles." [44] "We must *conquer* the South," he said, and "to do this we must bring the Northern mind to a comprehension of this necessity." [45] War was "in the air," he later confessed, "and some of us breathed it." [46] As Congress gave more attention to compromise measures, Andrew hurried to Washington to consult with congressional radicals. There he heard from Charles Francis Adams that Southerners were preparing to seize Washington by force and prevent Lincoln's inauguration. A Virginia congressman, John Y. Mason, swore to Andrew that never could the South be induced to rejoin a Union of which Massachusetts was a member. Thus confirmed in his direst apprehensions, Andrew held conference, on Christmas Eve, with Senators Doolittle of Wisconsin, Trumbull of Illinois, and Sumner and Wilson of his own Massachusetts. Solemnly the radical coterie decided that the integrity of the Union must be preserved, "though it cost a million lives." [47]

The Governor-elect's impassioned and sanguinary pronouncements chilled conservative hearts in Massachusetts. Boston Brahmins were horrified and indignant: they distrusted Andrew, whom they believed to be wanting in good judgment, common sense, and practical ability. "What

[44] Andrew to Montgomery Blair, December 4, 1860, cited in W. E. Smith: *Blair Family in Politics*, I, 509.

[45] Andrew to F. W. Bird, J. A. Andrew MSS.

[46] S. Burnham: *J. A. Andrew*, p. 8.

[47] Pearson: *Andrew*, I, 133–6; J. T. Morse, Jr. (ed.): *Memoir of Colonel Henry Lee*, p. 177; *New York Times*, December 25, 1860.

was apprehension about Andrew," ruefully admitted Sam Bowles, "is now conviction. He wobbles like an old cart — is conceited, dogmatic, and lacks breadth and tact for government." [48] Democrats, sickened by the radicals' willingness to sacrifice other men's lives, asked whether people wished to die for the radical cause. [49]

The disdain of the conservatives did not ruffle war-minded Andrew. "Banks has delivered an execrable thing," he told Sumner, "but it doesn't disturb my soul at all." Determined to force the issue, to arouse the people to war, and to yield not an inch, Andrew prepared to take office. On inauguration day, the new Governor braved a New England blizzard to deliver his inaugural address. Enumerating Massachusetts' blessings one by one — its wealth, its freedom from debt, its prosperous agriculture, banks, and scientific institutions — he offered them all, as it were, on the altars of abolition. Refuting his predecessor's arguments, he maintained that the personal-liberty law was right, just, and proper, and the Fugitive Slave Act a wrong against the citizens of Massachusetts. South Carolina's secession was an injury to the Old Bay State, which was ready to endure once more, if need be, the sacrifices it had borne during the Revolution. So saying, the newly sworn Governor called on the legislature to arm the state for war. [50] The entire address, sneered the *Boston Post*, was a lamentable appeal to passion, combining "the narrowness of a mere lawyer, with the intenseness of a fanatic." It was "sophomoric in style, immature in thought, wretched in argument, and small in political knowledge." [51]

The crusading Andrew did not pause for reactions to his address but in high fever plunged ahead. On the morning of his inauguration he had received from Charles Francis Adams another alarmist note predicting that the revolution-

[48] Merriam: *Bowles*, I, 318–19.

[49] *New Hampshire Patriot*, January 2, 1861.

[50] Pearson: *Andrew*, I, 138–44; Schouler: *Massachusetts in the Civil War*, pp. 9 ff.; *New York Times*, January 7, 1861.

[51] *Boston Post*, January 8, 1861.

ists would surely attack Washington. The moment he had
taken the oath of office, Andrew sent messengers out into the
howling storm to warn the other New England governors
and to urge them to place their states upon a war footing.
Late that night he began calling in the officers of his own
militia to tell them they must prepare their men for action.
In succeeding days he sent a messenger to Lincoln offering
troops, and another to General Scott to inquire how soon
troops were likely to be called, what routes they should take,
and what equipment they would need. He visited the ar-
mories, inspected militia companies, and complained to the
War Department about the inadequate protection of Boston
harbor. To assist him in his work Andrew chose four aides
— carefully culled from Harvard graduates and the better
families — bestowed military titles upon them, and put them
to gathering steamboats, purchasing supplies, and inspecting
the militia. On January 8, the anniversary of the Battle of
New Orleans, he ordered a salute fired in honor of Andrew
Jackson. The people, he said, must become used to the smell
of gunpowder.[52]

The other New England governors, Andrew's messengers
found, were on the whole less agitated. Sprague of Rhode
Island was willing enough to march off at the head of his
gaudy Zouaves, but was clearly a bit confused as to the issues.
In Connecticut the staid old Buckingham was not unduly
perturbed. Nor was Governor Fairbanks in Vermont. Without stopping to inquire where Fairbanks might be at the
moment, Andrew's courier plunged through the snowdrifts
to Montpelier, only to learn that the Governor was at his
home in St. Johnsbury. On the messenger pressed, pausing
only long enough at towns and hamlets along the way to re-
veal the secret purpose of his feverish journey. Rumors of
the mighty mission spread, and newspapers carried the story
until solemn denials came from Boston. The aging Governor of Vermont was courteous, but made no commitments.

[52] Pearson: *Andrew,* I, 142–5; Morse: *Memoir of Colonel Henry Lee,*
pp. 55–60.

After his visitor had departed, Fairbanks consulted with Governor Morgan on the crisis and asked Vermont's congressmen whether they thought a special session of the legislature necessary.[53]

Andrew's messenger arrived in New Hampshire on the eve of the Republican state convention. Ichabod Goodwin, finishing his second term, was a candidate to succeed himself. But the Governor, a former Whig, was too moderate for the radical clique who were now in control of the party. Unceremoniously they passed him by for one more passionately devoted to abolition principles. Nathaniel S. Berry, a former Free-Soiler, nearly seventy years old, had been inactive in politics for a decade. He had been "too ultra" for his party to support, the Democrats explained, until the Whig element had been sufficiently abolitionized. His nomination at this time they regarded as symbolic of the "rabid, unyielding spirit" that possessed the Republicans. At a moment when dissolution, civil war, anarchy, and general ruin threatened, the Republicans were determined "to progress even farther in the criminal course" that had brought the impending calamities. "To vote for Berry," added the Democrats, "is to vote to aggravate present difficulties, to oppose concessions for preservation of the Union, to invite and hasten . . . the bloody civil war." [54]

Even before New Hampshire's convention had chosen Berry, Andrew's messenger hurried on to Maine, where Israel Washburn, fresh from Congress, had just taken over the reins of the state. Scholarly in mien, Washburn was impressive as he declared that the South's demands were inadmissible and her course of action treasonable. He favored forbearance, he said, but could support no compromise that would be "moral treason." When Andrew's agent arrived, Washburn was in a mood to receive him. He had as good information as Andrew on the imminent danger to

[53] G. A. Benedict: *Vermont in the Civil War*, I, pp. 5 f.

[54] Lyford: *Rollins*, pp. 109 f.; Pillsbury: *New Hampshire*, II, 518; *New Hampshire Patriot*, December 26, 1860, January 16, 1861.

Washington, but after consulting Senator Lot M. Morrill he sent word to Andrew that "wherever Massachusetts leads, Maine will follow close, if she can't keep abreast." [55] To Lincoln Maine's governor expressed the fear that the Republican leaders were "unequal to the exigencies of the time." The party could only be saved by opposing all compromises with the South. [56] As Washburn thus accepted Andrew's leadership, conservative hopes in New England declined.

Thus by the beginning of the new year there was no concensus among the victors upon the meaning of their success. Abolitionists and secessionists alike agreed that Republican ascendancy marked the triumph of the principles that had moved William Lloyd Garrison and John Brown. Moderates did not concur, but their program of compromise recalled only memories of former well-meaning adjustments that had failed. To Abraham Lincoln, watching in Springfield, the counsel was still confused. In the weeks to come, he watched the reactions of other governors in other states.

[55] Schouler: *Massachusetts*, p. 17; *New York Tribune*, January 7, 1861; *New York Times*, January 7, 1861.

[56] Washburn to Lincoln, January 21, 1861, R. T. Lincoln MSS.

Chapter 7

Governors for War

IN the weeks between his election and his inauguration
Abraham Lincoln, President-elect of a dividing nation, did
not lack for advice. The first days of 1861 brought still more
new governors and new statements from old governors. As
the President-elect listened, the majority opinion began to
add up for a war upon the South. John Andrew's answer
had more support than Thurlow Weed's moderate counsel. By March, Abraham Lincoln was fully convinced that
the governors of the Northern states stood staunchly for
coercion.

From every side came the war call as the governors bade
defiance to the South. Into backwoods Lansing, Michigan's
legislators came in sleighs to witness the retirement of Moses
Wisner and the inauguration of Austin Blair. Both radicals,
the outgoing and incoming governors differed chiefly in the
intensity of their oratory and in their recommendations for
state expenditures. Wisner was going out under a cloud:
his administration had been a corrupt one, and the state's
treasurer was a fugitive from a grand jury. Yet Wisner, as if
to minimize the theft, proposed new and elaborate expenditures — even to appropriations for completing the last
twenty miles of a railroad to Lansing. Then, having counted
the state's wealth and suggested new ways of spending it,
he launched an attack upon the South — a diatribe filled
with "wicked bombast and defiance," according to Democrats.

Following Wisner, the new Governor — whose administration would have to shoulder the burden of expenditures — counseled prudence and economy. But in his observations on national affairs Blair was even more radical than his predecessor. The tall, gaunt, wizen-faced new Governor was master of a powerful voice, which he exploited to the fullest. Michigan was a sovereign state, and her first duty, he proclaimed, was to protect her citizens' right and liberties. The personal-liberty law was one of the safeguards the state had erected, and she was not called upon to justify it to the South. Moreover, if now the offending law were repealed, the motive would only be misunderstood. "The judgment of the country will be that it is done under the smarting of the Southern lash." Rather than yield that point of honor, the Governor urged the legislature to show "patriotic firmness and decision." As for secession, it was treason, and Michigan could be counted upon to uphold the Constitution and the laws.

"Oh," he cried, raising his voice as if to make himself heard even in Springfield, "Oh for the firm steady hand of a Washington, or a Jackson, to guide the ship of State in this perilous storm. Let us hope that we shall find him on the Fourth of March!" Descending to the practical, he recommended an increase of the militia and offered the state's militiamen to the president.[1]

At the same moment, on the other side of Illinois, the new Governor of Missouri took the oath of office. Retiring Governor R. M. Stewart, a native of New York and a moderate, assailed abolition fanatics and demanded that the North give guarantees to Southern property. Missouri, because of her geographical location, must take "the high position of armed neutrality." Far less moderate was the incoming Governor, Claiborne Fox Jackson. The state of Missouri,

[1] J. Robertson: *Michigan in the War*, pp. 10–13; Charles Moore: *History of Michigan*, I, 412–13; G. N. Fuller: *Governors of Michigan*, p. 94; *Detroit Free Press*, January 4, 1861; *New York Tribune*, January 5, 1861; *New York Times*, January 5, 1861.

he reminded his listeners, had slaves worth a hundred million dollars; hence her interests could not be divorced from
those of the other slave states. He advised calling a state convention to define Missouri's place in the Union, and a
Southern convention to propose amendments for the protection of the South. Jackson, too, had his eyes on Springfield.[2]

One by one the other Western governors made their positions known in messages to their legislatures. The Democratic Governor of Illinois, Wood, favored conciliation and
recommended repeal of the personal-liberty laws.[3] Indiana's
retiring Governor A. A. Hamond, a Buchanan Democrat,
gave assurances that his state would accord the South every
right in the territories and proposed a national convention
to mediate between the sections. He, too, charged that it
was Northern agitators who had fomented the controversy,
and he called upon the conservative elements to rally and
save the Union.[4] But these were echoes from the past that
Lincoln could afford to ignore; Hamond and Wood were
leaving office. On Jackson Day, while Andrew was burning
powder under New Englanders' noses, Governor-elect Lane,
watching a military parade in Indianapolis, cried that he
knew no other flag than that of his country: under it he
would lead his state to battle; under it he would live and
die![5]

From Ohio came a less oratorical, but equally emphatic
pledge of devotion to the Union. Governor Dennison had
been secretly supporting the Unionists in neighboring Kentucky, and his private advices had not been encouraging.
His message to the legislature was contrived to reassure Kentucky's Unionists and to disconcert the secessionists. He ad-

[2] S. B. Laughlin: *Missouri Politics during the Civil War,* p. 28;
New York Times and *New York Tribune,* January 5, 1861.

[3] *New York Tribune,* January 8, 1861.

[4] *Indiana Senate Journal,* 1861, pp. 27–8; *New York Times,* January 12, 1861.

[5] *New York Tribune,* January 9, 1861.

vocated modification of both the state's personal-liberty laws and the federal Fugitive Slave Act. Strongly he urged the state to increase its militia, and emphatically he denounced secession.[6]

Less restrained by proximity to the South and more closely connected with abolitionism were the governors of Minnesota and Wisconsin. As Minnesota's Ramsey viewed the situation, South Carolina had already levied war upon the United States, and the government must put down this treason before it considered any compromise.[7] Governor Randall, his red wig neatly in place for the ceremonies, solemnly proclaimed that "secession is revolution: revolution is war: War against the government of the United States is treason." On this platitudinous premise he argued elaborately against compromise. "The hopes of civilization and Christianity" — the familiar phrases rolled from his tongue — "are suspended now upon this question of dissolution." To save Christianity and civilization he proposed an immediate increase in the militia.[8]

Only in Iowa was there no legislative session to call forth a gubernatorial pronouncement. Considerations of economy had restrained Governor Kirkwood from yielding to demands for a special session. But he himself made a trip to Springfield to talk with Lincoln. In a private room in a hotel the two men talked far into the evening. Lincoln explained again that the Republicans could not afford to accept compromise, and Kirkwood returned to Iowa to gather arms and encourage the formation of local militia companies. Through Senator Grimes he offered Buchanan his nonexistent militia to coerce South Carolina.[9]

[6] Dennison to Giddings, January 8, 1861, Giddings MSS.; *New York Times*, January 8, 1861.

[7] J. H. Baker: *Lives of the Governors of Minnesota* (St. Paul), pp. 40–1.

[8] *Wisconsin State Journal*, January 15, 1861; E. B. Quiner, *Military History of Wisconsin*, pp. 36–7; *New York Tribune*, January 11, 1861.

[9] S. H. M. Byers: *Iowa in the Civil War*, p. 35; C. Cole: *Iowa through the Years*, p. 276; H. W. Lathrop: *Samuel J. Kirkwood*, pp.

To conservatives these gubernatorial pronouncements spelled the doom of compromise. Carl Schurz, carrying a torch through Pennsylvania, New York, and New England, found that the Republicans' increasing boldness was engendering a warlike spirit and that even timid men were no longer satisfied with timid measures. "There will be a fight," he smugly told his wife. As soon as sentiment was sufficiently crystallized, he planned to submit a plan of organization to the Republican governors.[10] By the first of January, Seward had abandoned hope and was speaking of "probable Civil War." Two thirds of the Republican senators, he estimated, were "as reckless in action as the South. They imagine that the government can go on, and conquer the South, while they themselves, sit still and see the work done."[11] The Washington correspondent of the *Boston Post* made hopeless summary of his observations in the nation's capital. "The Republicans," he repeated, "stand clutching their prize. They have fought for the patronage of a great government, and party discipline . . . prevents . . . conciliatory action. . . . They are today bent on coercion, and are prepared, as a party, to carry the torch and the sword into every seceding State."[12]

Confirmation of this judgment came from the boiling caldrons in the state capitols. With one accord the Republican-dominated legislatures resolved that secession was treason, debated bills to enlarge and arm the state militias, and offered troops to Buchanan to uphold the laws and preserve the Union. Wisconsin legislators pledged "our lives, our fortunes, and our sacred honor" to protect the Constitution. Michigan's radical legislature professed to regard the Southern states as traitors in open rebellion, to whom no concessions or compromises should be offered. In less trite phrases

---

105–9; Kirkwood to Grimes, January 12, 1861, in *Iowa Historical Record*, I, 39.

[10] Carl Schurz: *Reminiscences*, I, 169–78.

[11] Seward: *Seward*, pp. 496, 507.

[12] *Boston Post*, January 1, 1861.

other states expressed equally fervent patriotism. Only those
states dominated by Democrats or by moderate Republicans
seriously considered conciliation and compromise. New Jersey's legislature endorsed the Crittenden Compromise and
favored repeal of the personal-liberty laws. Tennessee deplored the rush of arms-giving. Virginia's Governor returned
the New York resolutions with the request that he be spared
any more such documents. Kentucky endorsed the proposals
for compromise and suggested that the state governors hold
a conference to save the Union.[13]

Still Lincoln gave no sign that he heard the radical chorus.
True, he had announced, early in January, that Seward was
to be Secretary of State; he had privately offered the Treasury to Chase, who was telling his friends about it and
assuring them that Lincoln was "a man to be depended
on"; [14] and he had come out against compromise. But none
of these moves proved that he had yielded to the pressure
of the radicals. Seeking light, all elements waited for Dick
Yates to speak, believing that he might reflect Lincoln's
views.

Richard Yates, however unworthy to be called a statesman, was an exceptionally shrewd politician, with a politician's knack for keeping an ear to the ground. Knowing that
he could be influenced, a number of men volunteered their
advice. Among them was a former colleague in Congress,
who urged him to be conservative and expressed the hope
that Lincoln would be. Nine out of ten Northerners, thought
this Ohioan, did not want to interfere with slavery. "I am
willing to concede any and every lawful thing for the sake
of *peace* and to preserve the Union," he declared.[15] Counter-
balancing such advice was the message the radical Trumbull

[13] C. Z. Lincoln (ed.): *Messages of the Governors of New York,*
pp. 305–31, contains all the resolutions. See also *Journals* of House
and Senate in the several states. *New York Times,* January 3, 12, 16,
1861.

[14] Chase: *Diary,* p. 295.

[15] John L. Taylor to Yates, December 12, 1860, Yates MSS.

sent from Washington. "Take strong Union ground in your message," urged the Senator, "and repudiate the idea of secession being anything else than revolution and rebellion." The legislature, he said, should pledge the state's men and means to the federal government.[16] One extremist in Illinois, where the radicals were circulating petitions for a reorganization of the militia, declared to Yates: "I am in favor of twenty years of War"; and another, Horace White, wrote effusively: "We live in revolutionary times, and I say God bless the revolution." [17] Many warned Yates that whatever he said would be thought to represent Lincoln's views. S. C. Fuller, who had concluded that "blood must flow" and that Republicans had the "high and holy mission" of protecting the Constitution, advised Yates to consult Lincoln and to announce Lincoln's position in his inaugural address.[18]

With a nation's eyes upon him, Yates delivered an address on January 14 which pleased the most extreme of the radicals. "The American people," he said, "need no assurance that the Republican party, valuing as it ought the triumph it has won, will never be disposed to yield its honors or avoid its duties. They not only claim, but intend to have the administration for the period of time allotted to them by the Constitution." The government could not be destroyed, and the people of the West would never permit the Mississippi River to fall into foreign hands. They would never allow the South to depart in peace. Then, knowing how impatient his listeners were for some word from Lincoln, Yates gave them the assurance they had been awaiting. "The administration of the incoming president, I have no doubt, will be characterized by wisdom and firmness." Never would Lincoln forget that "the whole material of the government, moral, political, and physical, if need be, must be

[16] Trumbull to Yates, December 19, 1860, Yates MSS.

[17] W. H. Hanna, December 19, and Horace White, December 30, 1860, to Trumbull, Trumbull MSS.

[18] S. C. Fuller to Yates, December 30, 1860, Yates MSS.

employed to preserve, protect, and defend the Constitution of the United States." Finally, Yates advised making ready the militia.[19]

On the same day Lane took the oath of office in Indiana. In his inaugural address, considerably milder than his neighbor's, he advocated the repeal of all laws contrary to the Constitution. Such "voluntary and prompt repeal" would be a "peace offering worthy of a great, intelligent, and free people."[20] But Lane, about to be appointed United States Senator, was to be Governor only for a day; the real Governor was the radical Morton. In his inaugural Morton dwelt at greater length on the state's condition than on the nation's. Convinced that war was coming, he advised reform in the state government. Almost his first official act was to demand of the War Department that the state be given her legal quota of federal arms. Almost at once, too, he began a reorganization of the state's finances, dismissing corrupt officials and cutting expenses in preparation for the bloody future.[21]

Last of the governors to speak was Curtin of Pennsylvania. Inaugurated on January 15, a day later than Lane and Yates, Curtin held a strategic position. Conservatives and moderates hoped he would eschew radical doctrines and stand firmly for compromise.[22] Radicals hoped he would become one of them. The night before he took office Curtin summoned five of his closest friends to advise him on his address. Together they framed a document that was a model of political fence-straddling. The Governor was for liberty and against all who would destroy it, "whether instigated by

[19] T. M. Eddy: *The Patriotism of Illinois*, I, 86–9; *Illinois Senate Journal*, 70–75.

[20] *Indiana Senate Journal, 1861,* pp. 56–7.

[21] W. H. H. Terrell: *Indiana in the War of Rebellion*, pp. 1–3; W. M. French: *Oliver P. Morton*, pp. 126–34; C. M. Walker: *O. P. Morton*, pp. 48 ff.; *Official Records of the Union and Confederate Armies in the War of the Rebellion*, Series 3, I, 41.

[22] *New York Times*, January 15, 1861.

hatred or ambition, by fanaticism or folly." He thought a situation of "mutual estrangement" between the sections had developed, which had been complicated by "precipitate acts and violent demonstrations of heated partisans." He said Lincoln's election did not justify secession, and Pennsylvania would support the government, but she was willing to join other states in considering honorable measures of conciliation. In the end, the Governor recommended repeal of the personal-liberty law and refrained from advising an increase of the militia. As a whole, the inaugural address was a triumph of oratory over consistency, and no one knew whether Curtin was a radical or a conservative. In fact, his message was directed more toward the Congress, which was debating the Morrill Act, than to the President-elect in Springfield.[23]

All the Northern governors had now spoken. Three of them, Curtin, Morgan, and Olden, had inclined toward moderation; the rest were radicals of varying degree. The outlook for peace was none too promising. But Lincoln had not yet made a clear declaration, and conservatives were willing to believe that Seward's appointment rather than Yates's speech was the significant straw in the wind. They still worked to commit the victorious Republicans to a policy of peace and conciliation. From the Senate floor Seward told the South, as much by his manner as by his actual words, that the incoming administration would put no obstacle in the way of a constitutional amendment guaranteeing slavery, and that the territorial question might be amicably adjusted.[24] In Boston a Union petition received nearly fourteen thousand signatures.[25] In Baltimore the Sun took comfort in the fact that the radicals had failed in their efforts

[23] Davis: Pennsylvania Politics, pp. 156–7; McClure: Old Time Notes, pp. 446–9; Egle: A. G. Curtin, pp. 39, 113–22; New York Tribune, January 15, 16; Philadelphia Inquirer, January 16, 1861.

[24] Seward: Seward, pp. 493–5; New York Times, January 14, 1861.

[25] New York Tribune, January 23, 1861.

to bring on a war when South Carolinians fired upon the *Star of the West*.[26]

In the six weeks that remained before Lincoln's inauguration extremists and moderates continued to struggle over the repeal of Northern personal-liberty laws and over the peace convention called in Virginia. On both issues the radicals won and forestalled the conservatives' efforts to save the Union by peaceful means.

The personal-liberty laws of the Northern states were important as symbols of sectional divergence and of Northern truculence. The total number of cases that arose under these laws was probably very small, but the orators of secession singled them out as violations of the Constitution and definite nullifications of the Fugitive Slave Act. The ordinances of secession all cited them as tangible evidence of Northern hostility to slavery. To Northern conservatives their repeal seemed a minor concession as compared with the blow that might thus be dealt the Southern position. Accordingly, the conservatives moved in the legislatures for repeal of the laws, and in so doing, they immediately aroused the radicals to opposition. When questioned about the laws, Lincoln declared that he had never read one, but if they were what Southerners claimed, they should be repealed. Then he solemnly asserted that as a simple citizen of Illinois he did not have the right to make suggestions to the states.[27]

Lacking direction from Lincoln, the radicals came to the defense of the personal-liberty laws. Maine's Governor Washburn, ignoring the Constitution, fell back upon the "grand and deathless truths of the Declaration of Independence" and opposed repeal.[28] In Michigan, Governor Blair, dispensing the minor patronage of the state, made support of the personal liberty law a test of Republican principles,[29] and Senator Zach Chandler, supporting Blair, declared that the

---

[26] M. P. Andrews: *History of Maryland*, p. 509.
[27] *New York Times*, January 14, 1861.
[28] *Boston Courier*, January 15, 23, 1861.
[29] *Detroit Free Press*, January 23, 1861.

people of Michigan would stand by the government —
"stand by it to blood, if necessary." [30] In Massachusetts the
conservatives brought in a petition for repeal signed by
dozens of prominent figures, among them the state's chief
justice, whose name headed the list. But Wendell Phillips
cried that Massachusetts would be disgraced by yielding to
South Carolina, Senator Sumner urged the state to maintain
its devotion to liberty, and Andrew stood firm.[31] In the end,
however, the General Court consented to minor modifications in the law — the removal of obviously unconstitutional
provisions.[32] Only one state, Rhode Island, repealed its statute. The radicals charged that Governor Sprague had purchased legislators' votes, but the Democrats thought they
had given a "manifestation of patriotism worthy of imitation
by the larger States." [33]

Meanwhile, as the states were considering, and rejecting,
proposals to repeal the personal-liberty laws, they were called
upon to decide whether they would send representatives to a
national peace conference. The Virginia legislature had issued a call for a convention in Washington, and Governor
Letcher invited his fellow governors to send delegates. The
executives of border slave states responded at once and instructed their delegates to work for concessions. The moderate governors in the free states also welcomed the suggestion. Governor Morgan told the New York legislature that
the great mass of the Northern people demanded that no
honorable effort to maintain peace be left untried. He proposed to select men "in whose character and patriotism the
people shall have full confidence" to represent the Empire
State. Opposing him, radicals in the legislature moved to

[30] Moore: *Michigan*, I, 415–16.

[31] *Boston Courier*, January 23, 25, 30; *New York Tribune*, January
23, 28, 31, February 2; *New York Times*, January 24, 25, 26, 1861;
Pierce: *Sumner*, IV, 20; V, 449; *Congressional Globe*, 36th Congress,
2nd session, pp. 152, 947.

[32] *Boston Courier*, March 14, 1861.

[33] *New Hampshire Gazette*, January 30, 1861.

instruct the delegates to accept no extension of the Missouri Compromise line. Some legislators were sure that the compromises would benefit only the South, but in the end New York accepted Virginia's invitation.[34]

The more radical governors were less disposed to co-operate. Dennison and Morton consulted the other governors before making recommendations to their legislatures. Andrew advised Dennison to ignore the movement, at least until after the inauguration. Yates consulted Lincoln, who told him to send no delegates. He would rather, said the President-elect, "be hung by the neck . . . on the steps of the capitol" than "beg or buy" a peaceful inauguration. But even Illinois found it politically expedient to send delegates. Sumner pleaded with Andrew not to "cave," but Charles Francis Adams recommended that Massachusetts and the other radical states send delegates to defeat the efforts of the peace men. Kirkwood, confessing that "the whole thing strikes me unfavorably," appointed Iowa's congressmen as delegates, instructing them, "if Compromise must be the order of the day," to accept the Missouri and the 1850 Compromise, but to impose a limit upon further territorial expansion. Wisconsin's legislature and Governor Randall fell into a deadlock over the appointment of delegates and sent no representatives. Minnesota and Michigan refused even to consider Virginia's invitation.[35]

[34] *New York Times,* January 25, 26; *New York Tribune,* January 25, 1861; *New York Senate Journal, 1861,* p. 94.

[35] *Appleton's Annual Cyclopedia, 1861,* I, 556; Quiner: *Military History of Wisconsin,* p. 40; Crockett: *History of Vermont,* III, 499–501; *New York Tribune,* January 22, 1861; A. C. Cole: *Era of the Civil War,* pp. 257–8; W. H. Herndon to Trumbull, January 21, 1861, Trumbull MSS.; *New York Times,* January 22, 30, 1861; *Ohio House Journal, 1861,* XLVII, 91; *Ohio Senate Journal, 1861,* XLVIII, 63; Pierce: *Sumner's Works,* IV, 14; V, 448, 465–6; Pearson: *Andrew,* I, 154; *Philadelphia Inquirer,* January 28, February 15, 1861; *Iowa Historical Record,* I, 375; *Annals of Iowa,* I, 505–25; Dennison to Yates and Morton to Yates, January 26, 1861, R. T. Lincoln MSS.; Lathrop: *Kirkwood,* pp. 109–11; Byers: *Iowa,* pp. 30–1, 37–9; Buckingham: *Bucking-*

On February 4, just a month before Lincoln's inauguration, delegates from twenty-one states assembled in Willard's Hotel in Washington. On the same day the founding fathers of the Southern Confederacy gathered in Montgomery, Alabama. They were a less distinguished, less able body of men than those gathered in Washington, but they were united in a grim determination to launch the Confederate States of America.

No such singleness of purpose inspired those who met with the ostensible purpose of preserving the United States of America. The radical governors of the North had made little pretense of sending balanced delegations of fair-minded and temperate men. The representatives of the border states, though sincerely willing to compromise, were intent upon breaking down the Republican position. Moreover, the Washington atmosphere was hardly conducive to peaceable discussion. Arriving delegations were rapidly infected with the pseudo-hysteria of the Republican congressmen. Vermont's awe-struck delegates listened in terror as one of their congressmen advised them, in a stage whisper, to carry weapons because Washington was filled with armed secessionists. At the meeting itself the radical congressmen, many of whom were also members of the peace conference, prevented Northern members from yielding on any Republican principle. They were not quite able to prevent all action, for eventually the conference presented Congress seven amendments to the Constitution. These were not, however, fundamentally different from Crittenden's proposals. Congress received them without enthusiasm, and rejected them with almost no debate.[36]

---

ham, p. 79; *Madison Argus and Democrat*, February 1, 4, 8, 9, 10, 14, 16, 21, 22, 1861; *Milwaukee Sentinel*, February 5, 1861; Smith: *Austin Blair*, pp. 50–1; *Boston Courier*, February 4, 5, 6, 7, 1861; Davis: *Pennsylvania Politics*, pp. 164–6; *Columbus Crisis*, February 7, 1861.

[36] L. E. Chittenden: *Recollections of President Lincoln*, pp. 19–25; Orville Browning: *Diary*, I, 451; *Leslie's Illustrated News*, March 2, 1861.

When for a brief moment it looked as if the convention might formulate some acceptable plan of compromise, the radicals in Congress were panic-stricken. Hurriedly the Michigan senators wrote Governor Blair that Michigan must send delegates. Blair deferred to his legislature and submitted the senators' letters. Democrats and moderates promptly seized upon one of them, Zach Chandler's, and gave it wide publicity as a summary of the radical position. "No Republican States should have sent delegates," the Senator had written, "but they are here and cannot get away. Ohio, Indiana, and Rhode Island are caving in, and there is danger of Illinois; and now they beg of us for God's sake to come to their rescue, and save the Republican party from rupture. I hope you will send *stiff-backed* men or none. . . . Some of the Manufacturing States think that a fight would be awful. Without a little blood-letting this Union will not, in my estimation, be worth a rush." [37]

Blood-letting was in the minds and plans of many. In these weeks the states were too preoccupied with martial preparations to give much thought to peace conferences and conciliatory gestures. Following Andrew's example, the governors had set about to accustom their people to the rattle of musketry and the fumes of gunpowder. Massachusetts' Governor, however, set a pace that was hard to follow. He corresponded vigorously with the other New England governors, retailing to them the stories of plots that came from Washington. Certain that war was coming, he tried to arouse General Scott, assuring him that Massachusetts' "patriotic citizen soldiers" would "respond with alacrity and force" if called upon to maintain "the integrity of the country." Particularly Andrew wanted to know just what routes the Bay State's troops should take in their march to Washington. While awaiting Scott's reply, he instructed a legislative committee to prepare for war and ordered officers of

[37] L. E. Chittenden: *Report . . . of the Conference Convention,* pp. 9, 468–9; *Detroit Post and Tribune, Life of Zachariah Chandler,* pp. 188–91; *Messages of the Governors of Michigan,* p. 442.

the militia to prepare rolls, fill vacancies, drill and uniform their men. In a frenzy of activity Andrew formed a military board, collected steamboats, protested to Washington on the defenseless condition of Boston harbor, and purchased two thousand overcoats for his militiamen. As earnest of the state's willingness to make sacrifice, he induced the legislature to offer a hundred thousand dollars to the federal government.

The climax of this delirium came on a Saturday late in January. Theodore Parker, the abolitionist preacher, had bequeathed to Massachusetts two muskets found on the battlefield of Lexington, which Andrew was to accept on behalf of the state. In his office that morning, as he contemplated the rusty relics of ancient carnage, Andrew yielded "to a perfect tempest of emotion" and wept. In the same mood, his blue eyes brimming with tears, the Governor appeared before the legislature. As the muskets were handed to the chairman, Andrew pushed forward, seized one of them, raised it to his lips, and kissed it.[38] Cold chills seized the Harvard graduates present.

Democrats were moved to remark that the Governor's enthusiasm did not involve personal sacrifices; less than a month after his inauguration Andrew had obtained a private secretary, and his friends were advocating a raise in his salary. One sarcastic observer remembered that he had "heerd tell that Rome was once saved by the gabble of geese. I have a fine flock, and you can 'tell John Andrew' that he can have the lot for the salvation of his party." Workingmen of Massachusetts, fearing that Andrew might make a valiant offer of their services, adopted an address condemning the abolitionists.[39]

[38] Andrew to Scott, January 12, 1861, in *Official Records*, Series 3, I, 36–7; W. Schouler: *Massachusetts in the Civil War*, pp. 18–22, 34–6; P. C. Headley: *Massachusetts in the Rebellion*, p. 96; Pearson: *Andrew*, I, 147–59.

[39] Morse: *Memoir of Lee*, p. 56; *Boston Post*, February 13, 1861; *Boston Courier*, February 11, 21, 1861; Merriam: *Bowles*, I, 318.

But disgust with Andrew did not deter the radicals from falling in with him. Throughout the North, military preparations proceeded steadily. Wisconsin revamped her militia law, and Minnesota considered ways and means of raising troops. In Iowa local military companies — many of them remnants of the Wide-Awakes — drilled to protect themselves from the Indians and to snatch the Mississippi River from the secessionists. Governor Kirkwood offered to send the troops to Washington and appealed for arms. Morgan of New York, who preferred peace and compromises to war and bloodshed, offered to garrison New York harbor should the regulars stationed there be called to Washington. Governor Buckingham, facing a campaign for re-election, issued a proclamation warning Connecticut's companies to fill their ranks, refurbish their equipment, and be ready for service. "When reason gives way to passion, and order yields to anarchy," he said, "then civil power must fall back upon the military for support." Morton of Indiana scurried about looking for arms, and Yates of Illinois was horror-stricken when Frank Blair warned him that secessionists planned to seize the St. Louis arsenal. In New England, Fairbanks consulted with Buckingham on the imminent danger; in Michigan, Blair organized two regiments, and the legislature pledged all the state's "military power and material resources." Even in far-off California preparations were under way. Governor John G. Downey appointed H. W. Halleck, a West Point man and a student of military law, major general of militia. Halleck searched the state's records, but could not even learn who were his staff officers. Yet he was sure that a powerful secession plot to create a Pacific republic was brewing, and he urged Downey to give him authority to call out troops in any emergency. In Congress, Senator Chandler recalled that Jefferson had thought blood was the natural manure of the Tree of Liberty.[40]

[40] Quiner: *Military History of Wisconsin*, p. 48; *New York Tribune*, January 15, 1861; Scott to Morgan, January 17, 1861, in *Official Records*, Series 3, I, 41; W. A. Croffut and J. M. Morris: *Military and*

In the meantime, as the governors assembled their state militias, and muskets rattled in legislative chambers, President-elect Lincoln grew restless in Illinois. Every train arriving at the Springfield stations discharged a cargo of politicians — suppliants for office and well-meaning advisers who lurked in hotel lobbies and on street corners to press their views upon the new administration. Abraham Lincoln enjoyed people, and so far as he could he saw them all. But it was all very wearing, too. As he sadly took leave of his old law partner, he sighed: "I am tired of office-holding already." [41] Partly to escape the importunate hordes, partly to sample public opinion for himself, and partly to see the state governors, he had decided to leave Springfield early, visit the leading cities of the East, and arrive in Washington well before inauguration day. Before he left he had his inaugural address printed, and en route he sought advice on its wording from a few friends.

On February 11 Lincoln bade touching farewell to his neighbors. That evening he was in Indianapolis, and the next day he looked across the Ohio River at Cincinnati and addressed reassuring words to his native Kentucky. Thence to Columbus, to Pittsburgh, to Cleveland, Buffalo, Rochester, Syracuse, and Albany; and thereafter to New York, to Trenton, to Philadelphia, and to Harrisburg. En route, his train stopped while he showed himself to crowds at Tolono, Illinois, at Steubenville, Ohio, at Utica, Troy, Poughkeepsie, Hudson, Peekskill, and Fishkill Landing, New York, and at Jersey City, Newark, and Lancaster. He spoke to the legislatures of Pennsylvania, New Jersey, New York, Ohio, and In-

---

Civil History of Connecticut, pp. 33, 34; W. Weeden; *War Governments,* p. 143; White: *Trumbull,* p. 120; Foulke: *Morton,* I, 101–4; Kirkwood to Joseph Holt, January 24, 25, 1861, in *Official Records,* Series 3, I, 55, 57; T. S. Mather to Yates, January 29, 1861, Yates MSS.; Benedict: *Vermont,* I, 4–5; J. W. Halleck to J. G. Downey, January 21, February 11, 16, 1861, Elbridge MSS. collection; *Detroit Post and Tribune, Chandler,* p. 191.

[41] W. H. Herndon and J. W. Weik: *Abraham Lincoln,* II, 194.

diana; to visitors at the Astor House, to a delegation bearing an invitation from Wilmington, to the German Club of Cincinnati. He saw mayors of cities, governors of states, and the people of the United States.

But for the most part Abraham Lincoln's remarks on this journey were trivial. Usually they consisted of a half-humorous statement that he would not make a speech. "I appear before you that I may see you, and that you may see me; and I am willing to admit that so far as the ladies are concerned I have the best of the bargain." Occasionally he descended to a labored pun; refusing to mount a specially prepared rostrum in Syracuse, he said: "But I wish you to understand that, though I am unwilling to go upon this platform you are not at liberty to draw inferences concerning any other platform with which my name has been or is connected." Humbly he accepted the courtesies tendered him, acknowledging that they were given to his office and not to him. On the whole, his public appearances were undistinguished, his utterances insipid or vague.

Still, there was one sentiment that ran like a thread through the President-elect's public remarks. At each train stop he repeated, in one form or another, the injunction he delivered at Indianapolis: "It is your business to rise up and preserve the Union and liberty for yourselves, and not for me."

To the legislatures Lincoln spoke at greater length. He assured Indiana's solons that he meant to hold and retake federal property in the South, and he raised the question whether any "special sacredness" attached to the name of "State." In Albany and Columbus he explained that he was merely trying to gain "a view of the whole field," and that when the time came he would speak. He assured the New Jersey assembly that he was devoted to peace, but told them that it might be "necessary to put the foot down firmly. . . . And if I do my duty and do right, you will sustain me, will you not?" Finally, in Harrisburg he noted troops in the streets and hoped that it would never become their duty to shed blood, and most especially never to shed fraternal blood. "I promise that so far as I may have wisdom to direct if so painful a result shall in any wise be brought about, it shall be through no fault of mine." [42]

At Harrisburg Lincoln received news that Baltimore plug-uglies planned to assassinate him as he passed through the Maryland city. Allan Pinkerton, an excitable and ambitious young detective, reported that he had uncovered the plot. Without delivering the alleged plotters to the police or taking steps to insure Lincoln's safe passage through the metropolis, Pinkerton sent word to Governor Curtin. Hysteria was in the air, and Pennsylvania's governor did not find it hard to believe that conspiracy was afoot. Excitedly he whispered the news to Lincoln and advised him to flee. Lincoln's entourage caught the infection and added their frenzied voices to Curtin's. Yielding to their frantic pleas, the incredulous Lincoln consented to be hustled off to an evening train. In a darkened carriage he changed trains in Baltimore and in the early morning arrived in Washington to be welcomed by the anxious Congressman E. B. Washburne. [43]

The undignified ending of his uninspiring trip added nothing to Lincoln's stature. He had seen the radical governors and learned that they advocated strong measures. He had seen the people and learned that their opinions were not crystallized. But he had impressed no one as a man eminently fit for the heavy responsibilities that were to be his. Radicals were not sure of him, and conservatives were disgusted. Old Sam Medary of Columbus, Jacksonian editor and ex-Governor of Kansas, recorded in his new-founded *Crisis* that Lincoln compared unfavorably with Jefferson Davis. The acidulous Massachusetts editor Sam Bowles concluded that "Lincoln is a Simple Susan," and that the Re-

[42] A. B. Lapsley (ed.): *Writings of Abraham Lincoln*, V, 204–50.
[43] McClure: *Lincoln and Men of War Times*, pp. 51–4.

publican party could "go hang." [44] Marylanders, smarting
under the insult of Lincoln's flight, told one another that
he was seeking to escape the assortment of bores who filled
Baltimore's Republican ranks.[45]

If it was the bores Lincoln was hoping to avoid, he did not
succeed. In Washington during the week that remained before his inauguration he was besieged by visiting delegations, importunate office-seekers, and would-be confidants. It
was just as it had been in Springfield, except that now he
had a measure of protection. Senator Seward took him in
charge, guarded him from the more obnoxious political
pests, and gave valuable counsel on the inaugural address.
At Seward's suggestion Lincoln changed the tone of his closing paragraph from defiance to a moving, poetic appeal.

Encouraged by Lincoln's failure to endorse the radicals,
Henry J. Raymond made one last appeal to the new administration. With extravagant praise for Lincoln's "strength and
skill," "high integrity of soul," "clear, calm perception," and
"courage and ability," Raymond proceeded to outline a
sound policy to save the Union. A simple proposal it was:
if New Mexico were merely turned over to her own people,
they would oust slavery and the proslavery party. This would
settle the territorial question, defeat the Confederacy's con-
spirators in the border states, and encourage Unionists in
the disaffected South.[46] The solution was almost too simple,
but it recognized that the territorial question was the only
issue between the sections. It recognized, too, that the issue
could be divested of its emotional connotations and settled
in the normal course of political procedure.

But Abraham Lincoln was closer to the vortex than Henry
Raymond. Perhaps he hoped, as he read his inaugural ad-
dress with its appeal to the "mystic chords of memory" —
"We are not enemies, but friends. We must not be enemies"

[44] *Columbus Crisis*, February 21, 1861; Bowles to H. L. Dawes,
February 26, 1861, in Merriam: *Bowles*, I, 318.

[45] Scharf: *History of Maryland*, III, 387–8.

[46] *New York Times*, March 1, 1861.

— that the Southerners would reconsider their ordinances of secession. Perhaps, too, he hoped that Southern compliance would still the war-mindedness of his own radical partisans. But certainly he knew that the extremists of both North and South were eager for war, and that the radical governors — still the most powerful element in his party — were arming the states to coerce the South.

Chapter 8

Lincoln Takes Command

 AD omens attended the first moments of Lincoln's administration. Inauguration day dawned bleak and blustery, threatening rain. Only a few drops fell, but throughout the day the wind continued to blow strong from the northwest, eddying fiendishly through the streets and whipping dust into the eyes of the throngs gathered to see the new government ushered in. Yet only the facetious pretended to find meaning in the weather. More serious men engaged in the task, equally futile, of divining the future from the oracular pronouncements of the politicians or from the tea leaves of petty events.

The significance of one such event was overlooked. On the Saturday night before inauguration, representatives of his party's factions gathered in Lincoln's rooms. Among them was Governor Hicks, arguing strenuously that Henry Winter Davis was a better choice for the cabinet than Montgomery Blair. But old F. P. Blair, veteran of a thousand political conferences, was also present, to defend the claims of his son. Pennsylvanians alternately begged and demanded the Treasury Department for Cameron. Northwesterners divided violently over Salmon P. Chase. Altogether, it was the kind of conclave in which the prairie politician functioned best. Finally, at the moment the contending delegations became deadlocked, he stood up.

"Gentlemen," he said, "it is evident that someone must take the responsibility of these appointments, and I will do it. My cabinet is complete. The positions are not definitely assigned, and will not be until I announce them privately to the gentlemen whom I have selected as my constitutional advisers." [1]

The delegations, accepting this as a dismissal, withdrew at once, but without appreciating the full import of Lincoln's words. They still failed to grasp the fact that Lincoln intended to make his own decisions, that he was to be the actual as well as the titular head of his party and of his administration.

The first weeks of the new administration were rife with confusion. The new office-holders, fresh and untried in public office, made more mistakes than the Democratic bureaucracy and were inclined to be irritatingly breezy about them. Crowds of office-seekers pressed their claims upon the new incumbents, and Lincoln and his cabinet worked far into the night parceling out the spoils of victory among the innumberable factions that had to be harmonized. For the President and his secretaries had much at stake. They sought to bind party men to the national government and to build a machine, independent of the state organizations, for future national campaigns.

To the state governors, the active heads of the Republican Party, the federal patronage was of greatest moment. One by one they arrived in Washington to visit the White House and the departments, to see for themselves how the land lay, and to bolster the claims of their constituents. Kirkwood of Iowa worked to get the Treasury for Chase; Minnesota's Ramsey, who had a faint hope of being made secretary of the interior, realized that his senatorial ambitions would be injured — as indeed they were to be — by the wrong man in the Land Office. [2] Curtin arrived early and labored

[1] G. L. P. Radcliffe: *Governor Thomas H. Hicks of Maryland,* pp. 29, 48–9; *New York Times,* March 4; *Chicago Tribune,* March 6; *New York Tribune,* March 6, 1861.

[2] H. W. Lathrop: *Life and Times of Samuel J. Kirkwood,* p. 108; W. W. Folwell: *A History of Minnesota,* I, 67 ff.

hard to keep Pennsylvania offices from Cameron. Leland
Stanford, who hoped to become governor of California,
struggled to keep Oregon's Senator Baker, an old friend of
Lincoln's, from controlling the California patronage.[3] Other
office-seekers appealed to Yates, to Congressman E. B. Washburne, and to Senator Trumbull to use their supposed influence with Lincoln.[4]

But in distributing jobs Lincoln was more inclined to give
ear to national than to state office-holders. At an early date
he announced that applicants must have the endorsement of
their congressmen. Where there were contests the President
attached no weight to gubernatorial endorsements but settled the matter by selecting men who would strengthen the
national party. Governor Andrew, when pressed to lend support to various contenders for collector of the port of Boston, was forced to reply that he had no control over the
customs house, though he did manage to get a job there for
his brother.[5] Nor could Sprague get favorable consideration
for his candidate for postmaster of Providence. Rhode Island's congressional delegation recommended another, and
Lincoln said to Sprague: "I followed the rule in this case." [6]

But even as he labored to build a national party through
a judicious apportionment of the patronage, Lincoln realized that more than a distribution of honors and emolu-
ments was needed to save his administration. The Southern
Confederacy was becoming a nation. Every step it took was
an implied insult to Lincoln's government, particularly the
seizure of federal forts, mints, post offices, and customs
houses. Buchanan, hoping to maintain peace through the
time-tried processes of concession and compromise, had si-

[3] *New York Times,* March 14, 1861.

[4] A. S. Eccles, March 8, 1861, to Yates, Yates MSS.; for samples of
letters, cf., A. R. Adams, Mathew Blain, C. W. Copeland, C. C. Du-
Puy, J. W. Fish, March 5–10 to E. B. Washburn, Washburn MSS.;
Alonzo Huntington to Trumbull, March 12, 1861, Trumbull MSS.

[5] H. G. Pearson: *John A. Andrew,* I, 171–2; Harry J. Carman and
Reinhard H. Luthin: *Lincoln and the Patronage,* p. 65.

[6] *Complete Works of Lincoln,* I, 270.

lently acquiesced as the seceding states occupied army posts and bristling forts. Silent, too, was Lincoln as President-elect, but in his inaugural he announced that all his powers would be used to "hold, occupy, and possess the property and places belonging to the government."

Specifically this meant Fort Sumter in Charleston harbor, which Major Anderson held with a handful of men. The situation in Sumter was acute, for the garrison had almost exhausted its food supply. Immediately after his inaugura-tion Lincoln consulted General Scott, an aged veteran with an unprofessional distaste for war. Scott advised that it was impractical to supply or reinforce the fort. Ten days later the President appealed to his cabinet for advice. Mont-gomery Blair wanted the government to show "firmness" and send an expedition. Chase favored sending an expedi-tion if it could be done without provoking war. Seward, Cameron, Welles, Smith, and Bates opposed. Two weeks later, on March 29, the cabinet gave substantially the same advice.[7]

Democrats generally and a bare handful of Republicans echoed the cabinet's conciliatory sentiments. The Demo-cratic *Chicago Times* welcomed the vague "reservations and exceptions and promises" in Lincoln's inaugural and hoped that "honest Old Abe will yet compel us to throw up our hat for him."[8] Among the Republicans those within Sew-ard's circle opposed coercion. Sam Bowles thought that the Republicans could "afford" a national convention to settle the issues,[9] and Thurlow Weed was sure the inaugural ad-dress aligned Lincoln against the abolitionists and radicals in the party.[10] New York's Governor, E. D. Morgan, took occasion to send to his legislature a proposed thirteenth

---

[7] R. E. West: *Gideon Welles*, pp. 95–107; F. W. Seward: *Seward at Washington*, pp. 528 ff.; E. Bates: *Diary of Edward Bates*, p. 180; W. E. Smith: *The Francis P. Blair Family in Politics*, II, 15–16.

[8] *Chicago Times*, March 9, 1861.

[9] G. S. Merriam: *Life and Times of Samuel Bowles*, I, 319.

[10] Weed: *Memoir of Thurlow Weed*, II, 325.

amendment to the Constitution that would guarantee slavery
where it existed and reassure the border states that the
North had no desire to interfere with Southern domestic
institutions.[11]

Seward himself worked to prevent Lincoln from taking
drastic action. "I would not provoke war in any way now,"
said the Secretary of State. Instead he proposed conciliating
the South and building up Southern Unionist support. This,
he recognized, would "demoralize the Republican party itself," but surely "no patriot and lover of humanity could
hesitate to surrender party for the higher interests of country and humanity."[12] Finally, in desperation, he sent Lincoln, on April 1, "Some Thoughts for the President's Consideration," proposing war against Spain and France as a
device for diverting popular attention from the slavery question to the problem of the Union. But Lincoln made short
shrift of Seward's "Thoughts." He denied that his administration lacked a policy, and he asserted his own responsibility. Thereafter Seward abandoned all hope of preventing
civil war.[13]

The movement for conciliation was weak and disorganized, and most of the proposals for compromise came from
Democrats. The coercionists were better organized and more
articulate. The *New York Tribune* humbly hung its head
at the humiliation of abandoning Sumter,[14] and the *Chicago
Tribune* found it hard to believe the rumors of abandon-
ment that seeped out from Washington. Coercion must be
resorted to, said the Chicago paper; "the very word Government means coercion."[15] Editor Raymond of the *New York
Times* changed tune before the rising clamor and harangued
the city's Republican Club to pass a resolution calling on

[11] *Boston Daily Courier*, March 23, 1861.
[12] *Complete Works of Lincoln*, II, 11–14.
[13] *Writings of Lincoln*, V, 278 f.
[14] *New York Tribune*, March 12, 1861.
[15] *Chicago Tribune*, March 4, 12, 1861.

Lincoln for immediate war. Republican editors generally pleaded eagerly for bloodshed.[16]

From the state governors came similar demands for action. O. P. Morton hurried on from Indianapolis to urge a vigorous policy and a prompt decision for war. His militia was organized, he said, and would be ready to march as soon as it had five thousand muskets. Secretary of War Cameron ordered the arms to Indiana's Governor.[17] Governor Andrew's plea for coercion took the form of a message to his legislature congratulating the Massachusetts delegates to the peace conference for their "patriotic adherence to principles fundamental both in morals and politics."[18] He too reported that his militia was ready.[19] Randall of Wisconsin went to Washington to give assurance that he would support a policy of coercion; he returned to Madison to consult with Republican legislators on further reorganization of the state's militia.[20]

More significant than the importunities of warmongering governors were the spring elections in New England. Republicans watched closely the campaigns in New Hampshire, Rhode Island, and Connecticut to learn whether a policy of coercion would have popular approval. In New Hampshire the Democrats nominated General George Stark, descendant of a Revolutionary soldier, on a platform favoring union and compromise. As he accepted the nomination in the middle of January, Stark declared that this would be the first opportunity for the citizens of a Northern state to ex-

[16] E. B. Hunt to Howell Cobb, March 7, 1861, U. B. Phillips (ed.): *Correspondence of Robert Toombs, Alexander H. Stephens, and Howell Cobb*, p. 548.

[17] W. D. Foulke: *Oliver P. Morton*, I, 113–14; W. B. Weeden: *War Government, Federal and State*, p. 145; C. M. Walker: *Sketch of O. P. Morton*, pp. 51–3; W. H. H. Terrell: *Indiana in the War*, p. 3; *Official Records*, series 3, I, 64.

[18] *Boston Daily Courier*, March 26, 1861.

[19] Pearson: *Andrew*, I, 173.

[20] *Wisconsin State Journal*, March 30, April 2, 6, 1861.

press themselves on the expediency of continuing "the dangerous sectional agitation" that had produced secession.[21]

New Hampshire's Republicans, refusing to renominate the relatively moderate Ichabod Goodwin, selected Nathaniel S. Berry, Free-Soiler and abolitionist, to oppose Stark. Berry's sixty-five years had brought him success as a tanner and minor honors as a politician. He had served as a state legislator and, though untrained in the law, as an associate justice of the Court of Common Pleas and as a probate judge. But he had failed four times between 1847 and 1850 to win the governorship on the Free-Soil ticket. Democrats scorned his extremism and declared that a vote for him was a vote to "aggravate present difficulties" and to produce a bloody civil war.

The election came a week after Lincoln's inauguration. Berry's victory, said the Democrats bitterly, was a "triumph of the most radical and uncompromising type of black Republicanism." It revealed that the "imminent peril" that the Republicans had brought to the country had not lessened their "pride of consistency," party passion, and greed for office. The only consolation Democrats could find was in the slight reduction in the Republican majority since the previous November.[22]

The elections in Connecticut and Rhode Island were held during the first week in April. "Connecticut will join New Hampshire," predicted the Republicans, "in avowing that she has no apology to offer, no repentance to be felt" in electing Lincoln. The party renominated William A. Buckingham, while James C. Loomis led a somewhat distraught Democracy to defeat. "Coercion" was the key-word of the campaign, and the coercionists won a majority of 2,000 in a total vote of 84,000. The endorsement was not ignored in Washington.[23]

[21] *New Hampshire Gazette,* January 23, 1861.

[22] Ibid., February 13, 27, March 13; *New Hampshire Patriot,* January 16; *New York Times,* March 13, 1861.

[23] W. A. Croffut and J. M. Morris: *Connecticut during the War,*

In contrast, the results in Rhode Island's election were less clear-cut. Governor Sprague's friends claimed that he was the handsomest man in New England, and even his enemies admitted that he was the richest. But his political concepts were badly muddled. He had begun as a Democrat, supported by moderate Republicans. Under his influence Rhode Island had repealed its personal-liberty law and had sent a conciliatory delegation to the peace conference. To the disgust of the radicals, he seemed to support Seward's program. But Sprague had money and a willingness to spend it on elections. His nomination by the Republicans was therefore a foregone conclusion, and when the Democrats also endorsed him it seemed certain that he would be re-elected without opposition. A handful of "straight-out" Republicans, however, could not stomach the Governor. They dismissed him as a political charlatan and nominated James Y. Smith, an estimable, able, and less wealthy manufacturer. When the voters, as expected, re-elected Sprague, New England Democrats professed to have won a victory over "John Brownism, Helperism, and black Republicanism." The election of moderate congressmen to replace two coercionists seemed to confirm their contention. But the moderates' victory in Rhode Island was too slight to compensate for the extremists in the other New England states. The Republican Party of New England would follow the precepts of John Andrew.[24]

Simultaneously with the New England elections came a new outcry from the metropolitan press. Under headlines: "Wanted: A Policy," the *New York Times* proclaimed that the administration had not met public expectations. "The President must adopt a more clear and distinct policy." The government must lead the people, and "it is the high, the

---

p. 37; S. G. Buckingham: *William A. Buckingham*, p. 91; *New York Times*, March 14, 30, 1861; Buckingham to Lincoln, April 15, 1861, R. T. Lincoln MSS.

[24] *New York Tribune*, February 13, March 28; *New York Times*, March 29, 30; *New Hampshire Gazette*, April 16, 1861.

imperative duty of President Lincoln, in this solemn crisis
of the nation's fate, to give the American people this guid-
ance and leadership." In the *New York Tribune* Horace
Greeley echoed his rival's demand and insisted upon a program "to bring matters to a focus." [25] So inspired, the state
governors renewed their protests against abandoning Fort
Sumter.[26]

Amid the rising demand for coercion, and without again
consulting his cabinet, Lincoln ordered the preparation of
expeditions to relieve both Fort Sumter at Charleston and
Fort Pickens at Pensacola. Then, while the ships whose appearance would be sure to provoke war were under way, the
President summoned Pennsylvania's Governor Curtin to
Washington. At the moment the legislature at Harrisburg
had before it a bill to reorganize the militia. The President
wanted the bill passed. He told Curtin he had information
that Southerners were planning to seize Washington, and he
would need Pennsylvania troops to protect the capital. Curtin agreed to prod the legislature, and hurried home to
write the necessary message. Before he had written it, Lincoln wired him: "I think the necessity of being ready in-
creases. Look to it." Soon afterward Curtin urged the legislature to establish a military bureau at Harrisburg, to modify
the militia laws, and to make it possible to distribute the
state's arms to volunteer companies. "Pennsylvania offers
no counsel and takes no action in the nature of a menace.
Her desire is peace and her object the preservation of
the personal and political rights of citizens, of the true
sovereignty of States, and the supremacy of law and order."
Inspired by this combination of rhetoric and hysteria,
the legislature, one day before Sumter, passed the mili-

[25] *New York Times,* April 3, 1861; *New York Tribune,* April 6,
1861.

[26] *New York Times,* April 8, 1861. The *Detroit Free Press,* April
13, 1861, quoted the *Baltimore Sun* as saying that Greeley had begged
Western governors to come to Washington and say the Republican
Party would be ruined if Lincoln did not make war on the South.

tia bill and appropriated half a million dollars to carry it out.[27]

While Lincoln was stirring Curtin to action, the relief expedition was on its way to Fort Sumter. The President took care to notify South Carolina's Governor, who sent the news to the Confederate capital. At Montgomery, Jefferson Davis consulted his cabinet, and Secretary of War L. P. Walker ordered General P. G. T. Beauregard to demand the evacuation of the fort. Major Anderson — who had not been informed that relief was coming — refused to surrender. At daybreak on April 12, Confederate batteries opened fire on the harbor's fort. The next evening Anderson surrendered.

Thus Lincoln had succeeded in making the Confederates appear to be the aggressors. Davis and Walker and Beauregard had given Lincoln's administration the policy demanded by the Northern governors.

Three months earlier the same guns that were to reduce Sumter had fired upon the *Star of the West,* but President Buchanan, eager to preserve peace, had not yielded to the pressure to declare the nation's honor violated. By the middle of April, however, the spirit of coercion had grown so strong that no one seriously suggested dismissing Sumter's fall as just an irritating incident. No voice, North or South, now spoke out for conciliation or compromise. Now men of all sections agreed that war was inevitable. "Fort Sumter is lost, but Freedom is saved," exulted Horace Greeley.[28] Governor Curtin, hastily summoned to Washington, told Lincoln that Pennsylvania could send 100,000 men to defend the capital, and Ramsey of Minnesota, in Washington on a patronage mission, quickly offered Secretary Cameron a thousand men.[29]

[27] J. G. Blaine: *Twenty Years of Congress,* I, 306–7; W. H. Egle: *Andrew Gregg Curtin,* pp. 41–2, 123; Angle: *New Letters of Lincoln,* p. 227; *Appleton's Annual Cyclopedia, 1861,* I, 569–70; *New York Times,* April 10, 1861.

[28] *New York Tribune,* April 20, 1861.

[29] *Official Records,* series 3, I, 67.

On April 15 Lincoln called on the governors to furnish 75,000 militia for three months' service to suppress rebellious combinations in seven states. Secretary of War Cameron hurriedly assigned quotas to the states and wired the governors to assemble the men at designated points. He called for one regiment, 37 officers and 743 men, from each of the states of Maine, New Hampshire, Vermont, Rhode Island, Connecticut, Delaware, Arkansas, Michigan, Wisconsin, Iowa, and Minnesota; two regiments each from Massachusetts, North Carolina, and Tennessee; three from Virginia; four each from New Jersey, Maryland, Kentucky, and Missouri; six apiece from Indiana and Illinois; thirteen from Ohio, sixteen from Pennsylvania, and seventeen from New York. He assigned no quota to Kansas, which had been a state for less than three months, nor to Oregon, California, or the District of Columbia.[30]

The governors responded promptly. Some were businesslike in their replies; Connecticut's Buckingham was almost brusque: "Your request will receive immediate attention." New Hampshire's Goodwin promised "vigorous measures to form companies"; Fairbanks would raise one Vermont regiment with promptness. Andrew, most laconic of all, wired: "Dispatch received. By what route shall I send?"

Others used the occasion to strike a dramatic pose. Washburn wired assurance that "the people of Maine of all parties will rally with alacrity to the maintenance of the Government." Dennison rashly pledged that Ohio "will furnish the largest number you will receive. Great rejoicing here over your proclamation." O. P. Morton tendered with bombast "for the defense of the Nation and to uphold the authority of the Government, 10,000 men." [31] Flushed with his electoral triumph and eager for martial acclaim, Sprague offered to lead personally a thousand men.[32] Governor Kirkwood rose to the occasion more slowly. He was working, in

---

[30] *Official Records,* series 3, I, 68–9.
[31] Ibid., I, 70–5.
[32] *New York Times,* April 15, 1861.

overalls and boots, on his farm near Iowa City when a congressman brought him Cameron's telegram. "Why the President wants a whole regiment of men!" he exclaimed. "Do you suppose, Mr. Vandever, I can raise that many?" He wired to Cameron to explain that the legislature was not in session, and to ask if the government would pay expenses. But he quickly discarded doubt and caution to measure up to the situation. Soon he sent Cameron word that "Two days ago we had two parties in this state; today we have but one, and that for the Constitution and the Union unconditionally." [33]

Immediately the governors issued proclamations calling their citizens to arms. Dennison proclaimed: "Your flag has been insulted and the Constitution of the Union treasonably defied," and called upon Ohioans to "meet the gravest responsibilities, and it may be sacrifice, to preserve your free institutions and your national independence." [34] Governor Yates, whose mind ran to melodrama, detected a vile conspiracy in secession. "Impelled by bold and sagacious leaders, disunionists at heart, they spurned in advance all proffers of compromise." But, said the chief magistrate of Illinois, "the spirit of a free and brave people is aroused at last. . . . Fully justified in the eyes of the world and in the light of history, they have resolved to save the government of our fathers. . . . Our people will wade through seas of blood before they will see a single star or a solitary stripe erased from the glorious flag of our Union." [35] Yates, Dennison, and most of the other governors convened their legislatures at the same time they called for troops.

But not all the governors were enthusiastic. Perhaps no one expected Ellis of North Carolina, Rector of Arkansas, Harris of Tennessee, or Letcher of Virginia to comply with Lincoln's requisition. Certainly in the six weeks of its ex-

---

[33] H. W. Lathrop: *Samuel J. Kirkwood*, p. 115; D. E. Clark: *Kirkwood*, p. 181; C. Cole: *Iowa through the Years*, p. 277.

[34] *Appleton's Annual Cyclopedia, 1861*, I, 557.

[35] T. M. Eddy: *The Patriotism of Illinois*, I, 90.

istence his administration had made no gesture to win confidence or loyalty in these states. Instead of complying, the
Southern governors called conventions to speed secession.
The governors of the border states gave evasive or truculent
replies. Burton of Delaware delayed answering and belatedly
reported that his state had no militia law.[36] Jackson of Missouri replied — in terms similar to those used by Letcher,
Harris, and Ellis — "Your requisition, in my judgment, is
illegal, unconstitutional, and revolutionary in its object, inhuman and diabolical. . . . Not one man will the state of
Missouri furnish to carry on any such unholy crusade." [37]
More curtly, Beriah Magoffin answered: "Kentucky will furnish no troops for the wicked purpose of subduing her sister
Southern States." [38]

These refusals did not cripple the government. Northern
governors, embarrassed by the numbers who offered their
services, soon besought the War Department to accept more
and more troops. The states and their governors were, in
fact, more enthusiastic for the oncoming war than was the
administration at Washington. The federal government
lacked imagination and initiative. The states lacked neither,
and the governors undertook, with telegrams, letters, and
personal agents, to prod the War Department and the White
House into vigorous action.[39]

Governor Andrew was a model of energy, efficiency, and
enthusiasm. Acting on a warning from Senator Wilson, he
summoned his war council, and even before Lincoln's call
came they had decided which regiments to muster first and
had made arrangements for lodging, feeding, and transporting the troops. Early in the morning of April 16 four regiments marched in a sleet storm to Boston Common. Andrew

[36] *Official Records,* series 3, I, 114.

[37] Ibid., I, 83.

[38] Ibid., I, 70.

[39] Fred A. Shannon: *Organization and Administration of the Union
Armies,* I, 33 ff.

reluctantly placed the men under the command of Brigadier General Benjamin F. Butler, his Breckinridge Democrat rival in the last election. Butler, with political acumen and dramatic sense as keen as Andrew's, bent his efforts to surpass the Governor in martial endeavor. Together they had the first two regiments ready to leave — one by rail to Washington, the other by water to Fort Monroe — in twenty-four hours.

Another regiment was prepared for the next day, and the fourth for three days later. "We work as fast as men can be properly equipped and moved," reported the Governor.

So fast did Andrew work that even while he delivered a parting sentence to them — "We shall follow you with our benedictions, our benefactions, and our prayers" — tailors worked furiously between the ranks, sewing the last buttons on the tails of the men's overcoats.

Though he mustered and dispatched three thousand militia and a battery of artillery in a week, all this did not exhaust his energy. Immediately after receiving Lincoln's call, he proposed to the Secretary of War that the capacity of the Springfield armory be doubled and the tools and arms at the Harpers Ferry arsenal be removed to Massachusetts. He reported to the Secretary the result of experiments he had been conducting with a new projectile. He placed guards around the state arsenal in Cambridge to protect it against Harvard's Southern students, stationed a school ship in Boston harbor to challenge the approach of Jeff Davis's navy, ordered the commander of the Charleston navy yard to arrest any naval officers who refused to take an oath of allegiance, and wrote the Governor-General of Canada about a suspicious-looking vessel on Lake Ontario. He proposed to raise a special regiment to man the forts in Boston harbor. He offered money to the federal government, and he promised the departing soldiers "to guard the hearthstones you have left; and, whatever may be the future, we will protect the wives and children you may leave." John Albion Andrew was carrying the whole war on his shoulders, and the amazed Cameron sent his congratulations.[40]

No other governor quite equaled Andrew's zeal and efficiency, but some of them faced problems he did not have to meet. The long-time rivalry between Cameron and Curtin tied Pennsylvania's hands. Parties may have been — as the Republicans so loudly proclaimed — suspended for the duration, but personal rivalries and factionalism among the Republicans went on growing through the war. Lincoln understood the feud between his Secretary of War and Pennsylvania's Governor, and called Curtin a second time to Washington before he called for troops. Appeased, Curtin returned to Harrisburg and began to raise troops with enthusiastic abandon. Then he bickered with Cameron over arming and equipping them and sending them forward. Cameron preferred to send the soldiers over his own railroad; Curtin thought it better they march to Washington. But even as the old feud found new fuel, Curtin got off the first troops to defend the capital. They arrived early, ununiformed and unarmed.[41]

New England's other governors, though slower than Andrew, went about their work with great efficiency. Fairbanks called the Vermont legislature and ordered his adjutant general to select men for the state's single regiment. Meantime he raised a hundred thousand dollars from banks and private subscriptions and offered to purchase arms for his troops from the federal government.[42] Buckingham won Cameron's

[40] *Official Records*, series 3, I, 71 ff., 78–9, 85–6, 93–4, 100; J. T. Morse: *Memoir of Colonel Henry Lee*, pp. 233 ff.; Pearson: *Andrew*, I, 210, 183 f., 195; B. F. Butler: *Butler's Book*, p. 174; P. C. Headley: *Massachusetts in the Rebellion*, pp. 111 f., 120.

[41] A. K. McClure: *Lincoln and Men of War Time*, p. 65; S. L. Davis: *Pennsylvania Politics*, pp. 188–9; *Appleton's Annual Cyclopedia, 1861*, I, 571; *Official Records*, series 3, I, 77, 82, 105.

[42] G. G. Benedict: *Vermont in the Civil War*, I, 18, 22, 25; *Official Records*, series 3, I, 84, 90–1, 105.

hearty congratulations for his promptness, "patriotic ardor and energy" in raising Connecticut's regiment. In New Hampshire, where enthusiasm was likewise great, the state's adjutant general, asking for two thousand arms, announced confidently that he could raise twenty thousand men! [43] In Maine the popular enthusiasm outran Governor Washburn. Embarrassed by the response to his call, Washburn urged Cameron to take five Maine regiments. But Maine had problems, too. The citizens of Portland, like those of Boston, felt strongly that their harbor should be defended. Washburn asked permission to occupy the harbor forts and to take arms from the Kennebec arsenal.[44]

Neither in New Jersey nor in New York did the governors display any enthusiasm. Governor Olden, without histrionics, raised his quota and reported to Cameron that he could secure two more regiments in three days.[45] No such dispatch was possible in New York, where the legislature, in session when the call came, created a military board to share responsibility with Governor Morgan. The Governor and the board promptly fell to bickering over expenses, over uniforms, and over the acceptance of troops. The board refused to allow Morgan to accept troops even in emergencies, to select an agent to purchase arms in Europe, or to appoint officers. Day after day the board met to approve contracts, purchase "bullet machines," and provide for clothing and transporting the militia. Meanwhile the radical press upbraided the Governor for his slowness. "The hearts of our people already murmur at the delays," said Raymond's *Times*. "New York expected to be first in the van of the great battle of constitutional liberty. She will yield to Massachusetts, but she must not be asked to stand behind any other state in this awful emergency. . . . Let the governor see to it that *not a man is delayed an hour*. . . . Let us have

[43] *Official Records*, series 3, I, 103.
[44] Ibid., I, 88, 93, 103.
[45] Ibid., I, 94.

no delay from ignorance in high place. . . ." Despite such heckling, Morgan managed to dispatch the first two regiments to Washington in four days.[46]

Western governors set about their unaccustomed task of raising and dispatching troops with as much enthusiasm as their New England colleagues. Their efficiency, however, fell short of Eastern standards. Kirkwood had Iowa's regiment ready in two weeks and was urging the government to take more troops. He, too, joined the general clamor for arms and uniforms.[47] Ramsey of Minnesota hurried home from Washington to supervise raising his regiment, his haste being due, in part at least, to Lieutenant Governor Ignatius Donnelley's assumption of the title "Governor ad interim," and his presumption of the Governor's right to issue patriotic proclamations.[48] In Wisconsin, Alexander Randall showed a rare combination of fervor and proficiency. Speaking at a mass meeting in Madison, he announced that Charleston, where "the first act was rehearsed, should be the theater of the closing scene." Fort Sumter, he declared, should be retaken and held, "though it cost fifty thousand lives and a hundred million of dollars. What was money — what was life — in the presence of such a crisis?" Despite his bloody intimations, the people rallied, and he wired Washington offering more men and demanding uniforms and arms for those he had.[49]

Michigan and Ohio witnessed more difficulties. The state treasury at Lansing had been looted by the former treasurer, and Governor Blair had to raise a hundred thousand dollars from Detroit bankers before he could issue a call for troops. His people responded readily enough, however, and the Governor told Cameron his regiment would be ready in a month

[46] *Official Records,* series 3, I, 95; *New York Times,* April 22, 1861.

[47] S. H. M. Byers: *Iowa in War Times,* p. 45.

[48] *Official Records,* series 3, I, 103.

[49] *Wisconsin State Journal,* April 15, 23, 1861; *Wisconsin Daily Patriot,* April 16, 20, 1861; *Report of the Adjutant-General of Wisconsin, 1861,* pp. 5, 8, 13; *Official Records,* series 3, I, 91, 102.

"to be mustered into the service and pay of the United States." [50]

Governor Dennison was perhaps the most inefficient of the state executives, and his staff was thoroughly befogged by the new duties. The Governor accepted companies as fast as they were offered, and soon found that he had raised fifty instead of thirteen regiments. Ohio's commissary general hurried to Columbus, where the volunteers were assembling, but could think of nothing better to do with them than quarter them in hotels at a dollar and a quarter a day. Soon the men were complaining about having to wait until noon for their breakfasts in the harassed hostelries, and the Governor was begging the War Department to take them off his hands. "Owing to an unavoidable confusion in the first hurry and enthusiasm of the moment of our people in Ohio in defense of the government, I find that I have already accepted and have in camp . . . a larger force than the thirteen regiments named." Indeed, thought Dennison, it would seriously repress the ardor of the people to send them home, and he believed the government should take the men just to show the insurgent states "that the lion in us is thoroughly roused." [51]

At the other extreme of efficiency among the Western governors was Morton of Indiana. Within three days after Lincoln's call he sent off a thousand men and was insisting that the government accept at least six more regiments. In a week he had six thousand men in camp, but they had no arms or equipment. A month earlier, when in Washington, Morton had persuaded the War Department to allot him five thousand stands of arms. "Why has there been so much delay?" he now demanded. He had not a pound of powder, not a single ball, not a piece of equipment. Nearly half a week had elapsed, and there was not even a federal officer in In-

---

[50] C. Moore: *History of Michigan*, I, 416; J. Robertson: *Michigan in the War*, pp. 17–18; *Official Records*, series 3, I, 88, 97.

[51] *Official Records*, series 3, I, 77, 101–2; Reid: *Ohio in the War*, I, 28 ff.

dianapolis. "Allow me to ask what is the cause of all this?" Such energy set a pace the War Department could not follow.[52]

Since these governors were all Republicans, enthusiasm, if not efficiency, could be expected from them. The governors of the border states, however, lacked this partisan urge for the bloody crusade. Jackson in Missouri and Magoffin in Kentucky were avowed secessionists. In Delaware, Governor Burton raised a half-hearted call for volunteer companies to organize for the state's defense, and added that such companies might, if they wished, offer their services to the federal government.[53] Delaware was not helpful and Missouri and Kentucky were later to be troublesome, but Maryland was the first of the border states to pose a serious problem.

Maryland's geographical position made her attitude on secession a matter of vital concern to the Washington government. For months her secessionists had been denouncing Governor Thomas H. Hicks for not calling the legislature into special session. But Governor Hicks, opposing secession, feared the legislature would take the state from the Union. The Governor had been elected in 1857 as a Know-Nothing, and in 1860 had supported the Constitutional Union ticket. He resisted the secessionists, yet at the same time he had no sympathy for the warlike Republicans. He had supported the peace conference, and he continued to hope that war would be averted.

The firing on Sumter and Lincoln's call for four Maryland regiments brought Governor Hicks posthaste to Washington. He had a long conversation with General Scott, who assured him that the Maryland militia would be used only in the state and the District of Columbia. Back in Baltimore, the hesitant Governor wrote Lincoln for confirmation of this promise. Secretary Cameron promptly replied with the necessary assurance. Hicks made the limitation a part of his

[52] *Official Records*, series 3, I, 80, 90, 92, 102–3.
[53] Ibid., I, 114.

proclamation, and he besought Marylanders to avoid all re-crimination on the subject of the emergency.[54]

Baltimore's plug-uglies did not heed their Governor's appeal. On April 19 the Sixth Massachusetts Regiment — Andrew's first answer to Lincoln's call — marched through Baltimore from one station to another. The city's famed hoodlums disputed their passage, and the Massachusetts men, with fervor enough to delight even Andrew's heart, fired into the mob. By the time they had fought their way to the Washington train they had accounted for nine of the mob and were carrying the corpses of four of their own number with them.

In the blood-flecked streets of Baltimore the rioting continued throughout the day. Late in the afternoon Mayor Brown and Governor Hicks tried to quiet the mob. The Governor repeated the assurances of the proclamation and begged for quiet. But the mob howled for secession. This Hicks would not support, but he proclaimed: "I am a Marylander, and I love my state, and I love the Union; but I'll suffer my right arm to be torn from my body before I'll raise it to strike a sister state."

This declaration did not help matters. That night Mayor Brown and Marshal Kane, both sympathetic to secession, conferred with Governor Hicks. The day's scenes, they told the Governor, would be repeated on the morrow if more Yankee troops came into the city. Their solution was drastic: to burn the railroad bridges between Baltimore and Harrisburg and Philadelphia. Reluctant and dubious, Hicks gave conditional approval to the course. That night the bridges were destroyed.

The next day Lincoln called Hicks and the mayor to Washington, only to learn that neither would come and neither could promise to control Baltimore's mob. Instead, the Marylanders urged the President to bring no more troops through the city, and Hicks took occasion to beg Lincoln to offer a truce to the secessionists. He even suggested — to

[54] *Ibid.*, I, 79–80; *Appleton's Annual Cyclopedia, 1861*, I, 444.

Seward's horror — that Lord Lyons, the British Minister, be asked to mediate between North and South. Lincoln made no promises, but consulted General Scott. His Army head agreed that troops should be marched around Baltimore.

But this did not end Governor Hicks's troubles. Hardly had he got back to Annapolis from Baltimore when General Butler, commanding the Massachusetts troops, arrived by boat. Both Hicks and the commander of the Naval Academy advised Butler to go away, but the intrepid general landed his troops, seized the railroad to Washington, and sent his men forward. Hicks appealed once more to Lincoln, but got no support. He even told Butler that he feared the presence of the Massachusetts troops would cause a Negro insurrection. But Butler offered his troops to put down any such insurrection — earning thereby a rebuke from abolitionist Andrew.

Meantime Hicks called the legislature into special session. Butler begged Lincoln to allow him "to bag the whole nest of traitorous Maryland legislators," but this was farther than the President was willing to go. Expecting trouble at Annapolis, Hicks instructed the legislators to meet in Frederick. There, he explained to them that the Baltimore riots were the acts of an irresponsible mob, and the legislators voted to approve the acts of Baltimore's city fathers in the emergency. But in the meantime General Butler moved over to Baltimore, took control of the city, and sent word to Washington that troops could now be brought through.[55]

The Maryland disturbances cut off the Eastern states from the capital, and for a week the governors were free to chart their own course. In the emergency Governor Andrew, Gen-

[55] J. G. Nicolay and J. Hay: *Abraham Lincoln: A History*, IV, 93–4, 119, 138–9, 168–9; F. Seward: *Seward at Washington*, p. 554; W. L. Seabrook: *Maryland's Great Part in Saving the Union*, p. 23; G. L. P. Radcliffe: *Governor Thomas H. Hicks of Maryland*, pp. 54–6, 63–4, 71–85, 89; Buchholz: *Governors of Maryland*, pp. 174–5; *Writings of Lincoln*, V, 289–90; Butler: *Butler's Book*, pp. 209–10; W. R. Thayer: *Life and Letters of John Hay*, I, 100–1.

eral John E. Wool, and the Union Defense Committee of New York City assumed responsibility. General Wool, seventy-seven years old, was living in retirement in Troy when the New York Committee, to give some show of regularity to their proceedings, called him to Albany. The old general advised with Governor Morgan and ordered New York troops sent to Washington. He sent arms from the arsenals to Governors Curtin and Dennison, ordered Olden of New Jersey to send militia to Fort Delaware, and communicated with other governors about sending military forces to the capital. In fact, Wool displayed more energy than the War Department had been able to muster. As soon as communications were re-established, Cameron brusquely ordered him to go back to Troy.[56]

In Massachusetts, Governor Andrew constituted himself unofficial secretary of war for New England. He assumed responsibility for supporting his state's troops, chartered two ships to carry supplies, and called on the towns to provide rations. For a week the women of Massachusetts cured beef and pork, baked bread, roasted coffee, and packed vegetables to load the boats for Annapolis and Washington. Andrew consulted Wool and got permission to garrison the forts in Boston harbor. And he advised the other governors. He loaned equipment to Maine and reported to Wool when New Hampshire had a regiment ready for service.

While busy with these various tasks, the Massachusetts Governor attempted to reopen direct relations with Washington. He armed George S. Boutwell with a loaded revolver, gave him one hundred dollars in gold, and sent him off with a package of letters to Lincoln. When Boutwell got to New York, he wired for Vice President Hamlin to come to the city and hold himself ready lest something happen to the President. Then Boutwell proceeded to Washington, where he found that Lincoln and the cabinet knew nothing of the rising public sentiment. He reassured them that the states were active and then hurried back to Boston

[56] *Official Records,* series 3, I, 106–7, 124.

to reassure Andrew that the federal government really meant to prosecute the war.[57]

Meantime, while Maryland's problem disturbed the East, the Western governors worried over Kentucky. Governor Magoffin's refusal to furnish troops brought frightening visions to Dennison, Morton, and Yates. Hardly had the news of Sumter come to Cincinnati when citizens of the Queen City began to imagine the hills of Covington and Newport, just across the Ohio River, covered with batteries. "The war fever rages high. Cincinnati is good for ten thousand volunteers," one alarmed citizen wrote to Dennison. "But will it be wise to send away a single man?" he asked. Leading citizens repeated these fears to the Governor and suggested that even in Cincinnati there were many with Southern sympathies. Troops, they all agreed, should be immediately sent. "Since Washington is cut off, our state will have to act independent of the War Department," advised Richard Smith of the *Cincinnati Gazette*.[58]

Impressed by the danger, Dennison appealed to Cameron to send heavy guns from Pittsburgh. Then, to prevent arms going from the North to Tennessee, he ordered the presidents of Ohio railroads to hold all shipments of contraband. He instructed telegraph lines to stop every communication regarding troop movements, and he told Cincinnati's mayor to prevent munitions, provisions, or contraband from passing through the city. But he advised the mayor that he should not cut off legitimate intercourse with Kentucky.[59]

Governor Morton, too, was worried about Kentucky. Although he had no important river city to guard, he, too,

[57] Pearson: *Andrew*, I, 200–8, 214–18; G. S. Boutwell: *Reminiscences of Sixty Years in Public Affairs*, I, 28 ff.

[58] Ohio Executive Records, MSS. letters of Timothy C. Day, April 15, J. Todd, J. W. Clark, April 16, R. Smith, April 25, and J. K. Harnfeld, May 1, 1861, to Dennison.

[59] *Official Records*, series 3, I, 101–4; letters of G. C. Davies, April 22, Rufus King, April 29, M. B. Wright, April 29, 1861, to Dennison; and Dennison to Mayor George Hatch, April 29, 1861, Ohio Executive Records MSS.

appealed for artillery to place on the banks of the Ohio to protect Indiana's southernmost counties. He sent secret agents into the Dark and Bloody Ground, and they reported back that Kentucky's Unionists needed support.[60]

Meantime Kentucky's own Governor was in a quandary. There was a strong Unionist element in his state and a widespread fear that Kentucky was destined to become the battleground between the sections. Already, too, the Confederate government was calling for troops, and many Kentuckians were organizing companies to join the Southern cause. Although his own sympathies were with the South, Magoffin hoped still for compromise. He determined to make one more attempt to avert the impending catastrophe.

"Will you cooperate with me," Magoffin wired Governors Morton and Dennison, "in a proposition to the government at Washington for peace by the border states as mediators?" Both governors suspected Magoffin's purpose, yet neither was in a position to make a point-blank refusal. Dennison agreed to send agents, or to come himself, to a meeting with Magoffin, but Morton, seeing an opportunity to cast doubts on the Kentuckian's sincerity, refused to meet an agent and insisted on a personal conference with Magoffin. The governors agreed upon the Spencer House in Cincinnati as the meeting-place. Morton arrived early and consulted with Dennison on tactics. When a Colonel Crittenden appeared with full powers to act for the Kentucky Governor, Morton and Dennison refused to see him. Crittenden proposed that the three governors unite in asking Lincoln to suspend hostilities until Congress could assemble, but Dennison was willing to unite with Kentucky only in advising the Southern states to return to the Union. Morton answered: "I invoke the State of Kentucky, by all the sacred ties that bind us together, to take her stand with Indiana, promptly and efficiently, on the side of the Union."

When Magoffin found that the two governors had refused

[60] Terrell: *Indiana in the War*, p. 212; Foulke: *Morton*, I, 134-5; *Official Records*, series 3, I, 125-6.

to see his agent, he set out at once for Cincinnati. But Morton and Dennison had hurried away. Morton immediately charged that Magoffin's move was merely a trick to gain time while Kentucky gathered arms. He did not, he said, recognize the right of any state to act as mediator between the federal government and the South. "I hold that Indiana and Kentucky are but integral parts of the nation, subject to the government of the United States, and bound to obey requisitions of the President." Disappointed in his efforts to preserve peace, Magoffin blamed George D. Prentice, Unionist editor of the *Louisville Journal,* for the failure. The border-state governors had seemed willing to co-operate until the *Journal* announced that Kentucky was sending arms to the Confederacy. "How can they have confidence in me if you tell lies about me?" asked the Governor plaintively.[61]

If the Kentucky problem troubled Morton and Dennison, Governor Yates had doubled worries. Illinois faced slaveholding states on two sides, and even the rankest amateur in military science could perceive Cairo's strategic importance. Moreover the Democratic counties of Egypt, as southern Illinois was nicknamed, filled the Illinois Governor with dread. Hardly had the guns of Sumter ceased booming when alarmed Republicans in southern Illinois began to demand that Yates send troops and cannon to guard Cairo from seizure.[62] As volunteers poured into Springfield in numbers far surpassing the Illinois quota, Yates quickly got permission

[61] Terrell: *Indiana in the War,* pp. 7–8, 212 ff., 215, 221–2; Weeden: *War Government,* p. 163; Foulke: *Morton,* I, 134–8; W. M. French: *Life of Oliver P. Morton,* pp. 183–8; C. M. Walker: *Sketch of Morton,* p. 69; Nicolay and Hay: *Lincoln,* IV, 200, 229–31; *Detroit Free Press,* May 3, 1861; E. M. Coulter: *Civil War and Readjustment in Kentucky,* p. 63; correspondence of Magoffin and Dennison, April 25, 26, 1861, and Dennison to Thomas Crittenden, May 1, 1861, Ohio Executive Records, MSS.

[62] Letters of C. H. Ray, April 16, John Olney, April 15, T. S. Rodney, April 19, and others, May 2–9, 1861, to Yates, Yates MSS.

to send four regiments from Chicago to the river city. Then he ordered stopped all shipments through Cairo to the South.[63]

On the other side of Illinois lay Missouri, where Governor Jackson was promoting secession. Thoroughly alarmed, the entire state government of Illinois — Governor Yates, United States Senator Trumbull, the treasurer, the auditor, and the secretary of state — sent a joint letter to Lincoln on the desperate situation in Missouri. Missouri's Unionists were not armed, and civil war was imminent in St. Louis. The officials made two proposals: first, that the arms in the St. Louis arsenal be immediately removed to Illinois, and, second, that a separate army of twenty thousand men be assembled at Cairo. This, they said, would "save Missouri certainly," would embarrass the Confederacy, and would protect Illinois.[64]

The Illinois communication brought quick action. Cameron ordered Yates to send three regiments to support the garrison of the St. Louis arsenal, and he instructed the arsenal's commander to issue ten thousand arms to the Illinois troops.[65] The new commandant of the arsenal, Nathaniel Lyon, was an appointee of the Blair brothers and cooperated readily. On the night of April 25 the Illinois troops took from the arsenal 21,000 stands of arms, 111,000 cartridges, and two field pieces. These they sneaked across the river to Alton and hurried to Springfield.[66]

The activities of the governors in raising troops, in dispatching them to Washington, and in arousing the martial spirit of their people contrasted sharply with the slowness,

[63] C. M. Hawley to Yates, April 25, 1861. Yates MSS.; *Official Records*, series 3, I, 113; *Chicago Times*, April 20, 1861; Eddy: *Patriotism of Illinois*, I, 97–102.

[64] *Official Records*, series 3, I, 80–1.

[65] Ibid., I, 92.

[66] Ibid., I, 193–5.

confusion, and inefficiency of the Washington government. The governors raised men, but the War Department had no arms for them. The governors organized their troops into regiments, but the army sent no officers to muster them into service. The governors housed, fed, and clothed the volunteers, raising the necessary money on their personal security, but the federal government was dilatory in taking over the burden of their support. When Washington was cut off from communication, the governors handled the problem of sending troops and assumed the task of dealing with the border states.

To Sam Medary, skeptical editor of the Columbus, Ohio, *Crisis,* the whole war appeared a "Governor's Conspiracy." [67] To Count Adam Gurowski, a Polish émigré who had identified himself with the abolitionist extremists, the energy of the governors and the fire of the people seemed to reflect criticism on the "tepid, if not cold" conduct of the administration. Lincoln, he concluded, had "slow powers of perception." [68]

The governors, too, were disgusted with the administration's lack of co-ordination and with its timidity. To them it seemed that the popular enthusiasm should be immediately harnessed for victory. Governor Dennison touched a responsive chord when he invited all the governors west of New England to a conference in Cleveland on May 3. To the conference, Morgan and Yates, too busy to attend, sent agents, who met with Dennison, Morton, Curtin, Randall, and Blair.

The governors found themselves in thorough agreement in their criticism of the government and in their plans for action. They agreed to address the President on the need for more men, more efficiency, more enthusiasm, and a concrete plan of campaign. To Alexander Randall they delegated the task of presenting their demands to Lincoln. The governors met General George B. McClellan, whom Dennison had dis-

[67] *Columbus Crisis,* April 18, 1861.
[68] Adam Gurowski: *Diary,* I, 46.

covered in obscurity and had made commander of Ohio's troops. They were delighted with him and with his talk of vigorous measures against the rebels.

The spirit of the meeting was manifested in the evening, when the people of Cleveland gathered outside the governors' hotel for an impromptu serenade. Cleveland's mayor introduced Governor Dennison, who remarked — wholly out of character — that the time for speaking had passed and that Ohio would march sternly off to put down treason. Then Dennison introduced in succession Curtin, Randall, and Blair — none of whom could have agreed that the day of oratory was over.

Governor Curtin rose rapidly to the occasion. He assured the crowd that a just God was above them, who abhorred wrong and upheld right, and that every man in Pennsylvania was ready to take up arms for the national honor. "To Arms!" he cried. "The country of Washington shall defend the flag of Washington, and it shall wave on every fort, state, and capitol in the land!"

Wisconsin's Governor had a more concrete proposal. Randall invited his nocturnal audience to unite with him in stamping out treason in its home. The nation, he avowed, should "transport an army down the Mississippi, and blaze a broad track through the whole South, from Montgomery to Charleston." Then Charleston should be "razed until not one stone is left upon another, until there is no place left for the owl to hoot nor the bittern to mourn."

In the oratorical afterglow of Randall's speech there was little left to be said. But Blair of Michigan drove the traitors step by step into the Gulf, with Michigan shoulder to shoulder with Ohio and Pennsylvania. This done, he, too, planted the flag over the verbal ashes of Charleston.

Warmed by the display of forensic talent, the crowd called for General McClellan. The Ohio commander, with a military man's understanding of the practical obstacles before the country, feared to commit himself. He explained that he was no maker of speeches. He implied that he was a man of deeds. The time would soon come, he told the crowd, when his acts would speak for him.[69]

In their calmer moments, and without the stimulus of an enthusiastic audience, the governors faced their problems. They dispatched messengers to Washington, and they authorized Randall to urge "some more definite course of policy" upon Lincoln. "We are prepared," Randall told the President, ". . . to sustain you and your administration in every measure, however extreme, for the suppression of this untoward rebellion and for the punishment of treason." The governors understood the government's difficulties, "but now we wish to urge upon you the absolute necessity, since Washington is safe, of giving more attention to the country immediately contiguous to the line between the free and slave states."

Cairo and the Mississippi River, Randall went on, were essential to the safety and the commerce of the Northwest. This meant that men and munitions would be needed. The Northwestern states could raise 16,000 men in four weeks — "among the swarming millions . . . there is but one pulse beating today" — but they needed a better military organization, and a "military head to which it can communicate its necessities without tedious and mischievous delays." Unless the federal government took control — the threat was pointed — there "will be war between border states, which will lose sight, for the time of the Government." There was widespread dissatisfaction, Randall said in concluding. The President must call more men and furnish them arms and a policy.[70]

At the same moment that the governors met in Cleveland, the Union Defense Committee of New York City, at whose insistence General Wool had assumed direction of the New York war effort, reported to Secretary Cameron on the number of volunteers who had answered Lincoln's call to arms.

[69] *New York Times,* May 16, 1861; E. B. Quiner: *Military History of Wisconsin,* p. 64.

[70] *Official Records,* series 3, I, 167–70.

The committee, which had more information than the War Department, had figures from thirteen of the seventeen Northern governors. The governors had raised, and had under arms or in near prospect, sixty-three regiments and a few batteries of artillery. In addition, these governors, who were belaboring the Department with demands that it accept more troops, reported that they had accepted or had available thirty-eight more regiments.[71] The committee did not have answers from Illinois or Indiana, where the response to the President's call had been enthusiastic, nor from Delaware and New Jersey.

A situation in which an unofficial committee raised troops and reported to the War Department, and in which the governors assumed authority, negotiated with neighboring states, and instructed the commander-in-chief on his policy, was intolerable. Faced with the situation, Lincoln again — as he had on the eve of his inauguration and when he sent supplies to Sumter — assumed responsibility. On May 3 the President called for forty regiments of volunteers, increased the regular army by eight regiments, and called for eighteen thousand new sailors for the navy.

But there was a difference between this call and Lincoln's earlier one. These were no longer state militia called for ninety days to protect the public property. These troops were volunteers called to serve three years or for the duration of the war. They would be soldiers "subject to the laws and regulations governing the army of the United States." The governors might still commission officers, but henceforth the President would control and direct the army.[72]

This call for three-year volunteers and this enlargement of the regular army came as Lincoln's answer to the governors. More and more, as the war lengthened, the governors came to realize that by this act Lincoln had taken command.[73]

[71] Ibid., I, 148–9.

[72] Ibid., I, 151–7, 207–8.

[73] W. B. Hesseltine and H. C. Wolf: "The Cleveland Conference of 1861," *Ohio Archeological and Historical Quarterly,* LVI, 258–265.

Chapter 9

Governors at Work

LINCOLN's call for volunteers was a weathervane pointing the direction of the nationalist winds. It was the first
indication that the federal government rather than the state
governors would assume control and direction of the Union
armies.

But it was only a weathervane. Law and custom and political necessity stood in the way of any prompt and thorough
alteration of the military system. The clustered prerogatives
of states' rights guarded the liberties of a people who had
long feared a standing army. In 1861 the militia was a people's army, and the state governments were the people's
governments. And in 1861 the federal government was far
removed from the people, while a national army, even
though its rank and file came from their immediate neigh-
borhood, might menace the citizens of the states. Although
Abraham Lincoln called for volunteers in the name of the
Union, the people would answer only through their states.
The Civil War accelerated the movement for nationalism,
but even at its end the regiments in the field bore the
names of the states from whence they came, and when they
finally furled their battle-torn flags, they deposited them in
the state capitols.

At the beginning the state governors stood ready to deliver their soldiers to the Union, but they were prepared
also to defend their rights against the President, the mili-
tarists, and the bureaucrats of the federal government. An-

[166]

swering calls for volunteers, raising men and money for the war, equipping and dispatching troops, complying with orders and regulations from the War Department, and unraveling the endless tangles in red tape brought strange new duties to the governors. They had clamored for war upon the South, they had rejoiced over Sumter, and they had plunged with enthusiasm into their new roles as commanders-in-chief of the state militias. Their unaccustomed duties brought unwonted labors upon them, and they bent willing backs to their tasks.

Governor John Albion Andrew fairly reveled in his job. The war brought out his mirth, making him the very picture of joviality. He teased his assistants, sometimes offending the more fastidious among them by the direct quality of his fun-making. "He was country bred," sighed a Back Bay Harvard man on his staff as he noticed how the Governor held sway over the plain people. "He was a poet," remarked a cultured lady who knew no other way of explaining Andrew's behavior. Boston society was curious and invited the Governor to tea. Blissfully unconscious of hostility, Andrew could stride into such a gathering, salute his hostess heartily, and give an impression of guileless frankness. His booming voice — he took the lead in congregational singing and delighted in martial music — seemed to imply honesty, hope, and patriotic enthusiasm.[1]

And Andrew worked. His office in the state house, lighted by two west windows and by gaslights, was twenty-five feet square. Equipped with a massive table, a green plush sofa, many chairs, and a heavy carved walnut bookcase, the room scarcely gave the nervous, exuberant Governor space enough for pacing the floor. Samples of shoddy clothing and other martial equipment hung from the gas jets. Here, with two secretaries, the Governor sat, interviewing the people who crowded the anteroom and overflowed into the corridor,

[1] J. T. Morse: *Memoir of Colonel Henry Lee*, pp. 236, 253–4; W. Schouler: *Massachusetts in the Civil War*, pp. 216 ff.; J. L. Bowen: *Massachusetts in the War*, pp. 33–5.

dictating sulphurous letters of advice to Washington, investigating complaints, issuing commissions, interviewing contractors — the presiding genius of the war.[2]

To the Massachusetts Governor the supineness of the federal administration seemed a composite of inefficiency and
criminality. During the days when communication with
Washington was cut off, Andrew had been war minister of
New England, raising troops, borrowing money, buying
ships, creating an army, directing the neighboring governors, and sending agents to Washington to instruct the federal government. When the crisis passed, Andrew expected
more energy both from Simon Cameron's War Department
and from the troops in the field.

Yet the War Department lacked both Andrew's zeal and
his energy. Faced with new problems, embarrassed by its
own lack of plans, it never measured up to Andrew's expectations. Andrew himself worked without system, but the War
Department had neither order nor direction. Late in May
1861 Secretary Cameron replied, almost plaintively, to another of Andrew's voluminous suggestions: "You will have
no excuse to complain of the want of vigor in the prosecution of the expedition now on foot to suppress the rebellion
in our Southern states. The whole power of the government,
with all the resources of the Northern people united, will
be used to settle the disturbing element for all time to come.
I have no doubt of the result, and I feel that as the policy
of the government develops itself to the public it will leave
no doubt in your mind." [3] But doubting Andrew was never
able to see any vigorous plan unfolding from the government's acts. So far as he was concerned, the whole problem
of relations between state and nation remained unsolved.[4]

New England's other governors complained less than Andrew, but showed scarcely less efficiency. Governor Washburne, he of the scholarly mien, revolved so faithfully in

[2] A. G. Browne: *John A. Andrew*, pp. 142–4.
[3] *Official Records*, series 3, I, 244.
[4] J. H. Pearson: *Life of John A. Andrew*, I, 237, 246–8, 280 f.

John Andrew's orbit that Maine seemed but a satellite of Massachusetts. An extra session of the Maine legislature in April resolved to furnish ten militia regiments and offered a bounty of two months' pay to each man who enlisted. Under this law recruiting went on steadily, and the Governor gained a reputation for quiet efficiency.[5]

Governor Buckingham, too, worked energetically. He never failed to answer immediately each communication from the War Department, and his only complaint was that the federal government neglected to call on Connecticut for as many troops as she could raise. On his own personal notes the Governor borrowed money from the state's banks and with it purchased arms and equipment for the troops. Promptness was his special virtue: "By our delay the safety of our armies, even of the nation, may be imperilled," he declared in an early proclamation, as he sounded the rallying trumpet to "Close your manufactories and workshops, turn aside from your farms and your business . . . meet face to face the enemy of your liberties." [6]

Governor Goodwin, soon to retire, sent off New Hampshire's first regiment so fully equipped that it could have lived entirely to itself and conducted an independent campaign for weeks. Its baggage train had twenty-four wagons, and its medical department contained a "most serviceable assortment of implements, calculated for the scientific mutilation of all applicants for surgical treatment." The men were clad in uniforms of "rebellious gray" and the coats, according to the state's adjutant general, "like a practical joke were more pointed than elegant." [7]

Fairbanks of Vermont extracted a law from the Green Mountain legislature authorizing him to establish recruiting stations and empowering him, if the President's next call for troops were not filled in six days, to draft a sufficient

[5] Adjutant General of Maine: *Report,* 1861, p. 5.

[6] W. A. Croffut and J. M. Morris: *Connecticut during the War,* pp. 56–7, 63, 78; F. C. Norton: *Governors of Connecticut,* p. 252.

[7] *New Hampshire Adjutant General's Report, 1865,* I, 34.

number of citizens for military duty. It was the most concise and most direct of the early laws, and Governor Fairbanks reported to the War Department his complete willingness to comply with its thoroughgoing provisions. The Vermont Governor gave the War Department no trouble.[8]

More of a problem to the War Department was Governor Sprague. Having led Rhode Island troops to Washington in person, the young Governor strutted about the capital enjoying his momentary elevation. Visiting the "Rhodian heroes" with their "fierce" colored blankets became a capital fad. Lincoln's private secretary, John Hay, with a fatuous adoration for the rich, found Governor Sprague a "small, insignificant youth," but was impressed by the wealth represented in the Rhode Island regiment. There was "enough of breeding and honor" among them to "retone the society of the Gulf." When such men, Hay rhapsodized in his diary, could "leave their houses, their women, and their wine, harden their hands, eat crackers for dinner, wear a shirt for a week, and never black their shoes, for a principle," it was "hard to set any bounds to the possibility of such an army!" [9]

The Governor dallied awhile in Washington and then returned to Providence. When the army officials instructed General Ambrose E. Burnside to requisition any supplies his troops needed, that swashbuckling successor to Sprague replied: "We need nothing, Sir, from the government; Rhode Island and her governor will attend to their wants." [10]

But as soon as Lincoln called for three-year volunteers, Governor Sprague rushed back to Washington to make a curious proposal. He believed that if he were serving officially with the Rhode Island regiment, he could induce the men to enlist for another three months "and so continue until the expiration of the war." He therefore offered himself

[8] _Official Records_, series 3, I, 194–6.
[9] Dennett: _Lincoln and the Civil War in the Letters and Diaries of John Hay_, p. 12.
[10] _New York Times_, May 4, 1861.

as a major general, to serve without pay. Meanwhile he would endeavor to have the state law limiting service to three months repealed. He explained to Secretary Cameron, however, that the people of Rhode Island would not permit him to sever connections with them entirely, nor would they consent to his holding a lower rank in the national army than he held in Rhode Island. Of course, he added, were it not for the people, "I would as freely shoulder a musket as wear a sword."

And Cameron approved! But political considerations stood in the way. Lincoln and his advisers had determined to make Benjamin F. Butler the first major general from New England. Couldn't Sprague, asked the Secretary of War solicitously, arrange matters so that he could accept a brigadier-generalship? But if Sprague couldn't be a major general, he would not fight. "I am led to believe I can be of more service to the cause in my present position," he said.[11]

In New York, Governor Morgan continued to have trouble with his military board and with a city committee in Manhattan. Together, these interfering agencies blocked the Governor's effectiveness until, in the summer, Lincoln commissioned Morgan a major general and erected New York into a military district under his control.[12]

New Jersey's Governor experienced no such difficulties. In fact, Governor Olden showed Andrew's aggressiveness without the New Englander's bombast and a promptness that was almost up to Buckingham's standard. Olden stayed long hours at his job. In the first twenty-one months of the war he was absent from his office but two days. Methodically, conscientiously, he wrote his own letters, and kept a careful eye on military expenditures. When Sumter fell, Olden raised nearly a half million from New Jersey banks. The legislature met promptly, gave the Governor unlimited authority

[11] *Official Records*, series 3, I, 193, 207, 212.

[12] Weeden: *War Government*, pp. 184–7; C. Z. Lincoln (ed.): *Messages of the Governors of New York*, V, 406; *Official Records*, series 3, I, 547.

to raise troops, and appropriated money for ten thousand stands of arms and a six dollars a month allotment for soldiers' families. With confidence Olden could tell Lincoln: "This state will at all times be ready to support . . . the general government in its noble effort to maintain our priceless institutions." [13]

Less smooth was Governor Curtin's path. The Pennsylvania legislature, not so tractable as New Jersey's, continually gave trouble. Cameron men in the legislature opposed giving Curtin a half million for the state's defense and questioned his calls for troops. Moreover, Cameron himself threw obstacles in the Governor's way. When Curtin raised twenty-five more militia regiments than Cameron had specified, the Secretary of War refused to take them off the Governor's hands. Curtin organized them into the Pennsylvania Reserves, training and equipping them at the state's expense. But the contracts he let for clothing were soon subjected to scrutiny. The legislature appointed an investigating committee, which whitewashed Curtin himself, but found wholesale peculation and fraud. The general opinion, expressed by the *Pittsburgh Gazette*, was that the Governor was responsible for "gathering around him a set of men more rotten than the blankets of which we have heard, and fouler than the rancid old bacon." [14]

In the West as in the East the governors were all patriotic but not all efficient. In Ohio, Governor Dennison, though energetic as a politician, was completely befuddled by his duties as commander-in-chief. Recognizing his own inadequacy, he asked Cameron for military aides, but the Secretary of War, himself inept and inefficient, replied that he had no time to be detailing lieutenants to help governors. Dennison finally found competent military advice, but by that time he had lost the confidence of his people. [15]

[13] J. Y. Foster: *New Jersey and the Rebellion*, pp. 23–5, 65–6.

[14] A. K. McClure: *Lincoln and Men of War Times*, pp. 255–9; Davis: *Pennsylvania Politics*, pp. 224–5.

[15] W. Reid: *Ohio in the War*, I, 21–31.

In contrast to Dennison stood Indiana's Governor Morton — the John Andrew of the West. His huge black mustache, slanting like a roof end from his nose to his double chin, covered a mouth whose straight lines betokened stern determination. Morton had both efficiency and zeal and little patience with the slow-moving, bungling motions of the War Department. He complained without ceasing that the federal government gave him no arms, no money, and no support. He raised troops in advance of calls and beyond his quota, and pressed them upon the government. He established a state arsenal for making cartridges and sold the product to the national government. He appointed officers, even from among Democrats, and he urged them to emulate his own example of speed and energy. Withal, he was an irritating goad to the War Department.[16]

In Wisconsin, Alex Randall surprised even his friends by his energy. He left nothing undone for the comfort of his troops — although his legislature's appropriation was inadequate — and he made appointments to military offices with astonishing lack of partisanship. Even the highly critical Chicago Times found him a model for governors of the loyal states.[17]

In Illinois, Governor Yates was constantly haunted by the fears that his state's frontiers would be invaded and that Egypt would help the Confederacy. Impelled by these specters, he worked feverishly, raising more troops than he needed and more than the federal government called for. His position as Governor of Lincoln's home state made him conspicuous. Neighboring states complained that Illinois was a favorite with the administration. In fact, though Cameron seldom turned down a request from Yates, the Gover-

16 W. D. Foulke: Life of O. P. Morton, I, 150–3; C. M. Walker: Sketch of Morton, pp. 92, 114–15; W. H. H. Terrell: Indiana in the War, pp. 18–20.

17 Chicago Times, July 19, 1861; Madison, Wisconsin, Patriot, May 7, 1861; Wisconsin Adjutant General's Report, 1861, pp. 28, 48; E. B. Quiner: Military History of Wisconsin, pp. 51–2.

nor never seemed to have enough aid. He was free in his advice to the administration, and showed no hesitancy in appealing over Cameron's head to the Illinoisan in the White House. Yet, though Yates had advantages, his military arrangements were never efficient, and the Governor was a poor administrator. He took his position seriously, however, ordering for himself a major general's uniform, complete with sash, sword, saddlecloth, and spurs. The Chicago tailor who got the order laid aside the fixings for General McClellan's horse to sew furiously on the trappings for Governor General Dick Yates.[18]

Most harassed of all the governors was Iowa's Kirkwood. His state was still frontier, sparsely settled, and poor. Financial difficulties complicated the Governor's task. During the first part of his administration Kirkwood had done without a private secretary; with the war's burdens his administrative staff expanded beyond the state's budget. In the beginning the Governor planned to save expense by not calling the legislature into session, but it cost ten thousand dollars to raise the first militia regiment. In the middle of May the lawmakers assembled.

When they met, the Governor asked them to legalize his expenditures, provide for additional regiments, relieve the soldiers' families, and protect the state's borders against the Indians on one side and the Missourians on the other. The legislature authorized the issuance of state bonds, which, having only the credit of a poverty-stricken commonwealth behind them, promptly went begging on the market.

Thereafter Governor Kirkwood became a peddler of bonds and a general purchasing agent for the state. He made contracts for clothing in Chicago, he tried to float the bonds on the New York market, and he begged the people of the state and its banks to buy bonds. He was busy as a bee,

[18] F. A. Shannon: *Organization and Administration of the Union Armies,* I, 89; W. B. Hesseltine: *Ulysses S. Grant,* p. 20; Isaac McBride, May 20; and L. McGrath, May 27, 1861, to Yates, Yates MSS.

pleading with the quartermaster general to furnish arms and supplies, raising soldiers, scraping the treasury bottom to pay them, and trying to keep up his own and his people's enthusiasm.

The only bright spot in the Iowa scene was the state's adjutant general. Nathaniel Baker had been a successful administrator before migrating to Iowa. In his native New Hampshire he had been a court clerk, speaker of the House of Representatives, and for four years Governor. He might — had fortune's wheel not stopped on Franklin Pierce's name — have been president of the United States. With such a background, Baker's talents made a valuable supplement to Kirkwood's energy. Together they almost overcame Iowa's lack of resources.

Once, raising a regiment at Davenport, Kirkwood ordered the newly commissioned colonel to report immediately to take charge of the men. The colonel demurred, saying he must first go home to get a clean shirt. The Governor replied that the regiment needed its colonel worse than the colonel needed fresh linen. The colonel went home anyway. Some time later Baker explained to the Governor about the colonel: "He said that every man he met that was not personally acquainted with him, after looking at his shirt, called him Governor Kirkwood, and he had borne that thing as long as he could stand it." [19]

One thing all the governors had in common — hard work. Their incessant labors contrasted strangely with the confusion and lackadaisical inefficiency in the War Department. Secretary Cameron furnished neither inspiration nor direction for the hard-working governors. The governors took full charge of their troops and were not even able to get competent advice from the War Department. Secretary of the Treasury Chase assumed Cameron's functions and

[19] D. E. Clark: *Samuel J. Kirkwood*, pp. 206–10; H. W. Lathrop: *Samuel J. Kirkwood*, pp. 115–18, 120–7, 140 f., 204–5; S. H. M. Byers: *Iowa in War Times*, pp. 45–6, 57–8, 72.

guided the clerks in the War Department. It was Chase who drafted the orders for the volunteer army. It was the governors who organized regiments, selected and commissioned officers. Cameron's only assistance was to advise them to be careful to select moral men. "The higher the moral character and general intelligence of the officers," said the Secretary of War, "the greater the efficiency of the troops and the resulting glory to their respective states." The minimum age for officers, advised the Secretary of War, should be twenty-two for lieutenants, thirty for captains, thirty-five for majors, and forty-five for colonels! Such advice was small help for the straining governors.[20]

After Lincoln called for three-year volunteers, it took Cameron twelve days to determine the quotas for the several states. Meantime governors, congressmen, and ambitious colonels pressed new regiments upon the President and the War Department. To an alert secretary the call for a volunteer army might have offered an opportunity to set up a national system of recruiting, but Cameron made no effort to take responsibility from the governors. Inertia, rather than any respect for states' rights, led the Secretary to use the militia system and to rely on the governors in raising the new army.

Immediately the governors began to ply the Secretary with questions. How many regiments could be taken from their states? What should they do with three-months men who would like to go for three years? Were the troops to receive state pay before they were mustered into the federal service? Cameron gave conflicting answers to his questioners, and put most of them off by replying that neither the quotas nor the system had been fixed. Yet he yielded to pressures, accepting more regiments from New York than the state's fair proportion, and then, to placate the other irate governors, increasing their allotment. When, on May 16, 1861, he assigned quotas, he asked for 55 regiments of

[20] *Official Records*, series 3, I, 227; Shannon: *Union Armies*, I, 22, 26, 32, 34, 38, 45, 48, 53.

three-year men in addition to 72 regiments of three-months militia he had already accepted.[21]

None of the governors were satisfied with the announced quotas, and some of them, like Buckingham, Fairbanks, and Washburn, thought they had been promised the privilege of furnishing more men. When Dennison protested against New York's excess, Cameron agreed to raise Ohio's allotment from 9 to 21 regiments.[22] Then Morton protested against favoritism to Ohio [23] and enlisted the support of both Dennison and Yates in his insistence that Indiana be allowed to send more men.[24] Finally Lincoln intervened to raise Indiana's quota from 10 to 16 regiments. Meantime it turned out that New York was having difficulty raising its enlarged quota. The Union Defense Committee of New York City, acting independently of Governor Morgan, promised 10 regiments, but it was able to parade only 4,500 men before the War Department's inspector, General W. B. Franklin. The general reported confusion in New York and recommended that the department reduce the city's quota and send a competent officer to take charge.[25]

In addition, Governor Morgan began to argue with the War Department over the appointment of militia generals. By state law, generals for New York troops were to be elected by the officers of the brigades, and Lieutenant Governor Robert Campbell protested — in the name of New York's military board — that appointment by the federal government violated the state law, destroyed the distinct character of the militia, repudiated an agreement Cameron had made, and was an insidious slur upon the state. Cameron replied by refusing to accept Generals Wadsworth and

21 *Official Records*, series 3, I, 129, 130, 131–2, 145, 150, 161, 170–200 *passim;* Pearson: *Andrew*, I, 224; H. W. Pearson: *James Wadsworth of Geneseo*, pp. 61–2; Weed: *Memoir of Thurlow Weed*, II, 333; Yates to McClernand, May 18, 1861, McClernand MSS.

22 *Official Records*, series 3, I, 220, 227.

23 Foulke: *Morton*, I, 126, 129.

24 *Official Records*, series 3, I, 232.

25 Ibid., I, 235–8.

Dix, the state's appointees. The governor and his attorney general went to Washington to beard the Secretary of War in his confused lair. Their trip was inconclusive, and its failure did nothing to promote harmony and efficiency.[26]

Meantime Lincoln learned of dissatisfaction and near riots among the Ohio recruits. Governor Dennison, zealous to rival New York in furnishing troops, attempted to convert the ninety-day militiamen into three-year volunteers. He got Lincoln's approval by telling the President that this was the unanimous desire of the men themselves. But he had neglected to get the assent of the men, who began to mutter mutinously when they learned of it. Lincoln sent an agent who arranged for separating the volunteers from those whose "patriotic ardor" had waned at the prospect of thirty-six months in the army.[27]

From time to time Cameron called on the governors for information on the number of troops authorized and mustered into the service of the United States. So bad were the War Department's own records that the Secretary had no other means of keeping himself informed. Just before Congress met in July, Cameron reported on his activities to Lincoln. Probably he was as surprised as his chief to learn that under Lincoln's call of May 3 the War Department had accepted 208 regiments, which, with the regular army, made a total of 230,000 men signed up for the duration. Making no attempt to explain how an original call for 55 regiments had swelled to 208, the Secretary praised the volunteer system and thanked the governors for their whole-hearted co-operation.[28]

All these troops had been raised without authority of law. Yielding to the pressure of the governors, Abraham Lincoln had assumed responsibility for sending an expedition to Sumter, for calling the militia, for enrolling a volunteer army, and for enlarging the regular army. But he had not

[26] *Official Records*, series 3, I, 249–54.   [28] Ibid., I, 303 f.
[27] Ibid., I, 265–6.

encumbered himself with Congress. That body did not meet until July 4, and by that time the President confronted it with the *fait accompli* of a war and of an army with which to fight it. And in so doing he had also enabled the Republican Party to avoid an internal conflict between its diverse elements. He had, by his extra-legal acts, brought momentary unity both to his party and to the North.

Faced with unavoidable war, Congress could only ratify Lincoln's acts, make them legal, and implement his policies. After endorsing what he had done, Congress turned to drafting a statute for the volunteer army. By an act of July 22, 1861, Congress regularized the existing system. The law authorized the President to accept 500,000 volunteers to suppress the rebellion. He might issue proclamations, calling for troops in proportion to the population of the states. He might call men for any period from six months to three years. He should appoint major generals and brigadier generals, but the state governors should commission all field, staff, and company officers.[29]

Amid the debates, one lone voice was raised in behalf of the national army. An Illinois congressman deplored the "erroneous idea" that seemed to exist "in some gentlemen's minds about the dignity and importance of states." Representative Richardson thought that "all this call upon the governors of the states for troops is mere courtesy." He would have the President call directly upon the citizens.[30] But neither the administration nor the Congress was prepared to heed such nationalist sentiments. The raising of troops remained in the hands of the governors.

Yet even in the summer of 1861 it was evident that the governors, however much they may have wanted war, could not meet the demands upon them. In these early months of the war both the national and the state governments were inexperienced and inefficient, but already it was clear that

[29] *United States Statutes at Large*, 268, 274.
[30] *Congressional Globe*, 37th Congress, 1st session, p. 245.

the federal government, if it were to save the union, must itself become efficient and must control the state governments. It would be another year, however, before Lincoln, having achieved relative efficiency in the War Department, could force the governors' hands.

Chapter 10

The Governors Fail

OR a year after the passage of the act placing the raising
of volunteers in the governors' hands, the state executives
tried, with varying efficiency, to raise troops. In the thirteen
months between the Union defeats at Bull Run and second
Manassas, while McClellan fought on the Peninsula and
Grant's Western armies moved from Forts Henry and Donelson to Shiloh and Corinth, the governors struggled to meet
the army's constantly increasing demands for men. Steadily,
too, they resisted the pressures the federal government
brought upon them, and fended off, in the name of states'
rights, the government's efforts to play a direct role. In the
end the governors failed either to raise men or to preserve
the substance of states' rights. But before they yielded, they
had sought another source of men for the armies.

The act of Congress authorizing the governors to recruit
volunteers came at the very crest of the governors' influence.
The day before the act passed, the Union armies met defeat
at Bull Run. The first reaction to the battle news was an
outpouring of soldiers. Governors pressed regiments upon
Cameron, and the Secretary took all that were offered. Three
regiments from Maine, six from Illinois, and two from Wisconsin were ordered into service. Curtin, reporting that companies were coming from all sides, advised taking "the wave
at its height." [1] Morgan called for 25,000 troops and, believing himself free from his military board, asked Cameron

[1] *Official Records*, series 3, I, 343 f.

to guarantee the expense.[2] Fairbanks appealed to Vermonters,[3] Kirkwood promised that all who came forward would
be accepted.[4] Dennison asked again for West Pointers to
command the regiments he hoped to raise.[5]

Yet, despite the governors' new determination, troops
came slowly. The three-months men, whose terms were ex-
piring, showed less willingness to enlist for three years. In
Pennsylvania the militiamen rioted at the prospect of being
sent home without pay. Cameron quickly ordered his son,
a paymaster, to Harrisburg with money for the troops, and
Curtin took advantage of the situation to make political
capital against the Camerons.[6] Everywhere recruiting declined. In Massachusetts, where five regiments were being
raised, the stream of volunteers dried up to a mere trickle —
in two days in August only four men joined up![7] Morgan
asked the department to muster men in squads of ten, and
begged for permission to pay a bounty.[8] Bull Run's sobering
lesson that war meant bloodshed and death had been rapidly
learned.

At the middle of August 1861 Washington, just catching
its breath after Bull Run, had a new "scare" — based on
nothing but vague rumors of an approaching enemy. Cameron wired the governors to ask how many regiments they
could send at once. The replies were not encouraging.
Buckingham thought he could send a regiment in two weeks,
and three regiments in a month. Washburn would need
from two to four weeks. Andrew had one regiment ready
for service and five more partially filled. New Jersey, said
Governor Olden, might send one regiment a week, but
Berry was vague about fixing a date for New Hampshire.

[2] *Official Records,* series 3, I, 354, 361–2; *New York Times,* July 27,
30, 1861.

[3] *Official Records,* series 3, I, 404–5.

[4] *Iowa Adjutant General's Report,* II, 709.

[5] *Official Records,* series 3, I, 380, 387.

[6] Ibid., I, 350 f.

[7] Pearson: *Andrew,* I, 244.

[8] *Official Records,* series 3, I, 410–11.

Morgan had no men and would not have for a month, and Dennison admitted his disappointment in the slowness of recruiting. Randall blamed the season, and explained that he could not get more enlistments until after the harvest.[9]

Discouraged and frightened, Cameron begged the governors to rush all the troops they had without waiting for regiments to be filled. Lincoln ordered Morton to start four regiments to St. Louis. "Hasten everything," [10] said the President. And Cameron told Dennison: "We need the men . . . in the present emergency." Failing to get enough men, Cameron appealed to the governors for the militia again — or for home guards. But all but one of the governors told him that a new call for militia would seriously retard raising the volunteer force. The exception was Andrew, who thought the "moral effect" would be good. Quickly Cameron dropped the idea, but he continued to urge the governors to accept everyone and hurry the troops, regardless of red tape, to Washington.[11]

Partly because recruiting was slackening, and partly as a result of patronage pressures, the administration began to authorize individuals to raise their own commands. The practice was first used in Delaware, where Governor Burton, who had neither legal authority nor enthusiasm for raising troops, failed to answer the calls either for militia or for volunteers. Consistently Delaware's secretary of state answered Cameron's requests for information with the assurance that the Governor would "cheerfully furnish" reports, but he had "no official knowledge of any of the matters inquired of." [12] In the circumstances Cameron authorized General Robert Patterson of Philadelphia to enlist troops in Delaware and Maryland.[13] This procedure received congres-

---

[9] Ibid., I, 412 ff., 420–1.
[10] *Writings of Lincoln,* V, 352.
[11] *Official Records,* series 3, I, 425–34.
[12] Ibid., I, 638, 784.
[13] Ibid., I, 110, 124–5.

sional approval in the act creating the volunteer army. The law provided that the President could commission individuals to raise independent commands in those states where the governors failed to perform recruiting duty.

The practice of authorizing independent commands received additional impetus from the governors' efforts to bring pressure upon the War Department to increase their quotas. In the first lush enthusiasm for enlistment the governors offered commissions to ambitious colonels on condition that the aspirants could get Lincoln's or Cameron's approval. Many of the prospective colonels had political influence, which they promptly used in Washington. But along with the colonels who had the blessing of the governors went others they would not choose. They, too, frequently had political power, and they, too, received special permission to raise regiments. As recruiting declined, and as Washington quaked from successive "scares," Cameron and Lincoln accepted every offer in sight.[14]

But the acceptance of independent commands quickly brought protests from the governors. Morton found himself saddled with three colonels for whom he was expected to provide regiments, Blair had more colonels than men, and Curtin found, upon counting, that the War Department or the President had authorized 58 people to raise regiments, but had called on him for only 54. The upshot was that Pennsylvania had 70 regiments being recruited at the same time, and only enough recruits for 10 of them.[15] Governor Morgan, still embarrassed by the activities of New York City's Union Defense Committee, urged the administration to conform to the law and accept troops only from the governors.[16] And Dennison, upon hearing of one such case, hastily wrote to Cameron: "Is it possible you have authorized W. G. Sherwin to organize a regiment of artillery? If

14 *Official Records*, series 3, I, 225, 275.
15 Ibid., I, 224, 269, 290, 439–41.
16 Ibid., I, 410–11.

so, for God's sake withdraw the authority. Such a commission will make a farce of the public service!" [17]

When Curtin flatly refused to recognize one presidential appointment, Andrew joined him in protesting to the War Department.[18] But by that time the practice of commissioning independent regiments had become so common that the chief clerk in the War Department had forgotten that the law required raising troops through the governors. "We have accepted twice as many from individual colonels as from state executives," he said.[19]

The rising protests of the governors brought Cameron to apologize and to back down. He explained to Morton that the President and the department had not intended to embarrass him,[20] and he assured Dennison that Sherwin would be completely under the Ohio Governor's control.[21] Lincoln referred an offer of an artillery company to Buckingham, stating that he didn't want to accept independent troops until Connecticut's quota had been filled.[22] Cameron told Morgan that the department had been accepting independent commands only to remove the impression that it was unwilling to receive all that were offered.[23] Then, to settle the matter, the Secretary issued formal orders that independent regiments should be completely under the governors.[24] States' rights were again triumphant.

But just as the governors were freeing themselves from this interference, the administration began the practice of permitting generals to recruit their own commands. On September 1, Brigadier General T. W. Sherman appeared

[17] Ibid., I, 447.

[18] Ibid., I, 448, 474; W. Schouler: *Massachusetts in the Civil War*, pp. 228–9.

[19] *Official Records*, series 3, I, 390.

[20] Ibid., I, 290.

[21] Ibid., I, 447.

[22] Ibid., I, 464, 466.

[23] Ibid., I, 465.

[24] Ibid., I, 483–4, 489, 495, 817.

in New England, bearing Lincoln's authorization to call on the governors for regiments for a new army that was to undertake a special expedition on the Carolina coast. In Boston, Andrew welcomed Sherman and promised to raise five regiments for his command. Recruiting, reported the Governor, had been slow, but the war spirit was reviving, and if he could only pay a bounty to recruits, he could raise the troops. "But," he warned, "we must strike immediately." [25]

Hardly had Sherman departed for New England before Major General Benjamin F. Butler appeared at the White House with a new scheme. Already Ben Butler's flair for drama had brought him notoriety. As a member of the Charleston Convention, he had voted 57 times for Jefferson Davis for the presidential nomination, and as the "Breckinridge" candidate for governor of Massachusetts, he had confirmed his partisan devotion to the Democratic Party. Despite this background he had been among the first and loudest in rushing to arms, had led the Massachusetts troops to the valiant conquest of Annapolis and Baltimore, and had moved on to Fortress Monroe. There he had recently endeared himself to the abolitionists by announcing that fugitive slaves taking refuge in the Union lines should be received as "contrabands of war."

Trailing such clouds of glory, Butler informed Lincoln that only Republicans were volunteering, and that the party was losing its voters to the army. Thereupon the general offered to raise an army of New England Democrats whom he might lead to attack the Confederacy along the Gulf coast. Intrigued by the prospect, Lincoln authorized Butler to raise six regiments, and Butler promised to get every officer and three fourths of the men from the Democratic Party. Lincoln's only question was about the governors, but Butler assured him that all of them, except Andrew, would co-operate.

The prediction was completely correct. Governor Wash-

[25] *Official Records,* series 3, I, 443.

burn was ready to offer an infantry regiment and a battery
of artillery, and to appoint a colonel from among Maine's
delegates to the Charleston Convention. Governor Buckingham offered a turbulent regiment of Connecticut Irishmen,
which Butler promptly took, put under a Democratic colonel, and brought to discipline. Fairbanks was just retiring as
Governor of Vermont, but both he and incoming Governor
Holbrook agreed to co-operate. The Vermont legislature listened to Butler and unanimously agreed to extend the state
bounty to Butler's regiment. In New Hampshire Butler
met opposition from ex-President Franklin Pierce, and Governor Berry asked the general to delay a bit. Sprague of
Rhode Island had already furnished Democrats to the war
and at the moment was helping General Ambrose Burnside
raise a Republican contingent. Butler, therefore, left Rhode
Island alone and turned his attention to Massachusetts and
Governor Andrew.[26]

When John Andrew got word that Butler was coming, he
immediately told Lincoln and Cameron that Massachusetts
had made prior commitments to General Sherman. He
promised, once Sherman was cared for, he would help Butler
to the utmost. However, he asked the department to authorize only the states to raise regiments. Cameron replied with
conflicting orders. First he directed Butler to use his own
judgment to "fit out and prepare" troops. Then he placed
all independent commands under the governors of the
states. Andrew quickly issued an order forbidding any new
regiments to be raised in Massachusetts until those already
authorized were filled. He then asked the War Department
not to detail any particular regiment to Butler. The department agreeably consented — completely unaware that a
storm was brewing in the Old Bay State.

Having cleared the way for resisting Butler, Andrew told
Sherman that he had "almost by right" a claim upon the
first three regiments to be raised in Massachusetts, and he
asked Sherman to insist upon his rights. Then, when Butler

[26] *Butler's Book,* pp. 295–305; *Official Records,* series 3, I, 652–3.

asked for troops, the Governor offered him two regiments. One was an Irish regiment, Democratic and recalcitrant from color guard to file-closers, and the other a paper regiment without name but whose colonel was a "townsman and a personal and political friend of General Butler."

Butler accepted the Irishmen and ordered them into camp. But he did not want his fellow townsman for a colonel. His preference was for one Jonas H. French, an even more ardent Democrat.

"Why, French helped to break up a John Brown meeting," cried Andrew in horror.

"That is why I want him," answered Butler.

When Andrew refused point-blank to commission French, Butler replied that he would commission him on his own authority. He announced that French would raise a regiment, and appointed a place for a rendezvous. Andrew answered with an order that no regiments could be raised in Massachusetts without the Governor's consent. Then Butler went to Washington.

He returned with an order creating the Department of New England, and with instructions to paymasters, to give his recruits a half-month pay in advance. Immediately, as commander of the new department, he ordered all officers to report to him.

Then followed a riot of letter-writing. Butler asked Andrew to announce that Butler had a right to recruit. The Governor refused, but offered to appoint a colonel if Butler would send a list of captains. Butler refused, and he protested against allowing recruiting officers to pay private bounties for recruits. Andrew denied that his officers were doing so, but charged that Butler's men were guilty. "I shall furnish you troops as I have to Burnside and Sherman, but it must be done by the state," said Governor Andrew. "I cannot permit any officer of the United States to raise troops in Massachusetts."

Having raised the question of money, Andrew appealed to Cameron to know what right Butler had to pay a bounty.

Cameron admitted that Butler could pay a bounty, but denied Andrew permission to do likewise. The Governor was still writhing when Butler asked to be assigned a room in the statehouse. Of course the Governor refused.

Then Butler sought an interview to ask Andrew to commission his officers. Andrew declined to see the general and replied, through his military secretary, that "His Excellency, Governor Andrew" was busy.

General Butler pondered his rebuff for a week, then wrote "His Excellency, Governor Andrew" for permission to recruit a regiment and a squadron. Since the officers were to go with Butler, would "His Excellency" think it improper for the general to select them? "His Excellency" had promised aid, and Butler knew of no better way he could furnish it. The general had raised two regiments in ten days — the promptest recruitment Massachusetts had seen! Fourteen times in 575 words Ben Butler sneered at "His Excellency."

But the victory was not yet in Butler's hands. The mayor of Lowell gave Andrew a new weapon. Were Butler's troops, asked the mayor, entitled to relief from the state funds? Promptly the attorney general decided that only regiments raised and commissioned by the Governor could claim aid. Just as promptly Butler issued an order declaring his troops entitled to the state bounty.

Piously John Andrew rejected a new request to commission Butler's officers. The men had been enlisted in violation of the law, the War Department's orders, and the directives from the state capital. Butler had confused recruiting, prevented Massachusetts regiments from filling up, and been insubordinate. The Governor regretted, indeed, that his official duty had brought him "into collision with a gentleman whom in other spheres I have known so long . . . and between whom and myself there ought to be nothing inconsistent with cordial, patriotic, and friendly cooperation in support and defense of a cause, grand as the proportions of the heritage of our fathers and blessed as their own immortality of fame!"

But, as Butler reported it to the War Department: "This doctrine of secession did not seem any more sound uttered by a governor north of Mason and Dixon's line than if proclaimed by Governor Magoffin south." "Will you recruit your own men under your own authority, or will you allow the authority to be wrested from you by the states?" asked General Butler. "In fine," he added, "is it not the very matter, in another form, about which we are in arms?"

In addition to appealing to high principles, both protagonists appealed to Washington. Andrew sent Henry Lee — and then Frank Howe and Mrs. Andrew — and finally he went himself to see Lincoln.

"You mean that General Butler lies?" asked Lincoln in mock horror.

"That is precisely what I mean," replied the humorless Lee.

But Lincoln, unconvinced, only suggested that, since Butler was cross-eyed, he "didn't see things as other people did." Instead of repudiating Butler, the President suggested that Andrew should commission his regiments.

Andrew refused again, and when Lincoln met Mrs. Andrew at a White House reception, he asked: "Well, how does your husband and General Butler get on? Has the governor commissioned those men yet?"

"We are informed, Sir," spoke up Frank Howe as Mrs. Andrew hesitated, "that you have commissioned them."

"No," said the President, "but I'm getting mad with the governor and Butler both."

Meantime, as the epistolary battle in Massachusetts degenerated into an interchange of insults over military etiquette, the state's senators — stepping gingerly lest they attract the ire of either warrior — sought an adjustment. In January 1862 Edwin Stanton replaced Simon Cameron in the War Department, and Senator Sumner laid the matter before the new Secretary. Stanton called for the correspondence, studied it, and summoned Andrew to Washington.

Andrew came. He refused, however, to go to a White

House reception: he did not approve of frivolity amid war. But he told his story to Lincoln and Stanton and finally agreed to a compromise. He would commission Butler's officers; the government would disband the Department of New England and send Butler off to war.

This was another victory for states' rights. But from the episode the Massachusetts Governor emerged suspicious and wary. Never again would John Albion Andrew trust Abraham Lincoln! [27]

The Andrew-Butler controversy lasted from September 1861 to February 1862 and served during that time to divert some attention from the waning popular enthusiasm for the war. Even in the West, where recruiting was much better than in the East, there was a decline in enlistments. Kirkwood issued appeals, designed to be stirring, calling Iowans to rally to "the cause of government, of home, of country, of freedom, of humanity, of God himself." Still the men did not respond. Darkly the Governor began to hint at a draft.[28] Yates reported that apathy was "stealing over even Illinois," [29] and the Democratic *Chicago Times* proposed a draft to equalize Eastern and Western sacrifice.[30] One of Governor Yates's volunteer advisers thought a draft would "get Men not Boys for solgers" and declared that "Every able Boddyed man in the Union ought to of been Drilling for the last six months." [31]

Despite the decreasing fervor, the federal government was momentarily content. On December 1, 1861 Secretary Cameron reported to Lincoln that the volunteer and regular army numbered 660,971 men, and he added fulsome praise

[27] *Official Records,* series 3, I, 498, 502, 541, 551–2, 633, 637, 652–6, 658, 811–98; Pearson: *Andrew,* I, 283–310; Schouler: *Massachusetts in the War,* pp. 252, 280–2. *Butler's Book,* pp. 305–14; Morse: *Memoir of Lee,* pp. 74 ff.; Andrew to Lincoln, January 1, 1862, R. T. Lincoln MSS.

[28] Iowa Adjutant General's *Report,* II, 709–10; Shannon: *Union Armies,* I, 264; *Official Records,* series 3, I, 520, 560–2, 574.

[29] *Official Records,* series 3, I, 500.

[30] *Chicago Times,* September 18, 1861.

[31] S. W. P. to Yates, October 4, 1861. Yates MSS.

for the prompt patriotism of the loyal governors who had raised the troops.[32] Two days later General McClellan announced a new recruiting system. After the first of the year a special recruiting officer would take charge of each state. Their main duty would be to keep filled the ranks of regiments in the field. All this implied that the army was large enough. The governors evidently had done their work well.[33]

But while the political power and demonstrated energy of the governors made them immune from attack, the people's mounting dissatisfaction with military administration centered on Secretary Cameron. The Pennsylvanian had entered Lincoln's cabinet with a reputation for political shysterism and personal dishonesty. His conduct of the War Office — his inefficiency, ineptness, and peculation — had done nothing to dissipate the clouds that hung over his name. At last certain New York bankers demanded that Lincoln dismiss him.[34] Facing widespreading criticism, Cameron determined to make a bid for the support of the radical element of Republicans. In October 1861 he had instructed General T. W. Sherman, commanding troops on the coast of South Carolina, to employ fugitive slaves as laborers and even as soldiers. Somewhat later the Secretary suggested using Negro soldiers, and when he made his annual report to Lincoln, he inserted a paragraph — at the insistence of Edwin M. Stanton — elaborating this idea.[35]

The proposal to use Negro troops made special appeal to governors who were having difficulty raising white men for the army. Radicals in general were delighted and sought to force Lincoln to accept the idea. "We are carrying on the war on peace principles," advised the *Chicago Tribune*, which saw 600,000 soldiers "acting merely as policemen to

---

[32] *Official Records*, series 3, I, 698–708.

[33] Shannon: *Union Armies*, I, 265; *Official Records*, series 3, I, 722–3.

[34] R. M. Blatchford to Cameron, September 1861, Cameron MSS.

[35] T. H. Williams: *Lincoln and the Radicals*, p. 59.

prevent the escape of those who could dig the trenches for us." [36]

But Lincoln was not convinced. He wanted to preserve the Union, he said in his first annual message, but he did not want the war to "degenerate into a violent and remorseless revolutionary struggle," and he warned against the hasty adoption of "radical and extreme measures." [37] Believing that Cameron's usefulness was over, he arranged to get rid of the Secretary by sending him to Russia. For his place in the cabinet, the President chose Edwin McMasters Stanton.

Secretary of War Stanton had been a lifelong Democrat, and he had risen, through sheer genius for political intrigue, to a post in James Buchanan's confused cabinet. He was a past master at being all things to all men, and his elevation to the cabinet met the approval of radicals, moderates, and Democrats alike. Andrew asked only how Stanton stood "on the great question of general policy in the conduct of the war," [38] and, being reassured, praised the new Secretary's "high ability" and "patriotic services." [39] Behind Stanton's great black beard was a mind filled with animal cunning. Quickly he began to earn for himself a reputation for efficiency and for impeccable integrity. He had "boxes and files" for everything — "order upon order," complained one of Cameron's defenders, "all seemingly predicated upon the idea that everything heretofore was disorder and frauds." [40]

Stanton's administration immediately brought financial honesty and the appearance of efficiency to the War Department. It was appearance only, however, for beneath the Secretary's brusque and insulting manner lay confusion still. For a couple of months the new recruiting system, with only routine replacements to care for, worked well enough. Then,

[36] *Chicago Tribune,* January 10, 1862.
[37] *Writings of Lincoln,* V, 382–409.
[38] Andrew to T. D. Andrews, January 14, 1862, Stanton MSS.
[39] G. C. Gorham: *Life of Edwin M. Stanton,* I, 242.
[40] K. Prichett to Cameron, February 2, 1862, Cameron MSS.

in April 1862, in a move as inept as any of Cameron's, Stanton ordered the recruiting offices closed. He explained to Halleck that he intended the order to force reports from the governors. A month later he abruptly ordered the offices reopened.[41] It took another month to re-establish the offices, and before the new officers could take charge, crisis was upon the country.

In May, McClellan began to push up the Peninsula toward Richmond and demanded that the Washington government send him all available reinforcements. To relieve the pressure in Richmond, Stonewall Jackson began a brilliant campaign in the Shenandoah Valley which so alarmed the capital that Lincoln and Stanton refused to send troops to McClellan. At the same time, stricken with panic, the President and the Secretary of War called on the governors for troops.

To the question how soon they could raise and forward troops, the astonished governors made prompt but vague replies. Governor Curtin remarked that the state's recruiting offices had been broken up long ago. Washburn thought he could raise a regiment in two weeks; New Jersey's Olden would need three months.[42] Ohio's new Governor Tod had no idea about time.

Most emphatic were the replies from Wisconsin's Governor Edward Salomon and Massachusetts' John Andrew. Both of them demanded a statement of policy before they would raise more soldiers.

When Stanton's request arrived, Edward Salomon had been Governor of Wisconsin less than a month. He had succeeded to the office upon the death of Louis P. Harvey, who had been inaugurated in January. Governor Harvey had taken his duties seriously. When he heard that Wisconsin regiments were engaged in the Battle of Pittsburg Landing, he hastily gathered hospital supplies and surgeons and hurried off to the battlefield. En route he had joined

[41] *Official Records,* series 3, II, 3, 29.
[42] Ibid., II, 44 ff.

Yates and Morton, bent upon a similar errand of mercy.
The gubernatorial party made arrangements to care for the
wounded, and Harvey had about completed his labors when,
on the night of April 19, 1862, in stepping from one boat to
another, he fell into the Tennessee River and was drowned.[43]
His death brought to the Governor's chair a fighting Prussian Jew who was as irascible as Secretary Stanton.

Edward Salomon was only thirty-three years of age and
had been a citizen of the United States less than a decade
when fate made him Governor. He had learned the ways of
the United States quickly, and he did not need more than a
month in the governor's office to detect the defects in the
military system. Wisconsin, he told Stanton, had already exceeded its quota of soldiers, but it was "ready still to furnish
troops." He thought he could raise one or two regiments;
before he did so, however, he would have to have an understanding with the War Department.

The Governor presented a bill of grievances. Wisconsin
had had trouble getting reimbursement for money spent in
raising troops. The paymasters who disbursed federal funds
were unreliable. Then, too, Wisconsin soldiers needed
clothes, and tents, and camp outfits. The officers would have
to be paid from the date of their commissions. Unless improvements could be made, said Governor Salomon, there
would be difficulty in raising men or furnishing officers in
Wisconsin.[44]

After standing his ground for a month, the Governor
finally wore the department down. He got pay for his officers
(providing they raised their regiment in thirty days), forced
a change of paymasters, and blocked a War Department effort to raise an independent regiment in Wisconsin. Salomon refused to catch panic from Stanton or from his fellow
governors, and eventually the others rallied around him to

[43] *Wisconsin State Journal*, April 10 to May 9, 1862; E. B. Quiner:
Military History of Wisconsin, pp. 117–20; *Official Records*, series 3,
II, 23.

[44] *Official Records*, series 3, II, 48–9.

demand efficiency and financial support from the War Department.[45]

At the same moment that Salomon insisted upon administrative efficiency, Governor Andrew demanded a clarifica-
tion of war aims. General David Hunter, commanding the
Department of the South, had issued a proclamation emanci-
pating slaves in Georgia, Florida, and South Carolina. This
was going further than Frémont, some months earlier,
had gone in Missouri. Lincoln had revoked Frémont's order,
and radicals generally expected that he would repudiate
Hunter's. Andrew, however, hoped to take advantage of
Lincoln's new need for troops to force the President to uphold Hunter's proclamation.

"If our people feel that they are going into the South to
help fight rebels who will kill and destroy them by all the
means known to savages . . ." Andrew replied to Stanton's
request for information, "while they themselves must never
'fire at the magazine,' I think they will feel that the draft is
heavy on their patriotism." But, added the Governor, "if the
President will sustain General Hunter, recognize all men,
even black men, as legally capable of that loyalty the blacks
are willing to manifest, and let them fight, with God and
human nature on their side, the roads will swarm, if need
be, with multitudes whom New England would pour out to
obey your call." [46]

Lincoln, however, had no intention of yielding to radical
pressure. On May 19, 1862, the day of Andrew's truculent
letter, the President proclaimed that Hunter had acted without authority. The question of freeing slaves, said the President, "I reserve to myself." [47]

The Democrats lost no time in expressing their horror at
Andrew's threat. Copperhead Sam Medary rejoiced that at
last the abolitionists had been forced to show their colors.

[45] *Official Records,* series 3, II, 61, 69, 81, 90, 96, 106, 110–11, 143.
[46] Ibid., II, 45.
[47] Nicolay and Hay: *Lincoln,* VI, 94–5; *Official Records,* series 3,
II, 42–3.

"Here is the secret of the conduct of the Republicans for the last year," he announced, and he called on Ohio's Governor Tod to demand that Lincoln state what the war was for. Even in Massachusetts, Democrats cried out against Andrew. Boston's Democratic Mayor Wightman promptly wrote Lincoln that Andrew did not speak for Massachusetts, that Bostonians did not want emancipation, and that enlistments would fall off only if Andrew's views prevailed.[48]

But Stanton secretly gave encouragement to Andrew. "I am not disturbed," he assured the Governor, "by the howling of those who are at your heels and mine." [49]

While Andrew and Salomon engaged in argument with the War Department, Stonewall Jackson's foot cavalry lashed the Union forces in the Shenandoah Valley and panic seized Washington again.

"Send all the troops forward that you can immediately," Stanton frantically wired the governors. Militia, volunteers, home guards — everything — and in companies, even squads, if there are no regiments. "Banks is completely routed. The enemy are in large force advancing upon Harper's Ferry." [50]

Before the governors had a chance to respond, the scare in Washington passed as suddenly as it had come. Banks crossed the Potomac safely, the capital breathed easier, and Stanton changed his mind about needing the militia. He had concentrated enough men, he believed, to "capture the enemy."

But he urged the governors to continue to raise three-year volunteers.[51] The governors tried hard. Their citizens, however, had developed an immunity to patriotic appeals, and some other inducement than oratory was needed. Andrew pleaded with Stanton to allow two dollars a head to recruiting agents and to give one month's pay as a bounty to the troops.[52] Kirkwood asked the Iowa counties to provide

---

[48] *Columbus Crisis*, May 28, June 25, 1862.
[49] *Official Records*, series 3, II, 93–4.
[50] Ibid., II, 68, 70.
[51] Ibid., II, 85, 88.
[52] Ibid., II, 97–8, 100.

relief for soldiers' families. Other governors talked about a draft.[53] Responding to pressure, Congress authorized a two-dollar premium and a month's advance pay, and Stanton immediately notified the governors.[54]

Late in June, in the midst of the apathy, came McClellan's defeat before Richmond. Lincoln, Stanton, and Seward were even more alarmed than before, but experience had taught them that their own panic was no longer a stimulus to recruiting. They had cried "wolf" too often, and they must try other tactics. Believing he needed fresh troops, Lincoln told Seward: "I would publicly appeal for this new force were it not that I fear a general panic and stampede would follow, so hard it is to have a thing understood as it really is." [55]

So saying, Lincoln proposed to put a new face on the matter. There was victory in the West — at Donelson, Shiloh, Corinth, and New Orleans — and the only substantial force of the enemy was in the East. If the Western army were moved east, the Confederates would abandon Richmond and retake Kentucky and Tennessee. If the force at Washington were sent to McClellan, Washington would fall. Therefore, said Lincoln, the country should send another 100,000 men — for the shortest possible time — who could immediately aid McClellan and promptly end the war.

Armed with this new view, Seward, who had not previously been identified with panic, prepared to approach the governors. On June 28 he left for New York, wiring ahead for Governor Morgan and Thurlow Weed to meet him at the Astor House. June 30, 1862, with Curtin also present, Seward laid before them the scheme that Lincoln had devised. The governors should demand that the President call for more — 150,000 more — troops to grasp the victory that was already within reach. Seward showed them the memorial

---

[53] Shannon: *Union Armies,* II, 58.
[54] *Official Records,* series 3, II, 191, 206–7.
[55] Ibid., II, 180.

they were to sign and the reply Lincoln would make to their appeal.

Morgan was skeptical. Without a bounty, he did not believe the troops could be raised. Seward promptly wired Stanton to ask for money. The next day Stanton agreed to advance twenty-five dollars to recruits from the hundred-dollar bounty they were to receive at the end of their service. It was illegal, said the Secretary of War, but he would take the responsibility.

Meantime Seward and Morgan were telegraphing to the other governors. Seventeen replied promptly, and Seward sent the memorial to Stanton for him to issue it. But Stanton noted that Andrew had not signed — nor had Sprague or Kirkwood, who had not been reached. Stanton refused to issue the memorial until Andrew had consented.

Andrew had not signed because he, like his radical colleague Stanton, was suspicious of anything that came from such moderates as Seward, Morgan, and Lincoln. He was holding strongly for a program of freeing and arming the South's slaves, and he saw in this move only a trick to disarm the radical Republicans.

"With the utmost respect for the gentlemen interested in memorializing the president," he informed Morgan, "I cannot put my humble name to a paper unseen." Anyhow, he added, without a bounty of twenty-five dollars a new appeal for troops would be futile.

With Andrew and Stanton holding up the memorial, Seward journeyed to Boston and saw the Governor personally. Whatever Andrew may have thought, he could only make the best of the situation. On July 2 he consented to sign, and Stanton, reassured that his radical ally would not suffer from discrimination, released to the press the governors' letter and Lincoln's reply. The fictitious interchange was dated back to June 28.

The next day Lincoln called on the governors for 300,000 volunteers for three years. The new figure was double the one Seward had used with the governors and three times the

President's original estimate. Stanton, however, had insisted on 300,000, and Lincoln had yielded. But, as if to keep the governors from smarting too much under the trick, Lincoln privately informed them that "it was thought safest to mark it high enough." He explained, however: "I should not want the half of 300,000 new troops if I could have them now. If I had 50,000 additional troops here now, I believe I could substantially close the war in two weeks." [56]

The replies of the governors to this explanatory statement were outwardly co-operative if not enthusiastic. Washburn reported that recruiting for three-year men was "terribly hard." Andrew and Olden proposed calling militia. Buckingham issued a war-cry for Connecticut's men to rally once again. Seward and an assistant in the War Department interviewed the Western governors at Cleveland and got promises of support. [57]

But from the day of Lincoln's call the spirit was changed. Although the forms of states' rights remained intact, the substance was altered. The new regiments still bore the names of the states, and the soldiers still heard orations on muster day from the governors, but the new army was, in reality, a national army. Abraham Lincoln had taken control.

The new order was reflected in the changed attitude of the governors. On July 7, 1862 Stanton assigned quotas to the states. [58] In earlier days the governors had complained that they were not asked for enough; now they thought the assessments too high. Massachusetts complained about the regular army officers who came to muster in the troops and began to demand bands in the camps and floors in the tents. [59] In Illinois, Yates issued a flamboyant call for the people to

---

[56] *Official Records,* series 3, II, 179–86, 198, 200–1; Nicolay and Hay: *Lincoln,* VI, 117–19, VII, 3; Shannon: *Union Armies,* I, 269–71; Pearson: *Andrew,* II, 29 f.; G. W. Smith: "Generative Forces of Union Propaganda," Ch. iv; Seward: *Seward at Washington,* II, 103.

[57] *Official Records,* series 3, II, 202–6.

[58] Ibid., II, 208.

[59] Ibid., II, 209.

"rally once again for the old flag, for our country, Union and Liberty," [60] but he immediately began to complain that his quota was too large and that the state ought to have credit for her citizens in Missouri regiments.[61] Almost with one accord the governors reported that recruiting was slow and demanded a bounty.[62]

The solution for the problem was simple: only a draft would fill the ranks. The governors made the suggestion, but — with full knowledge of the political consequences — they proposed that the national government take the responsibility.[63] On August 4, 1862 the President called on the governors for 300,000 militia to serve nine months, and ordered the governors to draft from the militia to fill any gaps in the other call for 300,000 volunteers. The date set for the militia draft was August 15 — a bare eleven days away! The President was exerting pressure upon the governors.[64]

Troubles quickly followed. The governors did not question the President's authority to order a draft — which was of dubious legality — nor did they object when Stanton — with equal lack of authority — determined that, in the counting, one three-year volunteer was the equivalent of four nine-month militiamen. Instead the governors protested at the time allowed, and, citing many a dubious figure, they argued with the War Department over the proper quotas. The people protested, too. There were draft riots in Wisconsin, and threats of riots in Pennsylvania. Yielding to pressure, Stanton permitted the governors to postpone the draft — first for a month, and then indefinitely.[65]

[60] Eddy: *Patriotism of Illinois*, I, 121–3.

[61] W. A. J. Russel to Yates, July 19, 1862, Yates MSS.

[62] *Official Records*, series 3, II, 265 ff.

[63] Ibid., II, 289, 290.

[64] Ibid., II, 291.

[65] Shannon: *Union Armies*, I, 272, 277, II, 55–7; Davis: *Pennsylvania Politics*, pp. 256–8; *Official Records*, series 3, II, 204, 208, 210–11, 212–13, 223, 232–51, 265 f., 269, 280–2, 290, 291, 316–20, 350–69, III, 420, 592; Ohio Executive Records, MSS. Box 208, 212; *Wisconsin*

Under the combined operation of these two calls, the states raised 421,465 volunteers and 87,558 militia. By equating, on Stanton's four-to-one basis, the volunteers and militiamen, the states — with some serious inequalities between them — more than met the demand under both calls.[66] The threat of the draft and the promise of the bounty proved more effective in raising men than the pleas of the governors and the periodic panics in Washington.

The draft and the new levies weighed heavily upon the war-weary people and the harassed governors. More and more of them began to listen to another proposal for getting men to meet the military's endless demands. Governor Andrew, growing worried as he saw the best youth of Massachusetts slain on the battlefield, turned plaintively to Senator Sumner. "Is not a Negro, good enough for them," he asked, "good enough for us?"[67]

"Shall we love the Negro so much," echoed Horace Greeley in the *New York Tribune,* "that we lay down our lives to save his?"[68]

Indignantly, Governor Yates wrote to his constituent in the White House that "sterner measures" were needed. The government, said the Illinois Governor, should use every available means to crush the rebellion. "Summon to the standard of the Republic all willing to fight for the Union. Let loyalty, and that alone, be the dividing line between the nation and its foes."[69] And although the Democratic press of Illinois sneered that Yates suffered from "a combination of Negro and whiskey on the brain,"[70] the state's Republicans echoed their Governor's words.[71]

State Journal, July 19, 1862; February 10, 1863; Moore: *Michigan,* I, 422; *Columbus Crisis,* July 30, 1862.

[66] *Official Records,* series 3, II, 188, IV, 72–3.

[67] Pearson: *Andrew,* II, 23–4.

[68] *New York Tribune,* July 10, 11, 1862.

[69] *Official Records,* series 3, II, 218.

[70] *Chicago Times,* July 12, 1862.

[71] *Illinois State Journal,* July 14, 15, 17, 1862.

Governor Kirkwood was more direct. He said he wanted, when the war was over, some dead niggers as well as dead white men.[72] Governor Andrew appealed to Heaven's judgment. He told a Methodist camp meeting that he had noticed that, from the day Lincoln had repudiated Hunter's order, "the blessing of God" had been "withdrawn from our arms." [73]

Yet Lincoln was unmoved by these pleas to use the black men to save the whites. He discussed it with his cabinet, and he permitted commanders in the field to employ Negro laborers, but he refused to permit Governors Salomon and Sprague to organize Negro regiments.[74]

Since Lincoln would not budge, and since the necessity of using Negro troops pressed heavily, the radicals among the governors began to consult together. Andrew wrote to Curtin, and Yates wrote Salomon, proposing that the governors meet, confer, and concert their action.[75] The most extreme among them hoped to withhold troops until Lincoln agreed to replace the conservative McClellan with the radical Frémont and organize Negroes to fight the war. The governors agreed to meet at Altoona, Pennsylvania, on September 23, 1862.

Though they could not yet foresee it, this meeting was doomed to fail. Beneath the forms of states' rights the substance of national power had grown strong. With infinite patience Father Abraham was guiding the writing of Destiny's childlike hand.

[72] D. E. Clark: *S. J. Kirkwood, passim.*

[73] Pearson: *Andrew,* II, 44 ff.

[74] Nicolay and Hay: *Lincoln,* VI, 125, 462; *Official Records,* series 3, II, 297, 314, 397. Pierpont to Lincoln, June 20, 1862, Sprague to Lincoln, September 26, 1862, R. T. Lincoln MSS.

[75] Salomon to Yates, September 11, 1862, Yates MSS.

Chapter 11

Border State Policies and the Radicals

URING these months while Abraham Lincoln watched the governors' failure to raise troops, he watched with equal care and an even more practiced eye over the course of political events. In the beginning the Republican Party had had neither organization nor positive program. From 1854 to 1860 it had been a coalescence of contradictions, relying on state organizations, without national unity. In 1860, Democratic discords had elevated Lincoln to the White House, but neither the Republican Party nor the electorate handed him a mandate. After the inauguration radical governors had demanded war upon the South, while Douglas Democrats, moderate Republicans, and Bell and Everett Constitutional Union men had proposed compromise. Fort Sumter brought war — and for the first time the Republican Party had a positive national program.

Yet a war for the mere preservation of the Union did not satisfy the radical elements among the Republicans. The radicals, and the industrial and financial groups who backed them, looked forward to the complete destruction of the Southern economic system and the South's political power. Correctly they had identified slavery as the keystone of the Southern system, and they consistently directed their efforts to destroy the keystone. Their first task was to gain control of their party and of the government. Their greatest obstacle, whom they must either convert or circumvent, was Abraham Lincoln.

Immediately after Sumter, Republican politicians raised the cry that party politics must be stilled for the duration of the war. Insisting that opposition was treason, Governor Morton told the Indiana legislature that every man must take a position for or against his country, and he recommended the immediate passage of a law defining treason against the state.[1] Olden of New Jersey issued a proclamation denouncing traitors in his state,[2] Randall warned against disorders in Wisconsin,[3] and Yates instructed the Illinois legislature that the time had come "to crush treason wherever it raises its unsightly head." Curtin of Pennsylvania thought the rebellion's leaders were insane to expect success from a divided North, and Kirkwood sent word to Lincoln that there was but one party in Iowa.[4]

The politicians, talking bravely of unity, were reassured by the attitude of financiers and businessmen. Before Sumter many old, conservative banking houses had favored compromise and deplored the economic dislocations of war. But once war was upon them, they responded with patriotic zeal. Governors appealed to the legislatures for bond issues, and the banks promptly subscribed to state securities.[5] Senator

---

[1] William M. French: *Life, Speeches, State Papers and Public Services of Governor Oliver P. Morton*, pp. 154 f.; Charles M. Walker: *Sketch of the Life, Character and Public Services of Oliver P. Morton*, pp. 56–65; *Indiana Adjutant General's Report, 1861*, p. 8; William Foulke, *Life of Oliver P. Morton*, I, 118–19.

[2] *New York Times*, April 29, 1861; *Appleton's American Annual Cyclopædia and Register of Important Events of the Years 1861–5*, I, (1861), 516–17.

[3] E. B. Quiner: *The Military History of Wisconsin*, p. 47.

[4] *New York Times*, April 29, 1861; William Henry Engle: *Andrew Gregg Curtin: His Life and Services*, pp. 125–6; *Official Records*, series 3, I, 86–7.

[5] Cf., for example, French: *Morton*, pp. 134 f.; *New York Times*, April 29, May 1, 1861; William E. Smith: *The Francis Preston Blair*

W. P. Fessenden reported to Secretary Cameron that he had been surprised and gratified to find "that our most cautious and money-loving men say that now is the time to establish our Government upon a permanent basis." Blood shed to ensure such an establishment "is well shed." The only fear, reported the Senator, was that the Government would "stop short of its whole duty." The business community was afraid that "when the work is half done . . . parties will spring up . . . urging a compromise or something short of entire subjugation."

"This," said the men of business, "would be a betrayal of the cause of social order." [6] This, said the radicals, must not happen — and in Indiana they organized a "vigilance committee" to look after the "political morals" of the legislature and of the press and to see that there was no slump in patriotism.[7] In Cincinnati a mob threatened the office of the Democrats' *Inquirer,* and in Chicago a vigilance committee threatened the *Times.*[8]

This general harmony of patriotic businessmen and enthusiastic politicians was marred by discords in southern Illinois. Hardly had the echoes from Fort Sumter's guns penetrated Egypt when Governor Dick Yates began to hear stories of rioting and threats. Democrats, reported one anonymous observer, "say they are going to help Jeff Davis & others say they are going to hang cut throt and shoot every Republican in egypt." [9] Soon the Governor had reports of hog-stealing, horse-stealing, and depredation on Republicans' property. One man complained that he had been run out of a post office, another explained at length how a mob besieged his store until "I hawled down my countrys flag with an akeing heart." Companies were forming for the

---

Family in Politics, II, 55–6; Engle: *Curtin,* p. 453; *Harper's Magazine,* April 1861; G. G. Benedict: *Vermont in the Civil War,* I, 23–6.

  [6] *Official Records,* series 3, I, 181–2, May 9, 1861.

  [7] Foulke: *Morton,* I, 123.

  [8] *Chicago Times,* April 18, 26, 1861.

  [9] Richard Yates, MSS., April 16, 1861.

Confederate army in Egypt, said the panic-stricken Republicans, and the "Golden Circle of Knights," a Southern secret society, was actively organizing Democrats.[10]

While Republicans, especially those in Egypt, professed alarm at these conditions, Democratic observers saw no cause for excitement. The *Chicago Times* did not believe the situation serious, but warned the Illinois legislature to follow a moderate and conciliatory course. A soldier reported from Cairo that the Egyptian disaffection was a mere rumor and there was no armed secessionist in the region. The *Times* concluded that the Republican fervor of patriotism did not "assuage their party hatred of Democrats, or modify their patent right for lying." [11]

Governor Yates, however, had few critical capacities and little basis for making judgments. He believed the stories from Egypt, but he saw in them an excuse for coercion rather than an opportunity for political conciliation. He urged the federal government to send troops to Cairo, and importuned General Frémont in St. Louis to keep a consignment of troops there.[12] But the radical Governor made no effort to deny that it was his and Lincoln's intention "to pursue this war until the last dollar of money and the last drop of blood at the command of the administration are exhausted." [13]

Opportunity for conciliation came to the Governor within a few weeks. Stephen A. Douglas, Senator from Illinois, died on June 3. The "Little Giant" had held Lincoln's hat at the

[10] Letters from H. D. Brigham (Pana, Ill.), April 24; G. Wright (Mason), April 19, 25; T. G. Aleen (Chester), April 19; Rev. O. M. Lee (Red Bank), May 2; Lucinda Moss (Cameron), May 21; James M. Eaton (South America), May 3; Patrick H. Lang (Marion), May 28; A. C. Clayton, April 20; Parker Earle and Charles Colby (Cobden), April 21; T. M. Seawell, April 23; G. Garland, April 23; J. N. Merill (Neponset), June 4; W. R. Welkinson, June 6, 1861, etc., to Yates, Yates MSS.

[11] *Chicago Times*, April 18, 19, 25, 26, 1861.

[12] Yates to Frémont, August 1, 1861, Yates MSS.

[13] A. C. Clayton to Yates, April 20, 1861, Yates MSS.

inauguration ceremonies and had supported his old rival's policies before and after Sumter. As leader of the opposition party his support had been invaluable, and his death brought immediate demands that Governor Yates select a "Douglas Democrat" for Douglas's Senate seat. Letters poured in to Dick Yates — some pleading for a broad conciliatory policy, some insisting that only a staunch Republican should fill the vacancy. "Soon the old Democratic leaders will have a new compromise and they'll sell us out," warned one adviser, who added that Yates might remove some rival aspirant for the governorship by sending him to the Senate. Some advisers urged that the "Old Whig" element in the Republican Party needed representation — but it occurred to no one to suggest that Lincoln might be consulted. In the end Yates passed over David Davis, who had managed Lincoln's nomination, and over Swett, and Scammon, and Koerner, and Judd — all good Republicans and all "in the family way, too" — to select Orville H. Browning, an old-time Whig.[14] When protests came from one disgruntled observer, Yates snarled back: "I . . . say to you to mind your own business . . . you are guilty of meanness and falsehood — and I would thank you not to trouble me with your silly advice." [15]

But however much Dick Yates's proscriptive partisanship might have pleased his fellow radicals, the Illinoisian in the White House would follow no such policy. Lincoln was acutely conscious of the necessity for holding Yates's neighbors in Missouri and Kentucky — as well as his own in western Virginia, Delaware, and Maryland — in the Union. The radical program of war had already precipitated the upper South into the Confederacy: only a belated conciliatory movement and skillful political manipulation would pre-

[14] Letters from J. G. Pettyjohn, June 3; I. M. Know; "Twenty Soldiers," June 6; R. F. Adams, June 5; H. S. Thomas, June 7; C. Storrs, June 7; and others to Yates, Yates MSS.

[15] Yates to Hunter, June 18, 1861, Yates MSS.

vent the border slave states from following them. "I think," explained the President, "to lose Kentucky is nearly . . . to lose the whole game. Kentucky gone, we cannot hold Missouri, nor, as I think, Maryland. These all against us, and the job on our hands is too large for us. We would as well consent to separation at once, including the surrender of this capital." [16]

Kentucky's position as the Civil War approached was clear: neither Governor Beriah Magoffin nor a majority of the people wanted their state to become a dark and bloody battleground. Since Henry Clay, Kentucky had contributed repeated compromise proposals to the nation, and her senior Senator, John J. Crittenden, had pleaded unsuccessfully that secession be met by new adjustments. Even at the last moments, as Lincoln called for warriors, Governor Magoffin had sought to enlist Morton's and Dennison's support for a new negotiation.

Governor Magoffin's own sympathies were with the South. His legislature, however, was pro-union. The people of the state and their political leaders divided so sharply on the issues that they approved Magoffin's declaration that Kentucky would remain neutral. Kentucky's unionists, as unwilling as the Governor to engage in war, extracted assurances from Lincoln that he had no intentions of sending troops through the state.[17]

Neighboring governors, however, were eager to exert military pressure on the Kentuckians. Always a combination of alarmist and plotter, O. P. Morton sent spies into Kentucky to watch the secessionists, demanded that Secretary Cameron defend the Ohio River, and smuggled arms to any violence-seeking unionist who would receive them.[18] Then, having invited Dennison and Yates to Indianapolis, he

[16] *Writings of Abraham Lincoln*, V, 364.

[17] E. Merton Coulter: *The Civil War and Readjustment in Kentucky*, pp. 80 ff.

[18] French: *Morton*, pp. 188 f.

united with them in demanding that Lincoln take forcible possession of prominent points in Kentucky and along the railroads leading to the South. This, they said, would relieve the border, stop Confederates from recruiting, and save the Union.[19]

But Lincoln was not to be swept away by impassioned promises. He calmly told Morton that neutrality was at the moment the best Kentucky's unionists hoped for, and explained he was "not anxious to multiply our enemies." He suggested, however, that Morton might stop Indiana citizens from selling arms and provisions to Kentucky.[20] With equal patience Lincoln remained quiet when Magoffin told his legislature that the President was guilty of usurpation. The legislature, however, pleased Lincoln more. Although it did not reject neutrality — and Magoffin issued a formal neutrality proclamation — it passed a military bill creating a home guard and a board of military commissioners. This unconstitutional act effectively removed Magoffin's military power and took men away from General Simon Buckner's pro-Southern state militia.[21]

Meantime, Lincoln gave cautious encouragement to the unionists. He sent his old friend Joshua Speed into the state and posted Colonel Robert Anderson, wearing his fresh laurels from Sumter, at Cincinnati to enlist Kentuckians among the three-year volunteers.[22] On June 20, 1861 the President's policy bore fruit when congressional elections returned nine unionist representatives to one secessionist. Two weeks later, unionists won a three-fourths majority in the state legislature. Then Lincoln took another careful step and established Camp Dick Robinson in eastern Kentucky, with Thomas Bramlette in command.[23]

[19] *New York Times,* May 15, 1861; Foulke: *Morton,* I, 140–1; Whitelaw Reid: *Ohio in the War,* I, 38.

[20] *Official Records,* series 3, I, 158.

[21] Nicolay and Hay: *Abraham Lincoln,* IV, 235 ff.

[22] Ibid., IV, 238; *Official Records,* series 1 (part 1), p. 140.

[23] Coulter: *Civil War and Readjustment in Kentucky,* pp. 103–4.

As Governor Magoffin saw the war creeping nearer, he resolved on one more move to save his state. Late in August he sent two commissioners to Washington to protest against troops being raised and quartered in Kentucky. The troops, said the Governor, imperiled the peace the people desired. But Lincoln, emboldened by events, would make no more promises to Magoffin's commissioners. He replied that the troops were there at the urgence of loyal citizens, and he regretted that the Governor did not show more solicitude for preserving the Union.[24]

Thereafter, both Lincoln and the unionists grew bolder. Morton, who had constituted himself the special mentor for Kentucky, continued to watch events and to encourage Kentucky's unionists. Early in October he suddenly screamed that the Confederate General Zollicoffer had "invaded" Kentucky with a determination to subjugate the loyal people, and "seize for plunder and vengeance the wealthy and populous cities on the border of Ohio and Indiana." So saying, he called on Indianans to "stand by Kentucky in her hour of peril," drive out the invader, and carry the war into the heart of the rebel states.[25]

A few days later Ulysses S. Grant, who had been watching from Cairo, crossed over the river and seized Paducah. Already the Confederate Leonidas Polk had taken Columbus. With these events, the last semblance of Kentucky's neutrality was gone. Yet even then the Union's hold on Kentucky was precarious and Lincoln felt constrained to check his Mortons and keep a wary eye on Kentucky sentiment.

With Kentucky's neighbors in western Virginia, however, the President strangely showed no concern. He may have

[24] Nicolay and Hay: *Lincoln*, IV, 240–244; *New York Times*, August 20, 1861; *Appleton's Cyclopædia*, p. 398; Tyler Dennett: *Lincoln and the Civil War in the Diaries and Letters of John Hay* (hereafter referred to as Hay), p. 25.

[25] Walker: *Morton*, p. 71.

bargained, as critics later claimed, with Virginians not to relieve Sumter in return for Virginia's rejection of a secession ordinance,[26] but he sent the expedition and abided the certain consequences. Virginia seceded. Yet when disgruntled unionists from the western counties assembled in Wheeling to begin a movement for "restoring" a "loyal" government, the President gave them no notice. He accepted, and tolerated — and sometimes used — Francis H. Pierpont's nebulous state, but he took no direct part in promoting the Union cause in western Virginia.

It was Ohio's Governor Dennison who encouraged West Virginia's separatist movement. When the leaders of Virginia's mountain counties, refusing to follow the eastern Virginians into the Confederacy, assembled at Wheeling, Dennison sent a messenger to promise military aid. Secretary of the Treasury Chase gave his blessing to this promise and urged Dennison to station Ohio troops just across the river from Wheeling.[27] From Pennsylvania came Curtin's approval and an agreement to act with the Ohio executive in supporting western Virginians,[28] and Dennison advised General George B. McClellan, commanding the Department of the Ohio, to be ready to invade Virginia.[29] When the unionists called for help, McClellan crossed the river with Ohio's troops, routed the feeble Confederate forces, and supported the "loyal" Virginia government.[30]

Still without Lincoln's approval, but with Dennison's and McClellan's support, the unionists declared the western counties of Virginia loyal, denounced eastern Virginia as schismatic, and selected new men to fill the "vacant" state

[26] John Minor Botts Testimony, February 15, 1866, *Report of the Joint Committee on Reconstruction*, 1866, part 2, pp. 114–23.

[27] Reid: *Ohio*, I, 39; Chase to Dennison, April 30, 1861, Ohio Executive Records, MSS. Box 198.

[28] *New York Times*, May 15, 1861.

[29] Reid: *Ohio*, I, 47–8.

[30] John Campbell to Dennison, May 27, 1861, Ohio Executive Records, MSS. Box 199: *McClellan's Own Story*, pp. 50–3.

offices.[31] In July, Tennessee's "loyal" Andrew Johnson presented two new Virginia senators for the state's vacant seats.[32] Their credentials bore the signature of Francis H. Pierpont, Governor.

The new Governor of loyal Virginia was a native of the western counties who had spent all of his forty-seven years in the state. As a lawyer, coal operator, and dealer in firebricks and leather he had accumulated wealth. A Whig in politics, he had followed Henry Clay and given full endorsement to the American system. His Wisconsin-born wife had abolitionist leanings, and her influence confirmed Pierpont's own antislavery attitudes. All together he was well fitted to represent the anti-Southern, conservative interests of western Virginia. Abraham Lincoln was to find him a reliable — but by no means brilliant — supporter of the moderate elements in the Union.[33]

Although Lincoln could afford to remain indifferent to the unionist movement in western Virginia, he could not neglect Maryland. He endorsed the actions of the military authorities and, ignoring Chief Justice Taney's protests, suspended the writ of habeas corpus. When radicals applauded such vigorous acts and proposed "the same wholesome regimen" for the rest of the South, the administration stationed its armies of occupation throughout the state.[34]

Faced with the facts of military occupation, Governor Hicks abandoned his earlier vacillation. Relying on the support of the federal government, he parted company with his legislature, deprived the state militia of its arms, and refused to answer legislative queries about his acts. When the legislature asked what he had done to prevent the arbitrary arrest of some of its members, the Governor replied

[31] Charles H. Ambler: *Francis H. Pierpont, Union War Governor of Virginia and Father of West Virginia*, pp. 117–35.

[32] *Congressional Globe*, 37th Congress, 1st Session, pp. 103 f.

[33] Ambler: *Pierpont*, pp. 1 ff., 74–6, 117–30.

[34] Matthew Page Andrews: *History of Maryland: Province and State*, pp. 520–3; *New York Times*, April 29, 1861.

that he had no official information about it. But when unionists from the Eastern Shore organized military companies to deal with their secessionist neighbors, Hicks urged Cameron to furnish them arms.[35]

By September the hostility between the Governor, favoring the administration, and his querulous, anti-Lincoln legislature had produced a high degree of hysteria in Washington. Finally General McClellan proposed that several anti-administration leaders and some members of the legislature be arrested, and Cameron, with the approval of Lincoln and Hicks, ordered enough legislators seized to prevent the passage of resolutions of secession. The military arrested members of the legislature, set a non-English-speaking Wisconsin regiment to guard them, and held them prisoners until after the November elections.[36] Lincoln refused to be questioned on the matter: "the public safety renders it necessary that the grounds of the arrests should at present be withheld," he declared — but he denied that either "personal or partisan animosity" had motivated the federal forces.

In the meantime Maryland's unionists held a convention and nominated Augustus Williamson Bradford for governor. The candidate was an old-line Whig who had retired from active politics when Henry Clay was defeated in 1844, and who had been clerk of the Baltimore County court for many years. He had emerged as a unionist at the peace conference in Willard's Hall, where he made a strong pro-union speech.[37] Personally honest, making up in dignity what he lacked in distinction, Bradford was too moderate for many Maryland

[35] William L. Seabrook: *Maryland's Great Part in Saving the Union,* p. 38; George L. P. Radcliffe: *Governor Thomas H. Hicks of Maryland and the Civil War,* pp. 30, 89–100; Hicks to Cameron, August 28 and September 3, *Official Records,* series 3, I, 463, 480–1; *Congressional Globe,* 37th Congress, 1st Session, p. 42.

[36] Radcliffe: *Hicks,* pp. 100–16; John M. Brewer: *Prison Life,* pp. 1–5; *Appleton's Annual Cyclopædia, 1861,* p. 448.

[37] Heinrich Ewald Buchholz: *Governors of Maryland from the Revolution to the Year 1908,* pp. 178 ff.

radicals. Their support, however, was hardly necessary for his election.

The federal troops decided the Maryland election. Maryland soldiers received a three-day furlough to go home to vote, and when unionists feared that this would not be enough to turn the scale, General Dix ordered the provost marshals to arrest any disunionists or Southern sympathizers. On election day the soldiers guarded the polls, arresting known Democrats and intimidating others. Bradford won by a majority of 31,438 over General Benjamin H. Howard, his Democratic opponent.[38] "I am persuaded," came an encouraging echo from Kentucky, "that the only way these polluted and demoralized are to be brought to a *de facto* loyalty is by vigorous and even violent measures." [39]

Promptly after the election Hicks summoned into special session the newly elected, and now thoroughly unionist, legislature. The legislators approved the war, voted $7,000 for the families of Massachusetts men killed in the Baltimore riots, and approved Hicks's acts. As soon as Bradford was inaugurated, the legislature rewarded Hicks's unionism by sending him to the Senate.

In the meantime, as Kentucky, Maryland, and western Virginia were being saved for the Union, Lincoln, Yates, and the Blairs were snatching Missouri from the Confederacy. In sharp contrast to the situation in Maryland, where the full force of federal power was felt, events in Missouri brought the rival doctrines of states' rights and nationalism into sharp focus. In establishing a "loyal" government in Missouri, the unionists used the very state convention which had been called — under the best theories of states' rights — to take Missouri out of the Union. Lincoln, whose prac-

[38] John Thomas Scharf: *History of Maryland from the Earliest Period to the Present Day*, III, 456–9; Radcliffe: *Hicks*, pp. 116–17; Buchholz: *Governors of Maryland*, pp. 180–1.

[39] George Morrison to Bradford, November 18, 1861, Bradford MSS.

ticality surmounted paradoxes, did not even deign to notice the theoretical discrepancies underlying his different acts.

After General Nathaniel Lyon, on May 10, 1861, captured the militia encamped in St. Louis, the pro-Southern legislature passed a bill creating a new state militia of 50,000 men. Governor Jackson then sought an interview with General Lyon and proposed to disband the paper militia in return for a recognition of the state's neutrality. Lyon refused, and Jackson returned to Jefferson City to issue a call for the 50,000 to help drive the usurping federal troops from the state. Lyon proceeded to march slowly toward the capitol, seizing railroads and telegraphs as he went, and arresting a number of pro-Southern leaders. As he approached Jefferson City, Jackson hurriedly left, and the legislature peaceably, albeit precipitously, adjourned. Jackson repeated his call, and moved quickly southwest toward the Oklahoma and Arkansas border. Lyon moved into Jefferson City and reconvened the Missouri convention.[40]

From neighboring Illinois, Governor Richard Yates watched these events with increasing anxiety. When the Missouri legislature provided for a militia, Yates hurriedly sent John A. McClernand, long a leading Democratic politician, to Washington with a message to Lincoln. Illinois was in danger, cried Yates as he proposed sending Illinois troops to sustain Missouri's loyalists.[41] Moreover, the Governor urged Cameron to permit him to enlist more cavalry and artillery, for, he explained, "we want to be fully ready to take the starch out of the Missouri secession chivalry." [42]

Whereas Illinois troops were used in the campaign that resulted in clearing Missouri of organized secession forces, Governor Yates took no hand in reorganizing the Missouri

[40] Buel Leopard and Floyd C. Shoemaker: *The Messages and Proclamations of the Governors of the State of Missouri*, III, 324–5; *New York Times*, May 25, June 14, 16, 24, 1861.

[41] Yates to Lincoln, May 15, 1861, McClernand MSS.

[42] *Official Records*, series 3, I, 272.

government. That work was done by the state convention —
the same convention that had assembled in March to consider secession. Although a number of the members had followed Governor Jackson into the Confederacy, a quorum,
dominated by unionists, remained.

If, according to the states' rights theories, a convention
was the sovereign state itself and had power to take a state
from the Union, then, of a certainty, such a body could de-
cree that Governor Jackson and his associates had vacated
their offices. The convention, in theory, could do anything.
In fact, when it met, it proceeded to abrogate the laws of
the recent legislature, declared the state offices vacant, in-
stalled new provisional incumbents, and called for a general
election.[43]

The convention's new provisional Governor was Hamilton R. Gamble, a retired judge who was the brother-in-law
of Attorney General Edward Bates. He had had, in the full
span of Missouri's statehood, intimate experience in the
state's turbulent politics. He had practiced law and politics,
winning wealth in the one and a succession of public offices
in the other. In 1854 he had retired from the state's judiciary
and moved to Pennsylvania. The secession crisis brought
him back to make an effort to "save" Missouri for the Union.
In February 1861 he had been elected to the convention,
and in its first session he had led the conditional unionists
who favored compromise and opposed secession.

Governor Gamble was a fit representative of majority
opinion in Missouri. He was a former Whig who had supported Bell and Everett in the previous November, and he
had no use for the radical "Dutch" whom the Blairs were
organizing in St. Louis.[44] He believed in slavery and disap-
proved of Lincoln's policies. Although the provisional Governor expected to hold office only until November, he could
not bring sufficient order into the state to warrant holding

[43] Sceva Bright Laughlin: *Missouri Politics during the Civil War,*
pp. 55–6.
[44] Nicolay and Hay: *Lincoln,* IV, 224 f.

an election. After a month in office he recalled the convention and asked it to provide for a militia and for money for the government. The convention assumed the duties of a legislature, abolished some state offices to save expenses, provided for collecting taxes, passed a militia law, and postponed elections until August 1862.[45]

Proof that Missouri was following a states' rights course came with the organization of the new state troops. Gamble journeyed to Washington and arranged that the militia were to be paid and equipped by the federal government but were not to be used outside Missouri. Lincoln agreed that Gamble might appoint minor officers if the major general of the militia should always be the federal commander of the department. Under this arrangement the Governor raised troops to combat Missouri's secessionist guerrillas.[46]

Such truckling to border-state conservatives won no endorsement from the radicals of the North. Yates and Morton and Dennison preferred to march their armies into the border states and apply the bayonets' quick remedies to secessionists and slaveholders. They were eager, from the beginning, for direct and vigorous action.

"Is this an abolitionist war?" asked the *Chicago Times*[47] as it noticed Yates's partisanship. And the Governor, as if in reply, proclaimed that the war was for the "liberties of mankind." Although it would cost "blood and treasure," it would vindicate the national government. "It will be worth all it ever cost," he asserted, "though the rivers run with blood." Moreover, "if it has no other effect it will relieve our fellow citizens of the taunts of cowardice made by Southern traitors, and reassert the great democratic principle, that a Northern man is, in courage, and in every other respect,

[45] Laughlin: *Missouri Politics*, pp. 62 f.; Leopard and Shoemaker: *Messages*, II, 415–17.

[46] *Writings of Abraham Lincoln*, V, 375–8; *Official Records*, series 3, I, 618–20.

[47] *Chicago Times*, June 19, 1861.

the equal of a Southern man." [48] With such arrant non-sense Dick Yates would evade the question of abolition.

At the same time, in New England, John Andrew was publicly refraining from expressing his antislavery views. On Montgomery Blair's advice to "drop the nigger," the Massachusetts Governor sent a message to his legislature that barely mentioned slavery, but defended the war as "vindicating" the "rights of the people." [49] Privately, however, he was as eager as ever for abolition. Once he sent an agent to Curtin of Pennsylvania asking permission for one of John Brown's sons to recruit secretly a company that would organize a slave insurrection in Virginia. Curtin indignantly refused and ordered the agent from his office. "So far as I am concerned," he asserted, "this war will be conducted only by civilized methods." [50] This rebuff did not long discourage Andrew, and soon his spokesmen were advocating a force in eastern Virginia to arm forty thousand slaves and free Negroes.[51]

But when Ben Butler offered troops to Governor Hicks to suppress slave insurrections, Andrew could contain himself no longer. He vigorously rebuked his old-time adversary — who promptly and enthusiastically replied in kind. He was pledged, said Butler, to put down mobs of all kinds, and he did not propose to let the defenseless women and children of Maryland suffer the horrors of San Domingo.[52]

To Democrats of the old faith, such actions as Andrew's seemed fully to prove that the radicals wanted war only for partisan ends. "These fiendish, impudent, interfering, petty Governors" aroused the ire of old Sam Medary in Ohio,[53] and Democrats generally met the radicals' enthusiasm with

[48] *New York Times,* June 20, 1861.

[49] Henry Greenleaf Pearson: *The Life of John A. Andrew,* I, 249 f.

[50] W. B. Wilson in W. H. Egle (editor): *Andrew Gregg Curtin: His Life and Services,* pp. 347–8.

[51] Boston *Bee and Atlas,* quoted in *New Hampshire Gazette,* May 1, 1861.

[52] P. C. Headley: *Massachusetts in the Rebellion,* p. 131.

[53] *Columbus Crisis,* May 23, 1861.

skepticism. When a preacher piously proclaimed the conflict a "holy war," New Hampshire Democrats recoiled from the "shocking impiety." "Now that they've succeeded in provoking war upon a portion of our people — now that they've inaugurated a war in defense of their party platform, which is sure to result in the destruction of the Union, they are full of joy, full of cheap patriotism." [54] But such a war — "against the constitution and the rights of the states, and a crusade against negro slavery" — the Democrats could not accept.[55]

The hidden conflict between Lincoln and the radicals could not long remain quiet. Lincoln, if he were to save the Union, needed the support of both Democrats and the border states. The radicals wanted neither. Constantly the radicals moaned at Lincoln's lack of "vigor." Finally, with Lincoln's repudiation of Frémont's antislavery proclamation, the radical opposition broke its bounds.

Late in July 1861 Lincoln appointed General John C. Frémont to command in Missouri. The turbulent condition of the state, torn by guerrilla warfare, taxed the resources of the commander and the ingenuity of his brilliant wife. Frémont himself was politically ambitious, harboring resentment against the man who had replaced him at the head of the Republican Party. His friends were eager for contracts, and the odor of corruption soon filled the corridors of his headquarters. Moreover, he quickly earned the hostility of the Blair family, who brought pressure on Lincoln for his removal.

Partly to defeat his enemies in Missouri and partly to recommend himself to the radical element among Republicans, the general issued an order declaring free the slaves of Missouri's secession sympathizers. The order shocked the slaveholding unionists of the border states and confirmed all that Democrats had charged about Republican intentions. From

[54] *New Hampshire Gazette,* April 24, 1861.
[55] *New Hampshire Patriot,* July 3, 1861.

Kentucky came prompt demands for Frémont's head. Hiding his indignation, Lincoln requested Frémont to rescind his order.

But the radicals were overjoyed by this evidence of "vigor," and their applause emboldened the general to refuse Lincoln's request. If the President wanted the order revoked, Frémont told Lincoln, he could do it himself. Promptly the President issued his order recalling both Frémont's proclamation and its author as well. A new general, instructed to be moderate, cautious, and conciliatory, took charge in Missouri.[56]

The martyred Frémont, "sacrificed" on the altar of border-state conservatism, became the darling of the radicals. Morton and Yates agreed that the general's removal was disastrous, and Yates was sure that "the hearts of the soldiers and of the people are with Frémont." [57] Throughout Illinois the incident served to bring the radicals out into the open. The *Rock River Democrat* believed "the principle enunciated in the proclamation will yet have to be adopted by the Government — it is right." Chicago Germans praised Frémont, and Lincoln's law partner, William H. Herndon, declared the President could never "squelch out this rebellion" while preserving slavery.[58] Thereafter the radicals lost no opportunity to change the war into an abolitionist crusade. In the months to come they created a Committee on the Conduct of the War, carried on a persistent crusade for emancipation, built the accidents and incidents of warfare into a heinous catalogue of slaveholding atrocities, and won governors and politicians to the radical cause.

In the meantime, as Lincoln moved cautiously in the border states, the moderates and radicals struggled for control of the Northern states. In the months following Fort Sumter, eight

---

[56] *Writings of Abraham Lincoln*, V, 362–5.

[57] G. Koerner to Yates, September 18, and reply, September 23, 1861, Yates MSS.

[58] Arthur C. Cole: *The Era of the Civil War, 1848–1870*, pp. 292–3.

states held elections for state offices. In the West, Ohio, Wisconsin, Iowa, and Minnesota elected governors and legislators; on the Pacific coast California held state elections, and in New England, Maine, Vermont, and Massachusetts went through their annual routine. In addition, there were minor contests in each of the other states. In each state the radicals sought to proscribe unionists and to commit the Republican Party to abolitionism; yet caution stayed their hand, and where it was necessary they stifled their zeal for emancipation until after the election.

In California the political situation was almost completely unclouded by military events. The people "fiddled," as one correspondent explained, while the nation burned. But, he added, "as we have not hose enough to take our water to the fire, and as we have nothing else to do, why not fiddle?" [59] There were not, as General H. W. Halleck of the militia complained, enough secessionists in California to send a column after.[60]

Such splendid isolation enabled the Californians to give full play to politics. As summer approached and the politicians buckled on their harness, four political parties emerged. The weakest, an "irrespective Union Party," which hoped to unite Bell-Everett and Douglas men, soon found that it was drawing strength only from the Republicans and withdrew from the contest. The others nominated candidates. The Douglas Democrats, professing full support of the war, had to pass up Governor Downey, their strongest candidate. Downey had written a letter opposing the coercion of the Southern states and was therefore vulnerable to Republican attacks. The "Democratic-Union Party" nominated John Conness, an assemblyman who had early jumped

---

[59] *New York Times,* June 26, 1861.

[60] Halleck to General G. W. Cullum, July 18, 1861, Elbridge MSS. Collection. Halleck grieved as well because only politicians got military appointments. "To think of Fremont's being made a Major-General," he exclaimed. "Why, he isn't fit to command a regiment!"

on the union bandwagon. The Breckinridge Democrats, still proclaiming themselves the "true" Democrats, named a candidate on a platform declaring recognition of the Confederacy preferable to war.

The Republicans, confident that the rising union sentiment and the Democratic split would give them the election, saw no reason for raising the abolitionist issue. They nominated Leland Stanford, a lawyer and merchant who had been their candidate two years before. Then he had polled but 10,000 votes in a total of more than 100,000. But in 1860 Lincoln had carried California by a few hundred votes, while his three opponents divided two thirds of the electorate. The Republicans were not disappointed in their hopes: in November Stanford received 56,000 votes to 63,000 almost evenly divided between his opponents. The new moderate Governor was to "fiddle" with local affairs — and to use his position to found his own railroad fortune — rather than carry water to the distant fire.[61]

In Iowa, as in California, the Republicans scorned a union movement and relied on a divided Democracy to re-elect Governor Kirkwood. Although, just after Sumter, the Governor could assure Lincoln that there were no more parties in the state, Iowa Republicans soon found it desirable to force the Democrats to retain their own organization. Democrats, admitted to a union party, would have committed the state to support Lincoln's border-state moderation and have eschewed abolitionism. "I am well satisfied that a large (a very large) proportion of democratic leaders in Iowa are pro-slavery in principle and feeling," declared the radical J. M. Beck to Kirkwood. These were the people who were advocating a "grand Union party," but, said Beck, "they are continually talking of a humane, brotherly and defensive war" and "if a word be said against the evils of slavery, or in favor of slavery restriction, they throw up

[61] *New York Times,* June 25, 26, July 4, 7, 16, 20, 22, 1861; James G. Blaine: *Twenty years of Congress: From Lincoln to Garfield,* I, 308–9.

their hands in horror and charge Republicans with an intention of interfering with the constitutional rights of the South."

"This thing must be averted," he advised, "or we will end by being tied hand and foot to the Philistines." He believed that the rank and file of the Democrats would support the Republicans, and the Democratic ship would founder. "But if we join in union with them our true men will be turned out of positions of public trust . . . and . . . these pro-slavery leaders of the democracy will have the settling of the vital and most important questions which will be brought forth when the rebels are conquered." [62]

In this spirit the Iowa radicals rejected all overtures for a union party, loudly proclaimed the Republicans the only supporters of the Union,[63] and forced Democrats to retain their organization. The Democratic Party promptly succumbed to D. A. Mahoney and the Breckinridge faction. They declared the war a failure and nominated Charles Mason to oppose Kirkwood. The Republicans, their own organization saved by the maneuver, heaped the charge of treason on the Democrats and won an easy victory in November.[64]

In Minnesota and Wisconsin the Republicans, safely radical, saw no need of proscribing Democrats. The Republicans of Minnesota renominated Alexander Ramsey for Governor and re-elected him in November after a quiet campaign.[65] In Wisconsin, however, the Republicans were faced with a somewhat more difficult task. Although Governor Randall

[62] S. H. M. Byers: *Iowa in War Times*, pp. 52 f. *et passim*.

[63] *Chicago Times*, June 4, 1861, noticed that Kirkwood "indignantly spurns every peace measure and whips war measures" through the legislature "under the cry of 'no party' and under the cloak of patriotism."

[64] S. H. M. Byers: *Iowa*, pp. 48–89, 178; H. W. Lathrop: *The Life and Times of Samuel J. Kirkwood*, pp. 127–60; *New York Times*, May 27, July 28, 1861; Dan Elbert Clark: *Samuel Jordon Kirkwood*, pp. 195–7; *Dubuque Hawkeye*, September 4, 9, 26, October 1, 1861.

[65] William Watts Folwell: *A History of Minnesota*, II, 100; *Columbus Crisis*, September 19, 1861.

invoked both the aid of the Almighty ("These gathering armies are the instruments of His vengeance, to execute His judgments — they are His flails, wherewith, on God's great Southern Threshing-Floor, He will pound rebellion for its sins!") [66] and the support of the people, many of his efforts met criticism. The clothing furnished soldiers, said the critics, was inferior, and the Governor had been wasteful and extravagant.[67] Moreover, Randall had won the enmity of the railroads when he refused to turn over state lands to the La Crosse Railroad Company before it had complied with the terms of the grant. In addition he had had difficulty disposing of state bonds in New York, and the state's credit had suffered.[68] After the larger Milwaukee banks had brought riotous mobs upon themselves by refusing to take notes of smaller banks who had invested in Southern states' issues, Randall offered to substitute Wisconsin bonds for those of the seceded states.[69] The Democratic *Chicago Times* denounced him as "certainly an ass." [70] Under such fire Randall sought a military commission, but Lincoln appointed him Minister to Rome.[71]

Cognizant of the criticism and of the difficulties involved, the Republicans of Wisconsin adopted a cautious policy. They nominated Louis P. Harvey, the Secretary of State, for governor, and Edward Salomon for Lieutenant governor. Harvey was one of the most popular men in the state, and during several terms in the state Senate and one in the secretaryship of state he had shown a high efficiency. Moreover, as one journal fondly noted, his name had "never been associated with any dishonorable transactions." [72] Democrats, of course, promptly charged that the Chicago & Northwestern Railroad had nominated him and that he would "sell Mil-

[66] *Wisconsin Daily Patriot,* May 15, 1861.
[67] *Mauston Star,* quoted in *Wisconsin State Journal,* June 6, 1861.
[68] *New York Times,* July 7, 1861.
[69] Ibid., June 26, 1861.
[70] *Chicago Times,* June 29, 1861.
[71] *Wisconsin State Journal,* August 7, September 7, 1861.
[72] Ibid., September 27, 1861.

waukee to Chicago." [73] Edward Salomon was an able lawyer, a German of ten years' residence, a Democrat, and a regent of the university. He was expected to bring the German vote into the Republican fold. In November 1861 he succeeded where Carl Schurz had failed. The Germans gave Harvey a safe majority over Benjamin Ferguson, the Democratic nominee.[74]

In Ohio, too, the mounting criticism of the Governor forced the Republicans to still their abolitionist element and nominate a unionist ticket. Governor Dennison's martial zeal could not long conceal his incompetence, and exaggerated reports of excessive contracts for tin cups, shoddy clothing, and inadequate housing for troops gained universal currency. Admitting that Dennison was a liability, the Republicans called a Union convention and nominated David Tod, a lifelong Democrat. War Democrats joined the Union movement, leaving their party to an anti-war faction that nominated H. J. Jewett on a platform calling for a national convention to settle difficulties and preserve the Union. They denounced, in vigorous partisan phrases, the "corruption, extravagance, incompetency, and favoritism" of state and nation and condemned Lincoln for suspending habeas corpus.[75]

The Republican nominee was a Youngstown coal and iron dealer and a railroad promoter whose economic interests gave him sympathy for the more conservative branch of the Republicans. He had been a Douglas Democrat, however, and had presided over the rump convention in Baltimore that had nominated Douglas for the Presidency. Like

[73] Translated from Milwaukee *See-Bote* in *Wisconsin State Journal,* November 7, 1861; cf. Frederick Merk: *Economic History of Wisconsin during the Civil War Decade,* pp. 255–6.

[74] *Wisconsin State Journal,* November 7, 11, December 2, 1861.

[75] E. O. Randall and Daniel J. Ryan: *History of Ohio: The Rise and Progress of an American State,* IV, 170–1; Reid: *Ohio in the War,* I, 53–61; *Crisis,* June 13, July 11, 1861; *New York Times,* August 12, 1861; U. G. Mitchell to Dennison, July 17, 1861, Ohio Executive Records, MSS.

Douglas, he had supported the war, and in accepting the Republican nomination he excoriated the "sanguinary ambitious and designing leaders" of the South in terms that delighted his radical supporters. During the campaign he refused to debate Jewett, and the Republicans permitted the Democrats to spend their fire upon the discredited Dennison. In October, Tod polled 206,000 votes to Jewett's 151,794. The strategy of a union party had saved Ohio for the Republicans.[76]

In the New England states, tradition had long since made a farce of annual elections. By agreement, each governor was entitled to renomination for a second year in office, and the opposition parties only made serious efforts every second year. In Vermont, however, Erastus Fairbanks had served two years, and the Republicans, meeting in convention, replaced him with Frederick Holbrook, who, although younger and less wealthy, was as conservative as the St. Johnsbury patriarch. A native of Brattleboro, Holbrook had inherited mills, stores, paper factories, and a publishing business, but his own interests were in agriculture. He wrote articles for farm papers, and became president of the State Agricultural Society. As a Whig member of the Vermont Senate he had taken a lead in memorializing Congress to establish a federal department of agriculture. Such activities made him widely known, and his suave manner and kindly disposition made him universally liked. His success against only token opposition in Republican Vermont was a foregone conclusion.[77]

In Maine and Massachusetts the elections were routine and without interest. Both Israel Washburn and John Andrew were renominated and re-elected. In Massachusetts,

[76] *Crisis*, August 22, 29, September 12, 19, November 14, 1861; Randall and Ryan: *Ohio*, IV, 176–7; *New York Times*, August 19, 1861.

[77] *Vermont Phoenix*, February 15, 1895, clipping in Elbridge MSS. collection; Henry Clay Williams: *Biographical Encyclopædia of Vermont*, pp. 100–1; G. G. Benedict: *Vermont in the Civil War*, I, 4 *et passim*.

however, the Republican convention made a vain effort to attract Democratic support, and rejected Charles Sumner's effort to get abolitionism endorsed in the platform. A committee sought in vain for a War Democrat to run for lieutenant governor, but finally selected a former Whig. Massachusetts Democrats nominated Isaac Davis to oppose Andrew, but their platform, with solemn pledges to "conquer a peace," was almost more radical than the Republicans' convention statement. As soon as the votes were counted, however, Andrew claimed the result was the "first step" toward carrying out the antislavery program.[78]

Had Radicals like John Andrew taken the pains to analyze the political situation in 1861, they would have discovered that, outside New England, only the Iowa Republicans had proved strong enough to win without Democratic support. Such an analysis might have indicated that Lincoln's cautious policy, his conciliation of border-state unionists, and his support of War Democrats met the approval of the Northern voters. But cautious analysis was not the forte of the radicals; their strength lay in their determination to crush slavery and subjugate the South. The party, the army, and the national government were but tools for their purpose, and Lincoln's moderate program only an obstacle before their goal.

Too intent upon their goal to heed signs of caution, the radical elements impatiently demanded "vigor," denounced the "imbecility" of the War Department, and applauded each arbitrary step toward violence. One of Yates's volunteer advisers, recounting how the "nights of the Golden Circul" were organizing in southern Illinois, demanded immediate and effective steps to "brake up this rebel rabel." [79]

[78] Pearson: *Andrew*, I, 320 ff.; William Schouler: *A History of Massachusetts in the Civil War*, pp. 243 ff.; *Appleton's Cyclopædia*, I, 450, II, 557–8.

[79] S. S. Warmoth to Yates, October 30, 1861, Yates MSS.

On a more literate level, Count Adam Gurowski, Polish refugee who talked democracy while advocating authoritarianism, secretly recorded in his diary that Lincoln had "plenty of good will" and might, "perhaps," be honest. But he was not a man of "transcendent power," and was completely under the thumb of the moderate Seward. It was Andrew, thought the radical Count, who was the incarnation of the "genuine American people," [80] who were all restless under Lincoln's hesitant rule. The *New York Times* editorially demanded that not an instant be lost in "repeating upon the soil of Virginia, the experiment so successfully tried in Maryland." And, added the editor: "a Government that has no power, or that will not put forth any, is not a Government." [81]

But as the radicals called for vigor, Democratic critics pointed to the dangers of arbitrary government and warned that abolitionists intended to destroy the liberties of the country. "We ask our people to reflect calmly and ask themselves where they are being led," said the *New Hampshire Patriot*. "Let no man be deterred from the inquiry by the parrot-cry of tory or traitor." [82] In Congress, Vallandigham of Ohio, a Douglas Democrat who would not follow Douglas, warned of a "conspiracy" to overthrow the federal government and "establish a strong centralized government in its stead." [83] At the same time Kentucky's Senator Powell foresaw an intention to reduce the Southern states to provinces and to send Northern governors supported by the "iron heel" of military power to rule over them. [84] In New York, Democrats in convention denounced both secession and abolition as destructive of the Union, and Horatio Seymour thought that loyal men would have to fight against

[80] Adam Gurowski: *Diary*, pp. 42, 44, 54, 63, 94.

[81] *New York Times*, May 2, 1861.

[82] *New Hampshire Patriot*, July 3, 1861.

[83] *Congressional Globe*, 37th Congress, 1st Session, p. 58.

[84] Ibid., 69.

both North and South. Like the radicals, he believed Lincoln a weakling who needed "stiffening." Seymour, however, would stiffen him in his border-state policy.[85] From Chicago came the echo that abolition assured "absolute and unlimited power for the Federal Government," and that Democrats opposed any violation of the Constitution that would overthrow states' rights.[86]

As if to confirm Democratic fears, Secretary of War Cameron embodied a strange proposal in his annual report to the President. "Wisdom and true statesmanship," he averred, demanded that the states surrounding the national capital be reshaped. He proposed extending the District of Columbia into Virginia, giving Virginia's counties between the Chesapeake and the Blue Ridge to Maryland, adding Maryland's mountain counties to Virginia, and putting the Eastern Shore of Maryland and Virginia in Delaware.[87] Democrats might well have shivered at such cavalier disdain of states' rights.

But radicals paid no heed to Democratic fears. A Michigan radical advised Governor Blair, when he heard of Frémont's removal, that he had "but little hopes of the country" unless the people took "the defense of the country into their own hands and set at defiance the old grannies at Washington." [88] And one of Ohio's abolitionists, beside himself over the treatment of Frémont, threatened that "a few more such beheadings of meritorious officers, added to the timid, vacillating and cowardly policy pursued by the Government and an indignant people will rise up and . . . hurl the whole concern into the Potomac; and call upon some daring, brave, intrepid and gallant leader. . . ." [89]

From the date of Frémont's removal, the radicals could

---

[85] Stewart Mitchell: *Horatio Seymour of New York*, pp. 237–43.

[86] *Chicago Times*, November 25, 1861.

[87] *Official Records*, series 3, I, 707–9.

[88] I. P. Christaney to Blair, October 18, 1861, Blair MSS.

[89] Israel Green to W. T. Barcom, November 7, 1861, Ohio Executive Records, MSS. Box 202.

hardly contain themselves, and as soon as the election returns were in they burst forth with new demands for vigor and with more open avowals of their antislavery aims. "Oh God! for a Cameronian battle-cry; for a grand, inspiring, electric shout . . . " prayed John Andrew. "This people must be *welded* together with the fire itself, both of the spirit and the flesh." [90] Horace Greeley, as if in answer, declared openly that no reconstruction of the Union would be worth having at the cost of slavery.[91] Charles Sumner had earlier advised Andrew to keep Massachusetts ahead, and "let the doctrine of emancipation be proclaimed as an essential and happy agency in subduing a wicked rebellion." Yet, for the moment, Andrew hesitated, relying — as he told a friend — on the "stern necessity of the logic of the war," which would force the administration to grapple with slavery and turn its guns on the institution itself.[92]

To speed the stern necessity, Andrew and the radical governors looked to Congress. When that body assembled in December 1861, Lincoln took cognizance of the growing strength of the radicals and proceeded to grapple with the slavery issue. He explained his border-state policy, reiterated his determination to preserve the Union, and proposed that Congress consider colonizing the blacks who had been freed by the Confiscation Act.[93] The radicals were incensed and promptly gave proof that such moderate policies were obnoxious. The Senate began to discuss a more drastic confiscation bill, while the House heard Thaddeus Stevens offer a resolution demanding emancipation as a military measure. Congressmen attacked generals who expelled fugitive slaves from their commands. Then, with criticisms of military reverses as an excuse, the radicals forced the creation of a joint Committee on the Conduct of the War. The

[90] Schouler: *Massachusetts in the War,* pp. 234–5.

[91] *New York Tribune,* October 31, 1861. Cf. also *New York Illustrated News,* November 11, 1861.

[92] Pearson: *Andrew,* II, 1–4.

[93] Nicolay and Hay: *Lincoln,* VI, 356–7.

committee, dominated by radicals, was to become the direct-ing junto in the abolitionist drive against the President.[94]

The party that Abraham Lincoln had united with a war was threatening to split over the war's objectives — and threatening as well to convert or to destroy the man who had united it.

[94] T. Harry Williams: *Lincoln and the Radicals*, pp. 50–65.

Chapter 12

Abolitionism and Arbitrary Arrests

By the beginning of 1862 the abolitionists had grown disgusted with Lincoln's cautious border-state policy. Not all the developments of 1861 had been to their liking, and they began the new year with a new determination to destroy slavery, to rid the nation of the dangers of Southern domination, and to control the South. "The thing we seek," explained a Massachusetts colonel to Governor Andrew, "is *permanent* dominion: & what instance is there of a permanent dominion without changing, revolutionizing, absorbing, the institutions, life, and manners of the conquered peoples?" And he added with scorn: "They think we mean to take their *slaves*. Bah! We must take their *ports,* their *mines,* their *water power,* the very soil they plow, and develop them by the hands of our *artisan* armies. . . . We are to be a regenerating, colonizing power, or we are to be whipped. Schoolmasters with howitzers, must instruct our southern brethren that they are a set of d—d fools in everything, that relates to . . . modern civilization." The migration and settlement of Yankees on Southern soil, explained the colonel, must follow success in battle.[1]

Thus the lure of loot infused a crusade whose banners bore the words of freedom. On the day after New Year's,

[1] J. G. Randall: *Lincoln the President,* II, 205–6; Lt. Col. S. Sergent to Andrew, January 14, 1862.

Horace Greeley lectured in Washington, and Abraham Lincoln, Salmon Chase, and half of Congress heard him proclaim that the real object of the war must be slavery's destruction. The audience, fully packed with an abolitionist claque, applauded loudly each time he proclaimed slavery "the sole purpose of the fight," and it gave vehement approval to the orator's assertion that "rebels had no right to own anything." This, explained Greeley, was Andrew Johnson's opinion — the enunciation of a patriot and the wisdom of a statesman.[2]

"The world moves and the Yankee is Yankeeized," added the *Chicago Tribune* as it urged its readers to write their congressmen.

And at the same time New York was talking about the speech of Wendell Phillips. Just before Christmas the abolitionist orator rose to damn the whole idea of reconstructing the Union with slavery. "Reconstruction becomes the subjection of the North!" cried the impassioned speaker. "Any statesman who leads these states back to reconstruction will be damned to infamy!" Then, remembering that bankers were meeting near by at the moment, Phillips warned that "if the country comes together again, on anything like the old basis, we pay off Jeff Davis' debts as well as our own."[3]

In Congress, where the radical Committee on the Conduct of the War was preparing to launch its career as director of the abolitionist crusade, men heard repeated talk about reducing the Southern states to territories, appointing Northern governors to rule over them, and maintaining an army of occupation to implement the eventual exploitation of the conquered land.[4]

In the New England states the first days of January saw the radical governors giving their vigorous assent to the

[2] *Chicago Tribune*, January 4, 1862.

[3] *New York Illustrated News*, January 4, 1862.

[4] *Crisis*, January 16, 1862; George W. Smith: "Some Northern War Time Attitudes toward the Post-Civil War South," *Journal of Southern History*, X, 253–74 (1944).

antislavery drive and preparing to add their influence to force Lincoln's hand. From the Senate chamber Charles Sumner advised John Andrew to "keep Massachusetts ahead" in abolition. "Let the doctrine of emancipation be proclaimed as an essential and happy agency in subduing a wicked rebellion." The governor turned to his legislature with assurance, announcing that a mortal blow to slavery would be struck by the war.[5] Although Andrew was more cautious than was his wont, and less emphatic than Sumner had wished, he was still offensive to the Democrats. "Governor Andrew is an ass," announced the Democratic *Chicago Times* as it declared that Massachusetts' chief part in the war had been in provoking it.[6]

Other New England governors gave assent to Andrew's doctrines, but in less vehement words. Washburn was more concerned with warning Maine's legislature of Canadian hostility and urging defense against British attacks than he was with slavery.[7] In Vermont, too, the more pressing business of the state's finances occupied handsome Governor Holbrook's attention.[8] In New Hampshire, however, the Republicans were so sure slavery was doomed that they met in convention and renominated Governor Berry. The meeting was a "no party" affair, but few Democrats showed up for it. They, instead, nominated General Stark again, while a "Union Party," pledging its support to Lincoln's moderate, non-abolitionist policy, chose still a third candidate for the governorship. The poll in March proved the Republicans right: Vermont was still abolitionist, and Berry won by a safe margin.[9]

In the West, Blair of Michigan and Kirkwood of Iowa surpassed even Andrew in demanding war on slavery and on

[5] Pearson: *Andrew*, II, 5–6; Headley: *Massachusetts*, p. 20.

[6] *Chicago Times*, January 6, 1862.

[7] *Chicago Tribune*, January 8, 1862.

[8] Williams, *Vermont*, 101–2.

[9] *New Hampshire Patriot*, January 8, 15; *Chicago Tribune*, January 3, 1862; Lyford: *Rollins*, p. 130.

Southern property. Still smarting over his failure to get his party's endorsement for Michigan's vacant senatorship, Blair launched into a venomous attack on slavery. "No property of a rebel ought to be free from confiscation — not even the sacred slave," he proclaimed. The time for gentle dalliance was past, and the Union forces should be hurled like a thunderbolt at the rebels: pay the soldiers from the rebel's property, "feed them from his granaries, mount them upon his horses." And, as for the border states, he "would apologize neither to Kentucky nor to anyone else." If soldiers must die, they should die in battle — "Then will they welcome it as the tired laborer welcomes sleep." The legislature responded with enthusiastic resolutions to sweep slavery from the land.[10]

With only slightly less bloodthirstiness, Kirkwood, steadily growing radical, reviewed the history of the rebellion in his inaugural. Although he admitted that the war's primary purpose was to save the Union and confessed he would drop slavery if the war could be ended and the Union restored, he pronounced slavery the great cause of the rebellion and advocated the destruction of all rebel property. The federal government, he said privately, was controlled by men who were "more concerned to break down the Republican party than to defeat the Rebels." To commanders in the field the Governor deplored the use of the army to protect the persons and property of rebels. "We have been pelting them in the secession apple-tree with good words and grass for a long time, and they *won't* come down. I think the time has fully come to use stones." [11]

The three new moderate governors, elected in 1861 and inaugurated in January 1862 as the radicals began to organize their drive, were less violent than their colleagues. Sand-

[10] Smith: *Blair*, pp. 63–70; Moore: *Michigan*, I, 421–2; Robertson: *Michigan in the War*, pp. 20–2; *Chicago Tribune*, January 4; *Chicago Times*, January 13, 15, 1862; Blair to Charles S. May, January 12, 1862, Blair MSS.

[11] Lathrop: *Kirkwood*, pp. 180–201; Byers: *Iowa*, p. 90; *Chicago Times*, January 28, 1862.

wiched between Blair and Kirkwood, Louis P. Harvey of
Wisconsin was more concerned about the health and well-
being of his troops than he was about sending them to glorious deaths. Slavery, he admitted, was the cause of the war,
and loyal people would sacrifice life and property to defend
the government; yet the extinction of slavery "is yet in the
order of Providence, and not to be directed by our impatience." [12]

Ohio's War Democrat, David Tod, took the oath of office
before a large gathering. Sam Medary, fighting editor of the
Copperhead *Columbus Crisis,* viewed the incoming administration "with leniency, if not with favor," and affected to
believe that the assembled multitudes had a general feeling
of relief over Dennison's retirement. Editor Medary's hostility to Dennison had not been relieved by the departing
executive's farewell message, which had run to eighteen
columns and displaced many of Medary's own scathing comments from his paper. But Governor Tod was mercifully
brief. He praised Lincoln's border-state policy and depre-
cated immediate emancipation. Thereupon he settled down
to the work of extricating the state's finances from the confusion in which Dennison had left them.[13]

Even less an abolitionist was Maryland's new Governor
Bradford. He had been elected by federal bayonets and
came into office committed to Lincoln's program. In his inaugural he characterized both secession and abolitionism as
"twin miseries," and proclaimed anew Maryland's devotion
to the Union and the Constitution. In the months to follow
he was to be faithful to Lincoln, and he frequently pleaded
with his fellow governors to stop agitation for abolition in
their states.[14]

[12] *Chicago Tribune,* January 11, 1862; Quiner: *Military History of Wisconsin,* pp. 122–3.

[13] Reid: *Ohio in the War,* I, 62–5; *Crisis,* January 2, 9, 13, 16; *Chicago Tribune,* January 7; *New York Times,* January 10, 1862.

[14] Buchholz: *Governors of Maryland,* pp. 181–2; Scharf: *Maryland,* III, 461; *Chicago Times,* January 14, 1862; *Appleton's Cyclopædia,* II, 561.

From the elections of 1861 and the statements of the moderate governors the Democrats drew hopes while the radicals mustered determination. As the radicals created the machinery for their drive for emancipation, the Democrats prepared for the congressional and state elections of 1862. Their strength, despite the defection of War Democrats, was still great, and they counted on many things to bring them victory. In their armament they listed the Middle Westerners' distrust of New England, the farmers' fear of industrial dominance, the widespread fear that lesser men had of Negro equality, and the honest man's reaction to official corruption. Exposure and denunciation became the tactics of the Democrats, and in the end so many of their barbs sank deep that the Republicans, moderate and radical alike, resorted to suppression and to arbitrary arrests under a suspension of habeas corpus. When they did so, the Democrats promptly stepped into the role of defenders of personal liberty against the government's ruthless aggrandizement.

First to bear the full brunt of the Democratic assault was Governor Dick Yates. In January a constitutional convention, elected the previous fall, assembled in Springfield. The Illinois constitution needed revision, but the Democratic majority of the convention showed less zeal for improving the fundamental instrument of government than for exploring the financial irregularities of Yates's administration. Yates and the Republicans complained loudly, but the precedents were against them. In Missouri, during the summer before, a constitutional convention had assumed control of the state, declared state offices vacant, and filled them with good Union men. Such actions accorded with the best states' rights theories, and there was little Yates could do except protest. He admitted irregularities in clothing contracts for Illinois troops and pleaded that speed in getting the clothing was responsible.

The convention investigated Yates, considered gerrymandering the state's congressional districts, and proposed changing the tenure of state officers in order that Yates might be removed. Eventually, after months of dispute, they framed a new constitution, which contained some needed reforms and much partisanship. Particularly significant were sections forbidding Negroes and mulattoes to settle or vote in the state.[15]

Promptly the Republicans organized to defeat the constitution. Illinois congressmen franked anti-constitution pamphlets into the state, and every postmaster became a distributor of literature. Both sides stumped the state, and Democrats denounced Yates — "completely ruined by the immoderate use of whiskey and near the gate of that psychical state called 'delirium tremens.' " [16] They told, too, a story that Yates, en route to the battlefield of Shiloh with a party of surgeons and nurses, stopped the boat for four hours while he rambled and got lost in the woods with a lady whom he had recently appointed an honorary major.[17]

Yet such scurrility did not avail to give the Democrats their constitution. In June the voters rejected the instrument, although they gave a sizable majority to the anti-Negro sections. "We have gotten out of an awful scrape," sighed Medill of the *Chicago Tribune*. "Let us," begged the editor, "do nothing to impair our position. Let us husband our strength for the decisive struggle next fall." [18]

In other states the Democrats, drawing inspiration from

[15] *Chicago Times,* January 7, 27, 28, 30, February 1; *Crisis,* February 5, 1862; Cole: *Era of the Civil War,* pp. 267–77; Yates to T. G. Henderson, February 4, and reply, February 6; letters of Governor Hoffman, February 6; R. F. Adams, February 6; Schuyler Colfax, February 17; J. Medill, March 1, to Yates, and Yates to Ward, March 24, Yates MSS.; Yates to Washburne, March 17, 1862, Washburne MSS.

[16] Governor Hoffman to Yates, February 6, 1862, Yates MSS.

[17] *Crisis,* June 4, 1862.

[18] L. S. Church to "Friend" Cullum, March 29; Weed to "Dear Judge," May 20; letters of M. Bartley, March 30; G. W. Rives, April 9; Charles E. Woodward, April 19; John Moses, May 1; H. J. Adkins, June 12, George Lopers, July 1; R. W. Waterman, July 2; J. Medill, July 3; to Yates: O. M. Hatch and others to Lincoln, June 12, 1862, Yates MSS.; Cole: *Era of the Civil War,* pp. 270–2; *Chicago Times,* May 22, June 6, 1862.

Illinois, sought political capital in military incompetence and governmental aggressions on personal liberty. Indiana's Democrats held a conference in January to denounce abolitionists, the government's usurpation of power, the suspension of habeas corpus, and the arbitrary imprisonment of citizens.[19] Governor Morton hurriedly sent copies of the proceedings to Secretary Cameron, pointing out that the Democrats were trying to sabotage the war by breaking down confidence in the war leaders.[20] Before the month was over, Morton was assuring Cameron's successor that there was a disloyal semi-political organization in Indiana, ten thousand strong. He begged Secretary Stanton to send ten thousand arms for the state's militia and to take "immediate, vigorous, and effective steps" to break up such dangerous combinations.[21] The Governor's alarms were to grow into hysterical panic before the year ended.

In the East, too, the Democrats spoke out more vigorously. Some of them even took momentary hope from the appointment of Edwin M. Stanton, Pennsylvania Democrat, to Cameron's place in the War Department.[22] In New Jersey's Democratic legislature resolutions denouncing federal usurpation received approval and the legislature suggested peace be made with the South.[23] From New York, Horatio Seymour went to Washington to speak at the Smithsonian Institution and used the occasion to pay a suspicious visit to General McClellan.[24] And in New England the Democrats found encouragement in the spring elections. Berry, Buckingham, and Sprague were re-elected, but the last was still considered a Democrat, and in New Hampshire the Democratic proportion of the vote increased.[25]

[19] *Appleton's Cyclopædia,* II, 527.

[20] Morton to Cameron, January 13, 1862, Cameron MSS.

[21] *Official Records,* series 3, II, 176–7.

[22] *Crisis,* January 20, 1862; J. A. Briggs to Tod, February 20, 1862; Ohio Executive Records, MSS., Box 206.

[23] Foster: *New Jersey,* pp. 274, 278–9.

[24] Mitchell: *Seymour,* pp. 243 f.

[25] *New Hampshire Patriot,* March 11, 19; *Crisis,* March 19, April 9,

But such Democratic agitation and occasional minor successes of the Democrats did not deter the radicals in their drive to emancipate slaves and destroy Southern wealth. The Committee on the Conduct of the War, with Secretary Stanton's full support, began the campaign by investigating General C. P. Stone's responsibility for the military disaster at Ball's Bluff. Convinced that Stone was not in sympathy with radical war aims, the committee promptly charged him with treason. Finding him loyal to McClellan, the committee engineered his arrest and imprisonment in Fort Lafayette. Then the committee investigated Frémont's case and heaped praises upon the intrepid abolitionist. Accompanying these moves the committee began a smear campaign against McClellan — ostensibly designed to make him fight, but with the real purpose of his removal. By the end of July, after failure in the Peninsular campaign, the radical program succeeded, and John Pope became commander in the Eastern theater.[26]

These military matters were window dressing for the radicals. Behind the fanfare of military investigations the Jacobin forces pursued their real objectives. In April they pushed through Congress a bill for emancipation, with compensation, for the District of Columbia.[27] Then the radicals debated a bill for abolishing slavery in the territories, interspersing their discussion with fiery excoriations of generals in the field who returned fugitive slaves.[28] Finally, just before the session ended, they succeeded in passing an act confiscating the property of all persons engaged in rebellion. The slaves so confiscated should be immediately freed.

But just as this bill was about to pass, Lincoln let it be known that he would veto it. The infuriated Jacobins re-

---

1862; Croffut and Morris: *Military History of Connecticut*, pp. 186–7; Pillsbury: *New Hampshire*, p. 546; Knight: *Sprague*, pp. 47–8.

[26] Williams: *Lincoln and the Radicals*, pp. 93–156.

[27] *Congressional Globe*, 37th Congress, 2nd Session (1862), pp. 1526, 1629–31, 1640–9, 1446–51.

[28] Ibid., pp. 2041–64.

acted by denouncing the President, but on somewhat sober
second thought they listened to an emissary who had gone
to treat with the enemy in the White House. The emissary
reported that Lincoln would accept the confiscation bill
with modifications that eliminated retroactive features from
the law and the provisions for permanent forfeiture of all
property. The radicals raged, but they were forced to amend
the bill. Even then the President, although he accepted it,
sent to Congress the veto message he had prepared.

As passed, the Confiscation Act declared free the slaves of
all persons found guilty of treason after its passage, emanci-
pated all rebel-owned slaves who entered Union lines, seized
the estates of Confederate officials, and authorized the raising of soldiers among the freedmen. Two days before the
act passed, the radical leaders, mindful of the mounting
difficulties in raising white troops for the war, issued an
address demanding that Negroes be employed in a military
capacity.[29]

As the radical drive for emancipation and confiscation thus
got under way, and while the Democrats made political
capital of radical acts, Abraham Lincoln found himself
caught between their fires. He recognized that, if he yielded
to the radical demands, the border states would rebel. Yet
he recognized as well that the radicals had strategic strength.
They controlled the machinery of Congress, and their governors held a number of the key states. Already the abolitionist governors, hard pressed to raise troops, were showing
reluctance in furnishing men for a moderate Union-saving
war. It was as evident to Lincoln as it was to Wendell Phillips that the radicals were winning. At the "anniversary" of
the American Anti-Slavery Society in May, Phillips announced that "Abraham Lincoln only rules: John C. Frémont governs. . . . The real president of the American
mind does not live in the White House; he leads the Mountain Department of Virginia."[30]

[29] Williams: *Lincoln and the Radicals*, pp. 163–8.
[30] *New York Illustrated News*, May 24, 1862.

Thus threatened in his control over both his party and the nation, Lincoln met the challenge with a threefold program. First, he attempted to counter the abolitionists with a program of compensated emancipation. Second, he strengthened his control over the border states. And finally he sought for and announced a verbal formula that yielded the form of emancipation to the radicals while retaining the substance of power in his own hands.

The President's first proposal, devised as he faced the rising tide of abolitionism, was compensated emancipation. In March he sent a message to Congress urging an appropriation to purchase slaves from loyal owners in the border states. A congressional committee investigated the possibilities of compensated emancipation, and gave consideration to Lincoln's further proposal that the Negroes thus freed should be colonized either in Latin America or in the Southwest. The only result of the proposal was the bill for compensated emancipation for the District of Columbia.

Neither radicals nor border-state moderates were pleased with a proposal to pay owners for slaves. Adam Gurowski confided to his bitter diary his grief that "the friends of humanity in Europe" would credit the District of Columbia Act not to the noble pressure exercised by the high-minded Northern masses, but to this Kentucky ———." [31] Nor did the border states respond to the suggestion. There was talk among their representatives in Congress of withdrawing in a body in protest against discussions of emancipation and confiscation,[32] and they had only frowns for proposals that the government buy the slaves of their constituents. In July, four months after his compensated emancipation message, Lincoln called the border-state delegations to the White House.

Congress was about to adjourn, and the President wished to plead his case. If they had supported the gradual emancipation message in March, he declared, the war would "now

[31] Gurowski: *Diary*, I, 192.
[32] *New York Illustrated News*, May 24, 1862.

be substantially ended." It was not even yet too late, and the congressmen might still persuade their states to accept it. Slavery was sure to be ended. "The abolitionist pressure," he explained, "is still upon me, and is increasing." The border states, by accepting compensation — "I do not speak of emancipation at once, but of a decision at once to emancipate gradually" — could relieve both the President and the country of the pressure.[33]

The President followed up the conference by sending to Congress a bill to compensate any state that might abolish slavery,[34] but neither Congress nor the border-state congressmen gave heed to his advice. Already, in Missouri, Governor Gamble had presented the compensated emancipation scheme to a state convention. A proposal to free all slaves born after 1864 upon their reaching the age of twenty-five was considered and summarily rejected. Upon Gamble's protest that this action was "rudely discourteous," the convention passed a resolution thanking the federal government, but explaining that the members of the convention had no authority from the citizens to "take action with respect to the grave and delicate questions of private right and public policy presented." Meantime, Missouri radicals, in a mass meeting in Jefferson City, resolved to make emancipation the issue in the coming elections. With the lines thus drawn, the Missouri congressmen who heard Lincoln's plan rejected "the proposition in its present unpalpable form."[35]

As it became evident that the border states would not willingly accept emancipation in any form, Lincoln came to realize that only military force would keep them in line. In Maryland and Kentucky the military authorities ruled the states, and during the summer of 1862 they fastened their grip upon the political machinery. Maryland's Governor

[33] Nicolay and Hay: *Lincoln*, VI, 108–11.

[34] *Works of Lincoln*, VI, 91.

[35] Nicolay and Hay: *Lincoln*, VI, 370–1, 391–3; Laughlin: *Missouri Politics*, pp. 71 ff.

and legislature, elected in 1861 by federal bayonets, gave
no trouble, and gradually the state's judiciary was estopped
from independent pronouncements. In May one Judge Car-
michael, sitting in court at Easton, was literally dragged
from the bench by a provost marshal and a body of soldiers.
The judge, at a previous session, had instructed a grand
jury to inquire into the processes of the recent election. He
was confined in federal military prisons for six months and
released without any formal charges being preferred against
him. A month later Judge James L. Bastol of the Court of
Appeals spent several days in jail without explanation from
his military jailers. The two arrests, supplemented by frequent excursions of provost marshals against disgruntled citizens, effectively prevented the expression of opposition sentiment in Maryland.[36]

In Kentucky, as the county elections of the summer approached, the military forces assumed an even greater control. In May, Senator Powell got the Senate to ask Lincoln
for information on arbitrary arrests in Kentucky. The President replied with the standard formula — it was "not com-
patible with the public interest" to give the information.
In June, General Jere T. Boyle began to arrest Democrats
and Southern sympathizers, and by July the jails were full.[37]
Finally General Boyle issued an order that "no person hostile in opinion to the government" could be a candidate for
office.[38] The election that followed was a "military census,"
and the unionist candidates were uniformly successful.[39]

While the elections were proceeding, the governors of
neighboring states kept a careful eye on developments. When
a delegation of "highly respectable gentlemen" of Cincinnati assured Tod that there would be a raid on the Ken-

[36] Andrews: *History of Maryland,* p. 539; Scharf: *History of Maryland,* III, 489.

[37] Coulter: *Civil War and Readjustment in Kentucky,* pp. 150-2;
G. W. Frost to Tod, July 3, 1862, Ohio Executive Records, MSS.

[38] R. H. Collins: *History of Kentucky,* I, 114.

[39] Coulter: *Civil War in Kentucky,* p. 155; Collins; *Kentucky,* I,
102, 105.

tucky legislature, the Ohio Governor promptly advised
Secretary Stanton to send a couple of Ohio's three-month
regiments to Frankfort. Tod sent agents to Washington, and
kept Yates and Morton informed of developments. The Indiana and Illinois governors joined in advising Lincoln to
put gunboats on the Ohio River.[40]

The first result of the Kentucky election was the resignation of Governor Beriah Magoffin. A constitutionalist and a
Southern rights man, Magoffin had originally been a secessionist, but had embraced neutrality in good faith. His continued difficulties with the Lincoln government, however,
had almost driven him into the arms of Jefferson Davis. He
had had, too, more than his share of troubles with Kentucky unionists. They had effectively shorn him of his military power, and they had constantly threatened him with
impeachment and arrest. Even assassination had been darkly
hinted at. He had resisted all suggestions that he resign until
after the elections. Then, realizing that his effectiveness was
at an end, he yielded to the pressure on condition that he be
allowed to name his successor. The state's lieutenant governor having died, the speaker of the Senate was next in the
line of succession. Magoffin chose James F. Robinson as his
successor, the Senate elected him speaker, and the Governor
laid down his office.[41]

The new Kentucky Governor, a "distinguished and loyal
citizen," had little disposition for quarrels with the federal
officials. He held office for a full year, but the unionists
made no effort to remove the "military board" that they had
created to curb Magoffin. Arbitrary arrests continued and
crowded the provost marshal's courts with men and women
picked up on suspicion of disloyalty. Moreover, the army

[40] *Official Records*, series 3, II, 285; J. H. Bates to Yates, August 7,
1862, Yates MSS.; Yates to Tod, August 11, 1862, Ohio Executive Records, MSS. and Yates MS. Letterbooks.

[41] Coulter: *Civil War and Readjustment in Kentucky*, pp. 142–5;
Crisis, August 27, 1862.

began to meddle with the civil courts. This finally, near the end of his term, brought Robinson into outraged opposition to federal interference.[42]

As the summer drew on, Lincoln came to the realization that only military force and the suspension of the writ of habeas corpus would retain the technical loyalty and nominal support of the border states. But at the same time, as he had explained to the border-state congressmen, the radical pressure for emancipation was increasing. Some gesture toward the abolitionists was becoming necessary. The President sought for a means of making the gesture as harmless as possible.

Late in June, Lincoln sounded out Vice President Hamlin on what items ought to go into a presidential proclamation.[43] Then, on July 13, riding back from a funeral with Secretaries Welles and Seward, the President declared that emancipation was a military necessity and asked the secretaries' advice. Both the secretaries, remembering their long experience in politics, assumed a judicial air and declared with pretentious solemnity that the question was grave and important.[44] Both were ready with objections nine days later when Lincoln presented the cabinet a preliminary draft of a preliminary emancipation proclamation.

The cabinet members promptly divided into factions. Montgomery Blair wondered about the effect of such a proclamation on the border states. Edward Bates, the Missouri conservative, surprised his colleagues by giving his wholehearted endorsement, while the abolitionist Chase, in close touch with the most extreme radicals in Congress, did not favor a presidential pronouncement. He preferred to bring emancipation through the army commanders in the South. Finally, the moderate Seward raised the question of timing. At the moment, with federal arms unsuccessful, a proclama-

---

[42] Thomas D. Clark: *History of Kentucky*, pp. 482–5.

[43] Hamlin: *Hamlin*, pp. 428–9.

[44] Welles: *Diary*, I, 70–1.

tion would look like a foolish bid for a slave insurrection. Would it not, asked the State Department head, be better to wait for a Northern victory? With this suggestion the cabinet members — each for his own purpose — agreed, and Lincoln put the preliminary emancipation proclamation back in his desk.[45]

[45] Nicolay and Hay: *Lincoln*, VI, 127, 161–5.

Chapter 13

Altoona and Aftermath

ON Lincoln's desk the Emancipation Proclamation would probably have remained had it not been for the increased activities of the radicals and a new move from the governors. The President realized that the abolitionist drive to pervert the war from its original purpose of preserving the Union to a crusade for freeing the slaves and confiscating Southern property did not have the support of the Northern people. He realized, too, that if he yielded to the radicals, only the use of troops at the polls and the arbitrary arrest of discontented citizens would enable him to pursue his Union-saving objectives. But the radical governors, on the other hand, already failing to raise troops for the armies, hoped to use Negro soldiers in place of their white constituents, and they increased their pressure upon the President.

The radicals rallied behind Dick Yates, who began again to instruct his constituent in the White House. "The time has come," Yates told Lincoln on July 11, "for the adoption of more decisive measures." Generals should not be frittering away their time guarding the property of traitors, and the government ought not to spurn the Negroes as soldiers. "Mr. Lincoln," cried the Governor, "the crisis demands greater efforts and sterner measures." [1]

Promptly Yates's mail filled with applauding letters. "Mr.

[1] Yates to Lincoln, July 11, 1862; R. T. Lincoln MSS. Eddy: *Patriotism of Illinois*, I, 124.

Lincoln is a great and good man, but he does not seem to comprehend the awful crisis that is upon the nation," said one. "The government must impoverish traitors," said another. "May the good God direct Mr. Lincoln aright and save our country," prayed a third. Then, when Yates spoke in Chicago on the same theme, the chorus swelled again. "You have touched the cord that rings the bell of Liberty," wrote one admirer, while another declared that Lincoln's constitutional scruples were besotted "folly, idiocy, and blindness." [2]

The abolitionist pressure was not limited to Illinois. In Maine the Republicans nominated an abolitionist for governor when Washburn declined to apply for another term. Abner Coburn was, with his brother, the largest landowner in the state and he was president of the Boston-owned Maine Central Railroad. He had been a Whig legislator, but was one of the founders of the Republican Party. The Democrats nominated a Copperhead to run against him, and in September succeeded in cutting the Republican majority to less than four thousand. But even this strengthened the determination of the radicals.[3] In New Hampshire the abolitionist legislature passed resolutions demanding that the war be made one for emancipation and urging Congress to confiscate the property of traitors.[4]

Lincoln paid no attention to either Illinois' Governor or New Hampshire's legislature, but when Horace Greeley, on August 20, published a "Prayer of Twenty Million," the President made reply. According to Greeley, the people demanded that the President enforce the confiscation acts, use Negro troops, and abolish slavery.[5] To this assault Lincoln answered that he had not meant to leave anyone in doubt about his policy. "I would save the union. I would save it in

[2] Letters of North, and A. J. Cropsey, July 14; J. M. Kelly and J. S. Fowler, July 22; Henry Asbury, July 17; J. D. Peterbaugh, July 20; D. L. Linegan, August 6; V. C. Taylor, August 20; Barby Smith, August 24, 1862, to Yates, Yates MSS.

[3] Hamlin: *Hamlin,* pp. 437–9.

[4] *New Hampshire Patriot,* July 16, 1862.

[5] *New York Tribune,* August 20, 1862.

the shortest way under the constitution. . . . My paramount object is to save the Union, not to save or destroy slavery." In this statement there was no comfort for the abolitionists, nor did they relish the President's further statement that "if I could save the Union without freeing any slaves, I would do it; and if I could do it by freeing some and leaving others alone, I would also do that. What I do about slavery and the colored race, I do because I believe it helps to save this Union." [6]

Close upon this exchange of letters came the military disaster of the second Battle of Manassas. In Washington, McClellan, *bête noire* of the radicals, once more took command of the army, while Lee's forces crossed the Potomac and began to march slowly northward. As the news reached New York, panic seized the city, and the month-old National War Committee, dominated by radicals, met behind closed doors at the New York Chamber of Commerce. The committee was more conscious of the threat implied by McClellan's restoration than of Lee's invasion. Requests went to Washington to suppress the *New York Herald*,[7] and for troops to protect the city. Quickly the committee appointed a group of seven to urge the citizens to press new levies, and chose other members to interview state governors on recruiting problems and other matters. One member journeyed west to see Western governors, another went to Morgan and Curtin, while three hurried to Providence to meet the New England governors at the Brown University commencement.[8]

The governors of the New England states had not, as a group, shown previously any interest in "literary exercises." Nor were they concerned, at this moment, in the academic ceremonies of Rhode Island's Baptist university. They had,

[6] *Writings of Lincoln*, VI, 123–4.

[7] Dr. J. A. B. Stone to Chase, September 5, 1862, Chase MSS.

[8] George W. Smith: "Generative Forces of Union Propaganda: A Study in Civil War Pressure Groups," Ch. iv, unpublished doctoral dissertation, 1939, in the library of the University of Wisconsin.

however, many weighty problems upon their minds. The President had but recently forced the state executives to subscribe to a new call for troops. Moreover, instead of welcoming the abolitionist proposition to use Negro soldiers, Lincoln was threatening to force the governors to draft their own constituents. He had reinstated the hated McClellan in command, and he had persisted in his "border-state" policy in the face of the mounting Jacobin pressure. Clearly the governors needed to consult together in the calm shade of the Providence campus.

Vermont's Governor Holbrook did not attend, but Berry, Sprague, Washburn, and Buckingham met Andrew, who had planned the meeting. In the air were rumors, given circulation by suspicious Democrats, that the governors talked in conspiratorial tones about raising a new army of 50,000 men, placing it under Frémont's command, and making the abolitionist hero a military dictator.[9] Andrew came to the meeting fresh from a rally on Boston Common where, instead of repudiating his "conditional patriotism" letter on Hunter's proclamation, he had asked "how many more Massachusetts boys are to lie down in death on the gory plain before the blow shall be struck which gives liberty to you, which gives a future to your country, as it breaks the chains of the bondman?"[10] The assembled governors at Providence shared Andrew's impatience. They knew — the New York committeemen had it from Secretary Chase — that Seward and Montgomery Blair had slowed Lincoln's hand. The governors solemnly agreed that "the unanimous choice of New England was for a change of the cabinet and a change in the generals," and they instructed the New Yorkers to proceed to Washington with the message.

The committee went to Washington. First the members called on Chase, who welcomed them warmly but advised

[9] *New York Illustrated News,* September 20, 1862; *New Hampshire Patriot,* October 7, 1862.

[10] *Addresses by . . . John Andrew . . . and others Delivered at the Mass Meeting . . . August 27, 1862,* p. 6.

them to approach Lincoln cautiously. But the committee, interviewing the President on September 10, lashed out furiously against Seward. Lincoln quickly took advantage of their intemperance to put them in the wrong, accused them of being willing to do anything to get rid of Seward, and dismissed them.[11]

In the meantime, from a number of directions, there came proposals that the governors of all the loyal states should meet to discuss the conduct of the war. Just as he returned from Providence, John Andrew confided to the radical Count Gurowski: "I am sadly but firmly trying to organize some movement, if possible, to save the president from the infamy of ruining the country." To another, the Massachusetts Governor wailed that "imbecility — treachery almost — has done its worst." Lincoln had no conception of his duty, and while Seward remained, there was no hope. "Put Jo Hooker or some man of courage and sense at the head of the army," he urged — "a man who believes a little more on our side than he does on the rebels side." [12]

Meanwhile, in Illinois, Dick Yates was reading a letter from a private in an Illinois regiment: "Could not the governors of the loyal states act in common on the means to influence the president to drive his generals to a speedy termination of the war?" The soldier thought that "everybody is anxious to go home," and the war only helped the contractors. Lincoln, he advised, could be influenced by a convention of the loyal governors, which might ask the President to resign or threaten to call their volunteers home.[13]

[11] Smith: "Generative Forces of Union Propaganda," ch. iv; Hazel C. Wolf, "The Civil War Governors and Emancipation," ch. ii, unpublished master's thesis, 1941, in the library of the University of Wisconsin; William B. Hesseltine and Hazel C. Wolf: "New England Governors vs. Lincoln: The Providence Conference," *Rhode Island History*, V, 105–13.

[12] Andrew to Gurowski, September 6, and to an unknown, no date, Andrew Letter Books.

[13] A. B. Schaeffer to Yates, September 8, 1862, Yates MSS.

And at the same time Senators Trumbull of Illinois and Chandler of Michigan, both radicals and both close to their governors, were agreeing that McClellan's disaster on the Peninsula sprang from "treason, rank treason," and Chandler declared that "nothing will now save us but a demand of the loyal governors, *backed by a threat,* that a change of policy and men shall instantly be made." [14] The pressure was growing stronger, and a conference of the governors, under radical auspices, was in the air.

Even Curtin of Pennsylvania felt it and consulted Lincoln about a countermove. With Lincoln's consent, he opened negotiations with John Andrew. "In the present emergency," he asked, "would it not be well that the loyal governors should meet at some point in the border states to take measures for the more active support of the government?" Andrew promptly replied, agreeing with the idea and promising to attend. Other governors, receiving identical telegrams, made similar replies. Wisconsin's Governor Salomon consulted Yates before replying, but the Illinois Governor urged him to attend. [15]

Having received favorable answers from all factions, Curtin added the support of Governors Tod and Pierpont to an official invitation to a meeting. Tod himself had been much concerned over the rising tide of opposition to McClellan. He had visited Washington a few weeks before to talk with the members of the cabinet, [16] and upon returning home had begged Stanton: "For God's sake, stop the wrangling between the friends of McClellan and yourself in Congress. I ask this as the friend of both. [17] When Curtin approached him, Tod promptly asked Stanton's advice, but the War Secretary replied that he had no suggestions to make, though he hoped the conference would be productive of good. [18]

[14] Chandler to Trumbull, September 10, 1862, Trumbull MSS.
[15] Salomon to Yates, September 11, 1862, Yates MSS.
[16] Welles: *Diary,* I, 403.
[17] *Official Records,* series 3, II, 219.
[18] Ibid., II, 543.

Pierpont was completely under Lincoln's thumb; so the call for a conference of the governors went out under the auspices of moderates whom Lincoln could control. The place was set for Altoona, Pennsylvania, and the date for September 24.

The governors who converged on Altoona were of many different minds on the nation's problems. Berry proposed to Andrew that the New England governors, fresh from Providence, should go together to the meeting. They might have been prepared to insist upon the elevation of Frémont.[19] Yates had advice from one of his constituents to urge the removal of all proslavery generals "at least from the western department." [20]

But the outcome of the conference was not to be left to chance or to the deliberations of the governors. Two days before the conference met, Abraham Lincoln called his cabinet into session. As they gathered around the table, the President opened Artemus Ward's latest book. With full appreciation of the author's humor, Lincoln read the chapter on "Highhanded Outrage at Utica." The story, an item of less than a page, related that showman Ward was once exhibiting his waxworks in Utica when a burly fellow seized the figure of Judas "Iscarrot" from the representation of the Last Supper and began to pommel it. "What did you bring this pussylanermus cuss here fur?" asked the Utican. Ward answered: "You egrejus ass. That air's a wax figger — a representashun of the false 'postle." But the irate citizen, who was later indicted for "arson in the third degree," replied: "That's all very well for you to say, but I tell you, old man, that Judas Iscarrot can't show hisself in Utiky with impunity by a darn site!"

The cabinet members laughed politely. Perhaps none of them saw any significant connection between the story and

[19] Copy of telegram, Berry to Andrew, September 16, 1862, Blair MSS.

[20] H. M. Tracy Cutler to Yates, September 18, Yates MSS.

the President's next act. Closing the book, and changing his tone, Lincoln told the cabinet that he had called them together for advice on the wording of an emancipation proclamation. He had decided, he said, to issue a proclamation. He wished that the country was in a better position, and admitted that the action of the army against the rebels had not been quite what he would have liked. But he had promised his Maker, if the army should be driven from Maryland, to issue the proclamation. "The rebel army is now driven out, and I am going to fulfill that promise." [21]

The preliminary Emancipation Proclamation appeared in the papers the following day. John A. Andrew read it on the train that was carrying him to Altoona. Had the Massachusetts radical possessed a sense of humor and an appreciation of Artemus Ward, he would have discovered how much Lincoln was pommeling a wax figure. For the proclamation did not free any slaves, and it did not furnish black soldiers to take the place of white men on the battlefields. Instead, the President began with a declaration that "hereafter, as heretofore, the war will be prosecuted for the object of practically restoring the constitutional relation between the United States and each of the states." Moreover, he reiterated his intention of recommending compensation to loyal owners for freeing their slaves, and of promoting colonization. But on January 1, 1863 he would declare free all slaves in any state or part of a state that should then be in rebellion. Then he completed the proclamation with extended quotations from the articles of war relating to the return of fugitive slaves and from the latest Confiscation Act.[22] The preliminary Emancipation Proclamation was by no means what John A. Andrew and the radical governors wanted.

"The Proclamation," said Governor Andrew, "is a poor *document*, but a mighty *act*." It was slow, it was wrong to wait until January, but it was "grand and sublime after all." Now, he wrote his chief henchman in Boston, was the

---

21 Myers: *McClellan,* p. 362.
22 Nicolay and Hay: *Lincoln,* VI, 158–60.

time to take advantage of the mighty act. "We must take up
the silver trumpet and repeat the immortal strain on every
hill-top . . . of New England. Our Republicans must make
it their business to sustain this act of Lincoln, and we will
drive the conservatism of a proslavery Hunkerism and the
reactionaries of despotism into the very caves and holes of
the earth. . . . No bickerings, no verbal criticism, no doubting Thomases, must halt the conquering march of triumphant liberty." [23]

A dozen governors assembled in Altoona with the Emancipation Proclamation hanging over them. The astute Lincoln had cut the ground from under the radicals, and, politicians as they all were, they knew it. Governor Curtin's
humorous mouth and twinkling eyes had a playful expression as he met his colleagues at the town's only hotel. When
they gathered in the Logan House parlor, there were, in addition to Tod, Curtin, and Pierpont, a New England delegation of Andrew, Washburn, Sprague, and Berry, a midwestern group consisting of Yates, Salomon, and Kirkwood,
and Bradford of Maryland and Olden of New Jersey representing Eastern moderates. O. P. Morton had sent one D. J.
Rose as his personal representative. New York's governor
Morgan, no longer the leader of his state's Republicans, had
refused to attend. Connecticut's Buckingham was still en
route, and Michigan's Blair was attending the state Republican convention in Detroit and too busy securing his own renomination to journey to Altoona. The governors organized
by making Bradford their chairman. [24]

[23] Browne: *Andrew,* pp. 74–5.

[24] The only contemporary report of the meeting was made by the
correspondent of the *New York Herald.* His partisan account appeared
on September 25, under the heading "A Second Hartford Convention." Austin Blair has been hailed as the "historian" of the conference (cf. John Russell Young in Egle: *Andrew Gregg Curtin,* pp. 306–
23), and a manuscript account of the meeting, along with a *typed* copy
of the "Address," is in the Blair MSS. in the Detroit Public Library.
For Blair's presence at the Michigan Republican state convention on
the day of the Altoona conference, see the *Detroit Advertiser,* Sep-

Promptly they began to discuss the Emancipation Proclamation, and Andrew harangued the group for an hour on
the subject. Finally he proposed sending Lincoln a message
expressing the gubernatorial gratitude for the presidential
gesture. But Andrew could not omit his hatred of McClellan
from either his speech or his resolutions, and the radical
demand for McClellan's immediate removal soon had the
chief magistrates of the states snarling at one another. Who,
asked the moderates, would take McClellan's place? "Frémont," replied Andrew — and his fellow visitors at Brown's
commencement nodded agreement.

Governor Tod, mindful of Ohio's pride in her hero, made
strong opposition. The people, he said, would rise *en masse*
to McClellan's defense and repudiate the governors. Curtin
joined his conservative colleague, hailing McClellan as the
man who rescued Maryland from the rebels. Bradford declared the general had the "perfect and unqualified confidence" of Maryland's loyal men. Even if there were a blem-
ish on McClellan's character, this was no time to remove
him.

In the light of the opposition, Andrew modified his resolutions, but by that time Tod and Salomon had resolutions
of their own. The debate continued, with Bradford pointing
out that the Emancipation Proclamation would amount to
nothing beyond the federal lines except to give a handle to
the rebels and to become a Confederate rallying cry.

---

tember, 24, 25, 1862. Blair's statement first appeared in the *Altoona
Tribune* of September 24, 1912, the fiftieth anniversary of the governors' conference, though it had been used by John Russell Young in
1893. It is probable that Blair prepared his account at that time for
Young's benefit. Nowhere, however, does Blair state that he was at
Altoona. He did, however, join the other governors in Washington on
September 25. Cf. *Detroit Advertiser,* September 27, 1862. In 1891 Governor Kirkwood wrote, for the *Iowa Historical Record,* an account of
his part in the conference; cf. Lathrop: *Kirkwood,* pp. 227–30. A few
months later, on February 16, 1892, Curtin wrote an account of the
conference for his friend A. K. McClure; cf. McClure: *Abraham Lincoln and Men of War Times,* pp. 270–1, footnote.

In the end the governors found they could only agree on thanking Lincoln for the proclamation and on urging him to organize 100,000 reserve troops for such emergencies as Lee's recent foray. Accordingly they drafted a confused "Address," which they promptly wired to Washington. "After nearly one year and a half," they began, ". . . the duty and purpose of the loyal states and people continue, and must always remain as they were at its origin — namely, to restore and perpetuate the authority of this government. . . ." Then, as if to hush the rumors they were conspiring against the President, the governors solemnly pledged their "most loyal and cordial" support. "We recognize in him the Chief Executive Magistrate of the nation, the Commander-in-Chief . . . their responsible and constitutional head, whose rightful authority . . . must be vigorously and religiously guarded. . . ."

Only after this abject declaration of submission did the governors propose a reserve army. And then, having made obeisance, they expressed their "heartfelt gratitude and encouraged hope" over the Emancipation Proclamation. It would give "new life," "new vigor," and "new hopes" to the hearts of the people. Finally, the governors ended their address with new pledges of personal support, and new avowals of devotion to the national cause.[25]

There was no "conditional patriotism" in the address, no querulous mention of McClellan, no hint of rallying around Frémont's standard. Only Bradford of Maryland, balking at emancipation, refused to sign. Lincoln accepted the surrender with the magnanimity only a victor could afford — and invited the governors to Washington.[26]

[25] *Official Records*, series 3, II, 582–4.

[26] The account of the Altoona meeting is based on the *New York Herald* of September 25. The *Herald's* correspondent was the only newspaper representative in Altoona. He and his paper were convinced that the governors were conspiring to overthrow Lincoln. Despite his efforts to slant his story to confirm his hypothesis, his account of the actual discussions bears internal evidence of authenticity. The *Herald's* account was republished in Democratic papers and inspired

The governors accepted with alacrity and early the next morning boarded the train for Washington. There Austin Blair joined them, adding strength to the radical wing. Despite their verbal humility, the radicals had not yet abandoned hope, and when they met the President, on the afternoon of September 26, they were prepared to raise the issue of McClellan. But Lincoln forestalled them again. He met them formally and listened in patience while Andrew read the "Address." Then, with studied politeness, the President thanked the governors. This was not what the radicals had planned and they squirmed in their seats.

Finally Kirkwood blurted: "There is an impression out west, Mr. President, that you do not dare to remove McClellan."

Lincoln's rough-hewn face reddened perceptibly, but he calmly turned on the Iowa radical. "If I believed our cause would be benefited by removing General McClellan tomorrow, I would remove him tomorrow," said the President. "I do not believe so today, but if the time shall come when I shall so believe, I will remove him promptly, and not till then."

With that the interview ended. Having received a formal declaration of their subjection, the President did not intend to engage in further dalliance with the governors.[27] The "Address" was a valuable document for Lincoln, and he used it

---

indignant denials of the main thesis, but evoked no denials of the details. The accounts of Kirkwood, Curtin, and Blair, mentioned above, were not written until thirty years later. In 1913 Henry W. Shoemaker wrote a "Biographical Appreciation of Colonel William Sprague" entitled *The Last of the War Governors*, based on an interview with Sprague in 1913. The weird account indicated that the Rhode Island Governor grew more erratic through the years, but is worthless for information about the conference.

[27] Ambler: *Pierpont*, p. 157; Nicolay and Hay: *Lincoln*, VI, 164–7; Clark: *Iowa*, p. 247; "The Altoona Conference," Blair MSS.; Lathrop: *Kirkwood*, pp. 227–30; Byers: *Iowa in the War*, p. 176; Welles: *Diary*, I, 153.

to coerce the state executives. Andrew, in the uncomfortable position of its sponsor, solicited the signatures of the governors who had not come to Altoona. He got the signatures of Vermont's governor Holbrook, Connecticut's Buckingham, Minnesota's Ramsey, Kansas' Robinson, Oregon's Gibbs, and California's Stanford. But Robinson of Kentucky, Gamble of Missouri, Burton of Delaware, Olden of New Jersey and Morgan of New York joined Bradford of Maryland in rejecting the document.[28]

The failure of border-state and moderate governors to support the Emancipation Proclamation encouraged the Democrats. Their papers reiterated the charge that the Altoona conference was a conspiracy to replace Lincoln with Frémont — "a Second Hartford Convention" — and they declared that the conspiring governors had forced Lincoln to issue the Emancipation Proclamation. On Boston Common Judge Joel Parker, professor in the Harvard Law School, explained to a "People's Meeting" the procession of events from the New York War Committee meeting, through the Providence gathering, to the Altoona conference and the Emancipation Proclamation. The Democrats denounced the "Disloyal Governors of the Loyal States." [29]

As the Democrats drove home their charges, Governor Washburne suggested to Andrew that the governors unite in denying the allegations.[30] But, probably knowing they would not agree, the governors said nothing. In the absence of a statement from the governors, Republican papers pounced upon the "Address" as the answer to their Democratic critics. The "Address" proved the Democrats were "wretched calumniators" stirring up "counter revolution and anarchy." The governors actually were devising means for raising

---

[28] Copies of telegrams, dated October 2-30, in Blair MSS.

[29] *New Hampshire Patriot,* September 24, October 1, 15; *Crisis,* October 1; *Chicago Times,* September 29, 1862.

[30] Washburne to Andrew, October 2, 1862; copy in Blair MSS.

larger armies and for a better conduct of the war. The "malevolence" of the "foul and infamous aspersions of the Vallandigham press" deserved only contempt.[31]

This recriminatory interchange hardly convinced even Republicans, and when, months later, Mallory of Kentucky repeated the Democratic theory on the floor of Congress, the Republicans sent Congressman George S. Boutwell to Lincoln.

The President obliged with his own version. "The truth is," he told Boutwell, "I never thought of the meeting of the governors at all. When Lee came over the Potomac I made a resolve that if McClellan drove him back I would send the proclamation after him." [32] Boutwell promptly disposed of Mallory's charges by quoting Lincoln and showing that since the Emancipation Proclamation came a day before the Altoona conference, the governors could not possibly have brought pressure on the President.

And this version, sanctioned by Lincoln, became thereafter the orthodox dogma of the conception of the Emancipation Proclamation. Thirty years later three surviving governors remembered only that they had assembled to strengthen the hand of their wartime leader.[33]

Whatever the reason for the Emancipation Proclamation, Abraham Lincoln knew that the governors' endorsement would not fill the armies. The proclamation and the Altoona

[31] *Detroit Advertiser,* September 29, October 1; *Illinois State Journal,* October 7, 1862.

[32] Blaine: *Twenty Years,* I, 438–9; "Altoona Conference" in Blair MSS.

[33] Nicolay and Hay, in their *Lincoln,* pp. 164–7, labor valiantly to prove the governors had no influence on the *Proclamation.* The accounts of Blair, Curtin, and Kirkwood (*q.v.*) agree in emphasizing that the conference was only designed to express the loyalty of the governors. F. B. Carpenter: *The Inner Life of Abraham Lincoln,* pp. 83–4. William B. Hesseltine and Hazel C. Wolf: "The Altoona Conference and the Emancipation Proclamation," *Pennsylvania Magazine of History and Biography,* LXXI, 195–205.

"Address" only removed such obstacles as Andrew's "conditional patriotism." On the other hand, they strengthened the Democratic appeal to the war-weary, anti-Negro populace. The Emancipation Proclamation made it more necessary than before that Lincoln find new methods for recruiting soldiers and for combating Democrats.

Faced with this necessity, the President determined to extend the suspension of the writ of habeas corpus. For a long time the governors, especially in the Middle West, had been haunted by the specter of a nefarious, disloyal secret society — the Knights of the Golden Circle — whose members (their name was legion) had sold their souls to Jefferson Davis. Every criticism, be it pertinent, paltry, or partisan, was promptly ascribed by the governors to the order.[34] There were seven hundred lodges in Illinois alone,[35] said the Republicans, and Governor Yates solemnly filed each letter, however vague and dubious its contents, which came from constituents who claimed to know the inner secrets of the "nights of the sirculs." [36] Morton frequently grew hysterical over the danger that Kentucky guerrillas, whose lurking shadows he could always see across the Ohio River, might raid Indiana with the help of the local Knights.[37]

In these and other states local military officers, with the consent of the War Department and the urging of the governors, had been arresting critics of the administration. Governor Tod of Ohio got Seward's consent to arrest a Dr.

[34] For complete acceptance of the Republican charges that the Knights of the Golden Circle — sometimes known, in Republican propaganda, as the Sons of Liberty, the Circle of Hosts, or the Union Relief Society — see Foulke: *Morton,* pp. 231 ff.; Flower: *Stanton,* pp. 249–50; Wood Gray: *The Hidden Civil War;* and G. F. Milton: *Abraham Lincoln and the Fifth Column.*

[35] *Illinois State Journal,* July 12, 1862.

[36] Anonymous to Yates, August 18; "Union Forever" to Yates, August 25, Yates MSS., and see use made of such letters in *Illinois State Journal,* August 30, 1862.

[37] Robert Dale Owen to Stanton, June 6, 1862, *Official Records,* series 3, II, 109–10.

Edson B. Olds, onetime member of Congress, for treasonable utterances. He was "a shrewd cunning man," said Tod, "with capacity for great mischief, and should at once be put out of the way." [38] In Illinois, Yates advised that a man who had wished Lincoln was in the hands of Beauregard "should be hanged in ten minutes after he said it." And, he added with unaccustomed humor, "if he says it again he should be hanged in five minutes." [39] Yet when a sixty-three-year-old minister in Egypt wrote the Governor that arbitrary arrests had made the people "dejected, cast down, full of terror, distrustful," Yates promptly denied that he had anything to do with the arrests. The arrests had all been made by the United States marshal — but, added the governor, "No sympathiser with treason should be allowed TO LIVE IN ILLINOIS." [40] In Pennsylvania the editors of the *Harrisburg Patriot and Union* were seized, hurried off to Washington, and for sixteen days imprisoned without a hearing.[41] In New Jersey, however, Governor Olden departed from the gubernatorial standard by interfering to prevent federal officers from carrying off citizens on orders of the Secretary of War.[42]

With arbitrary arrests growing more frequent, Lincoln's order for a general suspension of habeas corpus lent support to the governors' neurotic imaginings that Golden Knights were encircling them. The order — it came on September 24, the day the governors met at Altoona — authorized the arrest of all persons discouraging enlistments, resisting the draft, "or guilty of any disloyal practice." The same day the Secretary of War provided for a provost-marshal-general and special provost marshals in the states and ordered them to arrest deserters, seize disloyal persons, detect spies, and report treasonable practices.[43] The ostensible purpose of sus-

[38] Randall and Ryan: *Ohio*, IV, 185.

[39] M. Bradley to Yates, and reply, July 31, 1862, Yates MSS.

[40] Elder J. Hartley to Yates, August 30, and Yates to Hartley, September 10, 1862, Yates MSS.

[41] Davis: *Party Politics in Pennsylvania*, pp. 248-9.

[42] *Chicago Times*, September 4, 1862.

[43] *Official Records*, series 3, II, 586-8.

pending the writ was to facilitate the drafting of troops, but the governors made use of their visit to Washington to get a postponement of the draft until after the elections. The first use of the new suspension of habeas corpus was the intimidation of voters in the fall elections.

Within a few weeks of the Emancipation Proclamation and the suspension of habeas corpus came the state and congressional elections. Six states — Massachusetts, New Jersey, Delaware, New York, Michigan, and Kansas — chose governors, and nearly all chose state legislators. The issues in these, as in the congressional and senatorial contests, were the conduct of the war, emancipation and the Negro, personal liberty, and national conscription. The verdict of the polls showed clearly that the people of the North were opposed to the Emancipation Proclamation, opposed to governmental encroachment on individual rights, and opposed to conscription. The elections offered the first general opportunity for popular expression on the developing Republican program, and with only a few exceptions the radicals suffered defeat.

Four gubernatorial contests had significance to the party's leaders. No one paid attention to frontier Kansas, where the Republicans — all radical sons of New England — nominated and elected Thomas Carney, an Ohio-born wholesale merchant.[44] Nor did New Jersey's contest inspire much interest. The state was so completely overshadowed by New York and Pennsylvania, both of which went Democratic, that few were surprised that Joel Parker, arch-Democrat, won the governorship. Parker's campaign denunciations of abolitionists, federal usurpation, and conscription conformed to the prevailing Democratic dogma, but neither his personality nor his intellect attracted notice.[45] Finding nothing of importance in New Jersey or Kansas, political observers ignored

[44] *Crisis,* November 5, 1862; "Carney" in *Dictionary of American Biography.*

[45] "Parker" in *Dictionary of American Biography.*

them to watch the campaigns in Massachusetts, New York, Michigan, and little Delaware.

The watchers on the political horizons of Massachusetts saw a strange phenomenon: the Emancipation Proclamation helped John Andrew retain his place! Early in September the Republican state convention met in Worcester. Although the call for the convention invited all who would "support the present national and state governments" and who were in favor of "all means necessary for the effectual suppression of the Rebellion," the delegates who assembled were not all of one mind. Old Whigs and moderates among them, nauseated by the radical extremism, opposed a resolution endorsing Senator Sumner for re-election. When they were overruled, they sent out a call for a People's Party to support the President against the radicals. The *Springfield Republican* endorsed the movement, and the schism frightened Andrew. But the Emancipation Proclamation saved him by cutting the ground from under his opponents. "Poor document" as it was, he recognized it as a "mighty act" upon which he might capitalize. His patriotism now knew no conditions, and he loudly avowed his support of Lincoln's policy. The People's Party organizers were taken aback, but they assembled in Faneuil Hall, listened to Joel Parker of Harvard denounce the Altoona conspiracy, passed resolutions favoring Lincoln's border-state policy, praised McClellan, and nominated Charles Devens for governor. Assembling later, the Democrats made no nominations, but endorsed Devens.[46]

In addition to his luck in the Emancipation Proclamation's confounding his enemies, Andrew had a further opportunity to take the wind from his enemies' sails. His opponents charged that the Governor's policy would bring Negroes into Massachusetts to compete with white workmen. But when General Dix at Fort Monroe, with Stanton's approval, proposed sending "loyal blacks" to Massachusetts to prevent their being recaptured, Andrew promptly pro-

[46] Pearson: *Andrew,* II, 53 ff.; Schouler: *Massachusetts,* I, 371; *Appleton's Cyclopædia,* II, 563–5.

tested. The best protection for the fugitive slaves was arms
in their hands: they should be taken into the army. But, said
the Governor, the Northern states were the worst possible
asylum for people who needed the climate of the South. If
they had to be moved, they should be sent to Hilton Head
in South Carolina, where they could retain their health, be
trained as soldiers, and labor economically.[47] This answer
enraged Democrats, who promptly damned Andrew for in-
consistency, but it pleased moderate Republicans and the
mass of the people.[48] In November, Andrew won another
year in office by a vote of 79,835 to 52,587 for Devens.

The other state to elect a radical was Michigan. On the
day of the Altoona conference, the Republican convention
heard Austin Blair reavow his abolitionism. Lincoln, said
Blair, had removed a great load from the hearts of the people with the Emancipation Proclamation. "I rejoice to say
that I can now, with my whole heart, support the administration and the President of the United States." The war had
become a "war of ideas." [49] Democrats promptly pounced
upon this statement and found in it proof that Blair had
been withholding troops to force the President into emancipation.[50] With equal fervor they seized upon Blair's statement, made in Washington, where he had joined the Altoona
governors, that the government should "send to France for
a guillotine to chop off heads" of the disloyal.[51] Neither of
these statements had much effect on the electorate. In fact,
the election in Michigan did not center on Blair. The radical warmongering of Senator Zachariah Chandler was, comparatively, so much more offensive to the Democrats that
they neglected Blair to concentrate on the Senator. Chandler had a good organization, and the Republicans campaigned with vigor, announcing that the voters must choose

[47] Schouler: *Massachusetts*, I, 376–7.
[48] *Crisis*, November 19, 1862.
[49] *Detroit Advertiser*, September 25, 1862.
[50] *Chicago Times*, September 29, 1862.
[51] *Boston Post*, September 29, 1862.

between patriotism and treason. At the polls, Chandler supporters won and carried with them Blair and five of the state's
six congressmen. It was the best showing the Republicans
made in any state. "We saved the state," exulted one successful candidate for the legislature, "to stand by the side of
Massachusetts." [52]

In New York the attempt to elect a radical of the type of
Andrew and Blair met disaster. Governor Morgan's moderate administration had incensed the radicals and they determined to get rid of him. Perceiving the hopelessness of his
own cause, Morgan announced he would not be a candidate.
Then Thurlow Weed, in his own and Secretary Seward's
interests, hit upon a scheme to unite both Democrats and
Republicans behind General John A. Dix. But neither party
would accept Weed's moderate candidate. The radicals dominated the Republican convention, rejected all councils of
moderation, and nominated General James S. Wadsworth,
Stanton's right-hand man and military governor of the District of Columbia. In that capacity he had endeared himself
to the abolitionists by obstructing the operation of the Fugitive Slave Law in the District. He had been a "Silas Wright
Democrat," and he remained an uncompromising leader
even when it became obvious that his ideals were imperiling
his chances of success. [53]

To oppose the radical choice the Democrats chose Horatio
Seymour, a lawyer, dairy-farmer, speculator in Wisconsin
timber lands, and politician of the "Marcy" wing of the New
York Democracy. Seymour was gentle in speech, moderate in
manner, temperate in his judgments as in his habits. He
had more than an amateur's interest in science, keeping a
"polar microscope," a telescope, and sundry scientific appa-
ratus in the front parlor of his Utica home. He had been
Governor a dozen years before, and had been defeated for
re-election.

[52] H. H. Crapo, Sr., to W. W. Crapo, November 10, 1862, Crapo
MSS.; Moore: *Michigan*, I, 423–4; Smith: *Blair*, pp. 88–90.

[53] H. G. Pearson: *James S. Wadsworth of Geneseo*, pp. 140–1.

Seymour and the Democrats relied largely upon the Constitution in their campaign. While Wadsworth ostentatiously remained at his post of duty, Seymour harangued the citizens on the evils of arbitrary arrests and the Emancipation Proclamation. The latter was "a proposal for the butchery of women and children," for "arson and murder," for "lust and rapine." Moreover, Seymour assured the electorate, the Democrats had no desire to embarrass Lincoln — they only wanted to bring Washington to a realization that the war was solely for the suppression of the rebellion. It was not fought to change the social system of the states.

The climax of the campaign brought the contestants together at Cooper Institute a few days before election. At the beginning of the contest the radical managers had rejected Thurlow Weed's practical and experienced advice. But as the campaign went badly, they had invited him to their councils. Weed raised money and did what he could to revive the hopeless cause. When Wadsworth arrived for the Cooper Institute speech, Weed advised him to speak for Lincoln and the Union. But Wadsworth's principles were sounder than his judgment. He would have none of such "infamy." "We have paid for peace and freedom in the blood of our sons," he said, "let us now have it." His speech had fervor without poise, passion without compromise. Seymour spoke for Lincoln and the Union under the Constitution, and the bottom dropped out of the Republican cause. Two years before, Morgan had a majority of 50,000; on November 4, 1862 Seymour had 11,000 more supporters than his radical opponent.[54]

Seymour and Parker were the only Democrats to be elected governors in the fall elections, but the federal government saved the little slave state of Delaware by a narrow margin. Delaware was the last of the "border states" to be

[54] S. Mitchell: *Horatio Seymour of New York*, p. 244; D. G. Croly: *Seymour and Blair*, pp. 9 ff., 77 ff.; Barnes: *Memoir of Thurlow Weed*, II, 424–9; Pearson: *Wadsworth*, pp. 152–64; Welles: *Diary*, I, 154, 162–3; Blaine: *Twenty Years*, I, 442–3.

brought under control. Democratic Governor Burton had found no authority in the state's laws for raising troops and had responded to the government's frequent calls for men by pointing out this constitutional barrier. Volunteers, however, had been raised in the state. Throughout 1861 peace rallies had annoyed the government, and in June a peace convention in Dover adopted resolutions opposing the war and pointing out that the "doctrines and measures of the war party" would, whatever their apparent purpose, subvert the state governments and erect "a consolidated government on the ruins of the federal constitution." [55] In December, Secretary Cameron, while praising the "good sense and patriotism" of the people who had triumphed over traitors, proposed enlarging the state by giving it the Eastern Shore counties of Maryland and Virginia.[56]

Although this proposal received no attention, the subversion of the state went on. In March 1862 Colonel James Wallace, with Maryland home guards, took possession of the Dover Courthouse, and encouraged Unionists by arresting and imprisoning a number of leading citizens without trial. Later in the summer Delaware Unionists formed a "Union Party" and nominated William Cannon for governor. The candidate had long been a Democrat and had been a delegate to the Willard's Hotel peace conference, but with the firing on Sumter had become an ardent supporter of the war. The campaign promptly developed bitterness, and Unionists charged that secessionists from Maryland planned to invade the state on election day. As that day neared, Cannon and George P. Fisher, candidate for Congress, asked the War Department for troops. Promptly federal provost marshals, selected from Unionist ranks, began to operate, and 1,000 to 1,200 federal troops occupied the State fairgrounds at Dover. On November 4 the troops were guarding the polling places. Stationed before the windows of the polls, they

[55] Conrad: *Delaware*, I, 203–4.
[56] *Official Records*, series 3, I, 701, 708.

raised their drawn swords to permit the passage of voters who carried Unionist tickets. Democrats faced arrest, delays, and test oaths, or were deprived of their tickets and forced to cast Republican ballots. The result was Cannon's election by a bare majority of 111, while Fisher lost in the congressional race by 37 votes. Democrats won a majority of one in the state Senate, and of seven in the House.[57]

Although Seymour and Parker were the only Democrats elected governors in 1862, the Democrats won victories in the other states. The Emancipation Proclamation, growing radicalism, high taxes, increasing federal despotism, the imminence of the draft, and general war-weariness proved serious handicaps to the Republican candidates. In October, Ohio's citizens sent 14 Democrats and 5 Republicans to Congress, while in Pennsylvania the Democrats carried the state offices and elected half the congressmen. In Indiana, 7 of the 11 districts went Democratic and a new legislature had an anti-Lincoln and anti-Morton majority. By November the Republicans in the other states were desperately attempting to stem the tide with arbitrary arrests and soldiers' votes. Illinois soldiers were distributed near their homes and duly voted for Republicans on election day. But Illinois and Wisconsin went Democratic. Only Iowa and Minnesota, where soldiers in the field were permitted to vote, returned Republicans to Congress or state offices.

But when the votes were counted, it appeared that the Republicans would still control Congress. The border states, where the troops watched the polls and the voters balloted under the supervision of the provost marshals, had elected enough Republicans to overcome the Democrats. The people had rejected radicalism's destructive ambitions, had repudiated the Emancipation Proclamation and the Altoona

[57] Powell: *History of Delaware*, pp. 240–59; Conrad: *Delaware*, I, 197–8; *Report of the Committee of the General Assembly . . . of Delaware* (1863).

Address, and had rebuked the administration for its nationalizing tendencies — but the border-state policy had saved
the party's control of the government.

The lesson was clear enough. The governors had lost the
power to control their states; they could neither deliver men
to the armies nor voters at the polls. Only the President
could preserve the party — and he could save it only through
the methods that had been tested in Missouri, Kentucky,
Maryland, and Delaware.[58]

[58] Blaine: *Twenty Years*, I, 436–7, 441–4; Davis: *Pennsylvania Politics*, pp. 239–55, 260–3; Foulke: *Morton*, I, 203–7, 229; *Appleton's Cyclopædia*, II, 527–8; Weeden: *War Government*, p. 226; Cole: *Era of
the Civil War*, pp. 296–7; Reid: *Ohio*, I, 92; Folwell: *Minnesota*, II,
333; *Chicago Times*, August 13, September 27, 1862; Letters of J. L.
Camp, August 17; D. P. Ferry, August 19, September 17; F. Moro, August 20; M. G. Atwood, August 23; J. A. Wetherby, September 2;
A. Kitchell, October 9; G. I. Bergen, October 21; Soldiers at Camp
Jackson, October 23; Lewis Ellsworth, October 28; T. H. Phillips,
October 24; O. H. Browning, October 27, Yates MSS.; Nicolay and
Hay: *Lincoln*, VI, 381–2; Kenneth Stampp: "Indiana in the Civil War,"
p. 292, unpublished doctoral dissertation, dated 1941, in the library of
the University of Wisconsin.

Chapter 14

The Governors and Conscription

THE ELECTIONS of 1862 showed clearly that most of the governors no longer controlled their states. In 1860 they had been leading figures in the new Republican Party, and, despite divergent views among them, they had determined party policy and governmental action on the issues of compromise and war. As the war began, they had given it enthusiastic support, rallying men for the armies, urging their constituents on to sacrifice, and performing their manifold new duties with relative efficiency. But the exigencies of the war, and divided councils between the moderate and radical wings of the Republicans, had enabled Abraham Lincoln to assume and assert the leadership of both his party and the government. Whether this leadership could be consolidated into power depended, in part, on the President's ability to maintain the balance between his party's factions. In part, too, it depended on his ability to raise troops outside the agencies of the states.

By November 1862 the governors had reached the limits of their several abilities to raise men for the armies. The effects of initial confusion in raising, equipping, and training men and in supplying them with officers had been cumulative, and even after the original defects had been cleared away, the psychological effects on soldiers and civilians remained. Then too, military losses and the political squabbles over McClellan had served to take much of the glamour from the soldier's uniform. The uniform itself was made of expensive shoddy, and soldiers and civilians came to look askance at the shoddy contractors, huddled secretively about the government, who grew rich at the expense of soldiers, bond-buyers, and taxpayers. Moreover, there were always Democrats ready to point accusing fingers at Republican misfeasance and to ascribe immoral motives to all adherents of the opposite party.

It all added up to war-weariness. At the polls the voters cast votes, when they were permitted a free choice, against the radical program of emancipation and confiscation. At the recruiting stations, by failing to enlist, the war-weary people cast an even more effective vote. Against this wave of negation the governors had no weapons that they dared to use. Political considerations prevented them from coercing the people, and their reluctance to exercise power enabled Lincoln and the national government to step into the breach. The national government asserted and maintained the power to conscript men for the armies, and the state executives yielded to or co-operated with the Washington authorities. Eventually states' rights, weakened by war-weariness and rendered inarticulate by politics, died of attrition.

In the Southern Confederacy, where states' rights was an integral part of the political structure, the governors battled valiantly, and on the whole successfully, against the aggressive tendencies of the Richmond government. The Confederate government faced the same war-weariness, a similar factional bitterness, and the same growing hostility to national aggrandizement. In the South the governors headed the dissident groups, interposing the power of their states to protect individual liberties. In the North the governors generally fell in line with the national program and became mere agents — albeit querulous ones — of the national power. In the end, states' rights crippled the Confederacy and contributed largely to its defeat, while Lincoln's government effectively crippled the states.

The declining power of the states received significant illustration in August 1862 when the Indians of Minnesota went on the warpath. Long years of exploitation and injustice had bred a deep resentment among the Dakota tribesmen along the frontier. When this resentment came to a head and strong bands of red men attacked the white settlements, Governor Ramsey promptly appointed his old partner and political rival, Henry H. Sibley, to command Minnesota's militia. In a six weeks' campaign Sibley put down the uprising, captured more than a thousand Indians, and sentenced three hundred and three to death.

The Indians were clearly a federal responsibility, but the task of suppressing them fell upon Minnesota. Ramsey begged, almost in vain, for aid. "This is not our war; it is a national war," he told Lincoln. The War Department recognized its responsibility by creating a new military department and sending General John Pope, recently a failure in the Army of the Potomac, to take command, but the War Department and Pope allowed Sibley and the Minnesota troops to do the fighting.

Nevertheless, when the battles were over, the President interposed the federal authority to prevent Minnesota from lynching, within the forms of martial law, the wards of the nation. Pope and Sibley and Ramsey and the people of Minnesota were equally insistent upon prompt and condign execution of the savages. "It is my purpose utterly to exterminate the Sioux," proclaimed Pope with the bombast that had already won him fame in the East. "They are to be treated as maniacs or wild beasts." Pope himself had no concept that he could not execute the prisoners on the verdict of Sibley's drumhead court martial, but he sent, in a routine manner, the names of 303 condemned Indians to his commander-in-chief. Lincoln promptly demanded to see the complete records of the trials. When they arrived, the President turned them over to two competent advisers with orders to sort out those Indians guilty of violating women and of wanton butchery.

As it dawned on Minnesota that the President might stay the vengeance of the state, a popular outcry demanded the destruction of the prisoners. Ramsey, displaying an attitude toward minority groups in Minnesota that was quite different from his opinions on those in Mississippi, urged Lincoln to kill every Sioux. Otherwise, he threatened, "private vengeance" would dispatch them. As Lincoln delayed, the Minnesota Governor proposed: "Turn them over to me and I will order their execution." But Lincoln listened to Henry B. Whipple, Episcopal bishop of Minnesota, who told him "about the rascality of this Indian business" until, in Lincoln's words, "I felt it down to my boots." Then the President studied the trial records and concluded that only thirty-nine of the prisoners had committed crimes deserving death. These he ordered Sibley to execute; the others were held for a time and eventually released. Before this exercise of Presidential authority Ramsey, Sibley, Pope, and the Minnesotans grumbled, but they raised no hand to interpose state vengeance in the face of national clemency.[1]

Meantime, in neighboring Wisconsin, the Indian attack brought the normally calm Governor Salomon to the verge of panic. Wisconsin, too, had Indians, and Salomon presently heard rumors that they were growing restless. Suddenly succumbing to an unwonted hysteria, the Governor wired Stanton that Confederate emissaries were tampering with the Winnebago braves. The state needed arms and ammunition, and the Governor peremptorily demanded arms for the home guards and transportation for his troops. But Stanton was not to be rushed. He asked Salomon for "some satisfactory evidence" of a "reasonable necessity."

Such placidity enraged the Wisconsinite. Stanton's delays were "cruel," for the Secretary knew there were thousands of Indians in Wisconsin. "As executive of the State you must allow me to be the judge of the necessity for ammunition," said Salomon. But this only made the Secretary of

[1] W. W. Folwell: *A History of Minnesota,* II, 147–211, and especially pp. 147, 186–7, 191, 193, 197, 202–3, 204, 208, 209. Cf. also *Official Records,* series 2, V, 84, 86; W. P. Shortridge: *The Transition of a Typical Frontier,* pp. 150–1, 159–60.

War more stubborn. "You are entirely mistaken in supposing you are the exclusive judge," he replied coldly. Only the President could judge, and Salomon had not offered any facts for Lincoln's judgment. Instead, the Governor had contented himself "with giving imperious orders." Then, with an unaccustomed air of resignation, the Secretary added: "The Department has borne, and will continue to bear them patiently, and will act upon any facts you may communicate." [2]

The success of Sibley's campaign stilled any enthusiasm Wisconsin's Indians may have had for joining the outbreak, and Salomon's panic subsided. The incident, however, illustrated once again the waning authority of the states and the waxing assurance of the national government. Stanton's cold rationality confounded the overwrought Governor, and though the scene found both actors out of character, the curtain fell as another episode found the national government gaining prestige at the expense of the states.

The declining power of the states received further illustration as the governors faced the necessity of drafting their men into the state militias. Lincoln's call of July 2 for 300,000 men for three years had been based on a spurious "request" extracted from the governors. Despite their difficulties, the governors were making progress toward raising the men when, on August 4, the President, without warning, called on them to furnish an additional 300,000 militiamen for a period of nine months. If the quotas could not be raised by volunteering, said the President, the governors would have to raise the troops by a draft.

In actual fact, these two calls were not designed to raise 600,000 men. In truth, it was not 600,000 at all: for the war department allotted the quotas to the several states with a generous hand, and the assignments totaled 334,835 under each call. But, to confuse the situation still further, the second call was merely to supplement the first. Then the de-

[2] *Official Records*, series 3, II, 508–9, 518, 522–3.

partment determined that one three-year volunteer was equal to four nine-months militiamen, and informed some of the governors that any excess of volunteers could be used, at the ratio of four to one, to reduce the number of militia. Any deficit in the quota for either call, however, must be raised by a draft — and the department began to give the governors instruction on enrolling and conscripting the citizens.

None of the governors wanted to draft their constituents — though a number of them, seeing the 1862 elections approaching, wished they could find a way to draft Democrats. One of Dick Yates's voluntary advisers urged him to break up the Democratic opposition by such methods. "Take a son or brother cousin or nephew put him in the army and you find there is a growing interest amongst his friends for the welfare of our country." And, too, if they were drafted and made to "know their places," they would then "know that we have a government and that it has power." Yates thought this a "good letter" and may have wished he could impress the government's power on Democrats alone.[3]

The next best thing to drafting Democrats was to use the threat of the draft to discourage political opponents. Each governor sought and obtained permission to postpone the draft until after the elections, but in the meantime the enrollment for the draft went on. Citizens who obstructed enrollment officers were arrested and held without benefit of habeas corpus until after election day. In some places enrollment officers went to the polls to write down the names of the voters. Democrats were sure that these fraudulent activities were designed to suppress popular liberties.

To avoid a draft, the governors tried hard to raise their quotas by volunteering. In the end only the Eastern seaboard and Indiana, Ohio, and Wisconsin had to draft men into the militia. States, cities, counties, and townships offered bounties for enlistments, while every form of social pressure induced men to enter the ranks. Local pride com-

[3] Joab Porter to Yates, August 14, 1862, Yates MSS.

bined with national patriotism to urge men to enlist and avert the "shame" of conscription. So successful were these efforts that the governors raised 421,465 instead of the 334,835 volunteers called for. In addition they raised 87,588 militia. Since the excess of volunteers was credited against the militia call on a four-to-one ratio, the governors raised about six per cent more men than they needed to meet the two calls.[4]

Although the states successfully met the calls, they did not do so without troubles. Andrew faced the necessity of raising nearly 4,000 men by a draft. Expecting a riot in Boston, he held troops in readiness and asked Secretary Stanton to institute courts martial for dissatisfied citizens.[5] In Ohio the state's provost marshal used troops to break up one encampment of a thousand men who had assembled to resist the enrollment officers. Still, Governor Tod found that the draft went off harmoniously and that by offering bounties to the militia draftees he could get four fifths of them to enlist in the three-year regiments. He avoided further trouble by permitting conscientious objectors to pay $300 commutation, and with the $50,000 he collected from them he hired substitutes and provided care for the sick and wounded.[6]

In Schuylkill County, Pennsylvania, the enrollment officers met such resistance that Governor Curtin begged Stanton to call off the draft. The Governor feared the Molly Maguires, a secret Irish miners' society, which was well organized and strongly opposed conscription. Enrollment officers had attempted to get lists of workers from the mine-owners, but the employers, fearing retaliation from the workers, refused to co-operate. Stanton, however, who had no sympathy with Curtin's difficulties — and less with Curtin — ordered the Governor to enforce the draft, and he

[4] *Official Records*, series 3, II, 188, 271.

[5] Ibid., II, 640–1.

[6] Ibid., II, 650, 693; Carl Sandburg: *Abraham Lincoln, the War Years*, II, 156.

sent two regiments to aid the work. Then Curtin appealed
to Lincoln, who advised that "it might be well, in an extreme emergency, to be content with the appearance of exe-
cuting the laws." Curtin thereupon sent a commissioner into
the disaffected region to exempt men, and the "appearance"
of a draft was maintained.[7]

Wisconsin and Indiana also witnessed extended resistance
to the draft. In Indiana two enrollment officers were murdered, and in several places women met the state inquisitors
with a barrage of eggs, while rioting men used bricks, clubs,
and guns.[8] In Wisconsin, Governor Salomon's troubles were
more serious: in one county the boxes containing names of
potential draftees were destroyed, and it became extremely
hazardous for the draft officers to serve notices personally.
In Ozaukee County a mob assaulted a commissioner. Salomon issued a special proclamation to Milwaukeeans, warning them not to resist the draft and assuring them that he
would enforce the draft at any cost. Salomon begged Stanton
for 600 troops and for permission to serve notices by pub-
lication. The Governor arrested resistant citizens until he
had one hundred and fifty of them. Then he urged Stanton
to take them out of the state.[9]

Although the draft was subsequently enforced, Salomon's
troubles did not end. The prisoners whom he had confined
— and about whose disposal he could extract neither advice
nor aid from Stanton — appealed to the state Supreme
Court. The judges declared the President had no power to
suspend the writ of habeas corpus in Wisconsin, or to declare martial law therein, or to subject persons resisting the

　　[7] A. K. McClure: *Abraham Lincoln and Men of War Times*, pp.
80–4. For further conflict between Curtin and the War Department
over assigning drafted men to old regiments, cf. *Official Records*, series
3, II, 679, 696–7, 735, 739–40, 743.

　　[8] W. D. Foulke: *Life of Oliver P. Morton*, I, 199; Sandburg: *War
Years*, II, 156.

　　[9] *Official Records*, series 3, II, 704, 761, 765; *Wisconsin State Journal*, November 18, 1862; W. F. Raney: *Wisconsin: A Story of Progress*,
p. 162.

draft to court martial. Governor Salomon was a good constitutionalist, and his experience with the Ozaukee rioters
confirmed his cautious inclination to agree with the "loyal
and patriotic judges." He recommended that the President
discharge the prisoners and avoid a conflict between the
civil and the military authorities.[10]

But the national authorities could not afford to permit
state courts to limit the power of the national executive. Immediately Senator T. O. Howe wired the Governor and the
judges to suspend all proceedings until he could get to Madison to inspect the record for the President.[11] Arriving in
Madison, Howe requested Stanton to parole the prisoners,
while he prepared to argue the case before the Supreme
Court. In March the court unanimously reversed itself,
holding the draft and the suspension of habeas corpus alike
valid. Stanton thanked the Senator with "exceeding joy."
"Accounts from all parts of the country," he added, "show
that the national spirit is growing stronger and stronger." [12]

The nationalizing tendencies, illustrated by the punishment
of the Minnesota Indians and by the militia draft, soon met
a more vigorous and less amenable opponent than the Wisconsin Supreme Court. The Democratic upsurge in the elections of 1862, the widespread suspicion of the federal government's growing power, the deep popular objection to the
abolitionists and the Emancipation Proclamation were all
embodied in Horatio Seymour, newly elected Governor of
New York. As chief executive of the Union's most populous
state, Seymour was in a position to assume the leadership of
the states' rights forces — a leadership that might well place
him in the White House. To the tasks of crystallizing, or-

[10] *Official Records,* series 2, V, 174.

[11] Ibid., series 3, III, 17.

[12] Ibid., series 2, V, 190, series 3, III, 103. The ablest account of
the militia draft, as of all other aspects of raising troops, is Fred A.
Shannon: *The Organization and Administration of the Union Army,
1861–1865.* Cf. especially II, 288–92.

ganizing, and inspiring the opposition, Seymour brought an integrity that was incorruptible and a scholarly intelligence beyond the wont of politicians. Neither quality, however — even when backed by the mounting popular discontent and growing war-weariness — could prevail against the power and propaganda of the national government.

Abraham Lincoln beheld the rise of Horatio Seymour with well-placed apprehension. Shortly after the elections the President, in lowly mood, told Thurlow Weed that Seymour had greater power for good than any other man in the country. He could bring the Democrats into line, put down the rebellion, and save the government. "Tell him for me," said Lincoln as he dispatched Seward's alter ego to Albany, "that if he'll render this service to his country, I shall cheerfully make way for him as my successor." Greater love hath no man for his country than that he would lay down the Presidency for it, and Weed, impressed, hurried to take Seymour to the mountain top to show him the kingdom.[13]

Seymour heard the emissary in silence, giving no indication of his intended course. He did, however, look about for an adjutant general who would act in harmony with the national government.[14] But he neither listened to Weed nor consulted Lincoln about his inaugural address. Instead, he sought advice from fellow Democrats and heeded their counsels to make his initial speech a ringing denunciation of the tendencies of the day.[15] He would, he said in his first official utterance, strive "to maintain and defend the sovereignty and jurisdiction" of New York.

The Governor's inaugural address began by calling attention to his oath to support the constitutions of both the United States and New York. The dual nature of his duties was thus symbolized, said Seymour. Not only must the national Constitution be held inviolate, but the rights of the

---

13 *Memoir of Thurlow Weed*, II, 428.
14 Stewart Mitchell: *Horatio Seymour of New York*, p. 257.
15 Ibid., p. 267.

states must be sacred. A consolidated government, declared the Governor, would destroy "the essential home-rights and liberties of the people."

Thereupon Seymour launched into a discussion of the economic and political aspects of the war. The central and Western states, he contended, were opposed to the views of both the North and the South. So long as the war was for the preservation of the Union and the Constitution, these states supported Lincoln. When the administration abandoned the border-state policy it lost the support of the central and Western states. These states, with the greatest population and resources, were determined to defend states' rights and individual liberty at the same time that they saved the Union.

With a realism strange to the political oratory of war, Seymour placed the unionism of the central and Western states on economic grounds; the West needed the Southern markets. But there were constitutional implications as well in the situation. Division of the country would produce a centralization of power. The small states, explained Seymour — and by small states he meant New England — were more willing than the larger ones to centralize power, because they had a disproportionate power in the national government. A division of the Union, or the disfranchisement of the Southern states — making them territories — would enhance the power of the lesser regions. The six New England states, with New Jersey and Delaware, whose combined population was less than New York's, would balance, in the national government, the great producing states of New York, Pennsylvania, Ohio, Indiana, Illinois, Michigan, Wisconsin, and Iowa. And, in turn, this concentration of political power would place the national economy in leading-strings to the limited economic pursuits of New England. The national debt would be owned on the Atlantic seaboard and would divide the country into the "perilous sectional relations of debtor and creditor regions." Then, the Governor continued, the advantages of the protective tariff, growing out of this debt, would accrue to the same creditor states that enjoyed the excessive political power.

The only way to prevent these developments was the restoration of the Union — complete in all of its parts. "No section," proclaimed the Governor, "must be disorganized beyond the unavoidable necessities of war." The vigor of the war would be increased when the national effort was concentrated on restoring the Union, and not upon a "bloody, barbarous, revolutionary, and unconstitutional scheme" that gratified hatred, party ambition, and sectional advantage! [16]

Interspersed through this economic and political dissertation, and illustrating his exposition, were Seymour's comments on the unconstitutionality of the Emancipation Proclamation, arbitrary arrests, and conscription. The Governor clearly perceived his opportunity to place himself at the head of the discontented, furnish them ideological leadership and political direction — and to ride the wave, without Lincoln's help, into the White House. Promptly the address became a sensation, and men went mad in pairs over it. The legislature of Indiana, rejecting Morton's annual message, acknowledged Seymour as its leader. Border-state governors commented approvingly, while the *Journal of Commerce,* the *World,* and the *Chicago Times* were ecstatic. William Cullen Bryant of the *Post* ruminated that while Seymour spoke much truth on arbitrary arrests, yet these methods had saved Maryland, Kentucky, and Missouri for the Union. Fire, he thought, would have to be fought with fire. But Horace Greeley, eschewing any thought of rationality, denounced the address as "dexterous dishonesty" concocted of cowardice, drunkenness, and masked disloyalty by a demagogue.[17]

In Horatio Seymour, it was evident, the forces of national

[16] Lincoln (ed.) : *Messages from the Governors of New York,* V, 464–82.

[17] Mitchell: *Seymour,* pp. 265–7.

concentration had met a foeman worthy of their steel. Lincoln, as usual, approached his antagonist cautiously. He listened respectfully when John Seymour appeared at the White House as his brother's personal ambassador. The President explained with pointed patience that he had the same interest as the Governor in the life of the country. He pointed out that unless the Union were saved, there would be no next president of the United States. He pointed out that most of the officers in the army were Democrats — and he succeeded, in talking to Brother John, in keeping all discussion of Seymour's policies on a partisan level. Not once did he admit that the New York Governor had other objectives than the Presidency. Brother John could only sputter that Brother Horatio had no ambitions to be president. Abraham Lincoln probably smiled understandingly.[18]

But out of that interview grew the technique for handling Seymour — the Governor was never to be regarded as more than an ambitious schemer for power. Moreover, the very exigencies of the situation put Seymour at a disadvantage. His words — however scholarly — could not stand against Lincoln's Union-saving sentiments or the radicals' humanitarian gabble. Knowing this, Seymour sought to avoid letter-writing and to conduct business with Washington through personal messengers. But therein again he played into Lincoln's hands. The President was master of a literary style that Seymour, for all his oratory, could not match. And Lincoln, seeing that Seymour would not write, awaited an opportunity to put the Governor at a disadvantage.

Late in March the time came. Congress had passed a bill for national conscription, and Seymour had sounded his objections. Then Lincoln took up his pen and, ignoring the fact that he had talked long and intimately with Seymour's closest associates, wrote a letter whose sweet reasonableness must, one way or another, force Seymour's hand. "You and

[18] Ibid., 275 ff.

I are substantially strangers," began the President, "and I write this chiefly that we may become better acquainted. I, for the time being, am at the head of a nation which is in great peril, and you are at the head of the greatest state of that nation." Certainly, said the President, there could be no difference of purpose beween them, and if they differed on means, the differences should be as small as possible. Moreover, such differences "should not be enhanced by unjust suspicions on one side or the other." "Please," begged the President, "write me at least as long a letter as this, of course saying in it what you think fit."

Against so charming and disarming an appeal the Governor had no weapons. Defeated before he started, Seymour could only send another messenger. But he wrote a note saying he would reply, and promising support for any constitutional acts of the administration. Lincoln ignored the fact that Brother John again appeared to talk of arbitrary arrests. This was no letter as long as his, and, having waited a reasonable time, he gave his own letter to the press. In the situation, Seymour, champion of states' rights, was definitely worsted.[19]

In the meantime, as Lincoln sparred with Seymour, the government tried the experiment of raising Negro soldiers. A week before Seymour's inaugural the President issued the formal Emancipation Proclamation. The radicals, who had determined to accept the proclamation as a milestone, promptly began to push for further gains. In their opinion, the Negroes should be given an opportunity to prove on the battlefield their right to be free. In their effort to make soldiers of Negroes the radicals had the support of governors who were finding it difficult to persuade white men to fight for freedom.

Already by November 1862 a regiment of confiscated slaves had been enrolled in the Carolinas by General Rufus

[19] Nicolay and Hay: *Abraham Lincoln, a History*, VII, 10–12.

Saxton, while another, composed largely of free mulattoes, was forming under Ben Butler in New Orleans.[20]

Early in January, Cyrus Hamlin entered his father's office in Washington with a list of eight or ten officers who had declared themselves anxious to command Negro troops. Vice President Hamlin, ever eager to advance the radical cause, carried the list to Lincoln and begged permission for the officers to raise Negro regiments. Lincoln — to Hamlin's surprise — agreed, and sent Hamlin hurrying over to the War Department to break the news to Stanton. The great-bearded Secretary, who kept his emotions on tap for dramatic occasions, threw his arms about the Vice President. "Thank God for this," he exclaimed as he wept for joy. "Thank God for this."

But Lincoln's wry comment was: "I'm glad to know you both are satisfied." [21]

A few days later John Andrew was closeted with the Secretary of War. The Massachusetts Governor was having no easy time raising troops for the war he had so sedulously promoted. Learning that the government would accept Negroes, Andrew asked permission to raise a regiment, and, since Massachusetts had but few Negroes, the Governor proposed to recruit the regiment in North Carolina and Virginia. Stanton acceded to his fellow radical's suggestion, and Andrew hurried away to organize the Fifty-fourth Massachusetts Volunteers. Realizing the importance of the move, he selected officers carefully — and was soon beseeching Stanton to permit him to appoint Negro officers.

With Stanton's passive consent, Andrew appointed a Negro chaplain for his regiment. But even this did not produce a sufficient number of colored troops. As the sparse Negro population of Massachusetts failed to produce enough sol-

[20] *Official Records*, series 3, II, 663–4, 695; Shannon: *Union Armies*, II, 159.

[21] C. E. Hamlin: *Life and Times of Hannibal Hamlin*, pp. 431–2, tells the story. It is probably apocryphal.

diers, Andrew sent his recruiting agents into other states. This brought results, and by the middle of May the regiment was ready to march. Elated by this success, Andrew began to raise another regiment, but other governors objected to raids on their colored constituents and demanded that they be given credit on their draft quotas for the Negroes enrolled in Andrew's regiments. Then Andrew renewed his request to be allowed to recruit in Virginia, North Carolina, and the District of Columbia. When Lincoln demurred, Andrew protested that "Southern refugees" should be allowed to migrate to "high wage industries" of Massachusetts. Lincoln was not deceived by this high humanitarian tone, but he permitted Andrew to recruit Negroes, with Pierpoint's consent, in Virginia.[22]

Andrew himself believed that he was setting a worthy example in raising Negro regiments, and Stanton thought that Andrew's experiences would be useful to other governors. But other governors imitated Andrew in only a half-hearted manner and obtained but indifferent success. Stanton authorized Sprague of Rhode Island to raise a Negro regiment, but the troops never materialized.[23] Kirkwood wanted to raise Negro troops for Iowa in Arkansas and protested to Lincoln when the Union commander in the area interfered. If Negroes, said Kirkwood, were "willing to pay for their freedom by fighting for those who make them free, I am entirely willing they should do so." Moreover, the Iowa Governor could not "appreciate the policy that insists that all the lives lost and all the constitutions broken shall be those of white men when black men are to be found willing to do the work and take the risks." [24] Morton put the matter on the same practical grounds: Negroes were a means to an

[22] H. G. Pearson: *Life of John A. Andrew,* II, 71–91; Nicolay and Hay: *Lincoln,* VI, 462–3; W. Schouler: *A History of Massachusetts in the Civil War,* I, 407; *Official Records,* series 3, III, 36, 109–10, 117–18, 208–9, 423–4, 473–4.

[23] *Official Records,* series 3, III, 16, 38–9.

[24] D. E. Clark: *Samuel Jordan Kirkwood,* p. 294.

end, and if one more Negro went, another white man could stay home.[25] In Ohio, Tod at first met the demand for a Negro regiment by advising Negroes to enlist under Andrew. But when he found that Ohio could not get credit for them, he approached Stanton to raise a regiment. Stanton, however, advised delay until Andrew's regiments were raised and the Massachusetts experiment evaluated. After the Massachusetts troops marched off to the war, Tod began to recruit colored soldiers.[26]

But the major result of Andrew's experience was to show that the states could not effectively raise Negro troops. Early in the year the census bureau reported to the Secretary of the Interior that the Northern states had not proved a hospitable home for free Negroes, that the total number was declining, and that health conditions were poor among them. But, even so, if they enlisted at the same ratio as the whites, the Negro population of the North would only furnish 18,000 men.[27] Obviously, as Andrew was to learn from experience, the Negro troops would have to come from the areas where the Negroes lived. But when Andrew and other governors attempted to recruit in the border states, Governors Bramlette of Kentucky and Bradford of Maryland protested to Lincoln. Eventually the effort to raise Negro troops through the states failed.[28]

Since the Negroes were in the South, and accessible only where the Union armies had control, the national government, rather than the states, was the obvious agency for recruiting them. Just after the Emancipation Proclamation, the War Department authorized commanders in the field to enroll the Negroes. In March, Adjutant General Lorenzo Thomas went on a tour of inspection, visited contraband

[25] W. M. French: *Life . . . of Oliver P. Morton*, p. 73.

[26] W. Reid: *Ohio in the War*, I, 176–7; *Official Records*, series 3, III, 229, 372, 402.

[27] *Official Records*, series 3, III, 43–5.

[28] Nicolay and Hay: *Lincoln*, VI, 464–5; *Official Records*, series 3, III, 767–8, 787–9; Stanton to Lincoln, October 1, 1863, Stanton MSS.

camps at Cairo, talked to U. S. Grant at his Memphis headquarters, and ordered all commanders to assist in raising
Negro troops. He ordered white officers released to command the colored soldiers. In May the War Department set
up a special bureau of Negro recruitment, and thereafter
Negro soldiers were raised by the federal government. Except for the regular army and a few "independent" regiments raised early in the war, the Negroes were the first
troops raised by the national government without the intervention of the states.[29]

But while the government was seeking to tap this new source
of manpower, the armies so recently raised by volunteering
and by the draft were threatening to disintegrate. Like the
people from whence they sprang, the soldiers suffered from
war-weariness, and large numbers of them were disgusted
by the Emancipation Proclamation. Moreover, the new en-
rollees had been seduced by promises of bounties or coerced
by threats of conscription. Such soldiers had little patriotic
zest; they deserted as soon as they had collected their bounties. Substitutes collected their pay and disappeared from the
ranks. Others, tired of fighting, fraternized with the enemy.
One Illinois regiment in Mississippi suffered such desertions,
such lack of discipline, and such familiarity with the enemy
that it was put under guard. Another regiment, at Cairo,
dwindled by desertions to thirty-five men. The counties of
Egypt filled with deserters; one fugitive explained to his
brother: "I got tired of the war and came off home   I
have ben at home a bout a month and I have not ben both-
ered   This country is full of deserters   They are coming home every day." [30] Governor Yates, as usual, heard of
rumored uprisings, secret plottings, and weird night meetings of the Knights of the Golden Circle. In Ohio, Tod was

[29] *Official Records*, series 3, III, 3, 14, 46, 73, 82, 100, 118–24, 215–
16, 404, 418–20; Shannon: *Union Armies*, II, 162–4; Lincoln to N. P.
Banks, March 29, 1863, Lincoln MSS., Huntington Library.

[30] Elisha Ogden of Canton, Illinois, February 25, 1863, Yates MSS.

alarmed over the number of desertions and asked Lincoln to issue a proclamation granting amnesty to those who returned to their regiments in thirty days, and threatening punishment to those who remained in flight. Kirkwood was so alarmed that he wanted arms for loyal citizens to protect themselves from deserter bands, while Morton's provost-marshal-general told the War Department that "Southern Indiana is ripe for revolution. . . . The Government does not realize . . . the peril. The sooner the draft comes the better." [31]

The alarm over the desertion problem was reflected in Congress, where, in February, Massachusetts Senator Henry Wilson introduced a bill for national conscription. For a couple of weeks the House and Senate debated the measure, but they hurried their discussion in the full knowledge that the next Congress, product of the 1862 upheaval, would not adopt a national draft. Even so, Democrats and border-state men rallied to oppose this new, un-American assault on states' rights and individual liberties. When A. B. Olin of New York, sponsoring the measure in the House, declared that the government should not petition the state governments for the "boon" of troops, the Democrats objected. When Olin asserted that the idea of calling on the governors for troops was born of "the accursed doctrine of States Rights, State sovereignty, which has been chiefly instrumental in bringing upon the Republic our present calamity," the Democrats countered with excoriations of national concentration. This would, in Democratic eyes, establish an irresponsible despotism. Democrats declared that desertions were increasing and recruiting at a standstill because the Republicans endorsed tyranny; Republicans found the cause in the Democrats' advocacy of treason.[32]

---

[31] Sandburg: *War Years,* II, 157; Schouler: *Massachusetts,* I, 399; *Official Records,* series 3, III, 19–20, 37–8; W. H. Pierce to Yates, March 5, 1863, Yates MSS.

[32] *Congressional Globe,* 37th Congress, 3rd session, p. 1214; Nicolay and Hay: *Lincoln,* VII, 3–5.

Some Republicans, however, objected to conscription and its implications. Horace Greeley had regarded the scheme for a draft with skepticism, and shortly after it went into operation he informed Stanton that it must be changed. If, said Greeley, the pay in the army were raised from thirteen to twenty or twenty-five dollars, or even, if necessary, thirty dollars a month, the army would be filled. "Drafting is an anomaly in a free state," said the editor, and "it must and will be reformed out of our system of political economy." [33]

All such protests availed nothing. The Republican congressmen pushed the Enrollment Act through in the last minutes of the session. The act, for the first time, asserted the power of the national government to "raise and support armies" without state assistance. The law ignored the states and created enrollment districts that coincided with congressional districts. Over each was placed an assistant provost marshal, and the system was administered by a provost-marshal-general in the War Department. The provost marshals had instructions to enroll all men aged twenty to forty-five in their districts and had authority to arrest any who opposed the enrollments or the subsequent draft. The provost-marshal-general might assign quotas on the basis of the enrollment. Exemptions were offered to those who paid $300 commutation or who provided a substitute. Drafted men received the same bounty as volunteers. [34]

The only mention of the states in the act was a provision that quotas were to be assigned on the basis of the states' contributions under the several calls for volunteers. But this provision promptly opened the floodgates for gubernatorial protests. Lincoln appointed Colonel James B. Fry to be provost-marshal-general, and Fry assigned the assistant provost marshals. Most of them were already serving in the states, aiding the governors in apprehending deserters. Fry instructed the new officers to confer with the governors, and

[33] Greeley to Stanton, June 12, 1863, Stanton MSS.
[34] *United States Statutes at Large*, XII, 731–3.

to submit to them such records as might be necessary for the files of the states.[35]

The enrollment proceeded promptly and with more acquiescence than the officers expected. In West Virginia, Governor Boreman and the state officials protested against the enrollment and assured the provost marshal that a draft would drive as many into the Confederate as it enrolled in the Union army. In Delaware the enrollment officers received anonymous letters, and fifteen shots were fired into the house of one of them. Pennsylvania's dissenters resorted to fire, burning barns and sawmills of enrollment officers. One provost marshal tried to get mine-owners to furnish the names of their employees. The owners would have done so gladly, but feared the workers would burn the mines and destroy machinery. The owners suggested, however, that the provost marshal should come with troops and force the delivery of the names. In two districts of New Jersey the enrolling officers found it necessary to take a posse with them. Even then women slammed doors in their faces, men could not be found, and the officers gave up in disgust. The provost marshal began visiting factories, workshops, and contractors to obtain lists of the "laboring Irish." Irish workers in the marble quarries of Vermont attacked the officers. In Ohio, too, the enrollment officers met armed resistance, and when Governor Tod sent the militia to aid the provost marshal, the troops were ambushed. More armed conflicts came in Indiana, where two men were killed while enforcing the law. Fry ordered the local provost marshal to "punish unrelentingly, even cruelly," the resisters. In Illinois, General Burnside, with burning zeal, ordered harsh measures in advance of trouble. "Peace measures may be kept up too long," he told a provost marshal who advocated moderation. And Governor Yates, he of the ever trembling heart, told Secretary Chase that "the slightest cause, as the arrest of a deserter, is likely to cause revolution in the state." [36] In Mil-

[35] *Official Records*, series 3, III, 166–7.

[36] Ibid., III, 236–7, 361–2, 323, 351, 382, 400–1, 383, 349, 356, 403,

waukee the "Irish and Dutch" alarmed the timid provost marshal, who begged for troops to suppress the "resistance by the lower classes." An Irishman had hit an enrollment officer with a spade, and women had pelted the official with stones. The mayor thought that his police could maintain order, and Governor Salomon and General Pope in Madison were not alarmed. But Milwaukee, pleaded the provost marshal, "is thoroughly disloyal, and is controlled by mobs and has been for years." [37]

Despite the sporadic troubles, General Fry was satisfied that the enrollment had been made peacefully enough. By the time the figures were in, the provost-marshal-general proposed to Stanton that they test the system by a draft in those states that had a deficit under Lincoln's calls. Fry's figures showed an over-all excess of 13,542 — made up from the larger enlistments of some states. In the West only Wisconsin had a deficit, while in the East only New York and Rhode Island had oversubscribed the earlier calls. Yet the deficit from the Eastern and border states amounted to 87,103. In making the proposal, Fry suggested that the governors not be told of the quotas. It would, he said, only lead to arguments. [38]

Despite Fry's advice, the department told the governors their quotas, and the arguments the provost-marshal-general feared began. Governor Holbrook found Vermont had an excess instead of a deficit and promptly began an arithmetical disputation with Fry. [39] Curtin questioned Pennsylvania's assessment, [40] and Morton, not finding any discrepancies in Indiana's figures, found reason for alarm in the commutation clause. He feared that Democrats would all buy exemption, stay home, and vote, while Republicans would be

---

338, 392–4, 421–2, 464–5, 391–2; Yates to Chase, July 2, 1863, Stanton MSS.

[37] *Official Records*, series 3, III, 238–9, 247–8, 395–6.

[38] Ibid., III, 185–6.

[39] Ibid., III, 196–8.

[40] W. H. Egle: *Andrew Gregg Curtin*, pp. 60 ff.

drafted into the armies.[41] New Jersey's Governor Parker was horrified to learn his state was 12,000 behind in troops, and solemnly protested. Lincoln looked at Fry's mathematics and reduced the number to 8,700, but Parker remained dissatisfied.[42] New Hampshire led the New England states in demanding that the draft be assigned by towns instead of the congressional districts prescribed by law, and Andrew wanted to allow drafted men to volunteer in Massachusetts regiments and get the state's bounty. On the other hand, Minnesota's new Governor, H. A. Swift, protested against any draft at all. The families of drafted men, he explained, would all have to be moved and their farms abandoned to the Indians.[43] Confronted with such diverse troubles, Colonel Fry, harassed bureaucrat, might well have despaired of raising a national army.

But just then, as the returns from the enrollment officers were coming in and Fry was at his wits' end meeting the gubernatorial protests, General Robert E. Lee struck a blow for states' rights. The Confederate commander, fresh from the Battle of Chancellorsville, began a new invasion of the North. In advance of the main army, General Ewell began to cross the Potomac, and Governor Curtin took fright. Hastily he sent agents to Washington, where they infected the authorities with the Governor's panic. The emergency was too great for the slowly forming machinery of the national army to operate, and Stanton asked the governors of Maryland, Pennsylvania, Ohio, and West Virginia for 100,000 six-months militia. To confound the nationalists, it was the states'-rights Democrats who responded most rapidly to the call. Horatio Seymour hurried troops to Harrisburg — winning thereby Stanton's grudging thanks — and Joel Parker rushed troops to Curtin's aid and called on Jerseymen to take up arms to help a sister state. The federal authorities

[41] Morton to Stanton, March 6, 1863, Stanton MSS.

[42] *Writings of Lincoln*, VI, 362–3, 366–7.

[43] *Official Records*, series 3, III, 537, 549, 545–6, 577.

promptly added New Jersey's troops to the six-months militia, and Parker, protesting that they were state troops and not under Lincoln's call, ordered his men home.

But while the Democrats hurriedly sent citizen soldiers to Harrisburg, Curtin himself was having difficulty in raising the 50,000 Pennsylvanians Lincoln had summoned. "I will not insult you by inflammatory appeals," said Curtin. "A people who want the heart to defend their soil, their families, and their firesides are not worthy to be accounted men. . . . Show yourselves to be what you are — a free, loyal, spirited, brave, vigorous race." This was, after all, moderation for Curtin — and the people did not respond. Moreover, Curtin and the War Department began to argue, even in the face of the invader, over terms of service, quotas, credits, and bounties.

The other states had difficulties meeting the special call. Tod, exercising less restraint than Curtin, called on Ohioans to "meet this horde of rebels," and to "remember that our own sacred homes are threatened with pillage and destruction and our wives and daughters with insults." Bradford threatened a draft in Maryland, and a Massachusetts regiment — just home and still unpaid — mutinied. Rhode Island's Governor Smith dallied while he argued over the worth of a six-months militiaman on the state's draft quota.

Even greater intransigence came from the West. Morton thought that if six-months militiamen could be exempt from the draft while in the service, he could raise regiments at once. But it would be slow work if the men ran the risk of being folded into the army. He could, however, get no commitment from Fry that the militia would be exempt. Yates had other fears, besides. He told Stanton that he could not raise six-months troops. None but Union men would volunteer, he explained, and the Democrats who were left behind would control the state.[44]

[44] Ibid., series 1, Vol. XXVII, part 3, pp. 97, 111–13, 137, 138–41, 142, 164, 185–8, 190, 205–6, 241, 265, 342–7; series 3, Vol. III, pp. 360–5, 423; F. A. Flower: *Edwin McMasters Stanton*, pp. 198, 397–8;

Lee's invasion had produced a new and unexpected resurgence of states' rights at just the moment when the national government was prepared to assume exclusive control over the nation's military manpower. And although Lee was turned back at Gettysburg, he had made necessary serious modifications in the government's program. A few days after Gettysburg the citizens of New York City forced a further reconsideration of the draft.

Already the states' rights factions had begun to look to Horatio Seymour as their champion. The New York Governor had both dignity and intellect to recommend him as a leader. His iron-gray hair, his clean-shaven, full lips with good-humored dimples at the corners, his sensitive nose, and even his graying neck-whiskers framing his well-shaped head made him an impressive figure. Moreover, his personality inspired confidence: he seldom smoked, rarely drank wine, yet was no puritan. He was a cultured Christian gentleman — a type rare in politics, and a godsend to a Democratic opposition that sorely needed respectable leadership. Yet, as it turned out, Seymour's dignity, culture, personality, integrity, and oratory would not prevail against the shrewd and persistent "smear" tactics of the administration.[45]

From the beginning Seymour held that conscription was unconstitutional. The federal government should depend solely upon the states for troops. Moreover, as a strict constructionist, the Governor objected vehemently to the suspension of habeas corpus and the arbitrary arrests of citizens. Colonel Fry recognized that Seymour would furnish the most strenuous opposition to the draft, and the wary colonel instructed the provost marshals in New York to handle the Governor with gloves.

The first provost marshal to interview Seymour found the

J. Y. Foster: *New Jersey and the Rebellion,* pp. 766–8; Mitchell: *Seymour,* pp. 300 ff.; Welles: *Diary of Gideon Welles,* I, 331, 358; *Writings of Lincoln,* VI, 346; Stanton to Major General Charles Devens, July 3, 1863, Stanton MSS.

[45] D. G. Croly: *Seymour and Blair,* pp. 205 f.

Governor willing enough to raise troops and hoping that new state bounties would bring enough recruits to avoid a draft. Seymour, however, was casting suspicious eyes upon the state's quota, and the provost marshal suggested that any differences of opinion be adjusted quickly. Seymour himself told Stanton that he hoped to raise enough troops — through vigorous recruiting and bounteous bounties — to avoid a draft.[46]

But the War Department had no disposition to deal peacefully with the Democratic leader. Seymour denounced the draft and declared that neither the President nor the Congress had a right to force men "to take part in the ungodly conflict which is distracting the land." Moreover, the Governor condemned the administration for seizing and sentencing Vallandigham.[47] Stanton had no patience with such attitudes and resolutely faced the challenge. When the United States district attorney for New York held that evasions of the Enrollment Act were not punishable under the law, Stanton protested to Seward that even federal civil officers in New York gave no aid to the government in the war if they could find a "colorable pretext" for withholding it. Seward ordered the district attorney to support the government — and the stage was set for trying the draft in Seymour's bailiwick.[48]

July 11 fell on Saturday — a day, as it turned out, highly unfavorable for beginning the draft in New York City. The day before, Governor Seymour had been in the city inspecting the harbor defenses. He found them inadequate and, with the militia still in Pennsylvania, he feared that the Confederates might raid the city. He had, however, no intimation of the morrow's trouble and left for a visit in New Jersey. The next day the provost marshal's men drew the names for the draft. Sunday the names appeared in the papers, and indignant men began to assemble on street corners. Sunday afternoon and Monday a mob rioted in the streets.

[46] *Official Records*, series 3, III, 210, 214, 217.
[47] Nicolay and Hay: *Lincoln*, VII, 7.
[48] *Official Records*, series 3, III, 242–3.

It broke the windows of the *Tribune* office, wrecked the home of the provost marshal, burned a Negro church and a Negro orphan asylum, threw rocks, started fires, fought the police, terrorized half the city, and killed more than a dozen people. In the absence of the militia and of all troops, the police battled alone, and vainly, to restrain the mob. The mayor hurriedly called the Governor back to the city. Seymour promptly sent his adjutant general to Washington to ask a suspension of the draft and himself hurried to the troubled streets.

In the city Seymour consulted Mayor Opdyke and issued a proclamation ordering the rioters to disperse. At the city hall he addressed the mob. "My friends," he began as he pleaded with them to cease destroying property. Republicans pounced with glee on the phrase, which proved Seymour's affiliation with the rioters. But the rioters, friend or no, failed to disperse. Later in the day the Governor issued a second and more stringent order — and by that time troops had arrived and the mob dissolved.

The aftermath of the riot brought verbal confusion more clamorous than the mob. Everyone made capital of the situation — the Republican newspapers vied with one another in magnifying the horror of the riots and in counting the hundreds who died at the hands of the mob. The people of New York, inspired by the newspaper accounts, filed fabulous claims for damages against the city. And the Republican politicians, disguising partisanship as patriotism, dredged the sewers of their vocabulary for expletives against Seymour.[49]

Gideon Welles was sure of a connection between Seymour's opposition to conscription and the mob's violence. "This Sir Forcible Feeble is himself chiefly responsible for the outrage." [50] Countless radicals seized upon Seymour's

[49] Mitchell: *Seymour*, pp. 306 ff.; Nicolay and Hay: *Lincoln*, VII, 14–24; Shannon: *Union Armies*, II, 68; Flower: *Stanton*, pp. 241–2; *Official Records*, series 1, Vol. XXVII, part 2, pp. 875 ff.

[50] Welles: *Diary*, I, 369, 372.

"My friends" to prove the Governor's identification with "the lowest class of Democrats." [51] John Jay, abolitionist agitator with long experience in detecting imaginary plots of the slavocracy, solemnly told Stanton that the riots were part of a conspiracy to take New York out of the Union. The riot had got out of hand, but Stanton could rest assured the plotters would try again.[52] Seymour, said another alarmist, was in the hands of "the worst possible advisers," who wanted "collision between the general and state governments" thus to "console Jefferson Davis and the rebels for the defeats recently heaped upon them." [53]

Ex-Governor E. D. Morgan was unimpressed by the charges that Seymour was plotting secession and encouraging the mob. A moderate Republican, he too had suffered from radical barbs. But when he wrote Stanton in Seymour's defense, the Secretary of War imperiously informed him he had been "very much misinformed" about Seymour. Taking up the line Lincoln had already laid down, Stanton charged that Seymour had refused to co-operate. More than two months before, said Stanton, the War Department had tried to talk to the Governor. But Seymour had not come to Washington. "From the commencement of his administration until the present hour," said the Secretary in tones of injured piety, "this Department has treated Governor Seymour with the utmost deference and respect, and has availed itself of every opportunity to secure his cooperation." [54]

Soon the radicals added a new angle to the anti-Seymour campaign. Lincoln's private secretary, John Hay, began peddling rumors that "Seymour is in a terrible state of nervous excitement, and there is absolute danger of the loss of his wits." [55] And the provost marshal in New York informed Fry: "I know Governor Seymour personally, and have for

---

[51] Nicolay and Hay: *Lincoln*, VII, 13.
[52] *Official Records*, series 3, III, 540–2.
[53] James T. Brady to Stanton, July 18, 1863, Stanton MSS.
[54] Stanton to E. D. Morgan, July 17, 1863, Stanton MSS.
[55] T. Dennett: *Letters and Diaries of John Hay*, pp. 71 ff.

several years considered him to be a dangerous man with a mind congenitally disposed to lunacy." [56]

Seymour's insanity, however, was not evident from his acts. He first of all demanded that the draft be suspended until the rioters could be calmed. Then he sent Samuel J. Tilden to explain to Lincoln the situation in New York. Next he explained to an alarmed provost marshal that a drafted man had a right to the writ of habeas corpus and that the Governor would use all of his power, including the military, to enforce the right. If the courts held the law constitutional, then Seymour would use all his power to enforce it. The provost marshal advised the government to gamble on getting a favorable court decision. [57]

The government, however, preferred not to run the risks of a test case. On July 18 Stanton appointed General John A. Dix, a Democrat but no friend of Seymour's, to command in New York. Dix promptly told Seymour the draft would be resumed in New York, and asked point-blank "whether the military power of the state could be relied on to enforce the law in case of forcible resistance." [58] Seymour's reply was a letter to Fry asking the exact date of the draft, and another to Lincoln asking postponement until the governor could complete a letter he was preparing. [59]

Seymour had no real hope of avoiding a draft. "I am satisfied that [the administration] means to go on in a spirit of hostility to this state: that it is governed by a spirit of malice in all things great and small." Nevertheless, as he explained to Tilden, he had prepared a letter to Lincoln questioning the constitutionality and the fairness of the draft. "It will do no good, except in making up a record." [60]

The Governor's letter declared the draft was a harsh and unfortunate measure, and he pointed out that "at least one-

[56] *Official Records,* series 3, III, 608.

[57] Ibid., III, 561.

[58] Ibid., III, 592.

[59] Ibid., III, 575, 584–5, 607, 612; Mitchell: *Seymour,* pp. 340 ff.

[60] S. J. Tilden: *Letters and Literary Memorials,* I, 183–4.

half" of the people believed the Conscription Act was unconstitutional. He insisted that the judgment of the courts be obtained. Moreover, in regard to the draft in New York, the Governor charged the enrollment officers and the provost marshal's office with the grossest partisanship. The draft was designed, it appeared to Seymour, to take Democrats and exempt Republicans.[61]

Lincoln read the letter and his reply to his cabinet. Gideon Welles thought Seymour's a "party, political document, filled with perverted statements, and apologizing for, and diverting attention from, his mob." Lincoln's answer, on the other hand, seemed to Welles "manly, vigorous, and decisive." [62]

In his reply Lincoln refused to suspend the draft. He would have no objection to a Supreme Court decision, he said, but he could not spare the time. "We are contending with an enemy who . . . drives every ablebodied man he can reach into the ranks, very much as a butcher drives bullocks into a slaughter pen. This produces an army . . . with a rapidity not to be matched on our side." On the other hand, the President expressed his surprise at the figures Seymour presented to show the unfair nature of the assessments. The President proposed to reduce the number in all districts to the average — but he insisted that the draft would proceed.[63]

It had been the administration's contention that Seymour would not reply to friendly overtures. Hereafter, although the tone of the letters was hardly friendly, the administration had no complaint to make of Seymour's willingness to correspond frequently and at length. The Governor was making "a record," and he spared no pains to make himself clear. On the day Lincoln replied to his first letter, Seymour sent further figures showing the Democratic districts bore a heavier draft than Republican ones, and he added that he

[61] Nicolay and Hay: *Lincoln*, VII, 32–3.
[62] Welles: *Diary*, I, 395.
[63] *Official Records*, series 3, III, 635–6.

had detected the culprit among the enrollment officers who had padded the city's enrollment. The draft, said Seymour, would bring disgrace upon the American name and shame the administration. The honor of the country demanded that he continue to protest.[64]

Lincoln enrolled Fry in the epistolary battle. The provost-marshal-general denied that his officers had been guilty of partisanship, and he contended that Seymour had been given ample notice of the draft, and that the War Department had given New York credit for more soldiers than the state claimed. But Seymour was ready with more figures proving partisanship: nine Democratic districts had been assigned a total quota as large as nineteen Republican districts! It was part of a "manifest design to reduce the Democratic majority." [65] Lincoln in reply agreed again to reduce the quota of the Democratic districts to the average of the Republican districts, but again refused to postpone the draft.[66] Immediately Seymour came back with a demand that volunteers be accepted as substitutes for conscripts — a proposal that Lincoln professed to be unable to understand.[67] Seymour, however, was ready with another demand: that New York be given credit for its citizens serving in regiments from other states. Moreover, he complained that proper arrangements for reducing quotas were not made, and he declared that he had still not been given notice when the draft would take place.[68] Seymour was making his record, even though the material for it was running thin.

In the meantime, to make the record complete, Seymour carried on a vigorous correspondence with General Dix. The general, too, was interested in the record. He insisted, in frequent letters, that Seymour stop using the term "conscrip-

---

[64] Ibid., III, 636.

[65] Ibid., III, 639–54, 657–63.

[66] Nicolay and Hay: *Lincoln*, VII, 35–6; *Official Records*, series 3, III, 666–7.

[67] *Official Records*, series 3, III, 681.

[68] Ibid., III, 703–6.

tion," argued that secession was a crime, and demanded that the Governor give him assurances that the state would aid in enforcing the draft. Seymour persisted in charging the draft was political proscription, argued its constitutionality, and successfully dodged any commitment on the use of state troops. Finally Dix called for federal troops and suggested that Lincoln call out the state's militia over Seymour's head. When August 19, the date of the postponed draft, arrived, the federal troops were not on hand. The Governor, however, had warned that there must be no disorder, and Dix triumphantly wired the War Department that Seymour had caved in and the draft was proceeding peacefully.[69]

The victory, however, was not so complete as Dix and the War Department pretended. Already Lincoln had appointed an examining board to review Seymour's charges of corruption. The board denied the Governor's charges, whitewashed the administration, and found Seymour's figures true. Lincoln calmly ordered a reduction in the quotas to conform to the board's findings.[70]

Although the New York riots were the most serious — and for partisan purposes received the most attention — there were troubles as well in other cities. Rhode Island's draft came just before New York's, and passed off so well that Stanton thanked Governor J. Y. Smith for the patriotic spirit of his people.[71] The Rhode Island experience was disarming, however, and the government was unprepared for the New York troubles. After New York's draft riots the governors and the provost marshals took alarm and found premonitions of disaster in every transient grumble. The provost

[69] G. G. Gorham: *Life and Public Services of Edwin M. Stanton*, II, 112; Mitchell: *Seymour*, pp. 340–5; Dennet: *Hay*, p. 81; *Official Records*, series 3, III, 671–7, 685–6, 693.

[70] Nicolay and Hay: *Lincoln*, VII, 42. The original letters from Seymour to Lincoln are in the R. T. Lincoln MSS. Collection, Vols. CXIX–CXXI. Seymour's letter of August 21 contains Colonel Fry's penciled marginalia upon which Lincoln based his reply.

[71] *Official Records*, series 3, III, 483–4.

marshal in Detroit asked for troops in anticipation of disorders and consulted Austin Blair. The Michigan Governor
agreed that unless New York's mob was put down summarily, there would be resistance in Detroit. From Iowa came a
confirming echo. "For God's sake let there be no compromising or halfway measures," wired Governor Kirkwood as
he warned the War Department that the whole question of
conscription was at stake. Stanton gave assurance that the
draft would be properly enforced.[72]

In Massachusetts, John Andrew took warning from New
York. Fearful lest the Negro Fifty-fifth Regiment might ex-
cite rather than quell a mob, the Governor moved three
hundred men into Boston. Wearied from his work in preparing against trouble, the Governor went to Cambridge
for the Harvard commencement. As the salutatory orator
began his Latin sentences, the Governor nodded. Then,
when the salutatorian turned to address him, an aid poked
the gubernatorial ribs. Andrew jumped — and frightened
the Latin out of the speaker. Before orator and audience
had regained their composure, whispered word came of troubles in Boston, and Andrew, now wide awake, dashed off to
the city.

In Boston a mob had gathered before the arsenal in
Cooper Street. As the crowd swelled, someone began throwing
stones at the troops. It was not unlike the situation ninety-
three years before on the near-by Common, and, as in the
Boston Massacre, the soldiers fired into the crowd and several were killed. But the similarity ended there. The 1863
mob dispersed, and there was no Sam Adams of states' rights
to lead the populace to revolution. The danger passed as
quickly as it had risen, and John Andrew could sleep again.[73]

Almost as sleepless as Andrew was Wisconsin's Governor
Salomon, worried into insomnia by Milwaukee's timid pro-

[72] Ibid., III, 488–9, 494, 525.
[73] J. T. Morse: *Memoir of Colonel Henry Lee,* p. 255; W. B.
Weeden: *War Government,* p. 284; Schouler: *Massachusetts,* I, 476 ff.;
Pearson: *Andrew,* II, 133–4.

vost marshal. Although General Pope, who had moved to Madison after Minnesota's Indian campaign, assured both the Governor and the provost marshal that there were ample troops to prevent trouble, the Governor continued to worry. After a time he concluded that the draft could be avoided by volunteers, and began an argument with Stanton about paying the bounty to Wisconsin's troops. The belligerent Prussian liked nothing better than a scrap with the government over Wisconsin's rights, and the controversy diverted his attention from Milwaukee's discontent. The draft, when it came, passed off quietly enough.[74]

Meantime, as the draft proceeded, it became evident that the system of conscription was failing, more signally than the governors had done, to raise men. Only Seymour among the governors raised the theoretical question of states' rights and the law's constitutionality, but the other governors bickered over credits and quotas, over bounties, and over the conduct of the provost marshals until their combined complaints wrought more havoc than Seymour's open opposition. Moreover, as a result of the governors' continuous obstructions, the draft failed to produce men. Less than 36,000 men in the whole country came into the army as a result of the draft. Colonel Fry thought the fault was in the law itself, which was "essentially a law not to secure military service, but to exempt men from it." The best that its proponents could say for the system — looking ruefully at the pawky results — was that the draft had stimulated volunteer enlistments.[75]

In the end the administration abandoned its plans for a national army raised under the sole authority of Congress, and used the draft only to coerce the governors into redou-

[74] *Official Records*, series 3, III, 534-5, 544-5, 579-80, 592, 850-1, 863.

[75] Shannon: *Union Armies*, II, 115, 123-4; Weeden: *War Government*, p. 289; *Official Records*, series 3, III, 799-801, 893; Nicolay and Hay: *Lincoln*, VII, 7.

bled efforts to enlist troops. On October 17, 1863 Lincoln
issued another call for 300,000 men. Again the call was addressed to the governors, and the War Department assigned
quotas on a state basis. The draft was mentioned only as a
threat: if any state failed to raise its quota by January 1864,
a draft would be ordered.[76] This was victory neither for
states' rights nor for centralization, but a compromise by
which Colonel Fry and his provost marshals remained to
give impetus and direction to the governors. Under this direction the governors were recruiting agents. But the form,
if not the full substance, of states' rights remained.

The governors sprang with renewed energy to the new
task, and Horatio Seymour led all the rest. Three days after
Lincoln's call the New York Democrat trumpeted for citizens to do their duty, fill up the thinning ranks of the
armies, and give money for the cause. They should do it
cheerfully, "and not by a forced conscription or coercive
action on the part of the government." Even General Dix
had to admit that Seymour's patriotism did not falter on
volunteering.[77]

Democrat Joel Parker quickly followed Seymour's lead
and called on Jersey's citizens to volunteer. Salomon carefully explained the law in a recruiting proclamation that
lacked enthusiasm, and Coburn of Maine begged his constituents to prove that free men could "endure more and per-
severe longer" than traitors. War-weariness was evident, too,
in the failure of the other governors to strike fire with their
proclaiming pens. Abraham Lincoln would have his armies,
but it would take both state and national systems to recruit
them.[78]

[76] *Official Records,* series 3, III, 892.
[77] Ibid., III, 912, 913.
[78] Ibid., III, 911-12, 919-20, 941-3.

Chapter 15

Lincoln Saves the Governors

IN these months while the national government was reaching out to control the manpower of the states, the complexities of wartime politics made it imperative that Abraham Lincoln assume still more control over local and state politics. The adoption of national conscription reduced the state governors from a group of commanders-in-chief to a squad of recruiting agents. The exigencies of politics reduced them from political chieftains to subservient, albeit cantankerous, henchmen. Within a year after the Democratic successes of 1862 Abraham Lincoln had tightened his grasp on the Republican machine and had demonstrated to the governors that only he could carry elections and assure the continued dominance of the Republican Party.

In politics the dawn of 1863 saw Republican prospects at ebb tide. The arbitrary arrests, the threat of conscription, the upsurge of radicalism, and the preliminary Emancipation Proclamation had brought electoral success to the Democrats in November, and they began the new year with high hopes. The Republicans were correspondingly depressed: John Andrew feared that the administration lacked a "dauntless, constructive, business-like, working policy," [1] while one of Dick Yates's advisers confessed that "it looks gloomy indeed all over the land. Defeat after defeat and traitors running rampant all over the free states. My trust is in God," he added, "but I must confess that I see little of

[1] H. G. Pearson: *The Life of John A. Andrew*, II, 64.

his work." [2] Even far-off California, which Stanton referred to in his annual report as if it were a foreign country, felt the depression, and Governor Stanford, a "man devoid of ability, destitute of manly dignity," according to one of Halleck's friends, was unable to cope with a rising sentiment for a Pacific republic.[3]

In Washington on New Year's Day Lincoln issued the Emancipation Proclamation, but a visitor to the city found no unusual stir over it. The politicians, officeholders, clerks, and bureaucrats were all drunk.[4] In New Hampshire that same day the Republican convention met in a gloomy mood. The Democrats had already met in November and, capitalizing on the party's successes in other states, nominated Ira Eastman, a strong candidate opposed to the Emancipation Proclamation. For Governor the Republicans chose Joseph H. Gilmore, superintendent of the Concord Railroad, a man of business ability and political ambition, but lacking fire and enthusiasm. A considerable group turned from the convention in despair and began to seek a more acceptable candidate.[5]

In early January, John Andrew went to Washington, and gloom settled more darkly upon him as he found few men with "realizing sense, practical sagacity, and victorious faith." Salvation, it seemed to him, could only come after the party had passed "through a great purgation, only by a revival of the religion of patriotism, and the power of resurrection." The great cause of liberty would have to go down before Democratic, proslavery defeats and make its way back through travail of soul.[6] And Gideon Welles, without re-

[2] A. A. Terrell to Yates, December 25, 1862, Yates MSS.

[3] W. W. Stow to H. W. Halleck, December 30, 1862, Elbridge MSS. Collection.

[4] J. S. Robinson to L. Y. Hunt, January 2, 1863, Robinson MSS.

[5] J. O. Lyford: *Edward N. Rollins,* pp. 147 f.; Amos Hadley: *Life of Walter Harriman,* pp. 144–5; *New Hampshire Patriot,* January 7, 1863.

[6] A. G. Browne: *Sketch of the Official Life of John A. Andrew,* pp. 139–40.

sorting to camp-meeting vocabulary, was equally troubled.
Sadness overcame him as he surveyed calamity. The course
of good government and liberty was at stake, and the Democrats were playing politics.[7]

"Old Neptune" was especially perturbed by the governors'
messages, delivered to their legislatures in the first days of
the new year. None of them, except Tod — who merited a
note of thanks from Stanton [8] — had risen to the proper
heights. In Delaware, departing Governor Burton sent a farewell message to the legislature complaining about federal
military interference in the little state's election, and incoming Governor Cannon devoted his inaugural to justify-
ing arbitrary arrests and the army's acts. The matter had
already been debated in Congress, where Lincoln declined a
request for information, and the Delaware legislature investigated, denounced Cannon and the War Department,
and passed an "Act to Prevent Illegal Arrests." [9] In Michigan, Austin Blair almost neglected his radical evangelism
while he bored his legislature with a report on state finances,
business conditions, and crop prospects. Blair would have
liked, again, to have gone to the Senate, but the legislature
re-elected Zach Chandler and gave Blair a tea set as a consolation prize.[10] In Wisconsin, Salomon's message was equally
long, equally detailed, and equally uninspired.[11]

Whatever of inspiration there was in these early days of
1863 was among the Democrats. In Congress, Clement L.
Vallandigham of Ohio, hoping to be his state's next governor, took the floor of the House to denounce the war. The
causes that led to disunion were not eternal, he proclaimed,
and there was no irrepressible conflict between slave and

[7] Welles: *Diary of Gideon Welles,* I, 219.

[8] *Official Records,* series 3, III, 8.

[9] H. C. Conrad: *History of Delaware,* I, 207; F. Fessenden: *Life of
William Pitt Fessenden,* pp. 304–12.

[10] *Detroit Free Press,* January 8, 12, 1863.

[11] *Wisconsin State Journal,* January 15; *Milwaukee Sentinel,* January 15, 1863.

free labor. Peace, to his mind, was still possible.[12] In New Jersey incoming Joel Parker, who lacked a demagogue's quick wit but who had a sound education in the Democratic creed, spoke clearly against emancipation and arbitrary arrests. He admitted that abolitionist propaganda had driven the South to desperation, yet he denounced secession and promised to preserve the Union.[13] In the editorial offices of the *New York Tribune,* Horace Greeley noted that Parker promised to uphold the legal rights of New Jersey citizens and concluded that the speech was "as artfully in favor of the Rebels as the warmest Secessionist could desire." [14]

But neither Vallandigham's demagoguery nor Parker's caution gave adequate expression to the Democrats' rising spirits. That came from Horatio Seymour, whose penetrating analysis, rousing rhetoric, and scholarly exposition of states'-rights doctrines sent Democrats into ecstasy. It was, said Gideon Welles as he sank into despair, a "jesuitical" speech, "devoid of true patriotism, weak in statemanship, and a discredit to the position he occupies." [15]

The active response came quickly from the Middle West. In Illinois and Indiana the Democrats had won notable successes, and they prepared to fall into line under Seymour's leadership. O. P. Morton was especially alarmed as he faced the meeting of Indiana's Democratic legislature. In October 1862 he had warned Lincoln that the nation's house could not last more than another sixty days on a foundation of an irredeemable paper currency. The war must be won within that time, and the President must appoint generals, "convinced of the justice of our cause," who would crush the rebellion in two months.[16] Within a month Morton and

[12] *New York Tribune,* January 15, 1863.

[13] J. Y. Foster: *New Jersey and the Rebellion,* pp. 777–9.

[14] *New York Tribune,* January 21, 1863.

[15] Welles: *Diary,* I, 219.

[16] W. H. H. Terrell: *Indiana in the War of the Rebellion,* pp. 19–20; W. D. Foulke; *Oliver P. Morton,* I, 196–7.

Yates started for Washington to interest Lincoln in Kentucky matters, but turned back when they learned the President had removed Buell and appointed General Rosecrans to manage politics in the border state.

Morton, however, had other worries. "The fate of the northwest is trembling in the balance," he wrote to Lincoln; not an hour was to be lost. The Democratic politicians of Ohio, Indiana, and Illinois, assuming the rebellion could not be crushed, proposed to form a Northwest Confederacy to join the South. This would exclude New England, and the Democratic rabble-rousers were telling the citizens that the "people of New England are cold, selfish, moneymaking, and, through the medium of tariffs and railroads are crushing us into the dust." Since the Democrats were making much of the importance of the Mississippi River, the Indiana Governor urged a prompt campaign to capture the river and conquer the states on its western banks.[17] Finally in January, just as the legislature met, Morton solemnly informed the administration that the legislators would pass a joint resolution recognizing the Confederacy and urging the Western states to dissolve all ties with New England.[18]

"Morton is a good fellow," remarked Abraham Lincoln, "but at times he is the skeeredest man I know of." [19]

The Indiana legislature had no disposition to dally with the Confederacy, but it had no patience with Morton and the Lincoln government. The Governor prepared a solemn message giving an account of the state's war effort, recommending better care for soldiers' families, and suggesting improvements in the militia. With equal care, the Governor had the message printed and distributed to the newspapers, and on the proper day he sent it to the legislature. But the legislators had no desire to hear Morton's ranting words or

[17] Yates and Morton to Lincoln, October 25, 1862, R. T. Lincoln MSS.; Morton to Lincoln, October 27, 1863. Stanton MSS.; Foulke: *Morton*, I, 208–9.

[18] *Official Records*, series 3, III, 4.

[19] Carl Sandburg: *Abraham Lincoln: The War Years*, II, 244.

to heed his advice. A sufficient number of senators absented themselves to prevent a quorum, and the House decided that the lack of a Senate quorum prevented a joint meeting of the two houses. Then, several days later, they asked when Morton would appear to read his message. The outraged Governor refused to appear to read a message that had already been published in the newspapers. Thereupon the legislature condemned him and decided to adopt the "exalted and patriotic sentiments" of Governor Seymour. The legislature thanked the New York Governor and assured him that conservative Indianians were "looking with deep solicitude and confidence" to him to defend liberty against despotism and to uphold the sovereignty of the states.[20]

For two months, while Morton sputtered, the Indiana legislature investigated the Governor, denounced the Lincoln government, and debated bills to curb the Governor's power. Resolutions assailed the federal government for arresting citizens, rebuked the President for suspending habeas corpus, issuing the Emancipation Proclamation, interfering in West Virginia, and advocating conscription. Other resolutions declared Indiana would not furnish another man or dollar for "wicked, inhuman, and unholy" purposes, and proposed calling a national convention to end the war through compromise. The legislature investigated Morton's accounts — and especially those of the state arsenal — and reluctantly agreed that there were no financial irregularities.[21]

Morton himself was frantic. He loudly proclaimed that the Knights of the Golden Circle were organized in the state, and he made hysterical estimates of the membership of the nonexistent organization. He stimulated the provost marshal, H. B. Carrington, to arrest deserters, bounty-jumpers, and stragglers. Colonel Carrington was an ardent radical and as prone to panic as the Governor. In a few weeks he arrested 2,600, all of whom, he and Morton be-

[20] Foulke: *Morton*, I, 213; Terrell: *Indiana in the War*, p. 239.
[21] Terrell: *Indiana in the War*, pp. 239 ff.

lieved, were oath-bound knights.[22] But even Colonel Carrington's energy did not discourage Democrats, and Morton
begged to see Lincoln. He could not leave Indiana long
enough to go to Washington, but wouldn't Lincoln slip
away to Harrisburg for a few hours? Cagily the President replied that his absence would be noted and misin-
terpreted.[23]

Unable to see the President, Morton poured out his fears
in a letter to Stanton. The Democrats, he declared, planned
to offer the Confederates a new union without New England. The Democratic papers, said the Governor, were filled
with abuse of New England fanaticism and with allegations
that New England manufactures and railroads exploited the
West, whose natural markets were in the South. To counter-
act his argument, Morton proposed that the war be pressed
vigorously, the Mississippi River be opened, and the government undertake an elaborate propaganda campaign to show
that New England offered better markets than the South for
Western products.[24]

The administration paid no attention to Morton's proposals, but some encouragement came to the Governor from
regiments in the field. Twenty-two regiments adopted resolutions favoring the war, thanking Morton, and offering to
come home and "crush out all treasonable combinations
which defame the fair name of Indiana." The state Senate
promptly replied to the soldiers, telling them they had been
deceived by Morton and his clique. The people of Indiana,
said the senators, pointing to the polls, opposed the administration and repudiated Lincoln. The nation did not want a
war to free Negroes, but it did want an honorable peace.[25]

The spirit of the soldiers, it seemed to the legislature, was
the result of Morton's exclusive control over the state's

[22] *Official Records,* series 3, III, 19–20; Foulke: *Morton,* I, 243–4.

[23] *Official Records,* series 3, III, 23.

[24] Morton to Stanton, February 9, 1863, Stanton MSS.

[25] Indiana Senate *Report of Committee on Federal Relations,*
March 5, 1863.

forces. In order to control the Governor, the legislature considered a measure to reorganize the state militia under a
four-man board. This board — of which Morton could be a
member providing "there were enough honest men on it to
control it" — would have all authority to raise state troops,
commission officers, and direct their actions. But just as the
measure was about to pass, the Republican members, denouncing their colleagues, withdrew and broke the quorum.
Without a quorum the legislature adjourned.

With the end of the legislature, all financial bills died.
There was no appropriation for any state function, and no
authorization for taxes. The Governor was confronted by
the choice of running the state without funds or calling the
legislature into special session. In his dilemma he appealed
again to Lincoln. The national government had no desire
to have Indiana's Democrats reassembled, and Stanton found
$250,000 in the War Department funds. Morton organized
a Bureau of Finance and appealed to the people. Bankers,
railroads, and counties responded, and by January 1865,
when a new — and Republican — legislature met, the Governor had raised $1,026,321 and had spent, without author-
ity of law, $902,065. The Democratic legislators, intent upon
the preservation of state sovereignty, had overreached themselves. Indiana was completely subservient to the national
government.[26]

While the Indiana legislature was defeating its own purposes, Dick Yates was having comparable difficulties with
the Democrats in Illinois. The legislature was Democratic
and Yates's hopes of being elected United States senator
faded as the November returns came in.[27] The Governor
was convinced that only a secret society could have encom-
passed his defeat, and he listened credulously as rumors
from all parts of the state recounted the dark meetings of

[26] Terrell: *Indiana in the War*, p. 259; C. M. Walker: *Sketch of the
Life . . . of Oliver P. Morton*, pp. 100 ff.

[27] *Chicago Times*, November 11, 1862.

the dread Knights of the Golden Circle.[28] Yates prepared his legislative message with gloomy forebodings, recommending to the legislature appropriations for meeting the state's military expenses, reorganizing and strengthening the militia, and providing for the soldiers' vote. With an eye on the vote of the soldiers the Governor asked money for the Sanitary Commission, for a soldiers' home, and for increased bounties. He proposed that the state petition Congress to raise the soldiers' pay.[29]

The legislature paid little attention to these proposals. It proceeded to elect Congressman William A. Richardson to the Senate, and it passed, unlike their Indiana colleagues, the routine appropriation measures. It investigated Yates's corruption and found little to make into political capital. It passed resolutions opposing arbitrary arrests and the administration's conduct of the war. Then it demanded an armistice, and a national convention to make peace. Having done so, it adjourned until June.[30]

In the midst of the session Yates sought advice and consolation from his neighbor Morton. The legislature, he told Indiana's Governor, "is a wild, rampant revolutionary body" that would deprive the Governor of all power. "What is to be done in such a case? . . . Have you made any preparations for an emergency?" [31]

As the Governor listened to rumors, his alarm increased. He heard that Democrats were patronizing gun shops, and getting weapons repaired that had not been used for twenty years. He heard that lawyers refused to take oaths in the courts, that rebels were drilling in one county and were ready to unfurl the rattlesnake flag, that the Knights of the Golden Circle were meeting in the moonlight, that the army was filled with traitors, that threats to assassinate the Governor were boldly made. He listened to tales that three hun-

---

[28] H. Newburn to Yates, November 15, 1862, Yates MSS.
[29] T. M. Eddy: *The Patriotism of Illinois*, I, 127.
[30] C. A. Church: *The Republican Party in Illinois*, pp. 90–2.
[31] Yates to Morton, January 19, 1863, Yates MSS.

dred secret lodges met on Tuesday nights, that men called Lincoln a traitor, that men resisted the draft, that the Copperheads got a thousand guns from Springfield. He gave advice and comfort, if not aid, to those who asked arms to protect themselves against the secret enemy.[32]

Terrified by the evidences of things unseen, Governor Yates took heart when General John M. Palmer offered to come to Springfield to protect the state. Palmer had heard the rumors, too, and wrote Yates to ask about them. But the general advised caution lest some act of the Governor should be subversive of order.[33] Yates grabbed at the chance and asked Palmer to come immediately. Then he sent the general off to Washington to implore aid. At the same time the Governor sent word to Lincoln that the legislature would meet in June, take military power out of the Governor's hands, abolish the adjutant general's office, appoint a military board, and resist the draft. The Governor proposed bringing four regiments home, ostensibly for recruiting, but really to be ready to enforce martial law and disperse the legislature.[34]

When Palmer presented this proposition to Lincoln, the President told him an off-color story and asked: "Who can we trust if we cannot trust Illinois?" Getting no satisfaction, the general carried the Governor's proposition to Stanton. The War Secretary's suspicions were promptly aroused. "You are to command these troops, are you not?" he asked. But Palmer declared he had troops of his own, and he would not command troops against his own people.

"That shows the damned nonsense of the whole thing," cried the Secretary of War. "If you thought your own family

[32] Cf. Yates MSS., January to June 1863. On dozens of letters the Governor wrote endorsements indicating his complete acceptance of each rumor. None of the letters, indicating as they do the hysteria of the writers, furnishes specific information of the alleged meetings or plots.

[33] Palmer to Yates, January 18, 1863, Yates MSS.

[34] Yates's endorsement on William Buller and O. M. Hatch to Lincoln, March 1, 1863, Yates MSS.

and friends were in danger, you would be willing to command troops raised to protect them." [35]

Palmer reported his failure to Yates and returned to his troops in Tennessee. Governor Yates, however, could not be calm as he contemplated his plight. In the absence of sympathy and aid from Washington, the Governor began to encourage the formation of pro-administration and pro-war secret societies. Soon Union Leagues in Illinois counties were reporting that they had hundreds of men bound by oath to protect the government against the Copperheads. Each of them wanted arms.[36]

When the legislature reassembled in June, Yates still had no plan for dealing with it. The legislators began to discuss a bill to prevent illegal arrests, and another to prevent Negro immigration. It was in the midst of discussions on resolutions on federal relations when the two houses disagreed on the date of adjournment. Suddenly the Governor found a clause in the constitution that he could prorogue the legislature in case of such a disagreement. The situation hardly fitted the constitutional clause, but drowning Yates grabbed the straw. He prorogued the legislature and waited breathlessly to see if his act was respected. It was: the Senate accepted it and adjourned. The House remained in session two weeks, vainly filling the air with new denunciations of this "illegal, unconstitutional" usurpation.[37] A week later a Democratic convention in Springfield took up the cry, but no Knights of the Golden Circle were available to defend the Democrats. The shrewd Governor had safely weathered his imagined storm.

[35] John M. Palmer: *Personal Recollections*, pp. 152–3.

[36] Letters of C. H. Keller, Waterloo, March 20; W. J. Berkley, May 23; W. H. Cole, Clinton, May 28; R. D. Noteman, Centralia, June 26; A. B. Cherry, Colchester, June 30; "many Citizens" of Bond County, July 13; H. Silver, Peru, July 22; Thos. Moore, Metropolis, July 18, 1863, to Yates, Yates MSS.

[37] Yates to A. C. Fuller, June 10, 1863, Yates MSS.; A. C. Cole: *Era of the Civil War*, pp. 299–300; *Columbus Crisis*, June 24, 1863.

In the meantime, as Morton and Yates shook themselves free from their Democratic legislatures, the Republicans in the other states began to recover from their post-November melancholy. The spring elections in New England brought three new Republican governors and saved Connecticut's Governor Buckingham for the party. In New Hampshire the War Democrats, hoping to attract moderate Republicans, nominated a candidate to oppose Ira Eastman, and their 5,000 votes were enough to prevent Eastman from having a clear majority of the total vote. The choice was thrown into the legislature, which selected the radical Joseph A. Gilmore, who had 2,500 fewer popular votes than his Democratic opponent.[38] In Rhode Island the glamorous and erratic Sprague gave way to James Young Smith, another cotton manufacturer whom Sprague had defeated for governor two years before. In 1862 Sprague had been re-elected by an overwhelming majority, and had shortly after been elected to the United States Senate. In March 1863 he relinquished the governorship to Smith and went to Washington, where he had already successfully besieged the hand, if not the heart, of Salmon Chase's daughter, Kate. While the callow fledgling Senator and his ambitious and aggressive fiancée made the rounds of society before their November wedding date, the more competent and more prosaic Governor Smith tried to untangle the affairs of Rhode Island. Meantime in Vermont the spring elections brought another Smith, John Gregory Smith, a railroad president, into the governorship.

The New England victories, overcoming the hitherto exulting Democrats and lightening the Republican gloom, were more than mere spring harbingers of the autumn's harvest. They contained new lessons in political management and gave warning that state elections could only be

---

[38] *New Hampshire Patriot,* February 11, 25, March 11, June 10, 1863; Lyford: *Rollins,* pp. 147 ff.; Hadley: *Harriman,* pp. 144–51; H. Pillsbury: *New Hampshire: A History,* II, 546–7.

carried with federal aid. Rumor had it that New Hampshire's War Democrat was promised a brigadier general's commission if he would split the Democratic vote,[39] and the War Department peremptorily dismissed a lieutenant from the army for circulating Copperhead tickets — "doing all in his power to promote the success of the rebel cause." [40] In Connecticut, when Thomas H. Seymour, cousin of New York's Governor, waged a vigorous campaign denouncing the war and demanding peace, the federal government took a direct hand. Stanton promised Buckingham to furlough home as many Republicans as could be spared from the army, and Lincoln threw the federal patronage into the scales. A General Nye, foreseeing Seymour's victory, vowed to "buy up the damned state" and raised $100,000 in New York and Connecticut for the purchase. Just on the eve of the elections a brigadier general from the Ordnance Department put pressure on Connecticut's munitions manufacturers to force their workers to vote for Buckingham. In addition Union Leagues were organized a few weeks before the election.[41]

This combination of federal-inspired forces brought Buckingham a sweeping victory. "The Copperheads have sunk into their hides and hiding places," Buckingham exulted gratefully to Stanton.[42] Turning to the legislature, he told its members that the conflict must go on until the government should conquer. Civil war was cruelty and its fruits were desolation, sorrow, and death; but, said the Governor, the people must support the administration so that it might make fugitives and vagabonds of the Southerners. "Let the retribution be so terrible, that future generations shall not

[39] Hadley: *Harriman,* pp. 150–1.

[40] David G. Croly: *Seymour and Blair,* p. 126.

[41] T. H. Williams: *Lincoln and the Radicals,* pp. 280–3; W. A. Croffut and J. N. Morris: *Connecticut during the War,* pp. 322–7; Welles: *Diary,* I, 262, 306; *New York Tribune,* April 7, 1863; *Boston Courier,* April 5; *Detroit Free Press,* April 14, 1863; G. W. Smith: "Generative Forces of Union Propaganda," Ch. vi.

[42] Buckingham to Stanton, April 8, 1863, Stanton MSS.

dare to repeat the crime. Then, and then only, shall the wrong of an outraged people be avenged, human rights be vindicated, and constitutional authority be reestablished." [43]

By early summer the Republicans were able to assess their spring experiences in New England and the Middle West. By that time, too, the pattern for success had become evident. Eight states — Pennsylvania, Ohio, Wisconsin, Minnesota, Kentucky, Iowa, Maine, and Massachusetts — were to choose governors in the fall, and it was evident that only aggressive incumbent governors and the full influence of the federal administration could ensure Republican victories. Under the pressure of political necessity, the radicals and moderates closed their ranks and pledged support to the President. Abraham Lincoln, who controlled the army and the patronage, alone had the power to save the party in the states.

The pattern was already familiar as an integral part of the border-state policy, and it received its first demonstration in Kentucky. There no party called itself Republican, but the Union Democrats were close to Lincoln and received his blessing. In February the opposition, states'-rights faction tried to hold a convention in the House of Representatives, but the Unionist House refused them permission to use its chambers. When the states'-rights faction met in Metropolitan Hall in Frankfort, a detachment of federal troops drove them out. Somewhat later they succeeded in getting Charles A. Wyckliffe to declare himself a candidate for governor. Meantime the Union Democrats chose Thomas E. Bramlette, a radical only recently resigned from the federal army. His associations, both with Lincoln and with the army, were distasteful to the people, and his defeat seemed certain until the eve of the August elections. Then Governor Robinson issued a proclamation declaring that all Kentuckians who had expatriated themselves were disfranchised, General Boyle issued an order for the seizure of the rebel property — letting

[43] Croffut and Morris: *Connecticut during the War,* p. 328.

it be known that all supporters of Wyckliffe were *ipso facto* rebels — and General Burnside proclaimed martial law throughout the state. The military removed names from the ballots and in some counties suppressed the entire "peace" ticket. Voters and candidates alike were held in jails until after the elections. The result was 6,800 for Bramlette to 1,800 who had braved the bayonets to vote for Wyckliffe. "And thus," said old Sam Medary shudderingly from across the Ohio, "are the prerogatives of the people overthrown, the sovereignty of a State violated, our whole system of civil institutions mocked." [44]

Iowa's election, in contrast to Kentucky's, was carried with a minimum of federal interference. There was no less use of military force, however, to influence the election. Governor Kirkwood, radical to the core, had no intention of letting traitorous Copperheads win control of the state. Feelings were intense in the Hawkeye State, and frontier turbulence accompanied the discussions of political issues. Early in March, Kirkwood informed Stanton that it was "absolutely necessary" to have arms for the loyal men of Iowa. Unscrupulous individuals were organized to resist the draft, and there would be hostility to the government unless the loyal men were prepared to meet it. A few days later the Governor submitted letters from scattered partisans who declared with one voice that the Knights of the Golden Circle, 42,000 strong, were organized in every township. The leaders of these "active scoundrels" should be arrested, tried, and punished. [45]

Governor Kirkwood had no patience with Democrats who wore the liberty-head badge of their party. These Copperhead breastpins were "the emblems of moral treason," and it seemed to the Governor that the wearers must know that

[44] E. M. Coulter: *Civil War and Readjustment in Kentucky*, pp. 170–7; *Columbus Crisis*, August 12, 1863; Dennet: *Hay*, p. 125.

[45] *Official Records*, series 3, III, 62, 66–72.

they would create disturbances. Therefore, concluded Kirkwood, the Democrats were guilty of a constructive breach of the peace and should be punished for "an infraction of the law!" [46]

With such eagerness to use coercion, Kirkwood was prepared for the exigencies of the coming campaign. He continued to appeal to Stanton for arms, issued proclamations threatening Copperheads, and advised young ladies not to marry them. To the ladies the Governor explained that a man disloyal to his country would be unfaithful to his wife, and, besides, he wanted the breed to die out. [47]

Before the Republicans met to nominate a state ticket, Abraham Lincoln removed Kirkwood from the list of candidates by appointing him Minister to Denmark. The Governor accepted — though he never went — but insisted that he was needed for the campaign. [48] With Kirkwood out, the Republicans nominated Colonel William M. Stone, a judge who had left the bench to lead a regiment and had been wounded at Shiloh and before Vicksburg. [49] Six weeks later the Democrats, after being refused by one candidate, persuaded General James M. Tuttle to run for governor. The Democratic platform condemned the war — "unconstitutional and oppressive," a "prolific source of usurpation, tyranny and corruption" — and emancipation, but Tuttle confused the issues by announcing his support of Lincoln.

"He is far too good a man," moaned Kirkwood, "to be sacrificed by such a scurvy lot of politicians." Republican papers, which had been praising Tuttle before the nomination, feared that there would be a stampede for the general among the voting soldiers. They carefully gathered scathing condemnation of the general from regiments in the field and

[46] Kirkwood to Peter Dolbee, March 1863; H. W. Lathrop: *Samuel J. Kirkwood,* p. 240.

[47] *Davenport Gazette,* April 4, 1863.

[48] Lathrop: *Kirkwood,* pp. 277 ff.

[49] *Davenport Gazette,* June 20, 1863.

published them widely. Meantime, Kirkwood organized and armed the militia in each county.[50]

More significant than the expositions on the hustings were the martial aspects of the campaign. On August 1 George C. Tally, a Baptist preacher, spoke at a Democratic mass meeting in Keokuk County. As he passed through the town of South English, some Republicans attempted to take his "butternut" pin from him, and at the meeting Tally excoriated them for their violence. That afternoon, returning through the town, the preacher and his companions were again set upon by the mob and in the altercation Tally was shot to death. Two days later, hearing that Democrats were preparing vengeance, Governor Kirkwood sent forty stands of arms to the South English Republicans and started for the county with ten companies of infantry behind him. Lawyers came in to prosecute Tally's murderers, and Democratic companies followed. When Kirkwood arrived, he made a ranting speech threatening vengeance and punishment to all the Tally cohorts. Then the Governor, brave in the knowledge that his troops were coming, went to the hotel and sat quietly talking of the new steers he had just bought for his farm. The next day the troops arrived and were put under the command of a violent radical, Colonel N. P. Chipman. With the situation well in hand, twelve men were arrested for Tally's murder and released on bail.[51]

Flushed with his triumph in the Tally war, Kirkwood appeared in Dubuque to explain his concepts of law and order. In injured vein he declared that he had been accused of organizing companies to drive Democrats from the polls on election day. This was unjust: he was only attempting to vindicate the processes of the law as he had done in Keokuk. But, he added, the volunteer companies had another purpose. There had been threats of draft riots in Dubuque. "I

[50] S. H. M. Byers: *Iowa in War Times*, pp. 260–3; *Davenport Gazette*, August 5–19, 1863.

[51] Lathrop: *Kirkwood*, pp. 245–9.

want to talk long enough to tell you that it will be a bad thing to start a mob here in opposition to the draft." He had, he reminded them, sent ten companies and two pieces of artillery into Keokuk — "And not a blank cartridge. And I tell you if it becomes necessary for me to come here to Dubuque on the same errand, *I shall not bring a blank cartridge here.*" [52]

The result of Governor Kirkwood's vigorous campaigning was victory for Colonel Stone. In November the volunteer companies maintained the Governor's order at the polls, and 70,000 Iowans voted for the Republican candidate, while but 5,000 favored the Democratic general. Soldiers in the field ratified the civilians' choice by a vote of 16,791 to 2,904.

In contrast to the turbulence of Iowa's campaign, the contests in neighboring Minnesota and Wisconsin were mild and tame. In both states the Republicans normally had safe majorities, and although there had been draft riots in Wisconsin's lake-shore communities, the government had effectively suppressed the rioters and left little political capital for the Democrats. The Indian war, too, had frightened the populace into loyalty to the federal government.

In Minnesota the campaign was marked with little interest. Governor Ramsey and Lieutenant Governor Ignatius Donnelly, each heading rival factions of Republicans, left the state for Washington before the campaign. Donnelly was elected to the House of Representatives in 1862, and resigned as Lieutenant Governor the following March. In January, Ramsey was elected, after devious dealings in his party's caucus, to the United States Senate. When he quit the governorship in July, the president pro tem of the state Senate, Henry A. Swift, took his place. He served without disturbance or distinction until January, when the office passed to Brigadier General Stephen A. Miller, ex-merchant, former temperance lecturer, hero of the Virginia campaign from Bull Run to South Mountain, and executioner of the

[52] Ibid., pp. 265–6.

Sioux. The Republicans nominated Miller with confidence
and enthusiasm, and the Democratic nominee hardly both-
ered to contest the election. In November citizens and soldiers overwhelmingly endorsed the party's judgment.[53]

In Wisconsin the Democrats partially threw their cause
away by nominating a railroad lawyer who had figured prom-
inently in an earlier railroad scandal. The Republican press
unfolded Henry Palmer's record for the electorate and
pointed with pride to James T. Lewis, their own uncon-
taminated candidate. Lewis, who had been Secretary of
State, won his party's nomination over Governor Salomon
in a convention contest that involved personal rivalries
rather than ideological differences. In November the people
gave Lewis a majority of 16,000 and the soldier vote from
the field swelled his total by 8,000. The soldier vote, however, was significant in a choice for chief justice. The civilian
vote was cast for a Copperhead, but the soldiers reversed the
count and gave the judgeship to a corrupt tool of the railroad interests.[54]

More significant by far were the gubernatorial elections in
the October states of Pennsylvania and Ohio. And in these
states the full power of both the federal government and
Abraham Lincoln was needed to carry the day for the Republican Party. These were crucial states, and their loss
would have cost the party its control, ensured the election
of a Democratic president the next year, and defeated the
radical plans for economic exploitation of the South. In
these states the constitutional dogmas of states' rights fought
their last and fatal battle against the burgeoning power of
the national government.

The early weeks of the campaign in Pennsylvania brought

[53] J. B. Baker: *Lives of the Governors of Minnesota*, pp. 120–5;
W. W. Folwell: *History of Minnesota*, II, 106–8, 335 f.

[54] F. Merk: *Economic History of Wisconsin during the Civil War
Decade*, pp. 256–61; *Wisconsin State Journal*, April 13, August 20, 21,
October 14, November 28, 1863.

once more to the fore the ancient feud between Governor Curtin and Senator Cameron. As time had gone on, Cameron had become more radical while Curtin had grown closer to Lincoln. As a conservative, the Governor had gone so far as to disavow any connection with arbitrary arrests and he told his legislature that only Congress could suspend the writ of habeas corpus. Moreover, the Governor flirted with the idea of forming a Union Party and was even reported to be willing to withdraw in favor of a War Democrat.[55]

In April, rumors of Curtin's withdrawal received confirmation. For a long time the Governor's health had been bad, and Mrs. Curtin feared that he could not live through another campaign. She consulted A. K. McClure, and together they persuaded Curtin to retire from the governorship. McClure went to Washington and asked Lincoln to give Curtin a foreign mission. The President consulted Cameron, who welcomed a chance to be rid of his rival. Cameron suggested a second-class mission, but McClure won Lincoln's agreement to give a major embassy to the Governor. Thereupon Curtin announced to the legislature that he would not be a candidate.[56]

Immediately Cameron and his friends began to confer on a suitable radical candidate. They realized that only a strong man could carry the war-weary electorate, and they understood full well that if the Democrats won, "the hopes and destiny of the republic" were at stake. Then there would be "compromise and peace at the expense of liberty and the rights of the non-slaveholding States." But as they consulted, they were reluctantly forced to the conclusion that they had no strong man and that Curtin had unsuspected strength in

[55] G. W. Smith: "Generative Forces of Union Propaganda"; S. L. Davis: *Pennsylvania Politics*, pp. 279–80; McClure: *Lincoln and Men of War Times*, p. 261.

[56] Davis: *Pennsylvania Politics*, pp. 288–90; McClure: *Lincoln and Men of War Times*, pp. 261–2. Curtin to Lincoln, April 24, 1863, R. T. Lincoln MSS.

the rural areas. In desperation they appealed to Secretary
Chase to get Lincoln's advice. But when Chase brought the
matter up, the President cannily promised support for any
candidate the Union men of Pennsylvania chose. Finally,
with many misgivings, the Cameronites settled on "Honest
John" Covode, who had once won fame investigating Buchanan's "Lecompton swindle." [57]

Meantime Pennsylvania's Democrats nominated George W.
Woodward, Chief Justice of the Supreme Court, who had
declared the draft act illegal and the legal-tender system unconstitutional. Moreover, Democrats in the legislature proposed memorializing Congress to call a national convention
to restore the Union. Woodward's nomination, on the same
principles, inspired Democrats to a vigorous campaign, and
Republicans promptly concluded that the Knights of the
Golden Circle were organized in the state. Quickly, too, they
proposed arresting the leaders in order to intimidate the
rank and file.[58]

Woodward's nomination made it imperative that the Republicans choose their strongest man, and — to the horror of
the Cameronites — that appeared to be Curtin. Within a
few days of the Governor's announcement that he would
not be a candidate, the party members in leading counties
instructed delegates to the party's convention to draft Curtin. While Curtin and McClure were agreeing to support
Covode, party groups out in the state sent committees to
persuade Curtin to be a candidate. Moreover, Curtin and
his wife toured the state and met universal applause. Cameron began a countermovement, and invited Secretary Seward and Attorney General Bates, both moderates, to join
him in a trip through Pennsylvania over his railroad. Both

[57] S. P. Chase to B. H. Brewster, June 18, 1863; letters of Frank
Jordan, May 4, Jos. Casey, May 2, R. G. White, May 16, Thaddeus
Stevens, June 18, 1863, to Cameron, Cameron MSS.

[58] Davis: *Pennsylvania Politics*, pp. 281–2; *Official Records*, series 3,
III, 75.

declined. The Cameronite newspapers began to snipe at Curtin, demanding that he reiterate his renunciation, but the Governor's health had improved under acclaim. Ambition mixed with venom for Cameron sent the blood coursing faster through his veins, and he kept silent while the movement to draft him gained strength. In August, though Cameron fumed in frustration and his cohorts hissed in the galleries, the Republican convention rejected Covode and other Cameron-endorsed candidates and conferred the accolade of renomination on Curtin.[59]

In the meantime the campaign in Ohio was taking unpredictable shape. In March, Clement L. Vallandigham completed his congressional career with a rousing speech against the conscription bill and returned to Ohio. Soon he was on the stump denouncing the administration, the war that was being "waged for the purpose of crushing out liberty and erecting a despotism," and conscription. The ex-Congressman was the acknowledged leader of the Western Democrats. He was not Seymour's intellectual equal, but he possessed more energy and greater courage than the New Yorker. Democrats in Ohio rallied to his standard and it became evident that Vallandigham hoped to ride the wave of war-weariness into the executive residence.

The Democratic upsurge brought a curious episode in Ohio politics. Dr. Edson B. Olds, whom Governor Tod had had arrested the year before, filed an affidavit against the Governor. A grand jury in Fairfield County returned a true bill, and Olds proceeded to Columbus to arrest Tod in the Governor's office. Tod hurriedly appealed to the state supreme court and was released from custody on a writ of habeas corpus. The case dragged on until it was taken into the United States District Court at Cincinnati, where it was

---

[59] Davis: *Pennsylvania Politics*, pp. 242–4, 290–7; McClure: *Lincoln and Men of War Times*, pp. 261–2; Bates and Seward to Cameron, June 6 and 8, 1863; W. H. Egle: *Andrew Gregg Curtin*, pp. 160 ff.

dropped. At the same time Olds sued Tod for one hundred thousand dollars, but the case never came to trial.[60]

The boldness of the Democrats thoroughly frightened the military officials in the Ohio area. In March, Tod and O. P. Morton conferred with General Lew Wallace in Cincinnati, and the general assured them that eighty thousand enemies of the government were secretly organized in Ohio.[61] A month later General Ambrose E. Burnside, rabid radical and darling of the committee on the conduct of the war, issued an order that "treason, expressed or implied, will not be tolerated in this Department." The general had but recently failed in command of the Army of the Potomac and was burning to distinguish himself in the Department of the Ohio. Vallandigham continued to speak to Democratic rallies, and in May Burnside's men arrested him in his home and carried him off to be tried by court martial. The military court found him guilty of expressing sympathy for the South and of intending to hinder the prosecution of the war, and sentenced him to prison.[62]

The outcry from enraged Democrats almost overwhelmed the administration. Vallandigham applied to the United States Circuit Court at Cincinnati for a writ of habeas corpus, but the court refused on the ground that the military commander of the district had sole discretion in judging the need for his action. But Burnside's discretion was not highly regarded in Washington, where Lincoln determined to commute Vallandigham's sentence to banishment to the Confederacy.[63] Secretary Stanton, eager to protect a fellow radical, took occasion to warn Burnside to display more caution, to consult the governors before taking action, and to avoid newspaper controversies.[64]

[60] E. O. Randall and D. J. Ryan: *History of Ohio,* IV, 213–14; *Columbus Crisis,* March 25, April 15, 1863.

[61] *Columbus Crisis,* March 4, 1863.

[62] E. McPherson: *Political History of the Great Rebellion,* p. 162; W. B. Weeden: *War Government, Federal and State,* pp. 242–3.

[63] McPherson: *Political History of the Great Rebellion,* p. 162.

[64] Stanton to Burnside, June 1, 1863, Stanton MSS.

The immediate effect of Burnside's action was to ensure Vallandigham's nomination by the Democrats. Other candidates promptly withdrew, and while the exiled Democrat was making his way through Richmond and Havana to Niagara Falls, Canada, Democrats everywhere used the Constitution to cudgel the Republicans. Horatio Seymour wrote to a protest meeting in Albany that the government's actions had been "cowardly, brutal, and infamous." "It is not merely a step toward revolution," he declaimed, "it is revolution. It will not only lead to military despotism, it establishes military despotism . . . if it is upheld, our liberties are overthrown." [65]

On June 11, when the Democrats' convention met in Columbus, forty thousand men converged on the meeting. Moderate Democrats, recognizing Vallandigham's disadvantages, tried in vain to get the nomination for General McClellan or Hugh Jewett. Neither delegates nor irate mob would have a moderate man, and they cheered to the rafters as George Pugh, Vallandigham's lawyer, flayed Lincoln, Burnside, and the government in words that made Vallandigham's utterances seem mild and reasoned statements. The crowd demanded Vallandigham, and the convention gave him the nomination and sent a futile mission to Washington to beg Lincoln to restore the candidate to the state.[66]

A week after the Democrats made their choice, the Republicans assembled in Columbus. But there was no unanimity in their ranks on a candidate. Governor Tod had not proved a popular leader, the costs of government had risen in his administration, and he had been too zealous in making arbitrary arrests. Moreover, there were railroad interests to be considered behind the screen of national issues. Gov-

[65] S. Mitchell: *Horatio Seymour of New York*, pp. 289–90; J. G. Blaine: *Twenty Years of Congress*, I, 490–2; Nicolay and Hay: *Lincoln*, VII, 341–2.

[66] *Columbus Crisis*, June 3, 1863; Randall and Ryan: *Ohio*, IV, 228–9; W. Reid: *Ohio in the War*, I, 153–4; Nicolay and Hay: *Lincoln*, VII, 350–1.

ernor Tod was president of a railroad, but his company had
no interest in a consolidation scheme that would unite a set
of railroad lines from the Alleghenies to the Mississippi. The
leader of the consolidation plan was John Brough, president
of another road, who had once been a prominent Democrat,
a successful state auditor, and a newspaper editor. Republican managers and railroad consolidationists — frequently
the same persons — proposed to shift the party's affections
from Tod to Brough.

Brough possessed unusual ability in finance and had a
keen insight in politics. He was suspicious beyond the wont
of politicians, and tactless, even unscrupulous, in his treatment of men. His manners were bad. His weight was enormous, and, years before, waggish rhymesters had chanted a
ditty:

> If flesh is grass as the Scriptures say,
> Then Johnny Brough's a load of hay.

Despite his weight and his nearly sixty years, Brough was
an accomplished and vigorous speaker, and just as the Democrats were nominating their hero, the railroads' man appeared at Marietta, his birthplace, to make a strong Union
speech that endorsed Lincoln, emancipation, patriotism, and
arbitrary arrests. Promptly Cincinnati's papers spread his
speech upon their pages and proclaimed Brough their candidate. Quickly the railroads issued free passes to Columbus, and when the Republican convention assembled, there
was a crowd in the capital city that rivaled the Democratic mob.

In the convention Brough barely won the nomination
with 216 votes to Tod's 193. But Tod and his supporters
had no recourse, and they fell into line behind the new
candidate. The Governor wired Lincoln that opponents
would say that the Republicans had repudiated Lincoln.
"Do not believe it," said Tod. "Personal considerations alone
were the cause of my defeat. No man in Ohio will do more
to secure the triumphant election of the ticket nominated

than I will." Lincoln, who liked Tod, was sincerely regretful, but he promised Brough his full support.[67]

Three factors entered into the campaign in Ohio and Pennsylvania to bring success to the Republican candidates. The first was the Union victories at Gettysburg and Vicksburg. Grant and Meade were more effective vote-getters than the political candidates, and Democrats ceased denouncing the war as a failure. The second was the vigorous organizations of semi-secret societies; the third was the effective intervention of the federal government in the state campaigns.

As the campaigns got under way, the Republicans became excessively alarmed over the probable actions of the much feared Knights of the Golden Circle. This mysterious organization had never been identified, but in the fevered imagination of Republican partisans its members numbered hundreds of thousands. Lest the dragon society rise in its reputed strength and overthrow the government, Republicans banded themselves in "Strong Bands" and Union Leagues and begged governors and the federal government for arms. "The government does not realize the imminent danger of the peril," Indiana's Carrington told the War Department.[68] In Michigan, Democrats believed that Governor Blair was the head of the Strong Bands, whose purpose was to "overawe the peaceable citizens" of the state. The bands were both secret and military, and were controlled by "the most fanatical and desperate of former Republican leaders." [69] In Ohio Sam Medary charged that the Union Leagues were direct but "abolitionized" descendants of the Know-Nothing order.[70] In Illinois thousands joined the Strong Bands and

---

[67] *Columbus Crisis*, June 17, July 8, September 2, 1863; Reid: *Ohio in the War*, I, 166–7; Randall and Ryan: *Ohio*, IV, 231–4; *Official Records*, series 3, III, 380; *Writings of Lincoln*, VI, 331.

[68] *Official Records*, series 3, III, 75–6.

[69] *Detroit Free Press*, March 31, 1863.

[70] *Columbus Crisis*, February 18, 1863.

swore to sustain the government with arms. Chapter after chapter of the Union League asked Yates for arms, promised to "carry the State in the next election," and pledged themselves to "resist unto blood the treasonable practices of our rebel loving, Government hating neighbors." [71]

By the time of the elections the armed "dark lantern" societies were organized and able to combat the phantom organizations of the Democrats. In Ohio, George Pugh, candidate for lieutenant governor, who carried the burden of the campaign, asserted there would be fifty thousand "fully armed and equipped freemen of Ohio to receive their Governor-elect at the Canadian line and escort him to the State House." But Brough was sure of a different outcome. "For I tell you," he answered, "there is a mighty mass of men in this State whose nerves are strung up like steel, who will never permit this dishonor to be consummated to their native state." Old Sam Medary of the *Crisis* professed to be shocked by Brough's threat of civil war, and a Unionist mob raided and wrecked with impunity his newspaper office. [72]

In Pennsylvania, Union Leagues organized the voters from Philadelphia to Pittsburgh. Democrats jeered that secret orders of Antimasons and Know-Nothings had furnished the models for the new agency of violence. Replying to the Democrats, Curtin's friend John W. Forney admitted the leagues carried on propaganda which "enlightens the mind and instills mutual sentiments of respect and affection." Woodward's supporters doubted that the methods were confined to enlightenment. [73]

But a more potent factor in the Republican victories than either battles won or armed clubs was the national administration. Lincoln watched nervously and worried more than

[71] Letters of J. S. Wolfe, July 1; J. D. Bartlett and others, February 17; John Wilson, July 1; D. O. Mattice, July 2; G. H. Harlow, July 6; S. Park, July 26; A. D. White, July 27, 1863, to Yates, Yates MSS.

[72] Randall and Ryan: *Ohio,* IV, 236–7; *Columbus Crisis,* September 16, 1863.

[73] R. G. White to Cameron, September 18, 1863, Cameron MSS.; Davis: *Pennsylvania Politics,* p. 301.

he did over his own election in 1860.[74] And, in this case, he took more action. He authorized a fifteen-day leave for Ohio and Pennsylvania government clerks to go home to vote. The railroads gave passes, and the politicians assessed the clerks one per cent of their salaries. For two weeks public business was at a standstill.[75] Moreover, Lincoln and Stanton — the latter with a wry face — authorized commanders to furlough troops home to Pennsylvania.[76] Other members of the government, too, took an active part. Secretary Chase, for the first time since the war began, went home to Ohio and spoke repeatedly for Brough. Morton and Yates, too, laid aside their duties to lend a neighborly hand.[77]

On election day the polls were crowded. Union Leagues and soldiers inspected the voters. The workers of the Philadelphia arsenal were driven to the voting booths "like cattle to the slaughter." There were so many soldiers absent from the armies, said the Democrats, that Lee was tempted to raid Washington, and Meade had fallen back to the Potomac.[78]

That night Abraham Lincoln went over to the War Department's telegraph office to watch the returns. The votes from both states were favorable, and it was clear from the beginning of the count that Brough and Curtin were winning. About ten o'clock Lincoln wired to Columbus: "Where is John Brough?" Back came the word that Brough, too, was in a telegraph office. "Brough, what is your majority now?" wired Lincoln. "Over 30,000" replied the winning candidate. At midnight Brough answered: "Over 50,000." At five a.m. Brough answered: "Over 100,000." Back over the wire came the exultant message: "Glory to God in the highest. Ohio has saved the Nation. A. Lincoln." [79]

[74] Welles: *Diary*, I, 469.

[75] Davis: *Pennsylvania Politics*, p. 311.

[76] Ibid., pp. 315–16; Curtin to Lincoln, September 17, 1863, R. T. Lincoln MSS.

[77] Reid: *Ohio in the War*, I, 169; W. D. Foulke: *Oliver P. Morton*, I, 250–1.

[78] Davis: *Pennsylvania Politics*, p. 316.

[79] E. Hertz: *The Hidden Lincoln*, II, 914.

The episode may have expressed Lincoln's relief, but a more accurate outcome would have been a grateful ejaculation from Brough to the effect that Lincoln had saved Ohio. Andrew Gregg Curtin was in no doubt about the cause of his 15,000 majority over Woodward. In gratitude the victor went to Washington to thank Lincoln and Stanton. But just before he got to the War Department, one of his friends spoke to Stanton on Curtin's triumph. "Yes," observed the Secretary of War, "Pennsylvania must be a damned loyal State to give such a victory to Curtin!" Curtin heard the remark in time and did not waste his thanks on Stanton.[80]

With attention centered on Ohio and Pennsylvania, the elections in Maine and Massachusetts were anticlimactic. In Maine the Democrats adopted a platform of unqualified opposition to all the administration's acts. The Republicans, fearful that the opposition would capture the state, determined to replace Abner Coburn, with a War Democrat. The man of their choice was Samuel Cony, long a Democratic officeholder, who had joined the Unionist cause at the war's outbreak. His nomination won the support of Democratic politicians, and in September he was elected over Bion Bradbury by a substantial majority.[81]

Massachusetts Democrats entered the campaign with high hopes of capitalizing on arbitrary arrests, Andrew's Negroism, and conscription. They nominated Henry W. Paine of Cambridge, an old Whig who had never before attended a Democratic convention. The Republicans renominated Andrew, proclaimed their intention of supporting the government in all means to put down the rebellion and to continue the war until human slavery was driven from the land. In November the party had no need to call in outside help. Andrew won by a majority of 41,000 — the largest he had yet received.[82]

[80] McClure: *Lincoln and Men of War Times*, p. 261.

[81] *National Cyclopedia of American Biography*, VI, 314.

[82] W. Schouler: *Massachusetts in the Civil War*, I, 497–502; *New York Tribune*, November 5, 1863.

At the same time the victories in these solidly Republican states were reinforced by other successes in local elections. In Indiana, Republicans, aided by the provost marshals and the Union Leagues, won in county elections. More significant, however, was Republican success in New York. There, thanks to Seymour's prominence, the election of legislators and a secretary of state took on national importance. Seymour himself slowly lost ground as a Democratic leader. In April he vetoed a bill to allow soldiers to vote in the field, and Republicans sprang to the opportunity to portray the Governor as the enemy of democracy. Moreover, the Governor's attitude on the war was temporizing and inconclusive. He opposed conscription, yet was zealous in raising volunteers. He favored a vigorous prosecution of the war, yet displayed extreme sensitiveness about the methods used to secure liberty. Such a position, honest enough to a scholarly mind, was defective in political appeal. Adam Gurowski noticed that the "deep-dyed Copperheads and slavery-saviours" did not think Seymour "safe." In November the Democrats failed to respond to their Governor's appeals, while thousands of troops came home from Meade's army to vote against the party that would not permit them to vote in the field. For the next year Seymour would be saddled with an opposition legislature, and Republicans rejoiced at the Democrats' lost confidence in their leader.[83]

In these same local elections, as Seymour's challenge to national concentration declined, Lincoln's leadership received a new and emphatic demonstration in Maryland. Just on election eve Ex-Governor Hicks, now in the United States Senate and co-operating with the radicals, advised General Robert Schenck, in charge of the area, to place restrictions

[83] Mitchell: *Seymour*, pp. 288, 347–53; Welles: *Diary*, I, 231, 363; Croly: *Seymour and Blair*, pp. 124 f.; Lincoln (ed.): *Messages of the Governors of New York*, V, 513–16; Society for the Diffusion of Political Knowledge, *Pamphlet No. 7;* Adam Gurowski: *Diary*, II, 273; Dennett: *Hay*, p. 104; Nicolay and Hay: *Lincoln*, VII, 40; Blaine: *Twenty Years of Congress*, I, 497; *New York Tribune*, November 4, 5, 1863.

on disloyal voters in the state. At least, Hicks suggested, voters should be forced to take a stringent oath. Hearing that troops were being sent to Maryland to administer test oaths, Governor Bradford protested to Lincoln. But General Schenck, who had defeated Vallandigham in the congressional elections the year before and would soon take his seat in the House of Representatives, was as violent a radical as Burnside. He promptly ordered provost marshals to take troops to the polls, prevent disorder, and administer oaths to suspected Democrats. Bradford protested to Lincoln and issued a proclamation rescinding Schenck's orders. The general forbade the telegraph companies to transmit the Governor's order.

Lincoln replied to Bradford with a reminder that the Governor had himself been elected with federal bayonets the year before. Moreover, said the President, it was not enough that the candidates should be true men. "In this struggle for the nation's life" it was necessary that loyal men should have been elected only by loyal voters. Schenck himself, after consulting Stanton, told Lincoln that without military intervention "we lose this State." The President modified Schenck's orders slightly, but accepted the basic principle.

On election day the troops were at the polls. In Kent County, on the Eastern Shore, they arrested leading Democrats and scurried them across the bay. The commander issued instructions that only the candidates of the Union League convention were recognized by the federal authorities. In other places the soldiers administered oaths, arrested Democrats, and voted themselves.[84]

The result was not alone a victory in Maryland. It was a synthesis of the political developments of the year. The military power of the federal government, aided and supple-

[84] H. E. Buchholz: *Governors of Maryland*, pp. 175–6; McPherson: *Political History of the Great Rebellion*, pp. 308–16; T. H. Hicks to Schenck, October 26, 1863, Bradford MSS.; A. L. Knott: *Biographical Sketch of A. Lee Knott*, pp. 40–2; Dennett: *Hay*, p. 114; J. T. Scharf: *History of Maryland*, III, 569–70, 599.

mented by the organized Union Leagues and Strong Bands, could alone ensure electoral success in the more important Northern states. It did not need a repetition of the Maryland episode in Delaware's special congressional election, a week later, to emphasize the lesson.[85]

[85] W. H. Powell: *History of Delaware*, pp. 273–4; Conrad: *Delaware*, I, 211–12.

Chapter 16

The Soldier's Friends

By the last months of 1863 Abraham Lincoln had won the strategic heights in the struggle between national centralization and states' rights. In the arenas of both military control and politics the state governors had become agents of the federal government. National conscription had not been a success, and the governors retained a part of the form of states' rights in raising men for the armies, but the substance of state authority over the troops was gone. And, as the elections of 1863 had demonstrated, the President's military power could be translated, where necessary, into political might. There would be in the months — even years — to come renewed struggles between state and nation, and sometimes the national line would falter. But in each case the final triumph would rest with the forces whom Lincoln had led.

As the governors realized their new status, they felt their declining prestige more acutely than their loss of power. Grasping for some remnant of their former glory, they began to emphasize another aspect of their manifold functions. From the beginning of the war the state executives had shown a keen feeling for the welfare of the soldiers and had vied with one another for the title of "Soldier's Friend." Now they redoubled their efforts for the soldiers and spared no pains in portraying themselves as the champions of the men in arms. As the federal government assumed responsibility for raising armies and reduced the governors to mere recruiting agents, the executives assumed the role of protectors of their people from the unreasonable demands of the nation's war. As the casualties mounted in the last year of carnage, the governors became increasingly solicitous for the sick and the dead. In part the governors were politicians, transmuting tears — as they had once transmuted patriotism — into the golden majorities of the ballot-box. In part they were warm-hearted men, genuinely horrified by the graves and the crutches, the widows and the orphans, the inconsolable sadness and grief of war. Humanity combined with political profit to make the governors anxious for the well-being of their constituents in arms.

The governors undertook their intensified humanitarianism with a long background of experience. From the days when the first militiamen answered Lincoln's call for troops, the governors had showered care upon the soldiers of their states. Governor Buckingham visited each new forming Connecticut regiment to tell the men that the national government made ample provision for its defenders and to assure them that he would strive to get them all of their rights.[1] Wisconsin's Governor Randall appointed a state agent to march with each regiment to look after its welfare and to return the sick and wounded to the state. He invited other governors to follow his example, and he urged railroad and steamboat companies to give free passage home to all discharged soldiers.[2] Wisconsin's "Samaritans" displayed such efficiency that the surgeon general of the army protested that they snatched sick and wounded men from the hospitals before the surgeons could treat them. After a year the system was modified, but state agents continued to visit the armies and report on conditions.[3] Governor Ramsey early heard

[1] W. A. Croffut and J. M. Morris: *Military and Civil History of Connecticut*, p. 144.

[2] *Official Records*, series 3, I, 330–1.

[3] *Wisconsin State Journal*, February 7, 1862; *Official Records*, series 3, II, 40–1.

that Minnesota troops were without clothes, and hurried a personal emissary to Washington to demand relief.[4] Morton bent every effort to equip Indiana's troops with overcoats and warm underclothes, and complained vigorously to the War Department about its callous inefficiency.[5] Yates sent physicians on inspection trips,[6] while Andrew established agencies at Philadelphia and Baltimore and formed the Massachusetts Association to care for the wounded.[7] Once the Governor himself, hearing that a regiment without transportation was hungry in a New York fort, rushed to New York, hired a rowboat to take him to the fort, and announced that he was staying to starve with his men.[8]

When battles were fought, the governors rushed to the battlefields. Samuel Kirkwood heard that an Iowa company of 80 had lost 72 men at Donelson, and he dashed off to Tennessee with a surgeon, while the legislature appropriated three thousand dollars and sent a squad of medical men to the rescue.[9] Morton accompanied surgeons and nurses to Donelson, then hurried back to open a chain of hospitals leading to Indianapolis.[10] Yates sent surgeons and nurses to Donelson and six weeks later went twice to the Shiloh battlefield.[11] Tod and even Andrew rushed surgeons and medical supplies to Shiloh.[12]

It was on the trip to Shiloh that Wisconsin's Governor Harvey was drowned. His death made Wisconsin's people acutely conscious of the sufferings of the soldiers, and Har-

[4] W. W. Folwell: *History of Minnesota*, II, 31–2.

[5] W. M. French: *Life . . . of Governor Oliver P. Morton*, pp. 200 ff.

[6] Yates to Dr. D. M. Whitney, September 18, 1861, Yates MSS.

[7] W. Schouler: *Massachusetts in the Civil War*, pp. 302 f.

[8] H. G. Pearson: *Life of John A. Andrew*, I, 275.

[9] H. W. Lathrop: *Samuel J. Kirkwood*, pp. 207–8.

[10] C. Rall: *Indiana, One Hundred and Fifty Years of American Development*, II, 200.

[11] A. C. Cole: *The Era of the Civil War*, p. 284; T. M. Eddy: *The Patriotism of Illinois*, I, 252.

[12] Tod to Stanton, and Andrew to Stanton, April 10, 1863, Stanton MSS.

vey's successor, Salomon, devoted much time and money to the care of the state's soldiers. Although the "Samaritans" with each regiment proved an annoyance to the medical corps and were withdrawn, the Governor continued to appoint state agents to visit the camps and hospitals. The agents took charge of the distribution of gifts sent by the Sanitary Commission, arranged for wives to visit sick husbands, transacted business — especially transmitting money — for the soldiers, filed soldier complaints against brutal or incompetent officers, and sent the wounded and the bodies of the dead home to Wisconsin.[13]

Most famous of Wisconsin's state agents was Governor Harvey's widow. At a salary of three dollars a day, Mrs. Harvey threw herself wholeheartedly into the work of alleviating the miseries of Wisconsin's soldiers, sick and well. In September 1862 she arrived in St. Louis bearing wine, fruits, and comforting words for boys from the Badger State. She was diligent, faithful, and intelligent in her duties. She had a drunken surgeon removed from an army hospital. She found that Morton had sent a boat to take Indiana boys home, and she got a vessel for Wisconsin. She returned to Madison in the summer of 1863, threw herself into a campaign to raise more money, and went back down the river to Wisconsin's camps in the fall. She reported casualties to Governor Salomon, found a Catholic priest for a dying soldier, sent the Governor a tail feather from "Old Abe," eagle mascot of a Wisconsin regiment, and begged for boats to carry wounded soldiers from the fetid South to Wisconsin's "good air." Late in 1863 the War Department established the Harvey Hospital in Madison. Then Mrs. Harvey launched a campaign for an orphans' home, opened it in January 1866, and turned it over to the government in March.[14]

[13] Wisconsin Governors' Papers, MSS., contain hundreds of letters from and about the agents. Cf. Salomon to Lincoln, March 12, 1863, R. T. Lincoln MSS.

[14] Harvey MSS., Wisconsin Governors' Papers, April 1862 to April 1866.

The work of such state agents and of the governors brought political rewards. The governors won the hearts of the soldiers in the field and could count on them in political crises. Thus Morton could appeal, as the "Soldier's Friend," to the Indiana troops for support against his "disloyal" legislature. But the best example of the soldiers' rallying behind a governor came in Pennsylvania's 1863 election. Andrew Curtin may have been anathema to Cameron and only an "available" candidate to moderate Republicans, but he was the idol of the soldiers. He had raised money from the businessmen of the state and had lavished it on the soldiers. He had quarreled, on behalf of the soldiers, with Cameron and Stanton in the War Department. He had visited hospitals, had organized a state agency in Washington, and had personally answered thousands of soldiers' letters during the war. Having endeared himself to the soldiers, he got his reward when thousands of them deluged their relatives and friends with demands for his re-election. Not even the influence of "Little Mac" McClellan, cast into the scales for Judge Woodward at the last moment, could win the soldiers and their friends from the "Soldier's Friend." [15]

Curtin did not thank Stanton for sending the soldiers home to vote, but he sought in two ways to show his gratitude to the men themselves. First he proposed that the battlefield at Gettysburg be made into a national cemetery, and second he presented the legislature with a plan for a soldiers' orphanage. His fellow governors responded readily to Curtin's proposals to purchase the Gettysburg battlegrounds, and they appointed representatives to attend the dedication ceremonies.[16]

The Gettysburg dedication was planned to emphasize the

[15] W. H. Egle: *Andrew Gregg Curtin*, pp. 366 ff.; S. L. Davis: *Pennsylvania Politics, 1860–1863*, p. 309.

[16] V. T. Messner: "The Public Life of Austin Blair," pp. 43–4; letters of A. I. Boreman, November 12, and Joel Parker to Ward Hill Lamon, Lincoln MSS., Huntington Library.

role of the states in the war. The governors, the state commissioners, and the flags of the states occupied prominent places in the formal plans for the ceremony. But two weeks before the occasion Lincoln accepted an invitation to attend. His sudden and unexpected acceptance forced changes in the plans. Massachusetts' famed Edward Everett was the orator of the day, but the President had perforce to be given a place on the program.

Whether or no the governors had expected the occasion to redound to the glory of the states, Abraham Lincoln rose at Gettysburg to talk of the nation. He failed to mention that four score and seven years before, the fathers had brought forth thirteen independent states. He talked of the nation, "conceived in liberty and dedicated to the proposition that all men are created equal," and of the high resolve "that this nation, under God, shall have a new birth of freedom."

No one noted, then or later, that at the moment the President was pledging that "government of the people, by the people, and for the people shall not perish from the earth," General Robert Schenck's soldiers, less than a hundred miles away, were patrolling the polls in Delaware. But Lincoln knew that they were there, and that they, too, were upholding the nation. This was his theme at Gettysburg, and he thanked Everett for making an argument for the national supremacy and for excoriating the idea "of the general government being only an agency, whose principals are the states." [17] Andrew Curtin had his cemetery, but on that 19th of November, at Gettysburg and in Delaware, Lincoln by word and deed interred states' rights.

A week after Gettysburg, Governor Curtin began a new campaign to give symbolic expression to his gratitude for the soldiers' votes. That day he met two orphans of soldiers, and as he contemplated their miserable condition, he re-

[17] J. G. Randall: *Lincoln the President*, II, 303–20, has the best summary of the voluminous writings on the Gettysburg address.

flected that there were thousands of hungry and homeless children in Pennsylvania. Shortly after, Curtin heard Henry Ward Beecher plead for orphans and declare that the states must provide for their care. The Governor remembered that he had fifty thousand dollars in a special fund presented by the Pennsylvania Railroad for equipping soldiers. The road's president agreed to divert the money, but the legislature balked. Finally the Governor and the railroad flooded Harrisburg with orphans gathered from all parts of the state, and the legislature authorized the establishment of a number of soldiers' orphans' homes in Pennsylvania. The episode succeeded where Gettysburg had failed, and Curtin was securely crowned with the laurel "Soldier's Friend." [18]

Although care for the sick and wounded, honor for the dead, orphanages, and soldiers' homes brought the governors a large measure of goodwill, more than these were needed to ensure the soldiers' continued loyalty and political support. The governors, however, were equal to the occasion, and they slipped easily into their roles as defenders of the soldiers, real and potential, against the continued demands of the national government. Again Governor Curtin took the lead. A week after Gettysburg the Governor, alleging that he had always supported the President and that his recent re-election proved it, told Lincoln that the plan for raising troops under the recent call for 300,000 had already proved a failure. Accordingly he proposed a return to the system of using state authorities — the method that, he said, had proved successful since the war began. He proposed the consolidation of old regiments, gubernatorial control of recruiting, and state bounties. Moreover, thought Curtin, the most effective recruiting agents were the experienced soldiers, and he proposed that veteran regiments be sent home to fill their depleted ranks.[19]

[18] A. K. McClure: *Abraham Lincoln and Men of War Times*, pp. 266 f.

[19] *Official Records*, series 3, III, 1092–3.

Even before the Pennsylvania proposal came, the War Department had come to realize that the governors were essential agents in the recruiting process. Most of the governors had dutifully issued proclamations after Lincoln's latest call, but few of them had displayed more than a formal enthusiasm. Most of them, like New Hampshire's Governor Gilmore, had devoted more time to pointing to the rich bounties — $302 for new recruits and $402 for re-enlistments, plus $100 from the state — than to excoriating the rebels or to elaborating on the purposes of the war. Blair of Michigan had not mentioned the call until Democratic papers smoked him out with the charge that he preferred to fill the ranks with draftees. And then, alleging that federal bounties were sufficiently munificent, Blair withdrew the state bounty.[20]

Faced with the lack of gubernatorial enthusiasm, Fry instructed his provost marshals that it was "intended the governors take the leading part in the work" of raising troops, and that the department's plans would be modified to suit the governors' ideas.[21] Stanton told Governor J. Y. Smith of Rhode Island that it was the department's "anxious desire" to conform to the views and wishes of the governors. Yet neither Smith's request for the same bounties for new and veteran recruits nor Curtin's proposals met the department's approval.[22]

Curtin's proposals were but the first trickle of a flood of gubernatorial suggestions and protests. Gilmore wanted to pay Negroes the same bounty as white men; Thomas Carey, Governor of Kansas, wanted a regiment sent home to recruit its thin ranks; Seymour, backed by ex-Governor Morgan, wanted the draft apportioned to towns, the same bounties for new and old recruits, and a consolidation of veteran regiments with the surplus officers sent home to gather new commands; Morton grieved that the "spirit of reenlistment"

[20] Ibid., III, 993–4; *Detroit Free Press*, November 10, 13, 25, 1863.
[21] *Official Records*, series 3, III, 1012.
[22] Stanton to Smith, November 21, 1863, Stanton MSS.; *Official Records*, series 3, III, 1101.

was dying out, and wanted Indiana's men sent home for the winter so they could fill their ranks; thirty-five of Andrew's supporters united in a petition to raise Massachusetts troops among Southern refugees and Negroes; Gilmore protested against red tape and demanded that provost marshals be removed from New Hampshire. The governors showed fertility of ideas, ingenuity in devices for delaying, postponing, or modifying the draft, and persistence in presenting their protests and proposals to the War Department. To most of their suggestions, however, Stanton gave a decided veto.[23]

"You are too arbitrary," cried Curtin as he met frustration at every turn.

"I am not arbitrary enough," snarled Stanton. "War is arbitrary and cannot be managed except by such arbitrary rules as will prevent interference by men like yourself." [24]

Despite the failure of their protests, the governors continued to raise troops with one hand and to protect their citizens with the other. Under the law, the bounty paid recruits stopped on January 5, 1864, and on that day drafting should begin for all states that had not filled their quotas with "bounty bought" volunteers. Lincoln asked Congress to re-enact the provisions paying bounties, and Stanton and Fry furnished data on recruiting and lent support to the measure. The governors joined in the demand. Morton told Stanton that recruiting was going on better in Indiana than at any former time, and asked if the good work must be suddenly stopped. Andrew agreed, and wired: "We want thirty days and a free chance." Governor J. G. Smith reported that Vermont had exceeded her quota by 270, and Morton contended that he had raised 13,000 new and 5,000 old enlistments to exceed a quota of 16,141. He proposed that all enlistments after January 5 be dated back to that day in order that the men might collect the bounty. Under such pressure Congress extended the time of paying

---

[23] *Official Records*, series 3, III, 1096, 1098, 1100–1, 1162–3, 1165, 1167–9, 1187–9, 1196.

[24] F. A. Flower: *Edwin McMasters Stanton*, pp. 361–2.

bounties to March 1, and recruiting continued without a draft.[25]

But on February 1, while the states were still raising troops to meet the President's October call, Lincoln called for 200,000 more. The governors responded as well as they could. Gilmore told New Hampshire that there would never be another draft in the Old Granite State because "her sons will rise in their might, and, like an avalanche from their icy hills, sweep the last traces of armed treason into the Gulf of Mexico" before the Fourth of July.[26] Morton gave his hearty public approbation, promised to raise the men, but privately inquired whether it was right that the Western states should bear all the burdens of the war.[27] Kirkwood wired Lincoln: "There will be no draft in Iowa. You shall have our quota without it. We are coming, Father Abraham, with 500,000 more." [28]

The governors were finding the threat of a draft a compelling incentive to raise men. An exception, however, was found in Ohio, where blunt John Brough did not face the problem of re-election in 1864. Moreover, the recent election had shown him that Lincoln had the power to carry the Buckeye State. Freed from the political anxieties that weighed upon his colleagues, Brough had time to think of the costs of the recruiting program. Under the threat of the draft, states, counties, and townships had been giving bounties, bidding higher and higher for the lives of men, until it was possible for a potential soldier to obtain a thousand dollars for joining the army. The local communities were bankrupting themselves to avoid the draft of their citizens. The system, as Brough saw it, was destroying the confidence of the people in the government, was compounding corruption and undermining patriotism. Brough's solution, how-

[25] *Official Records*, series 3, IV, 8–10, 15–18, 26 f., 30–1.

[26] New Hampshire Adjutant General's *Report, 1865*, I, xxviii; *New Hampshire Patriot*, February 10, 1864.

[27] W. H. H. Terrell: *Indiana in the War of the Rebellion*, pp. 51–3.

[28] *Official Records*, series 3, IV, 72.

ever, was political suicide: Let the states fill their quotas by
their own drafts, and let them agree to a common bounty
policy.[29] When Stanton reported to Congress that the governors asked for delays in drafting, Brough hastened to dis-
claim any such intention. The financial situation was bad,
and recruiting had ceased: Brough wanted the draft made
promptly.[30]

But more than he wanted a draft Brough wanted an end
to the war. The bounty-bought enlistments did not produce
soldiers; they only contributed bounty-jumpers. Moreover,
Brough was thoroughly familiar with the war-weariness of
the people. Morton, too, was eager for the war to cease. In
January he wrote Lincoln that the war must end within
the year, and urged the President to call more men than
enough.[31] In April, Brough was in Indianapolis on private
railroad business, and the two governors conferred, and
agreed that some means must be found to free soldiers for
fighting. Accordingly they wired for Yates, Lewis of Wisconsin, and Stone of Iowa to join them. The five governors
united forces and descended on Washington, where they offered to raise 85,000 militia for one hundred days' service.
These men could be put on guard duty, and thereby veteran
soldiers could join the armies at the front. Lincoln, Stanton,
Halleck, and Grant approved, and Stanton extracted a special appropriation from Congress. The governors hurried
home to raise the troops, hoping that the men who answered
their call would be exempt from the draft, and hoping the
war would end before the hundred days were finished.[32]

[29] W. Reid: *Ohio in the War*, I, 205–7.

[30] *Official Records*, series 3, IV, 180.

[31] Morton to Stanton, January 18, 1864, Stanton MSS.

[32] F. A. Shannon: *Organization and Administration of the Union
Armies*, II, 120; C. M. Walker: *Sketch of the Life . . . of Oliver P.
Morton*, pp. 113; *Wisconsin State Journal*, April 22, May 2, 1864;
E. O. Randall and D. J. Ryan: *History of Ohio*, IV, 254; Reid: *Ohio
in the War*, I, 209; *Official Records*, series 3, IV, 237–8, 244 ff.; Terrell:
Indiana, pp. 35–9, 411, 412–13.

In the meantime, as the governors sought to win approval as Soldiers' Friends with humanitarian acts, and as they sought to guard their citizens from the government's demands, the political groundwork for the elections of 1864 was being laid. Four years before, state politics had been the determining factors in the national election. By 1864 the states had come to revolve so completely in the national orbit that the maneuvering and jockeying, the partisan squabbles, and the conflicting personalities in the states had little significance. State political leaders no longer gave directions to the national party. Instead, they took their cues from the party leaders in Washington.

From the night of the October 1863 elections in Ohio and Pennsylvania, Abraham Lincoln kept his eyes glued on the coming contest. Two days after the elections he was back in the War Department's telegraph office discussing political prospects. Taking a telegraph blank, he wrote the names of the states in two columns. In one he listed New York, Pennsylvania, New Jersey, Delaware, Maryland, Missouri, Kentucky, and Illinois, followed each with its electoral vote, and totaled the whole to make 114. The other column, which he might reasonably expect the Republicans to carry, added up to 117.[33] The President saw clearly that the election would be close.

The first development in the campaign was a Presidential proclamation of amnesty and reconstruction for the Southern states. On December 8 Lincoln announced that any person in the South — with the exception of high-ranking civil and military officers of the Confederacy — might be granted amnesty if he took an oath of allegiance to the United States. Moreover, whenever ten per cent of the population of any state had taken the oath, they might hold elections and establish a state government, which the President would recognize.

The political implications of the proclamation were im-

[33] P. M. Angle: *New Letters and Papers of Lincoln*, pp. 361–2.

mediately evident to both radicals and Democrats. Horatio Seymour perceived in it a new assault on popular liberties. In his January message to the legislature he pointed out that the arbitrary military power of the government was growing steadily. Moreover, every measure to pervert the war into a war against private property and personal rights at the South had been paralleled by claims to exercise military power at the North. He enumerated them: there was the Emancipation Proclamation for the South, and the suspension of habeas corpus for the North; the Confiscation Act for the South, and arrests, imprisonment, and banishment for Northern citizens; the claim to destroy political organizations in the South, and the armed interference in Northern elections. These acts against Northern liberties had been justified as necessary, but the government had given up no powers when the emergency passed. In fact, "more prerogatives are asserted in the hour of triumph than were claimed as a necessity in days of disaster and danger." The doctrine of Southern degradation, explained the Governor, "is a doctrine of Northern bankruptcy . . . it is a measure for lasting military despotism over one-third of our country, which will be the basis for military despotism over the whole land."

As for Lincoln's reconstruction program, Seymour saw it as a political device. The minority of one tenth in the states would be kept in power by the North's arms and treasure. There would be no motive, prophesied the Governor, to draw the remaining population into the fold; instead, "there will be every inducement of power, of gain, and of ambition, to perpetuate the condition of affairs." Moreover, it would be to the interest of the national administration to continue this system of government. Nine controlled states in the South with 70,000 voting population would balance in the House of Representatives and in the electoral college one half the population of the United States. Fourteen hundred men in Florida would balance New York in the Senate. Thus the nine states mentioned in Lincoln's proclamation, together with Pierpont's Virginia and West Virginia would constitute a system of rotten boroughs that would govern the nation.[34]

No less than Seymour, the radicals perceived the political potentialities of the President's proclamation. They saw, first of all, that amnesty would imply the restoration of confiscated property in the South, while a prompt reconstruction would prevent further predatory raids on Southern property. Then, too, they saw that the President's rotten-borough system would enhance the executive's power. In Congress the radicals immediately proclaimed that reconstruction was a congressional function, and they began to discuss a bill brought in by Henry Winter Davis and Ben Wade that would give Congress power over the conquered South.

Out of Congress the radicals generally began to look for a suitable Presidential candidate to replace Lincoln. Their eyes lighted, without difficulty, on the ambitious figure of Salmon Portland Chase. The Secretary of the Treasury was not a humble man, and he realized his own transcendent qualifications for the Presidency. His own view of his merits was shared by banker Jay Cooke, while Horace Greeley hopefully toyed with the idea of endorsing Chase. Radical governors, too, thought of supporting Chase: Governor Boreman thought the Secretary of the Treasury could surely carry West Virginia, Andrew was weary of Lincoln, Yates preferred a change in the White House, and Morton made speeches praising Chase and carefully sent them to him. In November 1863 Kate Chase's wedding to William Sprague added enormous private wealth to the Chase entourage, and Kate set up a social center — almost a salon — for the Chase

[34] Lincoln (ed.), *Messages from the Governors of New York*, V, 556–8; S. Mitchell: *Horatio Seymour of New York*, pp. 354–5. The *Detroit Free Press*, January 7, 1864, listed the number of voters necessary to control the Southern states under Lincoln's plan: Alabama, 9,036; Arkansas, 5,406; Florida, 1,436; Georgia, 10,637; Louisiana, 5,050; Mississippi, 6,912; Tennessee, 14,534; North Carolina, 9,628; Texas, 6,299.

movement in the $35,000 Washington house her fatuous
mate had purchased. Soon she had charmed Senator Trumbull into the Chase camp, and the Illinois solon wrote home
that the Lincoln movement was only a surface veneer. "You
would be surprised in talking with the public men we meet
here, to find how few when you come to get at their real
sentiments are for Mr. Lincoln's reelection." [35]

But perhaps none of the radicals really believed in Chase.
In December the American Antislavery Society heard
speeches alternately praising Lincoln for the Emancipation
Proclamation and damning him for supporting slavery in
the border states, but only a few of the prophets anointed
Chase for the succession.[36] Small-bore politicians in New
York organized a committee for the Secretary of the Treasury, but prominent leaders shied away from the movement.[37]
Newspaper correspondents found "ten times more work being done" for Chase than for Lincoln, but their editors were
unmoved by their reports.[38] Moreover, the Chase movement
met heavy attack. Montgomery Blair denounced Chase before the Maryland legislature,[39] and his brother, Frank, prepared to launch a violent attack on the Secretary on the floor
of the House of Representatives.[40] Finally the Chase boom
became a fiasco when a circular by Kansas' Senator Pomeroy, denouncing Lincoln and praising Chase, got into the
newspapers. Few editors found it convincing, and Chase,
embarrassed by the unfavorable response, offered to resign
from the cabinet. Lincoln, however, had no intention of
dignifying the Chase movement and kept his Secretary of

[35] T. Dennett: *Letters and Diaries of John Hay*, pp. 119, 129; D. V.
Smith: *Chase and Civil War Politics*, pp. 85–7, 106; *Milwaukee Senti-
nel*, January 7, 8, 1864; H. White: *Life of Lyman Trumbull*, p. 218;
T. H. Williams: *Lincoln and the Radicals*, p. 310.

[36] American Antislavery Society *Proceedings, 1863*.

[37] D. V. Smith: *Chase and Civil War Politics*, pp. 124–6.

[38] *Milwaukee Sentinel*, January 4, 1864.

[39] W. E. Smith: *The Francis P. Blair Family in Politics*, II, 253.

[40] St. Louis *Missouri Democrat*, January 29, February 5, 8, 1864.

the Treasury until the Republican convention was safely passed.[41]

Lincoln, however, had lost no time in building a fire in the rear of the Chase movement. He knew that the governors, restive under the pressure of the War Department, might welcome some new Republican candidate. But he knew, too, that he could count on the support of the army and of thousands of local politicians. The patronage, also, was in the President's hands and was an effective tool in coercing congressmen.

It was the patronage that caused Senator Lane of Kansas to jump on the Lincoln bandwagon. Governor Carney, who spent more time in his store in Leavenworth than in the capitol in Topeka, and whose major interest as governor had been in government contracts, wanted Lane's seat in the Senate.[42] But Lane enlisted Lincoln's aid in the contest, and got General Samuel Ryan Curtis appointed to command troops in the area. Curtis's arrival was made the signal for launching a Lincoln boom, and resolutions favoring Lincoln's renomination passed the legislature. After the fiasco of the Pomeroy Circular, Lane hurried back to Kansas, put himself at the head of the Lincoln movement, and got himself chosen to lead the delegates to the Baltimore Union Convention. In addition he got a solid Lincoln delegation sent to the Union League convention which would meet the day before the party convened.[43]

In other states Lincoln's agents went to work on the legislatures to get endorsements. Nomination by the legislatures was older in American custom than party conventions, and, however much it might smack of states' rights, it had the ap-

[41] Williams: *Lincoln and the Radicals*, p. 311; D. V. Smith: *Chase and Civil War Politics*, p. 118.

[42] *Official Records*, series 3, III, 1156–8.

[43] J. G. Nicolay and J. Hay: *Abraham Lincoln: A History*, IX, 54, 61; *Milwaukee Sentinel*, January 9, 1864; *Missouri Democrat*, January 18, 22, 25, 28, 1864.

pearance of springing from groups close to the people. In January the legislatures passed resolutions endorsing Lincoln. California's legislature contained thirteen Democrats, but only seven of them opposed the Lincoln resolutions. Wisconsin's legislature recognized the "liberal and enlarged views" of the President and promised him unanimous support from the state's union voters.[44] In Pennsylvania Cameron and Curtin, united for once, forced an endorsement of Lincoln through the legislature.[45] In New York the Union Central Committee, radical but shrewd, unanimously recommended renomination. In Nashville it was the Union League that nominated Lincoln for president and Andrew Johnson for vice president. In New Hampshire the Republican Party convention nominated Gilmore for another term, expressed confidence in Chase, but declared Lincoln the people's choice for president.[46] The Union Lincoln Association, headed by such New York merchants as Simeon Draper, Moses Taylor, and Moses Grinnell, called for mass meetings and legislative resolutions on Washington's Birthday.[47] In Indiana, Lincolnites in the Republican convention coupled endorsement of Lincoln with Morton's renomination for governor, and the radicals had, perforce, to take one with the other.[48] In Ohio the Lincoln moderates held a caucus without notifying the Chase men, adopted resolutions, and gave them to the press.[49]

Radicals throughout the country fumed in frustration as they witnessed the legislative upsurge for Lincoln. Their newspapers attempted to discount the movement, declaring that it was not good policy to commit the party before the

[44] *Milwaukee Sentinel,* January 28, 1864.

[45] Nicolay and Hay: *Lincoln,* IX, 53; McClure: *Lincoln and Men of War Times,* p. 166.

[46] Nicolay and Hay: *Lincoln,* IX, 55; *Milwaukee Sentinel,* January 6, 9, 12, 1864; *New Hampshire Patriot,* January 13, 1864.

[47] January 28, 1864, Yates MSS.; *Missouri Democrat,* February 12, 1864.

[48] Walker: *Morton,* p. 120.

[49] D. V. Smith: *Chase and Civil War Politics,* pp. 120, 122.

convention. The whole thing, thought the St. Louis radical *Missouri Democrat,* was in bad taste and worse judgment. The paper declared that Montgomery Blair's henchmen from the Post Office Department had appeared in Jefferson City and Topeka and made deals right and left to get the resolutions through the legislatures.[50]

Yet, despite the obvious nature of the movement, there was little the radicals could do. Senator Henry Wilson harped against Lincoln in private, but admitted the President was the popular choice.[51] Yates got confused reports from the Union Leagues of Illinois: one reported that the unconditional Union men were all for Lincoln; another concluded that Trumbull, having talked too much against Lincoln was *"ausgespielt"* and would even lose out in his own race for senator; but a third deplored that a number of "vere influansive News papers" had Lincoln as the "Republicken union Candidate" and proposed that Yates poll the league's membership for a nominee.[52]

Confirmation of the legislative resolutions came in New England's spring elections. New Hampshire's Republicans followed the lead of the state's "Loyal Leagues," adopted a platform endorsing the suspension of habeas corpus and Lincoln's ten per cent plan, and renominated Governor Gilmore and Abraham Lincoln. On March 8 the ticket won a complete victory — the result, said the Democrats, of palpable, shameless fraud, the denial of voting rights to hundreds of citizens, and the arrival of 4,000 soldiers home on furlough.[53] Governor Gilmore wired his gratitude to Stanton: "The soldiers of New Hampshire have aided civilians and citizens to achieve a great constitutional victory. . . . Our

---

[50] *Missouri Democrat,* February 3, 8, 12, 17, 1864.

[51] A. G. Riddle: *Recollections of War Times,* p. 267.

[52] Letters of W. D. Calloway, February 24; George N. Rutherford, February 26; and D. C. Scheer, February 29, 1864, to Yates, Yates MSS.

[53] J. O. Lyford: *Edward H. Rollins,* pp. 163–70; *New Hampshire Patriot,* December 2, 1863, January 13, March 9, 16, 1864. Gilmore to Lincoln, February 12, 1864, R. T. Lincoln MSS.

boys in blue will give no quarter to treason." [54] A month later, similar overwhelming victories in Vermont and Connecticut added further confirmation of Lincoln's popularity and retained the austere Buckingham and Vermont's railroad magnate, John Gregory Smith, in the governorships. In jubilant gratitude for Lincoln's aid in their states, Smith sent the President a can of Vermont maple honey, and Gilmore sent a jug of maple syrup — hoping it would "mitigate the bitterness and smooth the roughness of your official life." [55]

Before such evidences of political strength the radicals faltered. With Chase gone, they had turned their thoughts to Ben Wade, Ben Butler, and Frémont. But the leading radicals were wary of each of these movements, and no governor lent open support to the anti-Lincoln forces. Curtin, who was disgusted with his scurrilous treatment in the War Department, joined with some of the more sanguine radicals in proposing that the nominating convention be postponed. The administration forces trembled at the thought, but consoled themselves with the belief that the people would elect Lincoln as an independent if the party's convention rejected him.[56] Late in May, the radicals held a convention in Cleveland and nominated Frémont, and the Lincoln men breathed easier when they saw that no important political bosses endorsed the Pathfinder. Frémont himself accepted the nomination without much enthusiasm, and half promised to withdraw if the Republicans chose a man of right principles.[57]

Early in June the Republicans — calling themselves the Union Party — met in Baltimore. The delegations, some of them headed by state governors, represented the Union Leagues and the officeholders who had no disposition to disturb the current division of the spoils. The radicals who

[54] *Official Records*, series 3, IV, 160.

[55] Croffut and Morris: *Connecticut*, p. 630; Welles: *Diary of Gideon Welles*, II, 5; *Official Records*, series 3, IV, 217; Smith to Lincoln, March 19, and Gilmore to Lincoln, March 31, 1864, R. T. Lincoln MSS.

[56] Montgomery Blair to Cameron, April 12, 1864, Cameron MSS.

[57] Williams: *Lincoln and the Radicals*, p. 314.

attended were hopeless, and they voted listlessly with the majority. They did not even rally to the defense of Hannibal Hamlin, the abolitionist Vice President whom Lincoln had determined to discard in favor of Andrew Johnson of Tennessee. The new vice-presidential candidate had cooperated steadily with the radicals and was a more vigorous person than Hamlin. Moreover, the radicals were content with the platform's endorsement of their stand. Andrew and Blair, Yates and Iowa's Stone, Morton and Buckingham — radicals all — accepted the inevitable without comment.[58]

Within a month Lincoln added another blow to the radical cause. Secretary Chase became embroiled in a dispute over the patronage in New York, and when Lincoln took sides against him, the Secretary indignantly offered his resignation. To his surprise, the President accepted it and immediately nominated ex-Governor Tod to the post. Tod declined, and Senator William P. Fessenden took Chase's place in the cabinet. The radicals fumed in anger, but Chase had no popular support, and no one rallied in his defense.[59]

Nor did the radicals gain strength with the Wade-Davis bill that they forced through Congress in the closing hours of the session. The bill, challenging Lincoln's authority over reconstruction, received a pocket veto — to which the President added a patronizing statement that he thought the measure had its good features but he did not wish to be committed to any single plan of reconstruction. Wade and Davis met in New York to draft an irate "Manifesto" asserting anew the supremacy of Congress over the conquered South. The radicals hoped the document would strike fire, but their hopes faded as they found their assault on the President met no popular applause.

[58] C. E. Hamlin: *Hannibal Hamlin*, pp. 461–5; Andrew to Gurowski, April 24, 1864, Andrew MSS. Letter Books; Blaine: *Twenty Years of Congress*, I, 517; Cole: *Era of the Civil War*, p. 314; Hamlin to Cameron, June 18, 1864, Cameron MSS.

[59] L. E. Crittenden: *Recollections of President Lincoln*, pp. 369–77; Reid: *Ohio in the War*, I, 231–2; Dennett: *Hay*, p. 198; Welles: *Diary*, II, 62–3; D. V. Smith: *Chase and Civil War Politics*, p. 150.

Defeated in every effort to launch a campaign, the radicals prepared to rehabilitate themselves with the administration. Late in August the Democratic convention nominated General McClellan, and for a moment there was danger that the Republicans, radical and moderate alike, would be swept from office. The danger passed quickly, for General Sherman captured Atlanta and the Union's prospects brightened while the Frémont cause, never able to strike popular roots, lagged. Senator Zach Chandler, finding that Lincoln was willing to bargain, undertook to trade Frémont's withdrawal in return for Montgomery Blair's resignation from the cabinet. The devoted Blair was willing to be sacrificed, and with his withdrawal the Republicans closed ranks and the radicals supported Lincoln with energy and the semblance of enthusiasm.[60]

For the moment Lincoln was master of his party. As commander-in-chief of the army he could control the soldiers, and the radicals could not resist. In November the soldiers, supplementing the work of the patronage-holders and the Union Leagues, would reward the greatest of the Soldier's Friends.

[60] Williams: *Lincoln and the Radicals*, pp. 317–31.

Chapter 17

Lincoln Elects the Governors

IN the meantime, as Lincoln was capitalizing upon his popular support, rallying the Union Leagues to his cause, and demonstrating again that the army could be influential in elections, the campaign of 1864 in the states got under way. The state campaigns of 1864 showed fundamental differences from those of 1860. In the former year the Republican Party had been a series of state parties, the governors had been independent political figures, and they had nominated and elected Abraham Lincoln. But in 1864 the President was master of his party, and the governors depended upon him for their elections. In that year, in the East, Maine, Massachusetts, and New York were to choose governors, and in the West, Indiana, Illinois, Missouri, and Michigan. In other states local and congressional elections added to the confusion. In all the states able and experienced politicians directed the campaign, but each of them depended for direction and for ultimate aid upon the master politician in the White House.

Kentucky was the first state to hold elections after the Republican convention, and the Blue Grass State became the testing ground for the administration's power to win elections. In 1863 Thomas Bramlette, long devoted to the Union, had been elected Governor by federal bayonets. He began his administration with zeal for Lincoln and for the war, but hardly had he assumed office when he began to feel the restraining hand of the national government. In

January the new Governor protested when the removal of federal troops left the state defenseless before the Confederacy. By March he was having troubles trying to avoid a draft. He protested when Kentucky's quotas under the repeated calls did not take into consideration the numbers of men who had gone into the Confederate armies. He objected to the drafting of Negroes, and to recruiting agents of Northern states who came to fill their quotas with Kentucky's blacks. He protested so much that Morton's suspicions were aroused and the Indiana Governor asked Stanton about Bramlette's fidelity. "I believe the governor is a firm union man," cynically replied the Secretary of War, "especially as present appearances are not very encouraging to disloyalty." [1]

As the August elections approached, Bramlette came to see the full insignificance of his position. A month before the election the army took over the state. On July 5 Lincoln suspended habeas corpus and proclaimed martial law. Three days before the election the military arrested the Union Democratic candidate for chief justice and began seizing prominent Democrats. "Good Union men," reported one Kentucky preacher, "rejoice heartily at this and are brightening with the hope that the Government is at length fully alive to the great importance of crushing the rebellion in the rear." But the Democrats, who had seen military elections before, were not caught napping this time. When their candidate was arrested, they hastily wired the name of another to the polls and voted him in before the military had a chance to arrest him. But Bramlette had seen enough. He complained of the military arrests, of the banishments, the tyrannies, and the outrages of the army. "We are dealt with as though Kentucky was a rebellious and conquered province," he declared, and he recanted his early allegiance to Kentucky's son in the White House. After the elections the Union Democrats, who had been represented at Baltimore,

---

[1] E. M. Coulter: *Civil War and Readjustment in Kentucky*, pp. 179, 190–2, 200; *Official Records*, series 3, IV, 206, 416, 417; Lincoln to Bramlette, January 6, 1864, Lincoln MSS., Huntington Library.

sent a delegation to Chicago with instructions to support McClellan and Bramlette for president and vice president.[2]

The Illinois campaign bore fundamental resemblances to Kentucky's. Before it was over, Illinois was an armed camp in which skittish Republicans shied away from every dark bush. In May the Republican convention chose Richard J. Oglesby to succeed Yates as Governor and pledged the party to send Yates to the United States Senate. Oglesby, forty years of age, had been born in Kentucky and had been taken to Illinois as a child. He had had little schooling, but he had studied law and had practiced his profession until the Mexican War. After the war he first dug for gold in California, then returned to Illinois to enter Whig politics. He was early in the Republican Party, running for Congress in the 1858 elections, which had featured the Lincoln-Douglas debates. When the Civil War began, he left the state Senate to become colonel of the Eighth Illinois Regiment. He campaigned with Grant at Forts Henry and Donelson, was wounded at Corinth, and by the time of his nomination was a major general. His manner was bluff, his diction was crude, his wit and humor were tailored for the stump. He was as thorough a radical as Dick Yates.[3]

Although the party made much use of Oglesby's rough-hewn oratory during the canvass, the major interest of the Republicans centered on the fear that the Democrats would capture the state by violence. Governor Yates's mail was filled with alarmed reports of disaffection. Bounty-jumpers and deserters in Egypt were often lawless and generally loud, while Democrats were inclined to argue vehemently against the war and the administration. Such acts seemed treason to partisan Republicans, and their hysterical appeals for the Governor's aid reflected their panic. There were marauders,

[2] Coulter: *Civil War in Kentucky*, pp. 182, 186; George Schumarel to D. B. Henderson, August 4, 1864, Yates MSS.

[3] Charles A. Church: *History of the Republican Party in Illinois*, p. 92; William Pickering to Yates, June 18, and I. G. Wilson to Yates, August 27, 1864, Yates MSS.

thieves, gangs of cutthroats in numerous places, there were Copperheads organizing to resist the draft, there were Sons of Liberty threatening to win the elections. Sometimes Yates's informers gave the names of Copperheads whom they suspected of talking for the Confederacy. Mostly they complained of midnight drilling, secret arming, or vague threats made against Union men.[4] Sometimes it was women who carried their neighborly discussions to the Governor. Mrs. Fanny Hutchinson wrote Yates that "We have had Trouble and is having Trouble here with those Low Mean Copperheads that is worse then the meanest thing a person can think of   Treating people as they pleas and Threatening what they will Do with Women Murdering Them if They can get a Chance   There is some Two women down on Beck Crick that is and has turned Union women to be Copperheads and there Husbands in the service. Oh they are to lowlife to let walk on gods Green Earth. . . . They are Devils if I am Aloud to youse such an Expression."[5]

Governor Yates believed them all. He gathered the complaints and reported them to the War Department with demands for troops to quell the expected riots.[6] When Union Leagues asked for arms, the Governor made every effort to supply them or to have them supplied by the provost marshal, General E. A. Paine.[7] General Paine himself was thoroughly alarmed. His detectives told him of plots to carry the elections by foul means. "This is no cry of wolf," he told Yates, "but indisputable fact. . . . Now is the time to try our Union Leagues." The provost marshal demanded that Illinois be put under martial law.[8]

In July the Governor joined with General Rosecrans in appealing to Lincoln to suppress a new-found secret society.

[4] Letters of G. Williford, Eli Wiley, W. Homes, Reuben Carr, George Abbot, and others, January to August 1864, Yates MSS.

[5] Frances Mary Hutchinson to Yates, August 26, 1864, Yates MSS.

[6] *Official Records*, series 3, IV, 148–9.

[7] Eighteen letters, August 10–30, 1864, in Yates MSS.

[8] E. A. Paine to Yates, August 3, 1864, Yates MSS.

In St. Louis, Rosecrans had uncovered a secret conspiracy of the Order of American Knights, headed in the South by General Sterling Price and in the North by Vallandigham, which proposed to oppose the war in every way. Rosecrans's detectives reported 13,000 members of the O.A.K. in Missouri and 140,000 in Illinois. Under pressure, Lincoln sent his private secretary, John Hay, to hear Rosecrans's frantic story. But the President was unconvinced. He thought a secret shared by Rosecrans, Yates, Morton, Brough, and Bramlette, and by their staffs, and by sundry citizens was not much of a secret. It was as puerile, in the Presidential view, as the much-touted Knights of the Golden Circle.[9]

But Yates was not quieted by the President's calm. He insisted on holding troops, even the hundred-days men, in the state in defiance of the War Department. Stanton complained that Yates's course increased the troubles in Illinois, but the Governor was terrified.[10] "A large portion of my time is consumed by appeals to put down disloyal desperados," he told the Secretary of War. The people, he added, were losing confidence in the government, and nothing would restore it except a district commander. When Stanton suggested drafting men in delinquent districts, Yates replied that such a step would be revolutionary. The state had supplied more than its quota and universal dissatisfaction would result.[11] In September the Republican state central committee and the grand council of the state's Union League united in protesting against the draft. A draft would bring "sure and overwhelming defeat" upon the party. Yates added that he would not be responsible for the consequences; a draft would "hopelessly defeat us" in the coming election.[12]

So sure was Yates of Democratic plots that he saw no hope of carrying the state without the votes of the soldiers. Illinois

[9] Dennett: *Hay*, pp. 192 f.

[10] *Official Records*, series 3, IV, 426, 427.

[11] Ibid., IV, 558; Yates to Stanton, August 29, 1864, Yates MSS.

[12] Yates to Fry, April 30, 1864, Yates MSS.; *Official Records*, series 3, IV, 633, 700–2, 726–7.

law did not permit soldiers in the field to vote, and the Governor was afraid to call back the legislature, which he had prorogued. One adviser suggested that Yates extend the suffrage to the soldiers by proclamation, but the Governor did not dare the experiment. He could only beg the War Department to keep soldiers in the state until election time and to send others back to vote.[13]

In Indiana the campaign centered in the exposure of the work of the treasonable secret societies. For more than a year Morton had ruled Indiana as a despot, maintaining himself in power through his alliance with Provost Marshal Carrington, and financing his regime by gifts from the War Department and by forced contributions from the counties. The situation encouraged secret plots, and one of Carrington's spies, named Stidger, worked his way into the confidence of a little group who were actually trying to organize local chapters of the Sons of Liberty. In August, Morton and Carrington pounced upon the leaders and promptly remanded them for trial before a military commission. One leader proved his guilt by escaping from prison, and several others, found guilty on the strength of Stidger's imaginative testimony, were sentenced to death.

The treason trials furnished an excellent source of campaign material and threw a patriotic smoke screen over Morton's arbitrary and extra-legal administration. Morton was even on dubious legal ground in being a candidate. Indiana's forgotten constitution forbade two consecutive terms for a governor, but Morton contended that he had merely been filling out Lane's term and was therefore not violating the constitution. Fortunately, his Democratic opponent, Joseph E. McDonald, was a moderate Democrat and a personal friend and had no disposition to challenge Morton's unconstitutional acts. The two candidates traveled together

[13] Yates to Stanton, August 29, and M. C. Lane, March 6; Rock Island citizens, May 17, L. Nowland, July 28; Vandalia citizens, August 16; J. J. Richards, August 21; W. C. Flagg, August 22; G. I. King, September 9, 1864, to Yates, Yates MSS.

to a series of friendly joint debates. McDonald and the Democrats had no connections with the insignificant adventurers whom Carrington and Stidger had unearthed. As the election drew near, Morton and the Democratic leaders united in requesting Lincoln to send Indiana troops home to vote.[14]

In contrast to the martial spirit that prevailed in Kentucky, Illinois, and Indiana, the state campaign in Michigan was conducted in an aura of quiet and contentment. The Wolverine State was safely Republican and, since Chandler's re-election to the Senate, safely radical. Austin Blair led the Michigan delegation to Baltimore, dutifully voted for Lincoln, and returned home full of hopes for his own election to the Senate.

The successful aspirant for Blair's place was Henry Howland Crapo, a native of Massachusetts who had been a resident of Flint for less than seven years. At the age of fifty Crapo, who had held local offices in New Bedford for fifteen years, migrated to Michigan to look after his lumber business, run a store, operate farms, and acquire an interest in railroads. As a businessman, he was keen and alert. He acquired interests in salt mines and kept a watchful eye on the possibilities in petroleum. He had a New England businessman's horror of secession, but he found ways to turn the war, even in far-away Michigan, to profitable account.

When Crapo migrated to Michigan, he reversed the usual process of the westward movement by leaving his son behind in Massachusetts. To the son, who remained in charge of the family insurance office in New Bedford, the older Crapo sent a steady stream of letters recounting his economic successes on the frontier. In the fall of 1862 he proudly began to recount his political triumphs for his son's admiration. He

---

[14] *Official Records*, series 3, III, 19–20; IV, 228–9, 711–12, 716–17, 1286–7; Walker: *Morton*, pp. 106–8, 120 ff.; W. D. Foulke: *Life of Oliver P. Morton*, I, 365–77, 399–400, 419–21; Rall: *Indiana*, II, 230–3; G. F. Milton: *Abraham Lincoln and the Fifth Column;* Morton to Democratic nominees, July 25, 1864, Stanton MSS.

was nominated for the state Senate, he modestly wrote, because "I happen to be regarded in this part of the State as a
thorough business man, and in every sense reliable, and not
a politician; and am also popular among the farmers who
regard me as a 'working man.' . . . And I find that this popularity — unsought for and unsolicited as it has been — has
aided me very much indeed in my business. My sales and
my custom is steadily increasing." Moreover, he explained
that he could take time to go to the legislature; it only lasted
forty days, "and as I have some legislation of my own to
effect, and as I can make it tell in various ways to the interest of my business . . . I am inclined to think after all that
it 'will pay.' " [15]

Successful in the election, Crapo reported his oratorical
feats to his son. He was able to talk for two hours! [16] In the
legislature the elder Crapo was on the Committee on Banks
and Incorporations and on the Finance Committee. "Thus
you see I was placed in a position of no little power." Moreover, he worked hard, studied each piece of legislation, and
"this course, I could see very plainly, began to tell as the
session advanced, until I became, by a sort of common consent, a leading member, and my opinions and views began
to be sought on all important matters." Before the session
ended, leading Republicans requested him to run for governor, and since he did not want to hurt his friends, he consented.[17]

But other candidates offered themselves, and Crapo reported that "I regard the chances so small that it does not
occupy but a passing thought with me." With a little further
study, he concluded that he was not least among the six
candidates, but he was only afraid he might, after all, be
honored with the high office. Yet he continued to report on
his growing prospects and denied that he had "settled in my

[15] H. H. Crapo to William W. Crapo, October 19, 1862, H. H.
Crapo MSS.
[16] Crapo to Crapo, November 10, 1862, May 3, 1863, Crapo MSS.
[17] Ibid., February 28, 1864.

own mind" whether he wanted the nomination. But after the convention he regaled his son with a mock-modest account of how "victory has perched on the banner of my friends." He had carried a book with the names of the delegates to the convention, and he assigned names to each of his workers. "When we came to the convention the army of the Potomac was not better organized than my forces." He figured each vote correctly, but, he explained, "I did this merely to aid the efforts of my friends, without a *hope* or even a *wish* to succeed, and even now I regret the result." [18]

The Democrats of Michigan agreed with Crapo. The people, thought the Democrats, would be sorely puzzled by the candidate's peculiar qualifications. Mr. Crapo was tall, spare, hatchet-faced, and stooped; he wore green glasses, and was particularly sharp in money matters — but these hardly qualified him, according to the Democrats, to be governor of Michigan. The Democrats nominated William M. Fenton, a former Lieutenant Governor and a colonel of infantry — a man so well known that the "people do not have to go to a small insurance office in Bedford . . . to find out who he is." [19] But Crapo, watching carefully, was confident. "I can beat him," he told his son. "I've got a speech and a pack of notes and am going to make a canvass." [20]

The Republican candidate's confidence increased as he swung into action. Within a month he reported: "I do not hesitate to appear before any audience now. I have brought my voice under control and have become so familiar with the whole scope of the subject that I do not use notes." On the eve of the election he reported that he had stumped the state and made extemporaneous speeches lasting two to two and a half hours. "I am determined to make myself a reputation throughout the state which should command the respect . . . of the intelligent and influential men of the party." With so valiant a campaigner, Michigan Republi-

[18] Ibid., March 13, June 26, July 9, 1864.
[19] *Detroit Free Press,* July 8, 23, September 3, 1864.
[20] H. H. Crapo to W. W. Crapo, September 8, 1864, Crapo MSS.

cans scarcely needed Abraham Lincoln's aid to carry the state.[21]

In the other Midwestern states, where there were no gubernatorial contests, the campaign was almost as calm as it was in Michigan. Governor Brough did not face the problems that had harassed his predecessors, and he successfully raised his hundred-days men, upheld the draft, collected damages from Congress for losses caused by Morgan's raid, and set detectives to watch the activities of the Copperheads. For the most part, however, he was the Soldier's Friend, urging taxation for the welfare of the soldiers' families, sending agents to the troops, and getting into a quarrel with the Sanitary Commission. In this last he was still the guardian of the soldiers, protecting them from an agreement the Sanitary Commission had made to ship sick soldiers home over the Baltimore & Ohio Railroad. Brough thought that soldiers should be sent to their homes over the most convenient lines — including his own. Such activities kept the soldiers loyal supporters of the state and national administrations.[22]

Iowa's Governor Stone inherited a smooth-running state from Governor Kirkwood, and the new Governor took up his tasks without difficulty. He protested vigorously against drafting men in delinquent districts when the state's quota was filled, and he fell into the common panic as he learned, from Rosecrans's detectives, that there were 33,000 Sons of Liberty in Iowa. But Iowa was well organized, and the Democrats, after their defeat in 1863, were in no mood to force a repetition of the previous summer's Tally war. The campaign proceeded without enthusiasm.[23]

In Wisconsin, Governor Lewis divided his time between

[21] Ibid., September 30, October 9, 22, 1864.

[22] Reid: *Ohio in the War*, I, 183–6, 190–3, 202–3; Stanton to Brough, February 27, 1864, Stanton MSS.; *Official Records*, series 3, IV, 142–3, 405, 425, 494–5, 569–70, 598.

[23] S. H. M. Byers: *Iowa in War Times*, pp. 331–5; *Official Records*, series 3, IV, 89, 636–8.

trying to postpone the draft and visiting the state's soldiers. He was more emphatic than his neighbors in pledging full allegiance to the general government, but was as diligent as they in disputing about quotas and appealing, with ingenious arguments, to avoid a draft. In addition he made extensive trips to the hospitals, traveling to Washington, Fortress Monroe, Norfolk, and New Orleans. He succeeded in getting all Wisconsin's sick and wounded transferred to hospitals in the state. Returning from the trip, he threw himself with greater zeal than the occasion demanded into the campaign. Together with ex-governors Randall and Salomon, Lewis toured the state making speeches for Lincoln and Johnson.[24]

Minnesota was even less excited than Wisconsin over the campaign. Governor Stephen Miller performed the routine functions of his office without conflict, and made routine efforts to get Minnesota's wounded sent home from the field. He did not, however, display Lewis's solicitude for the sick, and he never became alarmed over the draft or over the stealthy movements of night-plotting Knights. He was more like Crapo in his desire to make his office "pay," though less scrupulous in his methods. Once he wrote to Simon Cameron about the possibilities of making money in Minnesota. An act of the legislature, he explained, had authorized the Governor to make a geological survey of the state. "There will doubtless be a number of valuable discoveries made, and I will have the first *advices* on the subject, and with capital I have not a doubt that a large amount can be made for myself and a few friends."

"One gentleman in Harrisburg," continued the Governor, "has authorized me to invest $10,000 for him, and gives me half the profits after refunding his principal and interest; and I am to attend to all the business and secure the titles in his name.

[24] E. B. Quiner: *Military History of Wisconsin*, pp. 193–4, 197–8; *Wisconsin State Journal*, January 4, 6, 14, April 30, October 7, 13, 21, 1864; *Milwaukee Sentinel*, January 6, 9, 13, 1864; *Official Records*, series 3, IV, 137, 682–4.

"Should the examination prove a success, I would be grateful for a similar arrangement with yourself or yourself and friends for $10,000 or $20,000; and you may rest assured that unless the prospects be very flattering I shall not invest a dollar. On the Lake and near it there will be Iron, Copper, and possibly Lead and silver. And in another portion of the State, near to a pacific Railroad route and known only to myself and one or two others there is a most flattering prospect of Coal." [25]

With such diversions to occupy his time, it was not surprising that Governor Miller gave little heed to the Presidential election.

Lying on the periphery of the Middle West was the slaveholding state of Missouri. Actually, Missouri occupied a place somewhere between the border states of Kentucky, Maryland, and Delaware and the neighboring loyal states of Iowa and Illinois. Like the border states, it had a considerable group of Confederate sympathizers, but, on the other hand, it had, like its loyal neighbors, strong elements of Democrats, and both moderate and radical Republicans. The state was rent with conflict between the Republican factions, and each sought to lay its cause before Abraham Lincoln. The President heard each in turn, worried much about the problems they laid before him, and scolded each for its partisan hatred of the other.

The Emancipation Proclamation split Missouri's Republicans into conservatives and radicals, gradual and immediate emancipationists. Earlier they had quarreled over the punishment for Confederate sympathizers, and General Curtis, commanding the department, and provisional Governor Gamble had emerged as heads of the respective factions. Lincoln struggled steadily to bring the factions together. In May 1863 he replaced Curtis with Schofield and instructed the

[25] Folwell: *Minnesota*, II, 335–6; James H. Baker: *Lives of the Governors of Minnesota*, pp. 136 f.; Miller to Cameron, August 8, 1864, Cameron MSS.

new commander to keep apart from the conflict. "If both factions, or neither, shall abuse you, you will probably be about right," said the President. The next month Gamble assembled the state convention to consider emancipation, and himself headed the convention's committee on slavery. The convention agreed to adopt gradual emancipation, and set July 4, 1870 as the date for slavery's end in Missouri.

Radicals in Missouri opposed the compromise solution, and Gamble resented Lincoln's dealing with him as merely the head of a faction. Both groups appealed to Lincoln for Presidential support. Gamble wrote an indignant letter to the President, and the radicals, assembling a party convention in September, endorsed Frémont and the Emancipation Proclamation, demanded Gamble's resignation and Schofield's removal, and sent, in pentacostal zeal, seventy men on a mission to Washington. The commission demanded that "Beast" Butler, distinguished for his radical malevolence in New Orleans, be sent to Missouri.[26]

Lincoln gave them a soft answer and they turned away in wrath. They returned to Missouri to wage a campaign against the moderates, hoping that November's elections would give them enough strength to impeach Gamble. But the conservatives won the elections by a narrow majority of seven hundred. When the legislators met in January 1864, Gamble was anxious to have them accept compensated emancipation. The Governor was watching a bill in Congress that would have given $300 compensation for each slave in the State. Gamble and some of the leading conservatives had

[26] Nicolay and Hay: *Lincoln*, VI, 375–6, 381–2, 385–9, 394, 397–8; *Writings of Lincoln*, VI, 177–8, 293, 295–6, 301–2, 333–4, 436–43; B. Leopard and F. C. Shoemaker: *Messages and Proclamations of the Governors of Missouri*, II, 444; *Columbus Crisis*, December 3, 1862; S. B. Laughlin: *Missouri Politics during the Civil War*, pp. 76–7, 79, 83–9; *Official Records*, series 3, III, 54; Dennett: *Hay*, pp. 71, 79, 101; Welles: *Diary*, I, 448, 471; Bates: *Diary*, p. 310; Stanton to Schofield, November 21, 1863, Stanton MSS.; J. L. Stephens to Jay Cook, December 7, 1863, Jay Cooke MSS., cited in G. W. Smith: "Generative Forces of Union Propaganda," p. 377.

plans to buy up the certificates of compensation at a discount of fifteen to forty per cent and had raised between $200,000 and $300,000 for the purpose. But Congress did not pass the bill.[27]

Late in January 1864 the personnel in Missouri changed. Lincoln attempted to heal the factional breach by removing Schofield, and Governor Gamble, harassed beyond his strength, died. The change benefited the radicals, for the new Governor, Willard P. Hall, though an able lawyer and the most genial of men, did not have the fighting qualities needed to lead the conservatives. The radicals gathered strength and in April elected the mayor of St. Louis. Supporting Frémont, then Chase, they sent a delegation to the Cleveland radical convention and a contesting delegation to Baltimore. Seated at Baltimore, Missouri radicals stood out against Lincoln and cast their votes for General Grant. The conservatives, repulsed at Baltimore, came home to join the Democrats, while the radicals took possession of the Republican Party and nominated Thomas C. Fletcher for governor. In November, Lincoln carried the state, but Fletcher ran well ahead of the Presidential ticket.[28]

In the Eastern states the campaign of 1864 was conducted without the accompaniment of spy scares and nocturnal plots, or even excessive emphasis on the governors' devotion to the soldiers' welfare. In New York, Horatio Seymour continued to oppose the arbitrary acts of the federal government and kept up his opposition to the draft. In May, General Dix suppressed two New York papers for publishing a bogus proclamation in which Lincoln allegedly called for 400,000 men and ordered a day of fasting and prayer. Seymour immediately attempted to have a grand jury indict Dix for false arrest. In July, when a new draft threatened, the Gov-

[27] Bates: *Diary*, pp. 321, 328; Laughlin: *Missouri Politics*, p. 90; Leopard and Shoemaker: *Messages of the Governors of Missouri*, II, 3–7.

[28] Laughlin: *Missouri Politics*, pp. 91–7.

ernor repeated all his old charges that the enrollment had been unfairly partisan and the state's quota excessive. In August the Governor attended the Democratic convention, hopeful that his own leadership in the cause of liberty would give him the nomination. Despite his pre-eminence in the fight, the party politicians passed over his claims to nominate General McClellan. Seymour favored neither the candidate nor the platform, and returned to announce that he would not run again for governor. But the Democratic convention nominated him by acclamation, and the Governor reluctantly took up the duties of the campaign, repeating endlessly and hopelessly his diatribes against despotism. The Republicans nominated Congressman Reuben Fenton, who, fully appreciating the necessity for removing Seymour, made an impassioned campaign.[29]

In Massachusetts the state campaign was a repetition of the 1863 performance. The Republicans assembled in Worcester adopted a platform pledging support of the war, listened to a speech declaring Sherman and Farragut were proving the truths of the Republicans' principles, and renominated Andrew with only three dissenting votes in a thousand. The Democrats met in Faneuil Hall, renominated their last year's candidate, endorsed McClellan, and praised the soldiers in Sherman's army. Neither candidate was enthusiastic about his party's Presidential nominee, and Andrew spent most of the campaign hoping that Lincoln would give way to a radical. The result in Massachusetts, however, was never in doubt, and the state campaign aroused no interest.[30]

In Maine, where there was never any likelihood of Democratic success, Governor Cony, renominated by the Republicans, attempted to frighten Stanton into postponing the

---

[29] *Official Records*, series 3, IV, 215–16, 401, 571–2, 600–5, 619–20, 629–30, 634–6; Mitchell: *Seymour*, pp. 358 f., 364, 373 f.; J. G. Nicolay and J. Hay: *Abraham Lincoln: A History*, VII, 43–4; D. G. Croly: *Seymour and Blair*, pp. 156 ff.; Stanton to Seymour, August 11, 1864, Stanton MSS.

[30] W. Schouler: *Massachusetts in the Civil War*, I, 587 f.

draft. When the Secretary of War, who no longer took fright easily, refused to permit Cony to retain drafted men for' coast defense, the Governor solemnly replied that he would greatly regret being obliged to tell the people of Maine "this pitiful favor has been refused them." But Stanton, unimpressed, was indifferent whether Cony told them that or whether he appealed to their patriotism to save the "national existence." Then Cony began to protest, in words close to Seymour's, that the assigned quotas were unjust. Moreover, he warned that the draft might induce the people "in the exercise of their power and in the frenzy of a canvass to do what might prove a source of endless and useless regret." Furthermore, if sailors could not be subtracted from the quotas, Cony warned, "you may look for political results agreeable neither to you nor to myself." Stanton, however, did not share the Governor's nervousness, and Cony changed his tactics. When, in September, Maine went overwhelmingly for him, he told Stanton the results were as good as fifty thousand reinforcements and prayed that the draft be delayed. But Stanton yielded nothing: "Having routed the enemies of the Union at the polls," he replied, "let the patriots of Maine hasten to bear their banner on to victory over the rebels in the field." The draft proceeded.[31]

The Maine victory may not have impressed the Secretary of War, but it came at a time to renew hopes among the Republicans. Throughout the summer the Union prospects were in a decline. Grant's armies, despite repeated reinforcements, made no headway, and the casualty lists from the Wilderness to Cold Harbor mounted alarmingly. Sherman, maneuvering in the mountains of Georgia, seemed totally useless. The radicals cheered for the Wade-Davis Manifesto and continued to pump gas into the leaky Frémont balloon. July and August saw Republican hopes at rock bottom.

Early in July, Yates's adjutant general missed his train in

[31] *Official Records*, series 3, IV, 33, 488, 544–5, 609, 623–4, 639, 714; Stanton to Cony, August 11, 1864, Stanton MSS.

Harrisburg and spent two hours with Governor Curtin. The Pennsylvania Governor was "down on things generally," and on the War Department in particular. Curtin saw no hopes: the general government seemed determined to "run the machine" and he proposed to let them do it. Already Curtin had told Lincoln that he would not consider himself responsible for raising troops or for carrying elections. Pennsylvania was 80,000 men behind in troops, and the Governor believed that a draft would meet general opposition from Republicans as well as from Democrats. Moreover, declared Curtin, he had been talking to Morton, and the Indiana Governor felt the same way.[32]

At the same time John Andrew was disgusted with the situation and was hoping to find some means of getting both Lincoln and Frémont to withdraw in favor of a third candidate. In his desperation he even wrote to Seymour, proposing that the two should consult together. The New Yorker went to Boston, spent a pleasant hour chatting, but failed to find any point of agreement with the Massachusetts radical. Andrew discussed the situation with radicals in New York, but they could not agree on any action. The canvass, thought Andrew, was "unspeakably dull." [33]

Apathy and disheartenment reached even into the upper circles of the party and penetrated the White House. Henry J. Raymond, editor of the *New York Times,* heard only discouraging reports and learned only of a general conviction that a change was needed. The consensus seemed to be that the war languished and Lincoln would not or could not bring peace. War-weariness and a desire for peace was everywhere. Something had to be done, Raymond told Cameron, to attract public attention. "Great victories might do it — but we are not likely to get them." Raymond asked Cameron's advice on another step: let Lincoln propose to Jeff Davis that both sides disband their armies and stop the

[32] A. G. Fuller to Yates, August 3, 1864, Yates MSS.

[33] Pearson: *Andrew,* II, 157–62; J. T. Morse: *Memoir of Colonel Henry Lee,* p. 237.

war *"on the basis of recognizing the supremacy of the con-stitution"* and refer all disputed questions to a convention of all the states! Raymond went to Washington to lay the proposal before the President,[34] but Lincoln did not accept it. Instead he wrote a memorandum, sealed it, had the members of the cabinet witness the envelope, and put it in his desk. The memorandum read: "This morning as for some days past, it seems exceedingly probable that this administration will not be elected. Then it will be my duty to so cooperate with the President-elect as to save the Union between the election and the inauguration; as he will have secured his election on such grounds that he cannot possibly save it afterwards." [35]

If Lincoln had in mind following Raymond's plan, he was merely adopting Seymour's proposals for negotiated peace. The prospect frightened John Andrew and he dashed about furiously writing letters to Yates and Brough and Morton, asking them to help him save Lincoln from evil influences. After the news of Sherman's victory, early in September, Andrew abandoned hope of another candidate. But he insisted that Lincoln must lead — at least through the election. Then he hoped that the radicals could "get hold of the machine" and run it themselves. He wished, he told Greeley, that Lincoln had the "quality of leadership," and was a "magnetic" and "a positive man, of clear purpose and more prophetic instinct," but he admitted that Massachusetts would vote for the President as he was.[36]

Sherman's victory before Atlanta reinvigorated the Republican campaign. Instead of heading, as he had hoped, a delegation of governors, Andrew went alone to the White House.

[34] H. J. Raymond to Cameron, August 21, and Russel Errett to Cameron, August 23, 25, 1864, Cameron MSS.

[35] Nicolay and Hay (eds.): *Complete Works of Abraham Lincoln*, II, 568.

[36] Pearson: *Andrew*, II, 162–72; George S. Merriam: *The Life and Times of Samuel Bowles*, I, 361–2; Schouler: *Massachusetts in the Civil War*, I, 575–6; Andrew to Greeley and Forbes to Andrew, September 3, 1864, Andrew MSS. Letter Books.

Lincoln listened to him, but he began to take actions that did not spring from Andrew's suggestions. The President wrote to Sherman to let Indiana's soldiers, "or any part of them, go home to vote at the state election." This was, Lincoln explained, in no sense an order. Sherman understood that it was a command. He sent soldiers home, and on election day in October the soldiers gathered at the Indiana polls. The Nineteenth Regiment of Vermont Volunteers voted in Indiana that day, but many a Democrat found his vote challenged. When the votes were counted, Morton had been elected by a majority of 22,000.[37]

On that same day the need for Lincoln's aid was illustrated in Pennsylvania. There it was not thought necessary to send the soldiers home. Early in the summer the legislature had provided for voting in the field. Under the law the Democratic minority had no rights, but Curtin, disgusted with the situation generally, determined to appoint some Democratic commissioners to collect the soldiers' votes. As the commissioners passed through Washington, however, the Democrats among them disappeared, under Stanton's orders, into the Old Capitol Prison. Despite this, Curtin's impartiality resulted in Democratic victories in local contests.[38]

In the evening of October's election day, Abraham Lincoln went again to the telegraph office to hear the returns. Ohio reports were coming in, and Republicans were winning in Cincinnati. The early reports were good in both Indiana and Pennsylvania, and Lincoln relaxed. For a time he read aloud from Petroleum V. Nasby, and then the Pennsylvania returns began "to be streaked with lean." Cameron, who had managed the congressional campaign in Pennsylvania, could not be reached, and the Presidential party

[37] McClure: *Lincoln and Men of War Times*, p. 93; B. R. Sulgrove: *History of Indianapolis and Marion County, Indiana*, p. 317.

[38] Egle: *Curtin*, pp. 173, 178; McClure: *Lincoln and Men of War Times*, pp. 177–8, 200; S. A. Purviance to Cameron, July 22, 1862, A. B. Hutchinson, August 31, and Captain Merrell, August 31, 1864, to Cameron, Cameron MSS.

waited nervously. Reports came in from the field and the hospitals where the Pennsylvanians were voting. Carver Hospital, in Washington, voted three to one for the Republicans. "That's hard on us, Stanton," said the President. "They know us better than the others."

Then Indiana returns began to show a flood of votes for Morton, and a message that Morton had 30,000 came in signed "McKin." "Who is that?" asked Lincoln. "A quartermaster of mine," answered Stanton. "He was sent there to announce that." In fact, explained the Secretary of War, a very healthy sentiment had been growing up among the quartermasters. One of Brough's nephews, promoted colonel and stationed at Louisville, had been reduced to a captaincy and sent to the front because he had bet against Morton. The assembled watchers nodded their unanimous approval.[39]

The results in Pennsylvania and Indiana pointed a clear direction. Lincoln conferred with Cameron and McClure and asked Meade and Sherman to send 5,000 men to Pennsylvania for the November election. The generals sent 10,000, and Lincoln carried the state by nearly a 6,000 majority, while the soldiers in the field added 14,000 more.[40] Already, before the October elections, Yates, too, had seen the need for having soldiers go home to vote. Stanton told an Illinois visitor that the state's soldiers in hospitals would be given furloughs, and Yates began compiling lists. But the sick were not enough. When a major asked to take a regiment home, ostensibly for recruiting but really to "conquer a peace with their bullets," the Governor applied to the War Department. From Egypt, Yates had word that the soldiers would be needed, and political workers came with assurances that only the soldiers could carry many localities. Finally the Governor appealed to Lincoln to send troops to vote. It was essential to elect a loyal state Senate, three congressional districts depended on the soldiers, and even the Presidential and the state tickets were unsafe without the uniformed voters. Defeat in Illinois,

[39] Dennett: *Hay*, pp. 227–8.
[40] McClure: *Lincoln and Men of War Times*, pp. 200 ff.

added the Governor, would be worse than defeat in the field. Under such pleas the soldiers came, and Lincoln carried his home state by 189,496 to McClellan's 158,730. The Republicans made a clean sweep of the state offices, and won eleven of the fourteen congressional seats.[41]

The soldiers' vote was crucial in many other states. New York allowed its soldiers to vote in the field, and each party sent three commissioners to Grant's armies. The Democratic commissioners, however, landed in Washington's Old Capitol Prison, where they remained until January. Moreover, the Democrats charged, many soldiers voted Democratic in their camps only to have their ballots switched in the post offices. The Democrats diligently dug up several sick soldiers who, having voted earlier in the hospitals, got home in time to vote — and found Republican ballots in their envelopes.[42] In addition, on the eve of the election, troops arrived on furlough from the Eastern armies. Even with this aid the vote was close. Seymour polled 54,000 more votes than he had got in 1862. The Republican vote, however, had swollen even more enormously, and Lincoln polled 368,000 to McClellan's 362,000. Without the soldiers New York would have remained in the Democratic column.[43]

In Connecticut, where Lincoln's majority was but 2,406 and 2,898 soldiers voted, the Democrats had a plausible claim to having carried the state for McClellan.[44] Maryland's vote was clearly the product of federal bayonets. In October the citizens of Maryland voted on a new constitution, providing for emancipation and bearing a drastic proscription

[41] Letters of B. C. Cook, September 19; H. Tompkins, September 26; E. Eno, September 27; F. W. Hutchinson, September 29; W. H. Howe, October 1; G. P. Smith, October 14; G. Borgan, October 20; J. Allison, October 22, 1864, to Yates, Yates MSS.; *Official Records, series 3*, IV, 871–2; C. A. Church: *Republican Party in Illinois*, p. 95.

[42] Croly: *Seymour and Blair*, pp. 131 f.

[43] Ibid., pp. 156 f.; *Official Records, series 3*, IV, 873; Mitchell: *Seymour*, pp. 373 ff.; McClure: *Lincoln and Men of War Times*, pp. 200 f.

[44] Crofutt and Morris: *Connecticut*, pp. 632, 636.

of Democrats. Although General Lew Wallace took control of the polls in Baltimore, the voters rejected the constitution by a majority of 2,000. But the proposed constitution had given votes to soldiers in the field, and 2,294 soldiers voted for it, and only 76 against. It took ten days to count the votes, but on October 29 Governor Bradford proclaimed the constitution in effect. This fortunate result came just in time for the November elections. On election day General Wallace again guarded the ballot boxes, and Baltimore cast nearly 15,000 votes for Lincoln to less than 3,000 for McClellan. The soldiers in the field completed the work, and Maryland gave Lincoln a majority of 7,000 in a total vote of 70,000.[45]

In Wisconsin and Iowa the soldiers' vote, overwhelmingly for Lincoln, did not affect the home vote.[46] Ohio's soldiers voted in the field, and the votes were sent home to be counted. But it was difficult indeed for soldiers to vote for Ohio's general. There were not enough Democratic ballots to go round in the camps, and the soldiers who wished to vote for McClellan must either clip a sample ballot from a newspaper or laboriously transcribe, often with a borrowed pencil, the names of the Democratic electors. Those who failed to copy the list correctly had their votes declared invalid by the officers who supervised the voting in the field. It did not matter a great deal, however. Many of the packages containing the soldiers' votes were never opened. Ohio was safe for Lincoln, and the election clerks at home merely guessed at the distribution of the army's vote.[47]

[45] A. L. Knott: *A Biographical Sketch of Hon. A. Lee Knott*, pp. 18–24, 43; W. L. Seabrook: *Maryland's Great Part in Saving the Union*, pp. 54–6.

[46] E. J. Benton: *Voting in the Field*, pp. 52–66; Byers: *Iowa in War Times*, p. 325; T. H. Williams: "Voters in Blue: The Citizen Soldiers of the Civil War," *Mississippi Valley Historical Review*, XXXI, 187–204.

[47] In the presence of officials of the Ohio State Archeological and Historical Society, I opened packages of soldiers' ballots, now in the

In McClellan's column, when the final tallies were made, were 21 electoral votes. Seven of them came from New Jersey, where Governor Parker had followed a cautious course which avoided giving a plausible pretext for federal intervention. The other McClellan votes represented, strangely enough, two of the border states where military intervention had first been tried. Late in October, Governor Cannon of Delaware had asked for the return of Delaware's soldiers. "Without the vote of our troops in the field it will be utterly impossible to carry our State," the Governor told Stanton. But the soldiers did not arrive, and Delaware's three electoral votes went to McClellan by a popular majority of 612.[48] Kentucky's eleven votes came as a clear revolt of Governor Bramlette. Three weeks before the election he issued a proclamation declaring that qualifications for voting were not to be fixed by military authorities. Citizens were to treat military orders "with indignant contempt," and sheriffs should arrest any soldiers interfering with voters. He would call off the election, said Bramlette, if it could not be free. Made bold by their Governor's bravery, 61,000 Democrats went to the polls to overwhelm the 26,000 Lincolnites.[49]

On election night Lincoln went back to the War Department. En route he heard the news from Indianapolis — 8,000 majority. It was 1,500 more than Morton had got three weeks before. During the evening the returns came in, and the President was in a buoyant mood. A year before, he had hoped to win 120 electoral votes; two months before he had expected defeat. Now he saw the returns add up to 213 votes in the electoral college, backed by a popular majority of

society's possession, and counted the votes of soldiers from Adams and Ottoway counties, Ohio. Many of the Democratic tickets were handwritten. The official returns of soldiers' votes from these counties bore no ascertainable relation to the votes actually cast by the men in the field.

[48] Cannon to Stanton, October 27, 1864, Stanton MSS.; H. C. Conrad: *History of Delaware*, I, 213.

[49] E. M. Coulter: *Civil War in Kentucky*, pp. 186–7.

nearly 400,000.[50] He had snatched victory from the brink of defeat, and Abraham Lincoln was master of a nation.

[50] Dennett: *Hay,* p. 233. The victory, however, was closer than either the popular or the electoral votes would indicate. Without the soldiers' vote in six crucial states, Lincoln would have lost the election. New York's 33 electoral votes were won by a popular majority of less than 7,000; Connecticut's 6 by 2,000; Pennsylvania's 26 by about 20,000; and Maryland's 7 by 7,000. Indiana's 13 and Illinois' 16 were carried by 20,000 and 30,000 respectively, but were probably due largely to the presence of soldiers as guards and as voters at the polls. Had these states gone for McClellan, he would have had a majority in the electoral college despite Lincoln's popular plurality.

Chapter 18

The Death of States' Rights

THE ELECTION of 1864 demonstrated, conclusively and finally, that Abraham Lincoln had made a nation. At the same moment on the battlefields of the Civil War the constitutional riddle of the American federal system was being resolved. Within a few months of the election Grant and Lee met at Appomattox Courthouse, and the Southern Confederacy — which had been founded upon the dogmas of states' rights — collapsed. But in the North, Abraham Lincoln had already determined that the nation was supreme and states' rights outmoded in theory and practice.

Under Lincoln's leadership the national government had won military control over the manpower of the states. A national economic system based on new national banks, the nation-made financial centers, government-subsidized railroads, and a protective tariff had grown strong during the war. And, of necessity, state politics revolved in the national orbit.

In 1860 the nation had been on the eve of dissolution. National institutions that had long existed had fallen apart. The Methodist and Baptist churches had divided, the Whig Party had disintegrated, and the Democratic Party had split. In that year the Republican Party, which Abraham Lincoln was to make into a new nationalizing agency, had only a nominal existence. It was, in truth, only a series of state parties, lacking either unity or a coherent program. Its orientation was in the states, and state politicians led it.

In 1860 the Republican platform had solemnly declared that "the Rights of the States . . . must and shall be pre-served," and had added: "the maintenance inviolate of the rights of the States, and especially the right of each state to order and control its own domestic institutions according to its own judgment exclusively is essential to that balance of powers on which the perfection and endurance of our politi-cal fabric depends."

And in 1860 the Republicans had taken pains to "de-nounce the lawless invasion by armed forces of the soil of any State or Territory, no matter under what pretext, as among the gravest of crimes."

Within four years the exigencies of the Civil War had made a mockery of these platform phrases. The governors of the states had elected Lincoln and had demanded war upon the states of the South. For a moment the war unified the Republican Party, but divisions between the party's rad-icals and moderates threatened again to tear it apart. The governors had failed to raise men for the armies by their un-aided efforts, and they had failed to keep political control of their states. As the governors' influence declined, Lincoln's power grew. By suspending the writ of habeas corpus, by conscription, and by the use of troops at the polls, Lincoln had saved the Republican Party and had made it an instru-ment to save the Union.

But states' rights were dead. Their death was clear in Janu-ary 1865 as the legislatures met and the governors, old and new, spoke again on the state of the Union. The contrast with 1861 was significant of the changes the war had wrought. In the January after Lincoln's first election the governors had given directions to the President-elect on the policies of his administration. Recognizing that they were the true spokesmen of the victorious party, and that Lincoln was President only by virtue of their successes in the states, they had forbidden compromise and called for war. But by Janu-ary 1865 experience had chastened the governors, and the torch of leadership had passed from their hands. Henry Crapo might boast to his son that he had become "one of the *strong men* in the rapidly growing and prosperous state" of Michigan, and that he was "commander-in-chief of sixty regiments," but even he reserved such swagger for his family circle.[1]

The new governors, Fenton in New York, Crapo in Michigan, Oglesby in Illinois, and Fletcher in Missouri, gave attention in their opening utterances to the newer problems before the nation. Governor Fletcher assumed an unexpected role by advocating a cessation of partisan hostility, and pleaded for liberality in dealing with Missouri's Confederates. A few days later, when the Missouri legislature abolished slavery, Fletcher joyfully issued a proclamation begging Southern sympathizers to co-operate in ending the institution.[2] In Illinois, Governor Yates delivered a garrulous farewell message reviewing his manifold achievements, and incoming Governor Oglesby surveyed the future of the nation from a radical vantage point. When the Southern people, he announced, laid down their arms and begged for peace, it would be time enough to arrange for them the terms of their re-entry into the union.[3] Fenton of New York merely proclaimed that the problems of the future were problems of the nation, and that the federal government would maintain republican governments in the Southern states.[4]

Austin Blair of Michigan was the only retiring governor who struck the old fire. He announced, as he reviewed the record of his administration, that the war's lessons had been useful. The relations between the federal and the state governments had been defined. The pernicious phrase "sovereign states" had once permeated the language and had

[1] H. H. Crapo to W. W. Crapo, November 12, 1863, March 19, 1864, Crapo MSS.

[2] Leopard and Shoemaker: *Messages of the Governors of Missouri,* II, 43, 48–53; Laughlin: *Missouri Politics,* pp. 102–3.

[3] A. C. Cole: *Era of the Civil War,* pp. 387, 388–9.

[4] Lincoln (ed.): *New York Governors' Messages,* V, 582 ff.

sapped loyalty to the national government. Now, he proclaimed, "There is, and can be, under the Constitution of
the United States, only one paramount sovereign authority."
This lesson, said Blair, was worth its cost. "Many a brave
hero has bit the dust . . . many a household has been
draped in mourning, and many a heart has broken," said
the proud Governor. "But who," he asked, "would take it
back? That is precious which is bought with blood." After
such an address the Democrats thought Crapo's inaugural a
model of sanity, and Crapo himself, who "tried to make it
decent" because he did not want to be "the smallest governor Michigan ever had," thought his message was a success.[5]

Two of the retiring governors, Yates and Blair, were candidates for seats in the United States Senate. The Illinois
legislature, now safely Republican, sent Yates to the national
capital to reap his reward for state services. Michigan, however, rejected Blair, and the old abolitionist retired from
public life.[6] John Andrew, too, hoped for national reward,
and looked forward to taking Welles's or Stanton's place in a
reorganized cabinet, but his hopes were dashed by Lincoln's
retention of his full staff of advisers.[7]

Before the end, there came one other change in the list of
governors. On March 1, 1865 William Cannon, whom federal bayonets had raised to Delaware's governorship, died
suddenly. His successor was Gove Salisbury, a physician who
had been speaker of the Delaware Senate, and a vigorous personality who might, had it not already been too late, have
struck still further blows for states' rights. His accession restored Delaware to the Democratic column.[8]

[5] *Detroit Free Press*, January 5, 7, 1865; Crapo to Crapo, January 1,
13, 1865, Crapo MSS.

[6] *Detroit Free Press*, December 3, 14, 1864, January 5, 6, 17, 1865;
letters of A. H. Rodman, December 9; W. D. Henderson, December
12; J. Medill, December 14, 1865, Yates MSS.

[7] Pearson: *Andrew*, II, 179.

[8] Conrad: *Delaware*, I, 214.

The governors, both old and new, continued to play the parts that the exigencies of the war had assigned them. In December, Lincoln called for 300,000 more troops, and the governors once more fell to arguing with the War Department over credits and quotas.[9] Curtin complained about the appointment of officers for Pennsylvania troops; Lewis that Wisconsin's draftees were escaping to Canada and that Western states were furnishing more than their share of soldiers; Miller that quotas were not assigned fairly in Minnesota; Brough that his legislature wanted credit for Ohio's hundred-day men; J. Gregory Smith that Vermont was unjustly assessed above New Hampshire. The harassed governors were mere recruiting agents of the national government, and the blows that killed states' rights had destroyed state enthusiasm for prolonging the war.

One complaint was particularly reminiscent of the states'-rights struggle against conscription. Governor Fenton, Republican though he was, took up New York's case just where Seymour had left it. The hated Democrat went out of office protesting again that New York was assigned an excessive quota. Fenton studied the figures, agreed with Seymour, and sent an agent to Washington with his protests. General Fry revised the quota upward by 60,000 and Fenton boarded a train for the capital while Republican legislators sent an angry delegation to the Governor. Lincoln yielded to the indignant pressure and reduced the quota by one fourth.[10]

Yet all of this merely confirmed the facts that Lincoln had triumphed over the governors, and the nation had emerged victorious over the states. The triumph was, in truth, the product of many factors. Among them, and fortunately for his Union-saving purposes, was the situation that had nearly always enabled Lincoln to deal with the governors individ-

[9] *Official Records*, series 3, IV, 1002–3.

[10] *Official Records*, series 3, IV, 1003–4, 1010, 1040–2, 1045–8, 1056–7, 1076–80, 1086, 1100–4; Tracy: *Uncollected Letters of Lincoln*, p. 251; Mitchell: *Seymour*, pp. 318 ff.

ually. Divided opinion between the conservatives and the radicals among them had made the President's moderating position easier. The governors, moreover, were not in the habit of consulting together, and their contacts with one another were comparatively few. Andrew dominated New England, and in the early days sent messages and couriers to his New England colleagues, but he seldom met them. Seymour once dropped into Andrew's office for an hour, but his visit was the only consultation between Massachusetts and New York. New Jersey normally followed either New York or Pennsylvania, but her governors never conferred with the chief executives of her neighbors. Nor did Curtin meet New York's Governors Morgan, Seymour, or Fenton to concert action between their states. In the West, at the beginning Morton, Yates, and Dennison conferred occasionally on Kentucky and Ohio River problems, but Blair in Michigan, Randall and Salomon in Wisconsin, Kirkwood in Iowa, and Minnesota's three governors were isolated.

Only three times did groups of governors assemble to formulate policy. The Cleveland meeting of Western governors and Curtin in May 1861 came at the height of initial enthusiasm for the war, and the governors merely demanded that more attention be given to the West. Lincoln accepted their pledge of co-operation and gave the governors so much work raising troops that they had no time for further consultation over campaign strategy. The Providence meeting of New England governors sent a committee to Lincoln to demand cabinet changes, but the President skillfully put the committeemen on the defensive and turned them away. Andrew led his neighbors from Providence to Altoona, but was unable to get agreement from other governors for schemes to use Negro troops and replace McClellan with Frémont. On the eve of the conference Lincoln issued the preliminary Emancipation Proclamation and cut the ground from under Andrew's radical plot. Thereafter the governors attempted no meeting, and Lincoln dealt with them individually.

In addition to the advantage of dealing with the governors

separately, Lincoln had an enormously swollen patronage to
dispense for national rather than state ends. The civilian
personnel of the departments grew under the needs of the
war, but no part of that patronage was at the disposal of the
governors. The President and the cabinet officers consulted
with congressmen on local appointments, but a governor's
recommendation was worthless to an office-seeker. Moreover,
the military patronage was at the President's disposal. Governors might appoint company and regimental officers, but
promotions from grade to grade and the selection of general
officers depended on the President. The army and the civil
patronage — as the experiences in the border states, in Ohio
in 1863, and in the campaign of 1864 proved — put the Republican Party exclusively in Lincoln's hands.

But in the long run Lincoln's victory over the governors
was the triumph of a superior intellect. Of the sixty-three
chief executives of the states with whom Lincoln dealt in
the four years of the Civil War, only Horatio Seymour could
approach the President in quality of mind. Seymour's par-
tial success in blocking conscription was a tribute to his intellectual power. Had he possessed Lincoln's understanding
of men and his political skill, Seymour might have prevented
the destruction of states' rights. But Seymour stood alone.
The other governors lacked the clear insight that Lincoln
and Seymour displayed. Andrew had emotion and energy,
but his judgment was weak and his enthusiasm outran his
capacity. Morton had zeal and ingenuity and administrative
skill, but his emotions were unstable, and he was frequently
filled with unwarranted terror. Curtin was orotund and confused, Yates was gullible, and Blair a fanatic lacking in political acumen. Most of the others were mediocrities who owed
their positions to "availability" rather than to ability. When
they became neurotic, hysterical, "skeered," or when they became contentious, arrogant, and imperative, Abraham Lincoln remained calm, keeping his balance — and keeping his
eye on the goal of saving the Union.

And this, above all, made Lincoln the architect of the

new nation. The victory of nationalism over localism, of centralization over states' rights, was, in the last analysis, a victory of a keener intellect over men of lesser minds. The new nation that emerged from the Civil War was not solely the result of the military defeat of the armies of Robert E. Lee. It was equally the result of the political victory that Abraham Lincoln's mind and personality won over the governors of the Northern states.

The last months of Lincoln's life were spent in the preliminaries of a new struggle; but it was a conflict in which the rights of the states and the state governors played little part. The war gave the nation supremacy over the states, but it neither solved the relations between the branches of the national government nor gave direction for the nation's future. The conflicts between the executive and Congress, and between moderates and radicals in the victorious party, remained to complicate and confuse the problem of reconstruction.

For both political and economic reasons the radicals were determined to circumvent Lincoln's program of reconstruction. Essentially Lincoln's ten-per-cent governments — announced in his proclamation of December 1863 and already in embryo in Tennessee and Louisiana — would be no better for the radicals than the border states. In Kentucky, Missouri, Maryland, and Delaware the President's handling of politics had prevented the success of the radical program. These states had passed from Presidential pocket-boroughs, controlled by the army, into conservative — almost Democratic — hands. The extension of a conciliatory border-state policy into the conquered area might well ensure the dominance of the moderate wing of the Republican Party. Moreover, such an outcome would effectively prevent Northern economic penetration of the South. Railroads would not bring profits to Northern capitalists, cotton would not seek Northern looms, and banks would not beg Northern credit. Instead, a moderate South, its politics controlled by a ten per cent dependent on Lincoln's patronage and directed by his army, might well combine with the border states to overthrow the national banks, reduce the wartime tariff, and pay the war-born national debt in greenbacks. The terrifying prospect of having the "results of the war" torn from their grasp impelled the radicals to a battle that, beginning early in 1865, was to rage with increasing intensity against President Andrew Johnson.

In that conflict for power Andrew Johnson would call in vain upon the dead dogmas of states' rights. He would attempt to resuscitate the states of the South and breathe new life into them. But the effort would fail, and Johnson might, in the end, have come to understand the symbolism of Lincoln's funeral.

On the night of April 14, in Ford's Theatre, insane John Wilkes Booth brought to a sudden end the last best chance of moderate, conciliatory reconstruction. Early the next morning Lincoln died, and the radicals quickly seized upon his body and paraded it indecently back along the route the President-elect had once followed from Springfield. They claimed to possess his spirit as well, and they planned the elaborate funeral to symbolize their pretensions. It was a national ceremony — and the radicals claimed that they had inherited the nation that Lincoln had made.

There were none to say them nay. The states raised no voice to claim the body of the man they had raised to leadership. Officers of the nation, senators and representatives, bore the pall between ranks of the nation's generals and admirals. They were followed by cabinet members and bureau chiefs. Far back in the crowds, mere spectators, were the governors of the once important states.

Bibliography

ABBOTT, STEPHEN G.: *The First Regiment New Hampshire Volunteers in the Great Rebellion* (1890).

ADAMS, CHARLES FRANCIS, JR.: *Charles Francis Adams, 1835–1915: An Autobiography* (1916).

Addresses by his excellency Governor John A. Andrew, Hon. Edward Everett, Hon. B. F. Thomas, and Hon. Robert C. Winthrop, delivered at the Mass Meeting in Aid of Recruiting, held on the Common under the auspices of the Committee of One Hundred and Fifty, on Wednesday, August 27, 1862 (1862).

ALEXANDER, DE ALVA STANWOOD: *A Political History of the State of New York* (Vols. II–III, 1906–1909).

AMBLER, CHARLES H.: *Francis H. Pierpont Union War Governor of Virginia and Father of West Virginia* (1937).

ANDREW, JOHN ALBION: *Correspondence between Gov. Andrew and Gov. Butler* (1862).

——: Manuscripts (Massachusetts Historical Society).

ANDREWS, MATTHEW PAGE: *History of Maryland: Province and State* (1929).

ANGLE, PAUL M.: *Lincoln 1854–1861, Being the Day by Day Activities of Abraham Lincoln from January 1, 1854 to March 4, 1861* (1933).

——: *New Letters and Papers of Lincoln* (1930).

——: *The Lincoln Reader* (1947).

Appleton's American Annual Cyclopædia and Register of Important Events of the Years 1861–5 (5 vols., 1864–70).

BAKER, JAMES H.: *Lives of the Governors of Minnesota* (1908).

BALTIMORE, MAYOR OF: *Communication from the Mayor of Baltimore, with the Mayor and Board of Police of Baltimore City* (1861).

BANCROFT, FREDERIC: *The Life of William H. Seward* (2 vols., 1900).

BARBER, E. W.: "Reminiscences of Governor Austin Blair" (Blair MSS., Burton Historical Collection).

[395]

BARINGER, WILLIAM E.: *Lincoln's Rise to Power* (1937).

——: *A House Dividing* (1945).

BARTON, WILLIAM E.: *President Lincoln* (2 vols., 1933).

BATES, EDWARD: *The Diary of Edward Bates 1859–1866*, edited by Howard K. Beale (1933).

BENEDICT, G. G.: *Vermont in the Civil War, A History of the part taken by the Vermont Soldiers and Sailors in the War for the Union, 1861–5* (2 vols., 1886).

BENTON, ELBERT S.: *Voting in the Field: A Forgotten Chapter of the Civil War* (1915).

BEVERIDGE, ALBERT J.: *Abraham Lincoln: 1809–1858* (2 vols., 1928).

BIGELOW, JOHN: *Retrospections of an Active Life* (5 vols., 1909).

BLAINE, JAMES G.: *Twenty Years of Congress: From Lincoln to Garfield* (2 vols., 1884).

BLAIR, AUSTIN: "The Conference of Loyal Governors at Altoona Pennsylvania in 1862" (Blair MSS., Burton Historical Collection, undated, after 1893).

——: Manuscripts (Burton Historical Collection).

Boston Post (1861–5).

BOUTWELL, GEORGE S.: *Reminiscences of Sixty Years in Public Affairs* (2 vols., 1902).

BOWEN, JAMES L.: *Massachusetts in the War 1861–1865* (1889).

BRADFORD, AUGUSTUS W.: Manuscripts (Maryland Historical Society).

BRENTS, J. A.: *The Patriots and Guerillas of East Tennessee and Kentucky* (1863).

BREWER, JOHN M.: *Prison Life* (n.d.).

BROUGH, JOHN: *Defenders of the Country and its Enemies* (1864).

——: *In Memory of John Brough, Proceedings of a meeting of citizens of Ohio* (1865).

BROWNE, ALBERT G.: *Sketch of the Official Life of John A. Andrew as Governor of Massachusetts* (1868).

BROWNE, ROBERT H.: *Abraham Lincoln and the Men of His Time* (2 vols., 1907).

BRUMMER, SIDNEY DAVID: *Political History of New York State during the Period of the Civil War* (1911).

BUCHHOLZ, HEINRICH EWALD: *Governors of Maryland from the Revolution to the Year 1908* (1908).

BUCKINGHAM, SAMUEL G.: *The Life of William A. Buckingham* (1894).

Burlington (Iowa) *Daily Hawk-Eye* (1861–5).

BUTLER, BENJAMIN F.: *Autobiography and Personal Reminis-*

cences of Major-General Benjamin F. Butler. Butler's Book
(1892).

——: *Private and Official Correspondence* (5 vols., 1917).

BYERS, S. H. M.: *Iowa in War Times* (1888).

CAMERON, SIMON: Manuscripts, 1861–3 (Library of Congress).

CARMAN, HENRY J., and LUTHIN, REINHARD H.: *Lincoln and the Patronage* (1943).

CARNEGIE, ANDREW: *Autobiography of Andrew Carnegie* (1920).

CARPENTER, FRANK B.: *The Inner Life of Abraham Lincoln* (1877).

CARR, LUCIEN: *Missouri, A Bone of Contention* (1888).

CARROLL, CHARLES: *Rhode Island: Three Centuries of Democracy* (2 vols., 1932).

CARROLL, HOWARD: *Twelve Americans* (1883).

CHANDLER, PELEG W.: *Memoir of Governor Andrew* (1880).

CHAPLIN, JEREMIAH and J. D.: *Life of Charles Sumner* (1874).

CHARNWOOD, LORD: *Abraham Lincoln* (1916).

Chicago Times (1861–5).

CHITTENDEN, LUCIUS E.: *Recollections of President Lincoln and His Administration* (1904).

CHURCH, CHARLES A.: *History of the Republican Party in Illinois, 1854–1912* (1912).

CLARK, CHARLES BRANCH: "Politics in Maryland during the Civil War," *Maryland History Magazine* (June 1942).

CLARK, DAN ELBERT: *Samuel Jordan Kirkwood* (1917).

CLARK, THOMAS D.: *A History of Kentucky* (1937).

COLE, ARTHUR CHARLES: *The Era of the Civil War, 1848–1870* (1919).

COLLINS, RICHARD H.: *History of Kentucky* (2 vols., 1877).

Congressional Globe, 36th to 39th Congress.

Connecticut War Record (2 vols., 1863–5).

CONRAD, HENRY C.: *History of the State of Delaware* (3 vols., 1908).

COULTER, E. MERTON: *The Civil War and Readjustment in Kentucky* (1926).

CRAPO, HENRY HOWLAND: Manuscripts (Michigan Historical Collection).

CRAVEN, AVERY: *The Coming of the Civil War* (1942).

CROCKETT, WALTER HILL: *Vermont: The Green Mountain State* (3 vols., 1921).

CROFFUTT, W. A., and MORRIS, JOHN M.: *The Military and Civil History of Connecticut during the War of 1861–65* (1869).

CROLY, DAVID G.: *Seymour and Blair, Their Lives and Services* (1868).

CURTIN, FRANCIS: *The Republican Party* (2 vols., 1904).

CURTIS, BENJAMIN R.: *Executive Power* (1862).

CURTIS, NEWTON MARTIN: *From Bull Run to Chancellorsville* (1906).

DANA, CHARLES A.: *Recollections of the Civil War* . . . (1902).

DAVIS, STANTON LING: *Pennsylvania Politics, 1860–1863* (1935).

DELAWARE, GENERAL ASSEMBLY: *Report of the Committee* . . . [*on*] . . . *the General Election* . . . *of November, 1862* (1863).

DENNETT, TYLER: *Lincoln and the Civil War in the Diaries and Letters of John Hay* (1939).

Detroit (Michigan) *Daily Advertiser* (1861–5).

Detroit (Michigan) *Free Press* (1861–5).

EDDY, THOMAS M.: *The Patriotism of Illinois* (2 vols., 1865).

EGLE, WILLIAM HENRY: *Andrew Gregg Curtin: His Life and Services* (1895).

FESSENDEN, FRANCIS: *Life and Public Services of William Pitt Fessenden* (2 vols., 1907).

FIELD, HENRY M.: *Life of David Dudley Field* (1898).

FISH, CARL R.: "Social Relief in the Northwest during the Civil War," *American Historical Review*, XXII, 309–24 (January 1917).

FITE, EMERSON DAVID: *The Presidential Campaign of 1860* (1911).

FLOWER, FRANK A.: *History of the Republican Party* (1884).

——: *Edwin McMasters Stanton — the Autocrat of Rebellion, Emancipation, and Reconstruction* (1905).

FOSTER, JOHN Y.: *New Jersey and the Rebellion* (1868).

FOULKE, WILLIAM DUDLEY: *Life of Oliver P. Morton* (2 vols., 1899).

FRENCH, WILLIAM M.: *Life, Speeches, State Papers and Public Services of Governor Oliver P. Morton* (1864).

FRY, JAMES B.: *New York and the Conscription of 1863: A Chapter in the History of the Civil War* (1885).

FOLWELL, WILLIAM WATTS: *A History of Minnesota* (4 vols., 1924).

FULLER, GEORGE N.: *Governors of the Territory and State of Michigan* (1928).

GIDDINGS, JOSHUA R.: Manuscripts, 1821–65 (Ohio State Archæological and Historical Society Library).

GOODRICH, DEWITT C., and TUTTLE, CHARLES RICHARD: *History of the State of Indiana* (1879).

GORHAM, GEORGE C.: *Life and Public Services of Edwin M. Stanton* (2 vols., 1899).

GRAY, JOHN CHIPMAN, and ROPES, JOHN CODMAN: *War Letters, 1862–1865* (1927).

GRAY, WOOD: *The Hidden Civil War: The Story of the Copperheads* (1942).

GUROWSKI, ADAM: *Diary*, from March 4, 1861 to November 12, 1862 (3 vols., 1862).

HADLEY, AMOS: *Life of Walter Harriman* (1888).

HALSTEAD, MURAT: *A History of the National Political Conventions* (1860).

HAMLIN, CHARLES EUGENE: *The Life and Times of Hannibal Hamlin* (1899).

HARRINGTON, FRED HARVEY: "The Life of N. P. Banks to 1861" (New York University Ph.D. dissertation, 1936).

HEADLEY, J. T.: *The Great Riots of New York, 1712–1873* (1873).

HEADLEY, P. C.: *Massachusetts in the Rebellion* (1866).

HENDRICK, BURTON J.: *Lincoln's War Cabinet* (1946).

HERRIOTT, F. I.: "Iowa and the First Nomination of Abraham Lincoln," *Annals of Iowa*, VIII, 81–115, 186–220, 444–466; IX, 45–64, 186–228.

——: "Republican Presidential Preliminaries in Iowa, 1859–1860" *Annals of Iowa*, IX, 241–283.

HERTZ, EMANUEL: *Abraham Lincoln — A New Portrait* (2 vols., 1931).

——: *The Hidden Lincoln* (1938).

HESSELTINE, WILLIAM B.: "Lincoln's War Governors," *Abraham Lincoln Association Quarterly*, IV, 153–200 (1946).

——, and WOLF, HAZEL, C.: "The New England Governors *vs.* Lincoln: The Providence Conference," *Rhode Island History*, V, 105–13 (1946).

——: "The Altoona Conference and the Emancipation Proclamation" *Pennsylvania Magazine of History and Biography*, LXXI, 195–205 (1947).

HOLCOMBE, JOHN W., and SKINNER, HUBERT M.: *Life and Public Services of Thomas A. Hendricks* (1886).

HUNT, GAILLARD: *Israel, Elihu, and Cadwallader Washburn* (1925).

Illinois State Journal (Springfield).

INDIANA SENATE: *Report of the Committee on Federal Relations* (1863).

JOHNSON, R. W.: *A Soldier's Reminiscences in Peace and War* (1886).

KNAPP, CHARLES M.: *New Jersey Politics during the Period of the Civil War and Reconstruction* (1924).

KNIGHT, BENJAMIN, SR.: *History of the Sprague Families of Rhode Island* (1881).

LAMON, WARD H.: Manuscripts (Henry E. Huntington Library).

LANE, J. ROBERT: *A Political History of Connecticut during the Civil War* (1941).

LAPSLEY, ARTHUR BROOKS (ed.): *The Writings of Abraham Lincoln* (8 vols., 1905).

LATHROP, H. W.: *The Life and Times of Samuel J. Kirkwood* (1893).

LAUGHLIN, SCEVA BRIGHT: *Missouri Politics during the Civil War* (1930).

LEA, HENRY C.: "Volunteering and Conscription," *United States Service Magazine* (Vol. I, March 1864).

LEECH, MARGARET: *Reveille in Washington* (1941).

LEOPARD, BUEL, and SHOEMAKER, FLOYD C.: *The Messages and Proclamations of the Governors of the State of Missouri* (1926).

LINCOLN, ABRAHAM: Manuscripts (Henry E. Huntington Library).

——: Manuscripts (Illinois State Historical Society Library).

LINCOLN, ROBERT TODD: Manuscript Collection (Library of Congress).

LINCOLN, CHARLES Z. (ed.): *Messages from the Governors* (Vol. V, 1857–68).

LUTHIN, REINHARD H.: *Lincoln's First Campaign* (1944).

LYFORD, JAMES O.: *Life of Edward H. Rollins* (1906).

MACARTNEY, CLARENCE E. N.: *Lincoln and His Generals* (1925).

McCLERNAND, JOHN A.: Manuscripts (Illinois State Historical Society Library).

McCLURE, A. K.: *Abraham Lincoln and Men of War Times* (1892).

McPHERSON, EDWARD: *The Political History of the United States of America during the Great Rebellion* (1865).

MENEELY, A. HOWARD: *The War Department, 1861: A Study in Mobilization and Administration* (1928).

MESSNER, VIVIAN THOMAS: "The Public Life of Austin Blair, War Governor of Michigan (1863–1894)" (M.A. thesis, Wayne University, 1935).

MERK, FREDERICK: *Economic History of Wisconsin during the Civil War Decade* (1916).

MERRIAM, GEORGE S.: *Life and Times of Samuel Bowles* (2 vols., 1885).

MILTON, GEORGE F.: *Abraham Lincoln and the Fifth Column* (1943).

Minnesota in the Civil and Indian Wars, 1861–1865 (2 vols., 1899).

MITCHELL, STEWART: *Horatio Seymour of New York* (1938).

MOORE, CHARLES: *History of Michigan* (4 vols., 1915).

MOORE, FRANK: *The Rebellion Record, a Diary of American Events* (10 vols., 1864–7).

MORSE, JOHN T., JR. (ed.): *Memoir of Colonel Henry Lee* (1905).

NEVINS, ALLAN: *Abram S. Hewitt* (1935).

NEW HAMPSHIRE: *Report of the Adjutant General . . . May 20, 1865* (2 vols., 1865–6).

New Hampshire Patriot and State Gazette (Concord, N. H., 1860–5).

NEW YORK: *Annual Report of the Adjutant General for 1862* (1863).

New York Journal of Commerce.

New York Times.

New York Tribune.

New York World.

NICOLAY, JOHN G., and HAY, JOHN: *Abraham Lincoln, a History* (10 vols., 1890).

—— (Eds.): *Complete Works of Abraham Lincoln* (12 vols., 1905).

NORTON, FREDERICK CALVIN: *The Governors of Connecticut* (1905).

OHIO ADJUTANT GENERAL'S OFFICE: Manuscripts (Ohio State Archæological and Historical Museum and Library).

OHIO EXECUTIVE RECORDS: Correspondence, 1860–5.

OLIVER, JOHN W.: "Draft Riots in Wisconsin during the Civil War," *Wisconsin Magazine of History,* II, 334–7 (1919).

PALMER, JOHN M.: Manuscripts (Illinois State Historical Society).

——: *Personal Recollections* (1901).

PATTON, JOHN: *Austin Blair, War Governor. An Address* (1898).

PEARSON, HENRY GREENLEAF: *The Life of John A. Andrew* (2 vols., 1904).

——: *James S. Wadsworth of Geneseo Brevet Major-General of United States Volunteers* (1913).

PHILIPS, JOHN F.: "Hamilton Rowan Gamble and the Provisional Government of Missouri," *Missouri Historical Review,* V, 1–14 (October 1910).

PHISTERER, FREDERICK (ed.) : *Statistical Record of the Armies of the United States* (1883).

PIERCE, EDWARD L.: *Memoir and Letters of Charles Sumner* (Vol. IV, 1894).

PILLSBURY, HOBART: *New Hampshire — a History* (5 vols., 1927).

POTTER, MARGUERITE: "Hamilton R. Gamble, Missouri's War Governor," *Missouri Historical Review* (October 1940).

POWELL, WALTER H.: *A History of Delaware* (1928).

PRATT, HARRY EDWARD (compiler) : *Concerning Mr. Lincoln, in which Abraham Lincoln is Pictured as He Appeared to Letter Writers of His Time* (1944).

QUINER, E. B.: *The Military History of Wisconsin* (1866).

RADCLIFFE, GEORGE L. P.: *Governor Thomas H. Hicks of Maryland and the Civil War* (1901).

RANDALL, EMILIUS O., and RYAN, DANIEL J.: *History of Ohio: The Rise and Progress of an American State* (5 vols., 1912).

RANDALL, JAMES GARFIELD: *The Civil War and Reconstruction* (1937).

——: *Lincoln the President from Springfield to Gettysburg* (2 vols., 1945).

——: "When War Came in 1861," *Abraham Lincoln Quarterly,* I, 3–42 (1940).

——: *Lincoln The Liberal Statesman* (1947).

RANEY, WILLIAM F.: *Wisconsin: A story of Progress* (1940).

REID, WHITELAW: *Ohio in the War* (2 vols., 1868).

Report of the Joint Committee on Reconstruction (1866).

RHODES, JAMES FORD: *History of the United States from the Compromise of 1850* (1896–1919).

RISSLE, ALBERT G.: *Recollections of War Times* (1895).

ROBERTSON, JNO.: *Michigan in the War* (1880).

ROBINSON, J. S.: Manuscripts (Ohio State Archæological and Historical Museum and Library).

ROLL, CHARLES: *Indiana, One hundred and Fifty Years of American Development* (5 vols., 1931).

SANDBURG, CARL: *Abraham Lincoln, The War Years* (4 vols., 1937).

SCHARF, JOHN THOMAS: *History of Delaware, 1609–1888* (2 vols., 1888).

——: *History of Maryland from the Earliest Period to the Present Day.* (3 vols., 1879).

SCHOULER, JAMES: *History of the United States under the Constitution* (6 vols., 1899).

SCHOULER, WILLIAM: *A History of Massachusetts in the Civil War* (1868).

SEABROOK, WILLIAM L.: *Maryland's Great Part in Saving the Union* (1913).

SEWARD, FREDERICK W.: *Seward at Washington as Senator and Secretary of State. A Memoir of His Life, 1846–1861* (1891).

SEYMOUR, HORATIO: *Public Record* (1868).

SHANNON, FRED ALBERT: *The Organization and Administration of the Union Army, 1861–1865* (2 vols., 1928).

——: "The Federal Government and the Negro Soldier," *Journal of Negro History,* XI, 570–80 (1926).

——: "States Rights and the Union Army," *Mississippi Valley Historical Review,* XII, 51–71 (June 1925).

SHOEMAKER, HENRY W.: *The Last of the War Governors* (1916).

SHORTRIDGE, WILSON PORTER: *The Transition of a Typical Frontier* (1919).

SMITH, GEORGE WINSTON: "Generative Forces of Union Propaganda: A Study in Civil War Pressure Groups" (MS. Ph.D. dissertation, University of Wisconsin, 1939).

——: "Some Northern Wartime Attitudes toward the Post Civil War South," *Journal of Southern History,* X, 253–74 (August 1944).

SMITH, WILLIAM E.: *The Francis Preston Blair Family in Politics* (2 vols., 1933).

SNEAD, THOMAS L.: *The Fight for Missouri* (1888).

SOCIETY FOR THE DIFFUSION OF POLITICAL KNOWLEDGE: *Papers from the Society,* etc. (1863).

STACKPOLE, EVERETT S.: *History of New Hampshire* (IV, 1917).

STAMPP, KENNETH M.: "Indiana in the Civil War" (MS. Ph.D. dissertation, University of Wisconsin, 1941).

——: "Lincoln and the Strategy of Defense in the Crisis of 1861," *Journal of Southern History,* X, 253–74 (1944).

STANLEY, R., and HALL, GEORGE O.: *Eastern Maine and the Rebellion* (1887).

STANLY, EDWARD: *A Military Governor among Abolitionists (A letter from Edward Stanly to Charles Sumner, 1865).*

STANTON, EDWIN McMASTERS: Manuscripts (Library of Congress).

STEPHENSON, ISAAC: *Recollections of a Long Life, 1829–1915* (1915).

STREETER, FLOYD BENJAMIN: *Political Parties in Michigan, 1737–1860* (1918).

SULGROVE, B. R.: *History of Indianapolis and Marion County, Indiana* (1884).

SWISHER, JACOB, and ERBE, CARL H.: *Iowa History as Told in Biography* (1932).

TERRELL, W. H. H.: *Indiana in the War of the Rebellion* (1869).

THAYER, WILLIAM R.: *The Life and Letters of John Hay* (2 vols., 1905).

TRACY, GILBERT A. (ed.): *Uncollected Letters of Abraham Lincoln* (1917).

United States Statutes at Large (1863).

UPTON, EMORY: *The Military Policy of the United States* (1912).

WALKER, CHARLES M.: *Sketch of the Life, Character and Public Services of Oliver P. Morton* (1878).

WALL, JAMES ALEXANDER: *A Sketch of the Life of Horatio Seymour, 1810–1886* (1929).

War of the Rebellion: A compilation of the Official Records of the Union and Confederate Armies (130 vols., 1880–1901).

WEED, THURLOW: *Life of Thurlow Weed including his Autobiography and a Memoir* (2 vols., 1884).

WEEDEN, WILLIAM BABCOCK: *War Government, Federal and State, in Massachusetts, New York, Pennsylvania and Indiana, 1861–1865* (1906).

WELLES, GIDEON: *Diary of Gideon Welles* (3 vols., 1864–9).

——: Manuscripts (Henry E. Huntington Library).

WEST, RICHARD S., JR.: *Gideon Welles: Lincoln's Navy Department* (1943).

WHITE, HORACE: *The Life of Lyman Trumbull* (1913).

WILLIAMS, HENRY CLAY (ed.): *Biographical Encyclopædia of Vermont* (1885).

WILLIAMS, T. HARRY: *Lincoln and the Radicals* (1941).

WILSON, HENRY: *Rise and Fall of the Slave Power in America* (3 vols., 1875–7).

WISCONSIN: *Annual Report of Adjutant General of the State* (1863–5).

WOLF, HAZEL CATHERINE: "The Civil War Governors and Emancipation" (M.A. thesis, University of Wisconsin, 1941).

WOODBURN, JAMES ALBERT: "Party Politics in Indiana during the Civil War," American Historical Association *Annual Report, 1902* (I, 223–51).

WRIGHT, EDWARD N.: *Conscientious Objectors in the Civil War* (1931).

YATES, RICHARD: Manuscripts (Illinois State Library).

Index

A NOTE ON THE TYPE

The text of this book has been set on the Linotype in a type-face called "Baskerville." The face is a facsimile reproduction of types cast from molds made for John Baskerville (Mdccvi–Mdcclxxv) from his designs. The punches for the revived Linotype Baskerville were cut under the supervision of the English printer George W. Jones. John Baskerville's original face was one of the forerunners of the type-style known as "modern face" to printers: a "modern" of the period A.D. *Mdccc.*

The typographic scheme and the binding design are by W. A. Dwiggins. The book was set up in type, printed, and bound by The Plimpton Press, Norwood, Massachusetts.

DATE DUE

DEMCO 38-296